MODERN ESSAYS:
A Rhetorical Approach

MODERN ESSAYS:
A Rhetorical Approach

Edited by

JAMES G. HEPBURN
Department of English
The University of Rhode Island

ROBERT A. GREENBERG
Department of English
Cornell University

New York
THE MACMILLAN COMPANY

Seventh Printing, 1965

Library of Congress catalog card number: 62–8154

THE MACMILLAN COMPANY, NEW YORK
COLLIER-MACMILLAN CANADA, LTD.,
TORONTO, ONTARIO

PRINTED IN THE UNITED STATES OF AMERICA

Foreword to the Teacher

Every text in reading and writing hopes to do something new. But the aims are ultimately the same: to provide good reading so that students can learn to do good writing. Sometimes students are advised to think before they write, and their text consists of thought-provoking essays. Or they are advised that writing is a craft, and their text is a sampling of finished products. Or they are not advised, but the teacher believes that unless his students are interested in their reading, they will not be interested in their writing, and so the text leads them to Plato by way of Julian Huxley. Yet the results are disappointing: student prose is rarely thoughtful, competent, or interesting. Something is wrong, most likely the high school education that the students received, and no text will right it. In despair, some teachers try to give their students a liberal education.

Nevertheless, the present text makes an attempt. It focuses upon writing as an art. With few exceptions the essays do not require major efforts at comprehension. They are meant to be thought-provoking but not brain-wracking. If some of them open up new worlds of ideas to the students, they do so without battering down the doors. At the same time, none of the essays was selected mainly because it dealt with an interesting subject such as organization men or lonely crowds. All of the subjects are meant to be interesting; some of them are more exciting than organization men; but the primary basis of selection was excellence.

What is excellence? There are many topic sentences in the following essays, developed through illustration and accumulation of detail. The accompanying questions for students often deal with these matters. But none of the essays was selected primarily to demonstrate some technical aspect of composition. Nor was overall competence the criterion. A host of modern writers write competently, but few of them move securely past craft into art. No teacher expects his students to become great writers, but if his students read excellent writers rather than competent writers, they may learn what no textbook can teach: that writing is always—properly—something of an art. The unity that a student strives for in a theme can come in part from his having examined the transitions in a piece of ephemeral journalism, but it must come in the end from a total awareness. Coherence, organization, and style are not parts to piece together but aspects of a whole that a writer attempts to create. The competent writer does not succeed as well at this paramount task as the excellent writer.

Not that the present text intends to make a mystery of writing. It divides writing into five parts and aims to be explicit about these parts in the introductory discussions. It also attempts, in the questions for students, to develop analytical skill. It is committed to dissection. The benefit of having essays that—mysteriously or not—possess excellence rather than competence is that they survive the operation.

Since teaching as well as writing is an art, a text that charts a path for the teacher may hinder more than it helps. The present text offers no rigid program. The editors themselves wait for more than three hundred pages to provide an introductory discussion on tone and style, but they imagine that most teachers will talk about the subject long before making it a focus of attention. Moreover, the questions for the essays in each section usually present opportunities to discuss other matters than the particular rhetorical problem of that section. At the same time, the text does offer patterns that may be useful. The five sections and the essays within each section are arranged in order of increasing complexity. Some of the later reading is itself easier than some of the earlier reading, but the questions about it should render the work more difficult. Secondly, the essays within each section concern subjects in roughly the same area, and the subjects as a whole move from public matters to private experience. The aim is to ameliorate discontinuity—the inevitable hazard in courses in reading and writing. The unity is loose and varied; it is an underlying one rather than an emphasized one; it is intended only to provide a sense of continuity. Occasionally this unity may be directly useful, as in the assigning of long papers on the subject-matter of three or four similar essays. Long papers can also be assigned on two or three essays by the same writer. Nine writers are represented by either two or three selections.

The editors hope that neither scheme nor apparatus will obscure the main purpose of the text: to provide good reading.

Introductory Note:
Three Problems in Writing

The basic problem in writing is having something to say. It may be helpful to know that there are, as some authorities tell us, four kinds of prose writing: narration, description, exposition, and argumentation. It may be helpful if the teacher assigns Question 5, to be answered in a paragraph of two hundred words. But the basic problem remains. Of course there is the young man who never has anything to say and never has any trouble saying it. He is to be envied: his talent is rare enough in people like Shakespeare who do have something to say. He hardly seems to affect the point. When it comes to writing, most students—most people—are strong silent types, who can't write unless they have something to say.

There may be some mistake about the young man. His glibness itself contains meaning. (Section 5 of the text will discuss the matter.) But given the ordinary interpretation of "having something to say," there is no mistake. And so it is clear that a text in reading and writing cannot solve the basic problem in writing. The obligation falls to the student.

The second problem in writing is training. Another young man has been reading poetry for years. He has acquired a large and ready vocabulary, knowledge of sentence patterns, an ear for tone and style. His training is informal, but it is real; and he is likely to obtain high marks in his course in reading and writing. Other students might think to overcome his advantage by harder work in the course. And if writing were a mechanical skill, they most certainly could. But writing is complex and subtle, and informal training is the best training possible. Courses in reading and writing are substitutes. Students will do well to supplement their text with poetry and novels.

The third problem in writing is pleasing the teacher. A student once wrote a theme that began in the following manner.

On the evening when I was first driven through the magnificent gates of Whitside College, thrilled at entering this portal to knowledge and yet saddened by memories of home, I was overwhelmed by the realization that in human existence great pleasures are accompanied by great pains.

His teacher red-pencilled the theme. The consequence was that for the rest of the term the student's writing was straightforward, plain, and dull. Neither teacher nor student was pleased.

There is, then, more than one kind of bad writing; and there is no charted path to good writing. A teacher is likely to advise his students to avoid Latinate vocabulary and passive constructions, but he knows that to eliminate Latin from English is to cut the language in half and that the passive voice is sometimes preferable to the active voice. His advice stems from broad rules of thumb: economy, straightforwardness, simplicity, and clarity. He knows that these rules are merely starting points towards good writing.

The standards of composition in courses in reading and writing are fairly uniform. They reflect modern tendencies in writing. (In another age writing tended towards richness, complexity, and subtlety.) It should be remarked, though, that among the few modern essayists who can lay claim to greatness in their art, some do not exhibit the modern tendencies: Henry James, Virginia Woolf. Such writers serve as well as Bernard Shaw and George Orwell as models that may enable modern students to progress beyond straightforward, plain, and dull writing.

The text treats writing according to five aspects: unity, coherence, and development; organization; strategy; point of view and assumptions; and tone and style. These are arbitrary divisions. In the course of studying them, the student will see that they overlap and involve one another. They are five ways for the student to look at one thing—while keeping three problems in mind.

Table of Contents

MODERN ESSAYS:
A Rhetorical Approach

SECTION I

Unity, Coherence, and Development

Unity, Coherence, and Development

The smaller part of writing a good essay is writing a good paragraph; and a well-written paragraph is one that is unified, coherent, and well-developed. Unity in a paragraph means singleness of subject. Consider the first paragraph in the Introductory Note as a small illustration. It opens with an assertion about the basic problem of writing. In the second and third sentences two other views on the problem of writing are offered. With the fourth sentence these alternative views are dismissed because—it is self-evident—they do not touch the basic problem; and the original assertion is made again. The next three sentences concern a seeming exception to the validity of the assertion. The final sentence re-states the assertion with a slight qualification to meet the exception. Thus the paragraph as a whole is a two-part examination of the validity of the opening assertion. It is a unified paragraph, marked in its unity by the first sentence, which thereby gains the title of "topic sentence." As the topic sentence, the first sentence provides the clearest expression of the view that is re-stated in the fourth and in the last sentence, and it is the basis for the comparisons in the second and third sentences and for the example in the fifth-to-seventh sentences.

Topic sentences are indicators of paragraph unity. Sometimes they occur in the middle or at the end of the paragraph rather than at the beginning; sometimes they exist as fragments of sentences or as two or three separate sentences covering separate parts of the paragraph; occasionally they turn up in the succeeding paragraph or in the preceding one; and frequently they do not turn up at all.

The absence of topic sentences in good writing can be regarded as a form of flattery: the writer assumes that the reader recognizes the unifying idea of a paragraph without its having to be made explicit. Few if any good writers think consciously about topic sentences. Topic sentences are mainly a pedagogical device. They are obvious guides to, and marks of, unified thought.

It is apparent that a unified paragraph must have several parts. Were its unity absolute, it would consist of a single sentence or a single word. The first paragraph in the Introductory Note, for example, moves from an assertion to a conclusion, offering comparisons and an example along the way. That the several sentences fit together to form a unified thought is due in part to a variety of linking devices. The operation of such devices contributes to what is known as paragraph coherence. The major linking devices—commonly called transitional devices—are the following: repeated words, synonyms, and other substitutes; conjunctive words and phrases; and parallel phrasing. Each of these devices is employed in the first paragraph in the Introductory Note. The word "writing" reappears several times after its use in the first sentence; it reappears in disguised form as "paragraph" in the third sentence and as "saying" in the fifth; it is embraced by the word "talent" in the sixth sentence. The phrase "young man" is referred to by the pronominal forms "he" and "his." With the conjunction "but" in the fourth sentence and with the phrase "of course" in the fifth, another kind of transition is effected. "But" heralds the rejection of the line of thinking in the two previous sentences; "of course" indicates that a concession will be made. They mark turns in the argument. Lastly, the repetition in sentence three of the opening words of sentence two implies that material of the same order (another apparent solution to the problem of writing) is being offered.

The handling of transitions is not always easy. The writer who wants his transitions to be utterly clear may bore his readers by unnecessarily repeating key words; the writer who employs subtle connections may confuse his readers. Consider whether the editors succeed in avoiding confusion about the relationship between the first and the second sentence in the first paragraph in the Introductory Note. The relationship is indicated indirectly by the related meanings of "problem" and "helpful." Perhaps the second sentence should have begun with a clear transition: Other problems, such as knowing the kind of writing to employ in a given circumstance. . . . As with the absence of topic sentences in good writing, subtlety of transition or absence of appropriate transitional devices can be considered a form of flattery. Until the student becomes competent at analyzing the subtle and unsubtle transitions used by other writers, he should refrain from trying to flatter his own readers.

Transitions from paragraph to paragraph are of the same nature as those within paragraphs. Using them presents the same difficulties. In the Introductory Note the transitional phrases at the beginning of the third and fourth paragraphs ("the second problem," "the third problem") are so straightforwardly repetitious as to risk boredom. When a student finds himself relying upon such transitions (including "also," "the next," "additionally," "in the third place"), he ought to ask himself whether he is writing a theme or a catalogue. The editors try to modify the suggestion of a catalogue in the Introductory Note: they present "the third problem" in a slightly humorous context that implies a special meaning of the word "problem"; and they balance the obvious transitional phrases with relatively subtle connections in the second and fifth paragraphs. What does "mistake," in the first sentence of the second paragraph, link to in the first paragraph? What exactly are the two elements in the fourth and fifth paragraphs linked by "then"?

Paragraph coherence depends upon more than transitional devices. Consistency of style and of point of view (matters to be discussed later) are also significant. More important is paragraph unity itself. If a paragraph is unified, it possesses the inherent coherence of related parts. In the first and second sentences of the first paragraph in the Introductory Note, "basic problem" and "helpful" are drawn together under a single implied subject: problems in writing. Unified thought will not necessarily produce coherent paragraphs, but it is a prime requisite for them.

By the time a writer has achieved unity and coherence in a paragraph, he has performed his other task: that of development. In order to develop a paragraph—in order to develop the idea that a topic sentence expresses—a writer must have further ideas and information at his disposal; but he should not regard his task as a filling in or a padding out of material: development ought to emerge from the desire or need to illuminate, explain, justify, elaborate. An understanding of the variety of means of development can make a writer conscious of the kinds and quality of material that he possesses or lacks. His freedom to employ one or another means of development is an opportunity to choose the most effective approach in a given context.

Several means of development are illustrated in the present discussion and in the Introductory Note. In the final paragraph below, the editors employ an analogy (comparing two very different things: paragraphs and men) as a means of illuminating a point. In the fourth paragraph in the Introductory Note the editors use a rudimentary anecdote for the same purpose. In the present paragraph and in the third paragraph above, the editors make use of classification and analysis (a means that sometimes amounts to no more than division and enumeration). Another means, similar to analogy, is comparison and contrast. As used here, comparison and contrast refers to a single rather than a dual subject. In the first paragraph in the Introductory Note, the subject—the basic problem in writing—is initially developed through a comparison with other problems. The focus of attention remains, however, on the basic problem. The most obvious and perhaps the most common means of development is example, or illustration. Much of the present discussion proceeds by means of examples; the first paragraph consists mainly of an example. Reason—a term used here to embrace cause-effect, logic, and implication—is a means that the second paragraph in the Introductory Note employs: but . . . and so . . . therefore (the last term being understood). And repetition, or restatement, is a means that the first paragraph in the Introductory Note employs. Repetition is a term that hardly suggests development; but some amount of repetition is essential in the development of an idea. Usually, as in the first paragraph in the Introductory Note, the repetition is either abbreviated or amplified. Among other means of development, the most common are accumulation of detail, allusion and quotation, and supporting data.

Paragraph development inevitably involves the question of paragraph order or arrangement. Do we want to begin with a topic sentence or do we want to lead up to it? If we have three examples, in what order shall we offer them? An answer to the first question usually requires an understanding of the relationship of the individual paragraph to the rest of the essay; and therefore it will not be considered here. The purely internal problem of order or arrangement can be met in a variety of ways. In some instances no preferred order emerges and none may be necessary: "His home bore evidences of culture. He possessed a library that. . . . On many walls hung paintings. . . . The piano that stood. . . ." But usually some sort of ordering is possible and desirable: "His home bore evidences of culture. Throughout the house hung paintings. . . . The shelves of his study. . . . In the center of his study stood a piano. . . ." What is the means used? Common patterns for arranging material include chronology, order of importance, space, and vision. The catalogue of means of development given in the previous paragraph proceeded alphabetically. Some material, it should be noted, automatically arranges itself according to demands of logic, narration, or process. In such cases the distinction between development and pattern disappears. (The problem of larger patterning will be taken up in the next section.)

If the student masters the means of paragraph development, and at the same time masters unity and coherence, he will be on the verge of writing ideal paragraphs. He should not try to go beyond the verge. Ideal paragraphs are written only in heaven, and five ideal paragraphs in a row would be as dull as a band of angels. In the real world, good paragraphs are like good men: they are usually too complex to be perfect, and they frequently make virtues out of limitations.

Florida, Missouri

MARK TWAIN

Samuel Langhorne Clemens (1835-1910), who wrote under
the name of Mark Twain, retains his position as the greatest
of American humorists. Born in Florida, Missouri, he left
school at the age of twelve, and began an erratic career as
apprentice printer, newspaper writer, soldier, steamboat pilot,
and business speculator—for a time he even thought of mi-
grating to South America to make his fortune. Success as a
writer came suddenly, with his famous tall tale, "The Celebrated Jumping Frog of Calaveras County," and was confirmed
soon after by *Innocents Abroad,* a humorously irreverent account of his tour of the Mediterranean and the Holy Land, and
Roughing It, a record of a trip through the West. Among his
best-known books are *Life on the Mississippi, A Connecticut
Yankee in King Arthur's Court,* and, of course, *Tom Sawyer*
and *Huckleberry Finn.* (Further headnote information on
Twain appears on pp. 66, 370.)

Most of the houses were of logs—all of them, indeed, except three
or four; these latter were frame ones. There were none of brick, and
none of stone. There was a log church, with a puncheon floor and
slab benches. A puncheon floor is made of logs whose upper surfaces have been chipped flat with the adz. The cracks between the
logs were not filled; there was no carpet; consequently, if you

dropped anything smaller than a peach, it was likely to go through. The church was perched upon short sections of logs, which elevated it two or three feet from the ground. Hogs slept under there, and whenever the dogs got after them during services, the minister had to wait till the disturbance was over. In winter there was always a refreshing breeze up through the puncheon floor; in summer there were fleas enough for all.

A slab bench is made of the outside cut of a sawlog, with the bark side down; it is supported on four sticks driven into auger holes at the ends; it has no back and no cushions. The church was twilighted with yellow tallow candles in tin sconces hung against the walls. Week days, the church was a schoolhouse.

There were two stores in the village. My uncle, John A. Quarles, was proprietor of one of them. It was a very small establishment, with a few rolls of "bit" calicoes on half a dozen shelves; a few barrels of salt mackerel, coffee, and New Orleans sugar behind the counter; stacks of brooms, shovels, axes, hoes, rakes, and such things here and there; a lot of cheap hats, bonnets, and tinware strung on strings and suspended from the walls; and at the other end of the room was another counter with bags of shot on it, a cheese or two, and a keg of powder; in front of it a row of nail kegs and a few pigs of lead, and behind it a barrel or two of New Orleans molasses and native corn whisky on tap. If a boy bought five or ten cents' worth of anything, he was entitled to half a handful of sugar from the barrel; if a woman bought a few yards of calico she was entitled to a spool of thread in addition to the usual gratis "trimmin's"; if a man bought a trifle, he was at liberty to draw and swallow as big a drink of whisky as he wanted.

Everything was cheap: apples, peaches, sweet potatoes, Irish potatoes, and corn, ten cents a bushel; chickens, ten cents apiece; butter, six cents a pound; eggs, three cents a dozen; coffee and sugar, five cents a pound; whisky, ten cents a gallon. I do not know how prices are out there in interior Missouri now, but I know what they are here in Hartford, Connecticut. To wit: apples, three dollars a bushel; peaches, five dollars; Irish potatoes (choice Bermudas), five dollars; chickens, a dollar to a dollar and a half apiece, according to weight; butter, forty-five to sixty cents a pound; eggs, fifty to sixty cents a dozen; coffee, forty-five cents a pound; native whisky, four or five dollars a gallon, I believe, but I can only be certain concerning the sort which I use myself, which is Scotch and costs ten dollars a gallon when you take two gallons—more when you take less.

QUESTIONS

1. What phrase or sentence identifies the topic of the first paragraph? What portion of the paragraph doesn't the phrase or sentence cover?

2. What is the subject of the second paragraph? Does the paragraph have a topic phrase or sentence? Identify the topic phrases or sentences of the third and fourth paragraphs.

3. Show how Twain uses repeated words and parallel phrasing in the first paragraph as means of transition. To what previous word—or words —might "winter" (in the last sentence) be said to link?

4. Point out the key transitional word or phrase in the opening sentence of the second, third, and fourth paragraphs, and show what it links to in the previous material.

5. In developing his material Twain employs comparison, classification and analysis, division and enumeration, and one or two other means. Identify them.

6. Do you see any pattern in Twain's description of the interior of his uncle's shop in the third sentence of the third paragraph? Can you see why Twain chose to present the three elements of the fourth sentence in a single sentence rather than in three short sentences? What would be the effect of shifting the woman to the third position in the sentence?

7. Do you see any pattern in the two lists of prices in the fourth paragraph?

8. Twain introduces occasional bits of humor into his description. Compare and contrast the kinds of humor in the following phrases: "dropped

anything smaller than a peach," "in winter there was always a refreshing breeze," "fleas enough for all," "to wit," "more when you take less."

9. Would you say that Twain's sentences are characteristically simple or complex? To what extent does he rely upon repeated constructions? Where —if anywhere—do you find the repetition at all awkward or tedious? What general quality does the repetition lend to the sketch?

New York

E. B. WHITE

Though he has published poetry and two children's books, E. B. White (1899—) is best known for his witty, informal, and very human essays on the passing scene. These were written largely for the *New Yorker* (whose staff he joined in the early 1920's) and have been collected under various titles —*Every Day is Saturday, Quo Vadimus?, The Second Tree from the Corner*. White's subjects change, but his point of view remains that of the city-man, worldly-wise and yet wistful, at ease in his surroundings and yet aware of another less complex and compromising setting.

The oft-quoted thumbnail sketch of New York is, of course: "It's a wonderful place, but I'd hate to live there." I have an idea that people from villages and small towns, people accustomed to the convenience and the friendliness of neighborhood over-the-fence living, are unaware that life in New York follows the neighborhood pattern. The city is literally a composite of tens of thousands of tiny neighborhood units. There are, of course, the big districts and big units: Chelsea and Murray Hill and Gramercy (which are residential units), Harlem (a racial unit), Greenwich Village (a unit dedicated to the arts and other matters), and there is Radio City (a commercial development), Peter Cooper Village (a housing unit), the Medical Center (a sickness unit) and many other sections each of which has some distinguishing characteristic. But the curious thing about New York is that each large geographical unit is composed of countless small neighborhoods. Each neighborhood is virtually self-sufficient. Usually it is no more than two or three blocks long and a couple of blocks wide. Each area is a city within a city within a city. Thus, no matter where you live in New York, you will find within a block or two a grocery store, a barbershop, a newsstand and shoeshine shack, an ice-coal-and-wood cellar (where you write your order on a pad outside as you walk by), a dry cleaner, a laundry, a delicatessen (beer and sandwiches delivered at any hour to your door), a flower shop, an undertaker's parlor, a movie house, a radio-repair shop, a stationer, a haberdasher, a tailor, a drugstore, a garage, a tearoom, a saloon, a hardware store, a liquor store, a shoe-repair shop. Every block or two, in most residential sections of New York, is a little main street. A man starts for work in the morning and before he has gone two hundred yards he has completed half a dozen missions: bought a paper, left a pair of shoes to be soled, picked up a pack of cigarettes, ordered a bottle of whiskey to be dispatched in the opposite direction against his home-coming, written a message to the unseen forces of the wood cellar, and notified the dry cleaner that a pair of trousers awaits call. Homeward bound eight hours later, he buys a bunch of pussy willows, a Mazda bulb, a drink, a shine—all between the corner where he steps off the bus and his apartment. So complete is each neighborhood, and so strong the sense of neighborhood, that many a New Yorker spends a lifetime within the confines of an area smaller than a country village. Let him walk two blocks from his corner and he is in a strange land and will feel uneasy till he gets back.

Storekeepers are particularly conscious of neighborhood boundary lines. A woman friend of mine moved recently from one apartment to another, a distance of three blocks. When she turned up, the day after the move, at the same grocer's that she had patronized for years, the proprietor was in ecstasy—almost in tears—at seeing her. "I was afraid," he said, "now that you've moved away I wouldn't be seeing you any more." To him, *away* was three blocks, or about seven hundred and fifty feet.

QUESTIONS

1. Both paragraphs have topic phrases or sentences. What are they? The first paragraph can be broken down into three or four smaller units. Identify these units and their topic phrases or sentences. Explain the relationship of these smaller units to the main topic of the paragraph.

2. What is the relationship between sentences one and two and between sentences two and three in the first paragraph? Identify the key transitional words and phrases in sentences two and three, and sentences four through nine.

3. To what elements in the first paragraph do "conscious" and "boundary lines" in the first sentence of the second paragraph relate? What is the broad relationship of the second paragraph to the first? Compare the last sentences of the two paragraphs. What function does their similarity serve?

4. Point out the accumulation of detail, anecdote, example, and comparison through which White develops the two paragraphs.

5. What seems to you to be the most convincing piece of evidence that New York is a neighborly place? What distinguishes it from the other evidence?

6. Examine the lists of "big districts and big units," small neighborhood stores, and missions that the man performs going to and from work. What basis do you see for the ordering of each of the lists? What feeling or attitude towards New York does White seem to express through the general degree of orderliness that he gives to the lists?

Seeing Life

ARNOLD BENNETT

Like many English novelists before him, Arnold Bennett
(1867-1931) was also a famous journalist. His political articles written during the First World War and his literary criticism written during the 'twenties were notable for their lucidity and intelligence. As a novelist, Bennett is known as a
realistic portrayer of English provincial life (*The Old Wives'
Tale, Clayhanger, These Twain*—works that have their setting
in the potteries of Staffordshire, where he lived as a youth);
but of equal merit are his fantasies (*The Glimpse*), impres-
sionistic sketches (*The Pretty Lady*), and psychological po-
traits (*Lord Raingo*). Bennett was content that the publ.
should think of him as a realist; privately he described all of
his novels as "variations on the theme of beauty." The following selection is the opening of a discussion on writing that was
intended for a popular audience.

A young dog, inexperienced, sadly lacking in even primary education, ambles and frisks along the footpath of Fulham Road, near
the mysterious gates of a Marist convent. He is a large puppy, on the
way to be a dog of much dignity, but at present he has little to
recommend him but that gawky elegance, and that bounding gratitude for the gift of life, which distinguish the normal puppy. He is

an ignorant fool. He might have entered the convent of nuns and had a fine time, but instead he steps off the pavement into the road, the road being a vast and interesting continent imperfectly explored. His confidence in his nose, in his agility, and in the goodness of God is touching, absolutely painful to witness. He glances casually at a huge, towering vermilion construction that is whizzing towards him on four wheels, preceded by a glint of brass and a wisp of steam; and then with disdain he ignores it as less important than a mere speck of odorous matter in the mud. The next instant he is lying inert in the mud. His confidence in the goodness of God had been misplaced. Since the beginning of time God had ordained him a victim.

An impressive thing happens. The motor-bus reluctantly slackens and stops. Not the differential brake, nor the footbrake, has arrested the motor-bus, but the invisible brake of public opinion, acting by administrative transmission. There is not a policeman in sight. Theoretically, the motor-bus is free to whiz onward in its flight to the paradise of Shoreditch, but in practice it is paralysed by dread. A man in brass buttons and a stylish cap leaps down from it, and the blackened demon who sits on its neck also leaps down from it, and they move gingerly towards the puppy. A little while ago the motor-bus might have overturned a human cyclist or so, and proceeded nonchalant on its way. But now even a puppy requires a post-mortem: such is the force of public opinion aroused. Two policemen appear in the distance.

"A street accident" is now in being, and a crowd gathers with calm joy and stares, passive and determined. The puppy offers no sign whatever; just lies in the road. Then a boy, destined probably to a great future by reason of his singular faculty of initiative, goes to the puppy and carries him by the scruff of the neck, to the shelter of the gutter. Relinquished by the boy, the lithe puppy falls into an easy horizontal attitude, and seems bent upon repose. The boy lifts the puppy's head to examine it, and the head drops back wearily. The puppy is dead. No cry, no blood, no disfigurement!

Even no perceptible jolt of the wheel as it climbed over the obstacle of the puppy's body! A wonderfully clean and perfect accident!

The increasing crowd stares with beatific placidity. People emerge impatiently from the bowels of the throbbing motor-bus and slip down from its back, and either join the crowd or vanish. The two policemen and the crew of the motor-bus have now met in parley. The conductor and the driver have an air at once nervous and resigned; their gestures are quick and vivacious. The policemen, on the other hand, indicate by their slow and huge movements that eternity is theirs. And they could not be more sure of the conductor and the driver if they had them manacled and leashed. The conductor and the driver admit the absolute dominion of the elephantine policemen; they admit that before the simple will of the policemen inconvenience, lost minutes, shortened leisure, docked wages, count as less than naught. And the policemen are carelessly sublime, well knowing that magistrates, jails, and the very Home Secretary on his throne—yes, and a whole system of conspiracy and perjury and brutality—are at their beck in case of need. And yet occasionally in the demeanour of the policemen towards the conductor and the driver there is a silent message that says: "After all, we, too, are working men like you, over-worked and under-paid and bursting with grievances in the service of the pitiless and dishonest public. We, too, have wives and children and privations and frightful apprehensions. We, too, have to struggle desperately. Only the awful magic of these garments and of the garter which we wear on our wrists sets an abyss between us and you." And the conductor writes and one of the policemen writes, and they keep on writing while the traffic makes beautiful curves to avoid them.

The still increasing crowd continues to stare in the pure blankness of pleasure. A close-shaved, well-dressed, middle-aged man, with a copy of *The Sportsman* in his podgy hand, who has descended from the motor-bus, starts stamping his feet. "I was knocked down by a taxi last year," he says fiercely. "But nobody took no notice of *that!* Are they going to stop here all the blank morning for a blank tyke?"

And for all his respectable appearance, his features become debased, and he emits a jet of disgusting profanity and brings most of the Trinity into the thunderous assertion that he has paid his fare. Then a man passes wheeling a muck-cart. And he stops and talks a long time with the other uniforms, because he, too, wears vestiges of a uniform. And the crowd never moves nor ceases to stare. Then the new arrival stoops and picks up the unclaimed, masterless puppy, and flings it, all soft and yielding, into the horrid mess of the cart, and passes on. And only that which is immortal and divine of the puppy remains behind, floating perhaps like an invisible vapour over the scene of the tragedy.

The crowd is tireless, all eyes. The four principals still converse and write. Nobody in the crowd comprehends what they are about. At length the driver separates himself, but is drawn back, and a new parley is commenced. But everything ends. The policemen turn on their immense heels. The driver and conductor race towards the motor-bus. The bell rings, the motor-bus, quite empty, disappears snorting round the corner into Walham Green. The crowd is now lessening. But it separates with reluctance, many of its members continuing to stare with intense absorption at the place where the puppy lay or the place where the policemen stood. An appreciable interval elapses before the "street accident" has entirely ceased to exist as a phenomenon.

The members of the crowd follow their noses, and during the course of the day remark to acquaintances:

"Saw a dog run over by a motor-bus in the Fulham Road this morning! Killed dead!"

And that is all they do remark. That is all they have witnessed. They will not, and could not, give intelligible and interesting particulars of the affair (unless it were as to the breed of the dog or the number of the bus-service). They have watched a dog run over. They analyse neither their sensations nor the phenomenon. They have witnessed it whole, as a bad writer uses a *cliché*. They have observed—that is to say, they have really seen—nothing.

QUESTIONS

1. Identify the subject of each of the first three paragraphs. To what extent is the subject of the second paragraph prepared for in the first? To what extent is the subject of the third paragraph prepared for beforehand? What topic phrases or sentences—if any—do the three paragraphs have?

2. What words in the second sentence of the sketch link it to the first sentence? Identify the words and phrases in the rest of the first paragraph that link to "inexperienced" in the first sentence (as synonym, antonym, example, consequence, etc.).

3. What is the most obvious transitional device that Bennett employs in the first paragraph? What effect does he achieve by its repetition? Where do you find basically the same device employed in the opening sentences of succeeding paragraphs?

4. What elements in paragraphs three and five stand parallel to each other? What is the essential contrast between the two paragraphs? What relationship do the two paragraphs bear to the fourth paragraph?

5. What pattern dominates the arrangement of most of the material in the sketch? Point out in paragraphs three and four the transitional words related to this pattern.

6. Bennett's sketch can be regarded as an illustration, a generalized anecdote, to support the assertion that he makes at the end. What do you think would be the effect of beginning with the assertion? If Bennett isn't merely trying to prove that people are unobservant, what is he trying to do?

7. At the beginning of the sketch, Bennett's puppy is about to enter a convent; at the end his immortal soul is divested of the flesh. What besides a kind of imagistic unity do these and the three or four other religious references contribute to the sketch?

8. From whose point of view is Fulham Road "a vast and interesting continent" (paragraph one)? To whom is the accident "impressive" (paragraph two)? Who thinks that the boy is "destined probably to a great future" (paragraph three)? To whom are the policemen "carelessly sublime" (paragraph four)? On the basis of your answers, would

you say that Bennett stands apart from the scene he describes? Does other evidence support or contradict your answer? Would you say that Bennett is present more in the scene or in the essay?

9. By what means does Bennett imply that the scene he describes is typical rather than unique? (Note, for example, the fact that except for the boy and the middle-aged man, Bennett gives no individual qualities to members of the crowd.) By what means does he achieve the vividness of a unique scene?

10. At the end of the sketch Bennett asserts that the crowd has observed nothing except a few details. Can you classify the kinds of things that Bennett himself has seen? Consider "glint of brass and a wisp of steam" (paragraph one), "blackened demon" (paragraph two), "whole system of conspiracy and perjury and brutality" (paragraph four), "while the traffic makes beautiful curves" (paragraph four). What prevents Bennett's assertion about the crowd's blindness from seeming arrogant?

The Kitchen

ALFRED KAZIN

Alfred Kazin (1915—) was born in New York City and received his education at the City College of New York and Columbia University. His comprehensive study of modern American prose, *On Native Grounds,* appeared when he was twenty-seven, and since then he has published innumerable essays and reviews (some collected in *The Inmost Leaf*) and edited books of criticism on Theodore Dreiser and F. Scott Fitzgerald. He has lectured and taught at many colleges and universities, and is generally considered one of the best of those critics who appraise literature from a social-historical point of view. The prose that follows is from the first volume of what will be an extensive autobiography.

In Brownsville tenements the kitchen is always the largest room and the center of the household. As a child I felt that we lived in a kitchen to which four other rooms were annexed. My mother, a "home" dressmaker, had her workshop in the kitchen. She told me once that she had begun dressmaking in Poland at thirteen; as far back as I can remember, she was always making dresses for the local women. She had an innate sense of design, a quick eye for all the subtleties in the latest fashions, even when she despised them, and great boldness. For three or four dollars she would study the fashion magazines with a customer, go with the customer to the

From *A Walker in the City.* Copyright, 1951, by Alfred Kazin. Reprinted by permission of Harcourt, Brace & World, Inc.

remnants store on Belmont Avenue to pick out the material, argue the owner down—all remnants stores, for some reason, were supposed to be shady, as if the owners dealt in stolen goods—and then for days would patiently fit and baste and sew and fit again. Our apartment was always full of women in their housedresses sitting around the kitchen table waiting for a fitting. My little bedroom next to the kitchen was the fitting room. The sewing machine, an old nut-brown Singer with golden scrolls painted along the black arm and engraved along the two tiers of little drawers massed with needles and thread on each side of the treadle, stood next to the window and the great coal-black stove which up to my last year in college was our main source of heat. By December the two outer bedrooms were closed off, and used to chill bottles of milk and cream, cold borscht and jellied calves' feet.

The kitchen held our lives together. My mother worked in it all day long, we ate in it almost all meals except the Passover *seder*, I did my homework and first writing at the kitchen table, and in winter I often had a bed made up for me on three kitchen chairs near the stove. On the wall just over the table hung a long horizontal mirror that sloped to a ship's prow at each end and was lined in cherry wood. It took up the whole wall, and drew every object in the kitchen to itself. The walls were a fiercely stippled whitewash, so often rewhitened by my father in slack seasons that the paint looked as if it had been squeezed and cracked into the walls. A large electric bulb hung down the center of the kitchen at the end of a chain that had been hooked into the ceiling; the old gas ring and key still jutted out of the wall like antlers. In the corner next to the toilet was the sink at which we washed, and the square tub in which my mother did our clothes. Above it, tacked to the shelf on which were pleasantly ranged square, blue-bordered white sugar and spice jars, hung calendars from the Public National Bank on Pitkin Avenue and the Minsker Progressive Branch of the Workman's Circle; receipts for the payment of insurance premiums, and household bills on a spindle; two little boxes engraved with Hebrew letters. One of these was for the poor, the other to buy back the

Land of Israel. Each spring a bearded little man would suddenly appear in our kitchen, salute us with a hurried Hebrew blessing, empty the boxes (sometimes with a sidelong look of disdain if they were not full), hurriedly bless us again for remembering our less fortunate Jewish brothers and sisters, and so take his departure until the next spring, after vainly trying to persuade my mother to take still another box. We did occasionally remember to drop coins in the boxes, but this was usually only on the dreaded morning of "mid-terms" and final examinations, because my mother thought it would bring me luck. She was extremely superstitious, but embarrassed about it, and always laughed at herself whenever, on the morning of an examination, she counseled me to leave the house on my right foot. "I know it's silly," her smile seemed to say, "but what harm can it do? It may calm God down."

The kitchen gave a special character to our lives; my mother's character. All my memories of that kitchen are dominated by the nearness of my mother sitting all day long at her sewing machine, by the clacking of the treadle against the linoleum floor, by the patient twist of her right shoulder as she automatically pushed at the wheel with one hand or lifted the foot to free the needle where it had got stuck in a thick piece of material. The kitchen was her life. Year by year, as I began to take in her fantastic capacity for labor and her anxious zeal, I realized it was ourselves she kept stitched together. I can never remember a time when she was not working. She worked because the law of her life was work, work and anxiety; she worked because she would have found life meaningless without work. She read almost no English; she could read the Yiddish paper, but never felt she had time to. We were always talking of a time when I would teach her how to read, but somehow there was never time. When I awoke in the morning she was already at her machine, or in the great morning crowd of housewives at the grocery getting fresh rolls for breakfast. When I returned from school she was at her machine, or conferring over *McCall's* with some neighborhood woman who had come in pointing hopefully to an illustration—"Mrs. Kazin! Mrs. Kazin! Make me a dress like it

shows here in the picture!" When my father came home from work
she had somehow mysteriously interrupted herself to make supper
for us, and the dishes cleared and washed, was back at her machine. When I went to bed at night, often she was still there,
pounding away at the treadle, hunched over the wheel, her hands
steering a piece of gauze under the needle with a finesse that always contrasted sharply with her swollen hands and broken nails.
Her left hand had been pierced through when as a girl she had
worked in the infamous Triangle Shirtwaist Factory on the East
Side. A needle had gone straight through the palm, severing a large
vein. They had sewn it up for her so clumsily that a tuft of flesh
always lay folded over the palm.

The kitchen was the great machine that set our lives running; it
whirred down a little only on Saturdays and holy days. From my
mother's kitchen I gained my first picture of life as a white, over-
heated, starkly lit workshop redolent with Jewish cooking, crowded
with women in housedresses, strewn with fashion magazines, patterns, dress material, spools of thread—and at whose center, so
lashed to her machine that bolts of energy seemed to dance out of
her hands and feet as she worked, my mother stamped the treadle
hard against the floor, hard, hard, and silently, grimly at war, beat
out the first rhythm of the world for me.

Every sound from the street roared and trembled at our windows
—a mother feeding her child on the doorstep, the screech of the
trolley cars on Rockaway Avenue, the eternal smash of a handball
against the wall of our house, the clatter of *"der Italyéner"*'s cart
packed with watermelons, the sing-song of the old-clothes men
walking Chester Street, the cries *"Árbes! Árbes! Kinder! Kinder! Heyse gute árbes!"* All day long people streamed into our
apartment as a matter of course—"customers," upstairs neighbors,
downstairs neighbors, women who would stop in for a half-hour's
talk, salesmen, relatives, insurance agents. Usually they came in
without ringing the bell—everyone knew my mother was always at
home. I would hear the front door opening, the wind whistling

through our front hall, and then some familiar face would appear in our kitchen with the same bland, matter-of-fact inquiring look: no need to stand on ceremony: my mother and her kitchen were available to everyone all day long.

At night the kitchen contracted around the blaze of light on the cloth, the patterns, the ironing board where the iron had burned a black border around the tear in the muslin cover; the finished dresses looked so frilly as they jostled on their wire hangers after all the work my mother had put into them. And then I would get that strangely ominous smell of tension from the dress fabrics and the burn in the cover of the ironing board—as if each piece of cloth and paper crushed with light under the naked bulb might suddenly go up in flames. Whenever I pass some small tailoring shop still lit up at night and see the owner hunched over his steam press; whenever in some poorer neighborhood of the city I see through a window some small crowded kitchen naked under the harsh light glittering in the ceiling, I still smell that fiery breath, that warning of imminent fire. I was always holding my breath. What I must have felt most about ourselves, I see now, was that we ourselves were like kindling—that all the hard-pressed pieces of ourselves and all the hard-used objects in that kitchen were like so many slivers of wood that might go up in flames if we came too near the white-blazing filaments in that naked bulb. Our tension itself was fire, we ourselves were forever burning—to live, to get down the foreboding in our souls, to make good.

Twice a year, on the anniversaries of her parents' deaths, my mother placed on top of the ice-box an ordinary kitchen glass packed with wax, the *yortsayt*, and lit the candle in it. Sitting at the kitchen table over my homework, I would look across the threshold to that mourning-glass, and sense that for my mother the distance from our kitchen to *der heym*, from life to death, was only a flame's length away. Poor as we were, it was not poverty that drove my mother so hard; it was loneliness—some endless bitter brooding over all those left behind, dead or dying or soon to die; a loneliness

locked up in her kitchen that dwelt every day on the hazardousness
of life and the nearness of death, but still kept struggling in the
lock, trying to get us through by endless labor.

With us, life started up again only on the last shore. There
seemed to be no middle ground between despair and the fury of
our ambition. Whenever my mother spoke of her hopes for us, it
was with such unbelievingness that the likes of us would ever come
to anything, such abashed hope and readiness for pain, that I finally
came to see in the flame burning on top of the ice-box death itself
burning away the bones of poor Jews, burning out in us everything
but courage, the blind resolution to live. In the light of that mourn-
ing-candle, there were ranged around me how many dead and dying—how many eras of pain, of exile, of dispersion, of cringing before the powers of this world!

It was always at dusk that my mother's loneliness came home most
to me. Painfully alert to every shift in the light at her window, she
would suddenly confess her fatigue by removing her pince-nez, and
then wearily pushing aside the great mound of fabrics on her machine, would stare at the street as if to warm herself in the last of
the sun. "How sad it is!" I once heard her say. "It grips me! It grips
me!" Twilight was the bottommost part of the day, the chillest and
loneliest time for her. Always so near to her moods, I knew she was
fighting some deep inner dread, struggling against the returning
tide of darkness along the streets that invariably assailed her heart
with the same foreboding— Where? Where now? Where is the day
taking us now?

Yet one good look at the street would revive her. I see her now,
perched against the windowsill, with her face against the glass, her
eyes almost asleep in enjoyment, just as she starts up with the
guilty cry—"What foolishness is this in me!"—and goes to the stove
to prepare supper for us: a moment, only a moment, watching the
evening crowd of women gathering at the grocery for fresh bread
and milk. But between my mother's pent-up face at the window
and the winter sun dying in the fabrics—"Alfred, see how beautiful!"—she has drawn for me one single line of sentience.

QUESTIONS

1. What do the first two sentences suggest will be the subject of the first paragraph? To what extent does the subject shift in the rest of the paragraph?

2. To what extent does the first sentence of the second paragraph serve as topic sentence? What chief divisions of subject do you see in the paragraph?

3. Examine the opening sentences of paragraphs two through eight. Compare the sorts of links that they establish with previous material. What broad movement of subject-matter do they suggest?

4. Point out the chief transitional words and phrases within the sixth paragraph. Then trace the shifts in subject from sentence to sentence. What broad means of development governs the movement? What relationship does the final sentence in the paragraph bear to the seventh and eighth paragraphs?

5. What means of development does Kazin employ in the next to last paragraph? What elements in the last paragraph link it to this one?

6. What are the four or five chief qualities that Kazin ascribes to his mother? Why do you suppose he presents them in the order he does?

7. Examine the transformations that the images of light and smelling undergo in the sixth paragraph. What contribution do they make to the paragraph as a whole? Where else in the sketch do you find a similar use of imagery?

8. On the basis of your answers to the first six questions, define the general degree of orderliness of Kazin's writing. What quality would you say it lends to the sketch: energy, seriousness, wit, openness, or something else?

Venice

HENRY JAMES

Henry James (1843-1916), probably the most influential of
modern novelists, was born in New York City, and was educated variously and informally at Albany, Newport, and Cambridge, as well as at Geneva, Bonn, and Paris. He early felt
the attraction of Europe, with its ancient and established cultures, and when in his thirties, he chose to make it his home.
He there wrote his many essays, short stories, and novels, in a
style subtle, refined, and increasingly more intricate and complex. His essays on literature and travel have been collected
in a number of volumes, including *Partial Portraits* and *Italian Hours*. Among his many well-known novels are *The Portrait of a Lady, The Ambassadors,* and *The Wings of the
Dove.* (Further headnote information on James appears on
pp. 232, 446.)

May in Venice is better than April, but June is best of all. Then
the days are hot, but not too hot, and the nights are more beautiful
than the days. Then Venice is rosier than ever in the morning and
more golden than ever as the day descends. She seems to expand
and evaporate, to multiply all her reflections and iridescences. Then
the life of her people and the strangeness of her constitution become a perpetual comedy, or at least a perpetual drama. Then the
gondola is your sole habitation, and you spend days between sea

From *Essays in London and Elsewhere* by Henry James. Reprinted by permission of Harper and Brothers.

and sky. You go to the Lido, though the Lido has been spoiled. When I first saw it, in 1869, it was a very natural place, and there was but a rough lane across the little island from the landing-place to the beach. There was a bathing-place in those days, and a restaurant, which was very bad, but where in the warm evenings your dinner didn't much matter as you sat letting it cool on the wooden terrace that stretched out into the sea. To-day the Lido is a part of united Italy and has been made the victim of villainous improvements. A little cockney village has sprung up on its rural bosom and a third-rate boulevard leads from Santa Elisabetta to the Adriatic. There are bitumen walks and gas-lamps, lodging-houses, shops and a *teatro diurno*. The bathing-establishment is bigger than before, and the restaurant as well; but it is a compensation perhaps that the cuisine is no better. Such as it is, however, you won't scorn occasionally to partake of it on the breezy platform under which bathers dart and splash, and which looks out to where the fishing-boats, with sails of orange and crimson, wander along the darkening horizon. The beach at the Lido is still lonely and beautiful, and you can easily walk away from the cockney village. The return to Venice in the sunset is classical and indispensable, and those who at that glowing hour have floated toward the towers that rise out of the lagoon will not easily part with the impression. But you indulge in larger excursions—you go to Burano and Torcello, to Malamocco and Chioggia. Torcello, like the Lido, has been improved; the deeply interesting little cathedral of the eighth century, which stood there on the edge of the sea, as touching in its ruin, with its grassy threshold and its primitive mosaics, as the bleached bones of a human skeleton washed ashore by the tide, has now been restored and made cheerful, and the charm of the place, its strange and suggestive desolation, has well-nigh departed.

It will still serve you as a pretext, however, for a day on the lagoon, especially as you will disembark at Burano and admire the wonderful fisher-folk, whose good looks—and bad manners, I am sorry to say—can scarcely be exaggerated. Burano is celebrated for the beauty of its women and the rapacity of its children, and it is a fact that though some of the ladies are rather bold about it every one of them shows you a handsome face. The children assail you for coppers, and in their desire to be satisfied pursue your gondola into the sea. Chioggia is a larger Burano, and you carry away from either place a half-sad, half-cynical, but altogether pictorial impression; the impression of bright-colored hovels, of bathing in stagnant canals, of young girls with faces of a delicate shape and a suscep- tible expression, with splendid heads of hair and complexions smeared with powder, faded yellow shawls that hang like old Greek draperies, and little wooden shoes that click as they go up and down the steps of the convex bridges; of brown-cheeked matrons with lustrous tresses and high tempers, massive throats en- cased with gold beads, and eyes that meet your own with a certain traditional defiance. The men throughout the islands of Venice are almost as handsome as the women; I have never seen so many good- looking rascals. At Burano and Chioggia they sit mending their nets, or lounge at the street corners, where conversation is always high- pitched, or clamor to you to take a boat; and everywhere they deco- rate the scene with their splendid color—cheeks and throats as richly brown as the sails of their fishing-smacks—their sea-faded tatters which are always a "costume," their soft Venetian jargon, and the gallantry with which they wear their hats, an article that no- where sits so well as on a mass of dense Venetian curls. If you are happy you will find yourself, after a June day in Venice (about ten o'clock), on a balcony that overhangs the Grand Canal, with your elbows on the broad ledge, a cigarette in your teeth and a little good company beside you. The gondolas pass beneath, the watery surface gleams here and there from their lamps, some of which are colored lanterns that move mysteriously in the darkness. There are some evenings in June when there are too many gondolas, too many lanterns, too many serenades in front of the hotels. The sere- nading in particular is overdone; but on such a balcony as I speak of you needn't suffer from it, for in the apartment behind you—an accessible refuge—there is more good company, there are more cig- arettes. If you are wise you will step back there presently.

QUESTIONS

1. Identify the several distinct units within the first paragraph. What topic phrases or sentences serve them? What is the general movement of the paragraph?

2. What are the key transitional words (a single word or phrase in each sentence) in the first twelve sentences of the first paragraph?

3. What is the means of development of the first seven sentences in the first paragraph? What are the two means employed in sentences seven through twelve? Which of the three means dominates the sketch as a whole?

4. What sentence in the first paragraph provides something of an outline for the structure of the second? Which of the two paragraphs is more unified? What is their general relationship to each other?

5. Trace the chronological movement of the sketch. To what earlier material do the last four sentences relate? In what sense do the last four sentences round off the sketch?

6. What quality do the following phrases have in common: "villainous improvements," "a compensation perhaps that the cuisine is no better," "restored and made cheerful, and the charm of the place . . . has well nigh departed"? Where else in the sketch do you find comparable phrases? To what extent would you say they define the overall quality of the sketch?

7. James' remarks about "villainous improvements" and the charms of desolation might suggest that he prefers old things to new and dead things to living. What is the evidence to the contrary?

8. How strongly does James object to the bad manners of the people on Burano? What is he basically concerned with in describing them? What appears to be his chief criterion regarding everything he judges in the sketch?

9. Which of James' senses are most engaged by Venice? Which sense most of all? Would you call him a sensualist?

10. James says that the cathedral at Torcello is "as touching in its ruin . . . as the bleached bones of a human skeleton washed ashore by the tide." Defend the appropriateness of the comparison from three stand-

points: its exactness and suggestiveness, its relationship to the broad comparison that James is making throughout the paragraph, and its relationship to the aspect of Venice that preoccupies his attention throughout the sketch. (You can perhaps most easily answer part of the question if you consider first some other comparison that he might have made: as touching in its ruin as a child's broken toy.)

Etna

D. H. LAWRENCE

The son of a coal miner, D. H. Lawrence (1885-1930) spent
his youth amid the poverty and brutality of an English mining
town, taught for a time in a secondary school, but early dedicated himself to writing. His first novel, *The White Peacock*,
appeared when he was twenty-six; three more followed in
rapid succession, including the largely autobiographical *Sons
and Lovers*, and also several volumes of poetry. With the end
of the First World War, he began a life of restless travel, settling for a time in Italy and Sicily, and then in Australia and
New Mexico. His last years he passed in different parts of Europe, dying in Southern France at the age of forty-four of the
tuberculosis he had contracted as a child. (Further headnote
information on Lawrence appears on pp. 265, 413.)

Comes over one an absolute necessity to move. And what is more,
to move in some particular direction. A double necessity then: to
get on the move, and to know whither.

Why can't one sit still? Here in Sicily it is so pleasant: the sunny
Ionian sea, the changing jewel of Calabria, like a fire-opal moved in
the light; Italy and the panorama of Christmas clouds, night with
the dog-star laying a long, luminous gleam across the sea, as if baying at us, Orion marching above; how the dog-star Sirius looks at

one, looks at one! he is the hound of heaven, green, glamorous and fierce!—and then oh regal evening star, hung westward flaring over the jagged dark precipices of tall Sicily: then Etna, that wicked witch, resting her thick white snow under heaven, and slowly, slowly rolling her orange-colored smoke. They called her the Pillar of Heaven, the Greeks. It seems wrong at first, for she trails up in a long, magical, flexible line from the sea's edge to her blunt cone, and does not seem tall. She seems rather low, under heaven. But as one knows her better, oh awe and wizardry! Remote under heaven, aloof, so near, yet never with us. The painters try to paint her, and the photographers to photograph her, in vain. Because why? Because the near ridges, with their olives and white houses, these are with us. Because the river-bed, and Naxos under the lemon groves, Greek Naxos deep under dark-leaved, many-fruited lemon groves, Etna's skirts and skirt-bottoms, these still are our world, our own world. Even the high villages among the oaks, on Etna. But Etna herself, Etna of the snow and secret changing winds, she is beyond a crystal wall. When I look at her, low, white, witchlike under heaven, slowly rolling her orange smoke and giving sometimes a breath of rose-red flame, then I must look away from earth, into the ether, into the low empyrean. And there, in that remote region, Etna is alone. If you would see her, you must slowly take off your eyes from the world and go a naked seer to the strange chamber of the empyrean. Pedestal of heaven! The Greeks had a sense of the magic truth of things. Thank goodness one still knows enough about them to find one's kinship at last. There are so many photographs, there are so infinitely many water-color drawings and oil paintings which purport to render Etna. But pedestal of heaven! You must cross the invisible border. Between the foreground, which is our own, and Etna, pivot of winds in lower heaven, there is a dividing line. You must change your state of mind. A metempsychosis. It is no use thinking you can see and behold Etna and the foreground both at once. Never. One or the other. Foreground and a transcribed Etna. Or Etna, pedestal of heaven.

Why, then, must one go? Why not stay? Ah, what a mistress, this

Etna! with her strange winds prowling round her like Circe's panthers, some black, some white. With her strange, remote communications and her terrible dynamic exhalations. She makes men mad. Such terrible vibrations of wicked and beautiful electricity she throws about her, like a deadly net! Nay, sometimes, verily, one can feel a new current of her demon magnetism seize one's living tissue and change the peaceful life of one's active cells. She makes a storm in the living plasm and a new adjustment. And sometimes it is like a madness.

This timeless Grecian Etna, in her lower-heaven loveliness, so lovely, so lovely, what a torturer! Not many men can really stand her, without losing their souls. She is like Circe. Unless a man is very strong, she takes his soul away from him and leaves him not a beast, but an elemental creature, intelligent and soulless. Intelligent, almost inspired, and soulless, like the Etna Sicilians. Intelligent daimons, and humanly, according to us, the most stupid people on earth. Ach, horror! How many men, how many races, has Etna put to flight? It was she who broke the quick of the Greek soul. And after the Greeks, she gave the Romans, the Normans, the Arabs, the Spaniards, the French, the Italians, even the English, she gave them all their inspired hour and broke their souls.

Perhaps it is she one must flee from. At any rate, one must go: and at once. After having come back only at the end of October, already one must dash away. And it is only the third of January. And one cannot afford to move. Yet there you are: at the Etna bidding one goes.

Where does one go? There is Girgenti by the south. There is Tunis at hand. Girgenti, and the sulphur spirit and the Greek guarding temples, to make one madder? Never. Neither Syracuse and the madness of its great quarries. Tunis? Africa? Not yet, not yet. Not the Arabs, not yet. Naples, Rome, Florence? No good at all. Where then?

Where then? Spain or Sardinia. Spain or Sardinia. Sardinia, which is like nowhere. Sardinia, which has no history, no date, no race, no offering. Let it be Sardinia. They say neither Romans nor Phoenicians, Greeks nor Arabs ever subdued Sardinia. It lies outside; outside the circuit of civilisation. Like the Basque lands. Sure enough, it is Italian now, with its railways and its motor-omnibuses. But there is an uncaptured Sardinia still. It lies within the net of this European civilisation, but it isn't landed yet. And the net is getting old and tattered. A good many fish are slipping through the net of the old European civilisation. Like that great whale of Russia. And probably even Sardinia. Sardinia then. Let it be Sardinia.

QUESTIONS

1. Show the relationship of the rest of the sketch to the two necessities that Lawrence mentions in the first paragraph.

2. Locate the topic phrases or sentences for the two main parts of the second paragraph. What are the topic phrases or sentences for paragraphs three and four?

3. Examine the opening sentences in the several paragraphs. Compare the sorts of links that they establish with previous material.

4. Examine the transitional devices in the third paragraph. Note particularly the parallel phrasing and the transformations that "dynamic" undergoes.

5. Where in the second paragraph do you find the answer to the question with which the paragraph opens? To what extent does the third paragraph provide the same answer? To which of the two paragraphs does the fourth paragraph seem closer?

6. Consider the following changes in material in the second paragraph: "the changing fire-opal of Calabria," "the Greeks called her the Pillar of Heaven," "the painters try vainly to paint her." On what basis could you say that the passages have been improved? On what basis could you say that they have been damaged?

7. In the fourth paragraph Lawrence compares Etna to Circe. Show how he builds up to this comparison in paragraphs two and three.

8. How appropriate does Lawrence's comparison of Etna to Circe seem? How appropriate does his comparison of European civilization to a fishing net seem? What exactly is he comparing in both instances? Would you say that he employs both comparisons in order to achieve vividness?

9. Lawrence employs analogy, illustration, and repetition in developing the fourth paragraph. Point them out. Identify his means of developing the seventh paragraph. Which of these means dominates the sketch? What quality does it lend to the sketch?

10. Analyze the sketch as a progression of questions and answers. How directly does Lawrence answer his questions? What general effect does he achieve by his repeated questioning? Can you relate your answer to this question to your answer to the last part of the ninth question?

Waxworks at the Abbey

VIRGINIA WOOLF

Though rather less esteemed than she once was, Virginia
Woolf (1882-1941) remains one of the more important of
modern novelists. A tireless experimenter, she reveals in such
novels as *Mrs. Dalloway, To the Lighthouse,* and *The Waves*
a sensibility alert to the most fleeting impression and nuance,
and a style delicate, intense, and thoroughly subjective. Similar qualities, somewhat subdued, are present in many of her
essays, which may be read in a number of collections, including *The Common Reader* (in two volumes), *The Death of the
Moth,* and *The Captain's Death Bed.* Among her other non-
fiction are *A Room of One's Own* and *Three Guineas,* both of
which champion the rights of woman, and *A Writer's Diary,*
a posthumous culling, by her husband, from her private journals. (Further headnote information on Virginia Woolf appears on p. 157.)

Nobody but a very great man could have worn the Duke of Wellington's top hat. It is as tall as a chimney, as straight as a ramrod, as
black as a rock. One could have seen it a mile off advancing in-
domitably down the street. It must have been to this emblem of in-
corruptible dignity that the Duke raised his two fingers when
passers-by respectfully saluted him. One is almost tempted to salute
it now.

The connexion between the waxworks in the Abbey and the Duke
of Wellington's top hat is one that the reader will discover if he goes
to the Abbey when the waxworks are shut. The waxworks have their
hours of audience like other potentates. And if that hour is four
and it is now a trifle past two, one may spend the intervening moments profitably in the United Services Museum in Whitehall,
among cannon and torpedoes and gun-carriages and helmets and
spurs and faded uniforms and the thousand other objects which
piety and curiosity have saved from time and treasured and num-
bered and stuck in glass cases forever. When the time comes to go,
indeed, there is not as much contrast as one would wish, perhaps,
between the Museum at one end of Whitehall and the Abbey at the
other. Too many monuments solicit attention with outstretched
hands; too many placards explain this and forbid that; too many
sightseers shuffle and stare for the past and the dead and the mystic
nature of the place to have full sway. Solitude is impossible. Do we
wish to see the Chapels? We are shepherded in flocks by gentlemen
in black gowns who are for ever locking us in or locking us out;
round whom we press and gape; from whom drop raucously all
kinds of dry unappetizing facts; how much beauty this tomb has;
how much age that; when they were destroyed; by whom they
were restored and what the cost was—until everybody longs to be
let off a tomb or two and is thankful when the lesson hour is over.
However, if one is very wicked, and very bored, and lags a little
behind; if the key is left in the door and turns quite easily, so that
after all it is an open question whether one has broken one's country's laws or not, then one can slip aside, run up a little dark staircase and find oneself in a very small chamber alone with Queen
Elizabeth.

The Queen dominates the room as she once dominated England.
Leaning a little forward so that she seems to beckon you to come to
her, she stands, holding her sceptre in one hand, her orb in the
other. It is a drawn, anguished figure, with the pursed look of someone who goes in perpetual dread of poison or of trap; yet forever
braces herself to meet the terror unflinchingly. Her eyes are wide

and vigilant; her nose thin as the beak of a hawk; her lips shut tight; her eyebrows arched; only the jowl gives the fine drawn face its massiveness. The orb and the sceptre are held in the long thin hands of an artist, as if the fingers thrilled at the touch of them. She is immensely intellectual, suffering, and tyrannical. She will not allow one to look elsewhere.

Yet in fact the little room is crowded. There are many hands here holding other sceptres and orbs. It is only beside Queen Elizabeth that the rest of the company seems insignificant. Flowing in velvet they fill their glass cases, as they once filled their thrones, with dignity. William and Mary are an amiable pair of monarchs; bazaar-opening, hospital-inspecting, modern; though the King, unfortunately, is a little short in the legs. Queen Anne fondles her orb in her lap with plump womanly hands that should have held a baby there. It is only by accident that they have clapped a great crown on her hair and told her to rule a kingdom, when she would so much rather have flirted discreetly—she was a pretty woman; or run to greet her husband smiling—she was a kindly one. Her type of beauty in its homeliness, its domesticity, comes down to us less impaired by time than the grander style. The Duchess of Richmond, who gave her face to Britannia on the coins, is out of fashion now. Only the carriage of the little head on the long neck, and the simper and the still look of one who has always stood still to be looked at assure us that she was beautiful once and had lovers beyond belief. The parrot sitting on its perch in the corner of the case seems to make its ironical comment on all that. Once only are we reminded of the fact that these effigies were moulded from the dead and that they were laid upon coffins and carried through the streets. The young Duke of Buckingham who died at Rome of consumption is the only one of them who has resigned himself to death. He lies very still with the ermine on his shoulders and the coronet on his brows, but his eyes are shut; his nose is a great peak between two sunk cheeks; he has succumbed to death and lies steeped in its calm. His aloofness compares strangely with the carnality of Charles the Second round the corner. King Charles still seems quivering with the passions and the greeds of life. The great lips are still pouting and watering and asking for more. The eyes are pouched and creased with all the long nights they have watched out—the torches, the dancing, and the women. In his dirty feathers and lace he is the very symbol of voluptuousness and dissipation, and his great blue-veined nose seems an irreverence on the part of the modeller, as if to set the crowd, as the procession comes by, nudging each other in the ribs and telling merry stories of the monarch.

And so from this garish bright assembly we run downstairs again into the Abbey, and enter that strange muddle and miscellany of objects both hallowed and ridiculous. Yet now the impression is less tumultuous than before. Two presences seem to control its incoherence, as sometimes a chattering group of people is ordered and quieted by the entry of someone before whom, they know not why, they fall silent. One is Elizabeth, beckoning; the other is an old top-hat.

QUESTIONS

1. Devise a topic sentence for the first paragraph. What phrase in the paragraph defines the topic most adequately?

2. Try to devise a topic sentence for the second paragraph. If it does not seem possible to devise a satisfactory one, divide the paragraph into its smaller parts and see whether topic sentences can be devised for them. What holds the paragraph together?

3. Examine the opening sentences of paragraphs two through five. What sorts of links do they establish with earlier material? Compare and contrast their forcefulness and smoothness as transitions.

4. By what means does Mrs. Woolf develop the first paragraph? Contrast it with the means by which she develops the third paragraph.

5. What pattern—if any—determines the order in which Mrs. Woolf describes the several wax figures in the room with Queen Elizabeth?

What pattern—or patterns—predominate in the broad arrangement of material in the sketch?

6. What are the two main connections between the Duke of Wellington and Queen Elizabeth discussed in the essay?

7. "Straight as a ramrod" (paragraph one) is a cliché. What makes it more than a cliché here? Rocks are perhaps not characteristically black. What justifies "black as a rock" (paragraph one)?

8. Point out the irony and exaggeration in the first three sentences in the first paragraph. What sort of man is the Duke of Wellington made to seem in the fourth sentence? Is there any material in the first four sentences that suggests that Mrs. Woolf means to be taken seriously in the fifth? To what extent do her irony and exaggeration serve to ridicule the Duke of Wellington? To what extent do they do something else?

9. The dramatic relationship between paragraphs one and two is similar to that between paragraphs three and four. Explain the relationship. What comment does the final paragraph make upon the relationship?

10. Mrs. Woolf leaves behind as strong an impression of herself as of Queen Elizabeth. What qualities does she reveal?

SECTION II

Organization

Organization

Often enough, organizing an essay seems to be a simple operation. "I organized this theme in four parts," says the student. "In the first part I described what it was like to be in a new school with two thousand other students instead of the two hundred there'd been in my grammar school. In the second part I told mainly about the Sophomore Hop. . . ." "No," says the teacher, "I don't mean how many parts or what's in each part. When I talk about organization I mean the basis on which you arranged those parts." The student finds another answer: "chronological." But this answer is not the whole answer.

If the student is writing up a physics experiment or explaining how to refine sugar, he may have no problem. He has followed a prescribed order in the conduct of his experiment, he has surrendered himself to the process of refining sugar. Suppose, though, that he is asked to describe Times Square. Well, he says to himself, if I organized my theme about high school chronologically, I'll organize this one spatially. But although "spatially" is a good descriptive word, it doesn't help much here. The student has yet to decide what sort of spatial order he prefers: left to right, top to bottom, looking down from the Times Building, or coming up from 38th Street. Even if he is writing his theme in a hurry, he is not likely to think that a spatial movement from left to right or top to bottom will do. "You've organized your theme spatially," he can hear his teacher say, "but you've also organized it mechanically. And by 'mechanically' I mean that it doesn't move." The student realizes that to describe Times Square from the Times Building might enable him to proceed on the basis of the relative visual prominence of several sights, or that coming up from 38th Street might provide a dramatic movement. He is on the verge of organizing his theme.

By this time the teacher is ready to ask: why in fact did you organize that high school theme chronologically? Chronology isn't a one-way street any more than space is—especially Times Square. Time goes backwards as well as forward, and it goes in circles. There is, in part, a chronological organization to Thoreau's *Walden:* the book begins with spring and goes through summer, fall, and winter, and then goes on to spring again because Thoreau associates spring with his view—which he wishes to emphasize at the end— that human life can undergo rebirths. The chronological order serves a higher principle.

There are many ways to organize essays. Few good essays adhere to a single pattern. Given material can be organized a dozen different ways by a dozen different writers, and each of the ways may be effective. (The resulting essays will have different meanings, too.) Some of the patterns of organizing are neatly defined by words like processive, chronological, spatial, and logical, which give a person a comfortable feeling that sometimes he ought not to have. Other patterns are suggested by terms such as causal and investigative. Whatever the pattern—and there are patterns for which there are no terms—the student will probably have failed to organize his theme well unless he can say: I employed this pattern because. . . . He should have a rationale for his organization. In a very short piece of writing, such as a single paragraph assignment, the rationale will be rudimentary. A paragraph that answers the question "Why did Thoreau go to the woods?" in three sentences—the first providing the answer, the latter two elucidating it—has directness and lucidity as its rationale. Similarly, in some forms of writing such as explanations of a process, the rationale may be implicit in the pattern-term (processive). But when the answer to the question "Why did Thoreau go to the woods?" is a long theme that explains practical, philosophical, psychological, and some other reasons, the writer ought to be able to say: I organized these parts in an order of increasing complexity because the simpler reasons were instrumental in explaining the more complex ones. To put the matter differently: why in fact did you organize that theme about high school chronologically? Was it to show a growth, a spreading of wings? If you had organized it in reverse chronological order, would it have been to trace more clearly a series of achievements back to a purposeful freshman? Or even to trace a series of failures back to him? Ultimately the rationale for the organization of an essay will refer to the overall purpose and conception of the essay. In deciding upon the organization of his theme about Times Square, the student is very likely coming to a clearer understanding of his exact subject (some bits and pieces of Times Square), the point of view he wishes to assume, the appropriate tone, and other aspects of his whole theme.

It is not always easy, perhaps not always possible, to state a clear-cut rationale for an organization. The fault lies in the occasional artificiality of the distinction between organization and rationale (processive organization, for example, has a built-in rationale), or in the ambiguity of terms (see the distinction between chronological and dramatic in the next paragraph). And sometimes when the task is easy, the ease is evasion. "I organized this paper logically," says the student, "because it was the best order." Perhaps he means: I organized this paper logically because it seemed logical to do so. What does the word logical mean to him? It may mean sensible. And sensible may mean the order in which the material happened to fall: helter-skelter. "Necessarily because I wrote this paper," says the student, "it is organized logically and in the best way."

The term development is frequently used in conjunction with organization—with a meaning different from that given to it in the preceding section of this text. Sometimes development and organization are used synonymously: I developed this theme chronologically. Sometimes development is used to suggest a unified, organic relationship of the elements of an essay. So used, it associates itself with rationale. Such a term as chronological suggests organization; such a term as dramatic suggests development. Together, organization and development imply purposive order: organization with a rationale.

Given below are some comments on a few terms that are frequently applied to organization.

Argumentation. Basically, an argument divides into three parts: assertion; evidence, illustration, or reasoning; and conclusion, or re-assertion. Usually the pattern is complicated through the use of, say, secondary illustration; and a well-argued piece of writing will take into account objections, counter-evidence, and so forth. If the writer is advocating an action, he will have to discuss the need for the action and the advantages of the particular action over other possible actions. The arrangement of the elements of an argument is not rigid; but need can be expected to precede evidence, and evidence can be expected to precede counter-evidence.

Cause-effect. This term more often describes the matter of an essay than the organizing principle behind it. If a writer deals with a single cause and its effect (the raid on Harper's Ferry and its repercussions), cause-effect gives him merely a beginning for arranging his material. (He is likely, of course, to proceed chronologically.) If he is dealing in multiple causes, he faces the problem of ordering them. Cause-effect is a significant organizing principle when the writer is dealing with a chain of several circumstances that he can link causally: Northern anti-slavery sentiment, the Kansas aid movement, the attraction of John Brown to Kansas, the murder by John Brown of pro-slavery men at Pottawatomie Creek, his raising of funds to continue such violence, his raid on Harper's Ferry, the development of Northern sympathy for him.

Characterization. See *Definition.*

Classification (and *Analysis*). As a preliminary act in the organizing of an essay, classification can be of the greatest help. A welter of causes of the Civil War (the Depression of 1857, the Kansas-Nebraska Bill, economic inequality between North and South, the Dred Scott decision, the election of Lincoln, the firing on Fort

Sumter, etc.) may be arranged under the headings of economic, political, and moral causes. After such classification, the writer will face a simpler organizational task with regard to his three categories.

Comparison and Contrast. The phrase has two meanings. It can refer to the method of developing a single subject that was mentioned in the previous section of the text, or it can refer to two or more subjects being examined together. In the latter sense, the phrase has limited usefulness organizationally. If the relationship between the subjects divides into two or more parts, the writer faces a problem of organization that the term comparison-and-contrast does not help to solve.

Definition. This term and *Characterization* are occasionally cited as patterns of organization. The terms seem rather to suggest categories of subject-matter (or perhaps kinds of writing, comparable to description and narration). If a writer undertakes a relatively formal definition, he will divide his essay into prescribed parts, but the arrangement of those parts—whether few or many—remains to be determined. If, as is more likely, a writer undertakes something different from a formal definition (Carl Becker in his essay "Progress" in this section), he even more clearly will have to cast about for an organizational scheme. It will help him in thinking about his definition and perhaps help him in organizing his material if he knows that there are several methods or aspects of defining: analysis, function, example, negation, and so forth.

Drama. In dramatic literature, the term conventionally refers to a progressive raising of tension to a climax, followed by a denouement. Just as there are many plays without climaxes in the conventional sense, so there are many kinds of dramatic order. And no clear names define or describe them. In two or three essays in the present section, the student will find significant dramatic order that complements another organizational pattern. "Marrakech" provides the most notable illustration.

Investigation. If an archaeologist comes upon a strange piece of statuary in the Egyptian desert, he sees it first as a physical object (a shattered face, two legs); he may then notice the quality of the countenance (kingly); next he may examine the sculptural technique (excellent); finally he infers from the nature of the technique that the statue probably was made during the reign of Ozymandias. A glance at the hitherto unseen pedestal that lies in the sand confirms his opinion. Another archaeologist may investigate the same subject differently, but the basic pattern he follows is likely to be the same: observation or inspection—analysis—comprehension or inference. Writers can follow such patterns from actual experience; they can create and modify them.

On the Aran Islands

JOHN MILLINGTON SYNGE

Born near Dublin, of cultured and established family, John Millington Synge (1871-1909) studied at Trinity College, Dublin, and spent much of his early manhood somewhat aimlessly in Paris. There he met William Butler Yeats, who persuaded him to visit the Aran Islands (in western Ireland) and to live among the islanders. His impressions and observations provided the impetus for the series of remarkable plays on peasant life that he wrote in the years 1903-1907: the most famous are *Riders to the Sea* and *The Playboy of the Western World*. *The Aran Islands,* from which the following are selections, is a record of his several visits, concerning which Yeats remembered his having said: "Is not style born out of the shock of new material?"

I

After Mass this morning an old woman was buried. She lived in the cottage next mine, and more than once before noon I heard a faint echo of the keen. I did not go to the wake for fear my presence might jar upon the mourners, but all last evening I could hear the strokes of a hammer in the yard, where, in the middle of a little crowd of idlers, the next of kin laboured slowly at the coffin. To-day, before the hour for the funeral, poteen was served to a number of men who stood about upon the road, and a portion was brought to me in my room. Then the coffin was carried out sewn loosely in sailcloth, and held near the ground by three cross-poles lashed upon the top. As we moved down to the low eastern portion of the island, nearly all the men, and all the oldest women, wearing petticoats over their heads, came out and joined in the procession.

While the grave was being opened the women sat down among the flat tombstones, bordered with a pale fringe of early bracken, and began the wild keen, or crying for the dead. Each old woman, as she took her turn in the leading recitative, seemed possessed for the moment with a profound ecstasy of grief, swaying to and fro, and bending her forehead to the stone before her, while she called out to the dead with a perpetually recurring chant of sobs.

All round the graveyard other wrinkled women, looking out from under the deep red petticoats that cloaked them, rocked themselves with the same rhythm, and intoned the inarticulate chant that is sustained by all as an accompaniment.

The morning had been beautifully fine, but as they lowered the coffin into the grave, thunder rumbled overhead and hailstones hissed among the bracken.

In Inishmaan one is forced to believe in a sympathy between man and nature, and at this moment when the thunder sounded a death-peal of extraordinary grandeur above the voices of the women, I could see the faces near me stiff and drawn with emotion.

When the coffin was in the grave, and the thunder had rolled away across the hills of Clare, the keen broke out again more passionately than before.

This grief of the keen is no personal complaint for the death of one woman over eighty years, but seems to contain the whole passionate rage that lurks somewhere in every native of the island. In this cry of pain the inner consciousness of the people seems to lay itself bare for an instant, and to reveal the mood of beings who feel their isolation in the face of a universe that wars on them with winds and seas. They are usually silent, but in the presence of death all outward show of indifference or patience is forgotten, and they shriek with pitiable despair before the horror of the fate to which they all are doomed.

Before they covered the coffin an old man kneeled down by the grave and repeated a simple prayer for the dead.

There was an irony in these words of atonement and Catholic belief spoken by voices that were still hoarse with the cries of pagan desperation.

A little beyond the grave I saw a line of old women who had recited in the keen sitting in the shadow of a wall beside the roofless shell of the church. They were still sobbing and shaken with grief, yet they were beginning to talk again of the daily trifles that veil from them the terror of the world.

When we had all come out of the graveyard, and two men had rebuilt the hole in the wall through which the coffin had been carried in, we walked back to the village, talking of anything, and joking of anything, as if merely coming from the boat-slip, or the pier.

One man told me of the poteen drinking that takes place at some funerals.

"A while since," he said, "there were two men fell down in the graveyard while the drink was on them. The sea was rough that day, the way no one could go to bring the doctor, and one of the men never woke again, and found death that night."

II

In some ways these men and women seem strangely far away from me. They have the same emotions that I have, and the animals have, yet I cannot talk to them when there is much to say, more than to the dog that whines beside me in a mountain fog.

There is hardly an hour I am with them that I do not feel the shock of some inconceivable idea, and then again the shock of some vague emotion that is familiar to them and to me. On some days I feel this island as a perfect home and resting place; on other days I feel that I am a waif among the people. I can feel more with them than they can feel with me, and while I wander among them, they like me sometimes, and laugh at me sometimes, yet never know what I am doing.

In the evenings I sometimes meet with a girl who is not yet half through her 'teens, yet seems in some ways more consciously developed than any one else that I have met here. She has passed part of her life on the mainland, and the disillusion she found in Galway has coloured her imagination.

As we sit on stools on either side of the fire I hear her voice going backwards and forwards in the same sentence from the gaiety of a child to the plaintive intonation of an old race that is worn with sorrow. At one moment she is a simple peasant, at another she seems to be looking out at the world with a sense of prehistoric disillusion and to sum up in the expression of her grey-blue eyes the whole external despondency of the clouds and sea.

Our conversation is usually disjointed. One evening we talked of a town on the mainland.

"Ah, it's a queer place," she said: "I wouldn't choose to live in it. It's a queer place, and indeed I don't know the place that isn't."

Another evening we talked of the people who live on the island or come to visit it.

"Father——is gone," she said; "he was a kind man but a queer man. Priests is queer people, and I don't know who isn't."

Then after a long pause she told me with seriousness, as if speaking of a thing that surprised herself, and should surprise me, that she was very fond of the boys.

In our talk, which is sometimes full of the innocent realism of childhood, she is always pathetically eager to say the right thing and be engaging.

One evening I found her trying to light a fire in the little side room of her cottage, where there is an ordinary fireplace. I went in to help her and showed her how to hold up a paper before the mouth of the chimney to make a draught, a method she had never seen. Then I told her of men who live alone in Paris and make their own fires that they may have no one to bother them. She was sitting in a heap on the floor staring into the turf, and as I finished she looked up with surprise.

"They're like me so," she said; "would anyone have thought that!"

Below the sympathy we feel there is still a chasm between us.

"Musha," she muttered as I was leaving her this evening, "I think it's to hell you'll be going by and by."

Occasionally I meet her also in a kitchen where young men go to play cards after dark and a few girls slip in to share the amusement. At such times her eyes shine in the light of the candles, and her cheeks flush with the first tumult of youth, till she hardly seems the same girl who sits every evening droning to herself over the turf.

III

In the autumn season the threshing of the rye is one of the many tasks that fall to the men and boys. The sheaves are collected on a bare rock, and then each is beaten separately on a couple of stones placed on end one against the other. The land is so poor that a field hardly produces more grain than is needed for seed the following year, so the rye-growing is carried on merely for the straw, which is used for thatching.

The stooks are carried to and from the threshing fields, piled on donkeys that one meets everywhere at this season, with their black, unbridled heads just visible beneath a pinnacle of golden straw.

While the threshing is going on sons and daughters keep turning up with one thing and another till there is a little crowd on the rocks, and any one who is passing stops for an hour or two to talk on his way to the sea, so that, like the kelp-burning in the summertime, this work is full of sociability.

When the threshing is over the straw is taken up to the cottages and piled up in an outhouse, or more often in a corner of the kitchen, where it brings a new liveliness of colour.

A few days ago when I was visiting a cottage where there are the most beautiful children on the island, the eldest daughter, a girl of about fourteen, went and sat down on a heap of straw by the doorway. A ray of sunlight fell on her and on a portion of the rye, giving her figure and red dress with the straw under it a curious relief against the nets and oilskins, and forming a natural picture of exquisite harmony and colour.

In our own cottage the thatching—it is done every year—had just been carried out. The rope-twisting was done partly in the lane, partly in the kitchen when the weather was uncertain. Two men usually sit together at this work, one of them hammering the straw with a heavy block of wood, the other forming the rope, the main body of which is twisted by a boy or girl with a bent stick specially formed for this employment.

In wet weather, when the work must be done indoors, the person who is twisting recedes gradually out of the door, across the lane, and sometimes across a field or two beyond it. A great length is needed to form the close network which is spread over the thatch, as each piece measures about fifty yards. When this work is in progress in half the cottages of the village, the road has a curious look, and one has to pick one's steps through a maze of twisting ropes that pass from the dark doorways on either side into the fields.

When four or five immense balls of rope have been completed, a thatching party is arranged, and before dawn some morning they come down to the house, and the work is taken in hand with such energy that it is usually ended within the day.

Like all work that is done in common on the island, the thatching is regarded as a sort of festival. From the moment a roof is taken in hand there is a whirl of laughter and talk till it is ended, and, as the man whose house is being covered is a host instead of an employer, he lays himself out to please the men who work with him.

The day our own house was thatched the large table was taken into the kitchen from my room, and high teas were given every few hours. Most of the people who came along the road turned down into the kitchen for a few minutes, and the talking was incessant. Once when I went into the window I heard Michael retailing my astronomical lectures from the apex of the gable, but usually their topics have to do with the affairs of the island.

It is likely that much of the intelligence and charm of these people is due to the absence of any division of labour, and to the correspondingly wide development of each individual, whose varied knowledge and skill necessitates considerable activity of mind. Each man can speak two languages. He is a skilled fisherman, and can manage a curagh with extraordinary nerve and dexterity. He can farm simply, burn kelp, cut out pampooties, mend nets, build and thatch a house, and make a cradle or a coffin. His work changes with the seasons in a way that keeps him free from the dulness that comes to people who have always the same occupation. The danger of his life on the sea gives him the alertness of the primitive hunter, and the long nights he spends fishing in his curagh bring him some of the emotions that are thought peculiar to men who have lived with the arts.

QUESTIONS

I

1. What organizational pattern covers the first two paragraphs and most of the rest of the sketch? At what points in the sketch is that pattern broken? What is the general character of the material that falls within that pattern? What is the character of the material that falls outside of it? How would you describe the overall pattern of the sketch—to include the material outside as well as inside the primary pattern? What sort of rationale can you offer for Synge's organizing the sketch the way he has rather than, say, putting the material that falls into the primary pattern first and then drawing together the other material into a unit?

2. Synge's relationship to the Aran people is indicated in two or three ways. What are they? If his relationship were different, what aspects of the sketch would be different?

3. Distinguish between the sort of description contained in the sentence that begins: "Then the coffin was carried out" and the sort in the sen-

tence that begins: "Each old woman." Which predominates in the
sketch? What connection is there between the predominance of the one
sort and Synge's relationship to the people?

4. Several of the paragraphs are unusually brief. Can some of them be
satisfactorily joined to others? What would happen to the organization
if they were joined? What quality do the short paragraphs give to the
sketch?

5. Synge says, "In Inishmaan one is forced to believe in a sympathy
between man and nature." Later he says that the people "feel their
isolation in the face of a universe that wars on them." Explain what he
means by each statement and show that the statements do not contradict each other. Which of the statements is applicable to the description of nature in the final paragraph? Of what relevance to the
depiction of nature is the fact that the dead woman is eighty years old
rather than, say, eighteen?

II

1. Express the central idea of the first two paragraphs in a brief sentence. What is the broad relationship of the first two paragraphs to the
rest of the sketch?

2. What are the main divisions of the material which follows the first
two paragraphs? Can they be rearranged with modification? What justifies their present order? Do the first two paragraphs have an orderliness
of parts that implies a particular order in the material that will follow?

3. To what previously in the account of the girl does the final paragraph
relate? In what way does the final paragraph make a satisfactory conclusion to the sketch? In what way doesn't it?

III

1. What broad organizational pattern governs the first four paragraphs?
What material within these paragraphs anticipates the breakdown in the
pattern that occurs with the fifth paragraph? Where does the pattern re-
establish itself? Is the material in the fifth paragraph echoed in any
subsequent material?

2. What would you say is the subject of the sketch? In which sentence
is the subject most clearly stated? Explain the relationship of the first
four paragraphs to the subject; then the fifth paragraph; then the succeeding paragraphs.

3. Compare the function of the final paragraph with that of the opening two paragraphs in the preceding sketch. Can this paragraph be more easily shifted to the opening position than they can to the closing position? Would you prefer to see this paragraph in the opening position? What rationale can you offer for the way Synge organizes each sketch?

4. The descriptive material in this sketch differs considerably from the material in the two preceding sketches. What aspects of the three are similar?

How Wealth Accumulates and Men Decay

GEORGE BERNARD SHAW

Though known principally as a playwright, George Bernard Shaw (1856-1950) produced a substantial body of prose, much of it, like the plays, polemical in character. Born in Dublin, he moved to London at the age of twenty, took to journalism, wrote unusually good music and drama criticism, wrote several unimpressive novels, and finally turned to playwriting. Meanwhile, he joined the Fabian Society, a socialist group opposed to revolutionary action, debated publicly for its principles, and wrote economic and political tracts. His views found expression in his plays—*Widowers' Houses, The Doctor's Dilemma, Mrs. Warren's Profession*—and though during a long life he advocated many causes and theories, his general orientation remained that of the Fabians. Offered below is a chapter from a study of socialism and capitalism, written when Shaw was in his early seventies. (Further headnote information on Shaw appears on p. 361.)

I want to stress this personal helplessness we are all stricken with in the face of a system that has passed beyond our knowledge and control. To bring it nearer home, I propose that we switch off from the big things like empires and their wars to little familiar things. Take pins for example! I do not know why it is that I so seldom use a pin when my wife cannot get on without boxes of them at hand;

From *The Intelligent Woman's Guide to Socialism and Capitalism* by George Bernard Shaw. Reprinted by permission of The Public Trustee and The Society of Authors, London.

but it is so; and I will therefore take pins as being for some reason specially important to women.

There was a time when pinmakers could buy the material; shape it; make the head and the point; ornament it; and take it to market or to your door and sell it to you. They had to know three trades: buying, making, and selling; and the making required skill in several operations. They not only knew how the thing was done from beginning to end, but could do it. But they could not afford to sell you a paper of pins for a farthing. Pins cost so much that a woman's dress allowance was called pin money.

By the end of the eighteenth century Adam Smith boasted that it took eighteen men to make a pin, each man doing a little bit of the job and passing the pin on to the next, and none of them being able to make a whole pin or to buy the materials or to sell it when it was made. The most you could say for them was that at least they had some idea of how it was made, though they could not make it. Now as this meant that they were clearly less capable and knowledgeable men than the old pinmakers, you may ask why Adam Smith boasted of it as a triumph of civilization when its effect was so clearly a degrading effect. The reason was that by setting each man to do just one little bit of the work and nothing but that, over and over again, he became very quick at it. The men, it is said, could turn out nearly five thousand pins a day each; and thus pins became plentiful and cheap. The country was supposed to be richer because it had more pins, though it had turned capable men into mere machines doing their work without intelligence, and being fed by the spare food of the capitalist as an engine is fed with coal and oil. That was why the poet Goldsmith, who was a far-sighted economist as well as a poet, complained that "wealth accumulates, and men decay."

Nowadays Adam Smith's eighteen men are as extinct as the diplodocus. The eighteen flesh-and-blood machines are replaced by machines of steel which spout out pins by the hundred million. Even sticking them into pink papers is done by machinery. The result is that with the exception of a few people who design the machines, nobody knows how to make a pin or how a pin is made: that is to say, the modern worker in pin manufacture need not be one-tenth so intelligent and skilful and accomplished as the old pinmaker; and the only compensation we have for this deterioration is that pins are so cheap that a single pin has no expressible value at all. Even with a big profit stuck on to the cost-price you can buy dozens for a farthing; and pins are so recklessly thrown away and wasted that verses have to be written to persuade children (without success) that it is a sin to steal a pin.

Many serious thinkers, like John Ruskin and William Morris, have been greatly troubled by this, just as Goldsmith was, and have asked whether we really believe that it is an advance in wealth to lose our skill and degrade our workers for the sake of being able to waste pins by the ton. We shall see later on, when we come to consider the Distribution of Leisure, that the cure for this is not to go back to the old ways; for if the saving of time by modern machinery were equally divided among us, it would set us all free for higher work than pinmaking or the like. But in the meantime the fact remains that pins are now made by men and women who cannot make anything by themselves, and could not arrange between themselves to make anything even in little bits. They are ignorant and helpless, and cannot lift their finger to begin their day's work until it has all been arranged for them by their employers, who themselves do not understand the machines they buy, and simply pay other people to set them going by carrying out the machine maker's directions.

The same is true of clothes. Formerly the whole work of making clothes, from the shearing of the sheep to the turning out of the finished and washed garment ready to put on, had to be done in the country by the men and women of the household, especially the women; so that to this day an unmarried woman is called a spinster. Nowadays nothing is left of all this but the sheep-shearing; and even that, like the milking of cows, is being done by machinery, as the sewing is. Give a woman a sheep today and ask her to produce a woollen dress for you; and not only will she be quite unable to do it, but you are as likely as not to find that she is not even aware of any connection between sheep and clothes. When she gets her clothes, which she does by buying them at a shop, she knows that there is a difference between wool and cotton and silk, between flannel and merino, perhaps even between stockinet and other wefts; but as to how they are made, or what they are made of, or how they came to be in the shop ready for her to buy, she knows hardly anything. And the shop assistant from whom she buys is no wiser. The people engaged in the making of them know even less; for many of them are too poor to have much choice of materials when they buy their own clothes.

Thus the capitalist system has produced an almost universal ignorance of how things are made and done, whilst at the same time it has caused them to be made and done on a gigantic scale. We have to buy books and encyclopedias to find out what it is we are doing all day; and as the books are written by people who are not doing it, and who get their information from other books, what they tell us is from twenty to fifty years out of date, and unpractical at that. And of course most of us are too tired of our work when we come home to want to read about it: what we need is a cinema to take our minds off it and feed our imagination.

It is a funny place, this world of Capitalism, with its astonishing spread of ignorance and helplessness, boasting all the time of its spread of education and enlightenment. There stand the thousands of property owners and the millions of wage workers, none of them able to make anything, none of them knowing what to do until somebody tells them, none of them having the least notion of how it is that they find people paying them money, and things in the shops to buy with it. And when they travel they are surprised to find that savages and Esquimaux and villagers who have to make everything for themselves are more intelligent and resourceful! The wonder would be if they were anything else. We should die of idiocy through disuse of our mental faculties if we did not fill our heads with romantic nonsense out of illustrated newspapers and novels and plays and films. Such stuff keeps us alive; but it falsifies

everything for us so absurdly that it leaves us more or less dangerous lunatics in the real world.

Excuse my going on like this; but as I am a writer of books and
plays myself, I know the folly and peril of it better than you do.
And when I see that this moment of our utmost ignorance and
helplessness, delusion and folly, has been stumbled on by the blind
forces of Capitalism as the moment for giving votes to everybody,
so that the few wise women are hopelessly overruled by the thousands whose political minds, as far as they can be said to have any
political minds at all, have been formed in the cinema, I realize
that I had better stop writing plays for a while to discuss political
and social realities in this book with those who are intelligent
enough to listen to me.

QUESTIONS

1. What is the organizing pattern of paragraphs two through four?
Where else does Shaw make use of the pattern?

2. Divide Shaw's discussion into about six major parts; then reduce
these parts to three. What organizing principle governs them? What
sort of rationale can you offer for Shaw's organizing the sketch the way
he has rather than, say, employing an investigative pattern?

3. Shaw states one advantage in talking about pins rather than wars.
Can you think of others? What are the comparable disadvantages?

4. Can you justify Shaw's giving the derivations of "pin money" and
"spinster"? Or is he just showing off his knowledge?

5. At what point does Shaw admit that the good old days were not so
good? To what extent does his admission invalidate his general argument?

6. Of what relevance to his main line of reasoning is Shaw's statement
in the sixth paragraph that many modern shopworkers "are too poor to
have much choice of materials when they buy their own clothes"? Re-
cast as an assertion by a defender of capitalism the sentence in the third
paragraph that begins: "The country was supposed to be richer."

7. What would be the effect of reversing the order of mentioning the "savages, Esquimaux, and villagers"? Compare Shaw's judgment that these groups are "more intelligent and resourceful" than wage earners and property owners with John Millington Synge's judgment upon the Aran islanders (at the end of the third sketch, p. 57). Are they the same judgments? Does one seem more convincing than the other? Why?

8. At the end of the seventh paragraph Shaw speaks of the contemporary need for movies "to take our minds off it [our daily work] and feed our imagination." What distinction, if any, is he making between mind and imagination? If you see a distinction, do you think it carries over into the next paragraph? Does Shaw's assertion that "we fill our heads with romantic nonsense" invalidate his earlier description of modern men as "mere machines" (paragraph three)?

9. What attitude does Shaw seem to take towards his readers? Does it seem to be an attitude especially designed for women readers? In what way does his attitude affect the seriousness of his argument?

Corn-Pone Opinions

MARK TWAIN

Twain's type of humor, based so often on the bold display of
incongruity, possessed from the start the possibilities of cyni-
cism, but it was not until the 1890's, long after he had
achieved success, that disillusionment and bitterness came to
dominate his work. The failure of his business ventures, the
sense of waning powers, the death of his daughter, the sickness
and death of his wife—all contributed to a blackness of mood
and pessimistic estimate of man, best seen at their extreme in
such works as *What Is Man?*, *The Mysterious Stranger*, and
The Man That Corrupted Hadleyburg. The last, a long short
story, may be especially compared with the essay reprinted
below. (Further headnote information on Twain appears on
pp. 8, 370.)

Fifty years ago, when I was a boy of fifteen and helping to inhabit
a Missourian village on the banks of the Mississippi, I had a friend
whose society was very dear to me because I was forbidden by my
mother to partake of it. He was a gay and impudent and satirical
and delightful young black man—a slave—who daily preached
sermons from the top of his master's woodpile, with me for sole
audience. He imitated the pulpit style of the several clergymen of
the village, and did it well and with fine passion and energy. To

me he was a wonder. I believed he was the greatest orator in the
United States and would some day be heard from. But it did not
happen; in the distribution of rewards he was overlooked. It is the
way, in this world.

He interrupted his preaching now and then to saw a stick of
wood, but the sawing was a pretense—he did it with his mouth,
exactly imitating the sound the bucksaw makes in shrieking its way
through the wood. But it served its purpose, it kept his master from
coming out to see how the work was getting along. I listened to the
sermons from the open window of a lumber room at the back of
the house. One of his texts was this:

"You tell me whar a man gits his corn pone, en I'll tell you what
his 'pinions is."

I can never forget it. It was deeply impressed upon me. By my
mother. Not upon my memory, but elsewhere. She had slipped in
upon me while I was absorbed and not watching. The black philosopher's idea was that a man is not independent and cannot afford
views which might interfere with his bread and butter. If he would
prosper, he must train with the majority; in matters of large moment, like politics and religion, he must think and feel with the
bulk of his neighbors or suffer damage in his social standing and in
his business prosperities. He must restrict himself to corn-pone
opinions—at least on the surface. He must get his opinions from
other people, he must reason out none for himself, he must have no
first-hand views.

I think Jerry was right, in the main, but I think he did not go far
enough.

1. It was his idea that a man conforms to the majority view of
his locality by calculation and intention.

This happens, but I think it is not the rule.

2. It was his idea that there is such a thing as a first-hand opinion,
an original opinion, an opinion which is coldly reasoned out in a
man's head by a searching analysis of the facts involved, with the
heart unconsulted and the jury room closed against outside influences. It may be that such an opinion has been born somewhere at

some time or other, but I suppose it got away before they could catch it and stuff it and put it in the museum.

I am persuaded that a coldly-thought-out and independent verdict upon a fashion in clothes, or manners, or literature, or politics, or religion, or any other matter that is projected into the field of our notice and interest is a most rare thing—if it has indeed ever existed.

A new thing in costume appears—the flaring hoopskirt, for example—and the passers-by are shocked, and the irreverent laugh. Six months later everybody is reconciled; the fashion has established itself; it is admired now and no one laughs. Public opinion resented it before, public opinion accepts it now and is happy in it. Why? Was the resentment reasoned out? Was the acceptance reasoned out? No. The instinct that moves to conformity did the work. It is our nature to conform; it is a force which not many can successfully resist. What is its seat? The inborn requirement of self-approval. We all have to bow to that; there are no exceptions. Even the woman who refuses from first to last to wear the hoopskirt comes under that law and is its slave; she could not wear the skirt and have her own approval, and that she *must* have, she cannot help herself. But as a rule our self-approval has its source in but one place and not elsewhere—the approval of other people. A person of vast consequences can introduce any kind of novelty in dress and the general world will presently adopt it—moved to do it in the first place by the natural instinct to passively yield to that vague something recognized as authority, and in the second place by the human instinct to train with the multitude and have its approval. An empress introduced the hoopskirt and we know the result. A nobody introduced the bloomer and we know the result. If Eve should come again in her ripe renown, and re-introduce her quaint styles—well, we know what would happen. And we should be cruelly embarrassed, along at first.

The hoopskirt runs its course and disappears. Nobody reasons about it. One woman abandons the fashion, her neighbor notices this and follows her lead, this influences the next woman and so on

and so on, and presently the skirt has vanished out of the world, no
one knows how nor why; nor cares, for that matter. It will come
again by and by, and in due course will go again.

Twenty-five years ago in England, six or eight wine glasses stood
grouped by each person's plate at a dinner party, and they were
used, not left idle and empty; to-day there are but three or four in
the group and the average guest sparingly uses about two of them.
We have not adopted this new fashion yet, but we shall do it
presently. We shall not think it out, we shall merely conform and
let it go at that. We get our notions and habits and opinions from
outside influences; we do not have to study them out.

Our table manners and company manners and street manners
change from time to time, but the changes are not reasoned out;
we merely notice and conform. We are creatures of outside influences; as a rule we do not think, we only imitate. We cannot
invent standards that will stick; what we mistake for standards
are only fashions, and perishable. We may continue to admire them
but we drop the use of them. We notice this in literature. Shakespeare is a standard, and fifty years ago we used to write tragedies
which we couldn't tell from—from somebody else's, but we don't do
it any more now. Our prose standard three quarters of a century
ago was ornate and diffuse; some authority or other changed it in
the direction of compactness and simplicity, and conformity followed without argument. The historical novel starts up suddenly
and sweeps the land. Everybody writes one and the nation is glad.
We had historical novels before; but nobody read them and the
rest of us conformed—without reasoning it out. We are conforming
in the other way now, because it is another case of everybody.

The outside influences are always pouring in upon us and we
are always obeying their orders and accepting their verdicts. The
Smiths like the new play, the Joneses go to see it and they copy
the Smith verdict. Morals, religions, politics, get their following from
surrounding influences and atmospheres almost entirely; not from
study, not from thinking. A man must and will have his own approval first of all, in each and every moment and circumstance of

his life—even if he must repent of a self-approved act the moment after its commission in order to get his self-approval *again*: but speaking in general terms, a man's self-approval in the large concerns of life has its source in the approval of the peoples about him, and not in a searching personal examination of the matter. Mohammedans are Mohammedans because they are born and reared among that sect, not because they have thought it out and can furnish sound reasons for being Mohammedans; we know why Catholics are Catholics, why Presbyterians are Presbyterians, why Baptists are Baptists, why Mormons are Mormons, why thieves are thieves, why monarchists are monarchists, why Republicans are Republicans and Democrats, Democrats. We know it is a matter of association and sympathy, not reasoning and examination; that hardly a man in the world has an opinion upon morals, politics, or religion which he got otherwise than through his associations and sympathies. Broadly speaking, there are none but corn-pone opinions. And broadly speaking, corn-pone stands for self-approval. Self-approval is acquired mainly from the approval of other people. The result is conformity. Sometimes conformity has a sordid business interest—the bread-and-butter interest—but not in most cases, I think. I think that in the majority of cases it is unconscious and not calculated, that it is born of the human being's natural yearning to stand well with his fellows and have their inspiring approval and praise—a yearning which is commonly so strong and so insistent that it cannot be effectually resisted and must have its way.

A political emergency brings out the corn-pone opinion in fine force in its two chief varieties—the pocketbook variety, which has its origin in self-interest, and the bigger variety, the sentimental variety—the one which can't bear to be outside the pale; can't bear to be in disfavor, can't endure the averted face and the cold shoulder, wants to stand well with his friends, wants to be smiled upon, wants to be welcome, wants to hear the precious words, *"He's* on the right track!"* Uttered perhaps by an ass, but still an ass of high degree, an ass whose approval is gold and diamonds to a smaller ass, and confers glory and honor and happiness and membership in the herd. For these gauds many a man will dump his life-long principles into the street, and his conscience along with them. We have seen it happen. In some millions of instances.

Men think they think upon great political questions, and they do; but they think with their party, not independently; they read its literature but not that of the other side; they arrive at convictions but they are drawn from a partial view of the matter in hand and are of no particular value. They swarm with their party, they feel with their party, they are happy in their party's approval; and where the party leads they will follow, whether for right and honor or through blood and dirt and a mush of mutilated morals.

In our late canvass half of the nation passionately believed that in silver lay salvation, the other half as passionately believed that that way lay destruction. Do you believe that a tenth part of the people on either side had any rational excuse for having an opinion about the matter at all? I studied that mighty question to the bottom—came out empty. Half of our people passionately believe in high tariff, the other half believe otherwise. Does this mean study and examination or only feeling? The latter, I think. I have deeply studied that question, too—and didn't arrive. We all do no end of feeling and we mistake it for thinking. And out of it we get an aggregation which we consider a boon. Its name is Public Opinion. It is held in reverence. It settles everything. Some think it the Voice of God.

QUESTIONS

1. The anecdote with which Twain begins his essay is related to his argument in ways both direct and indirect. Clarify the following relationships: the Negro youth's text and Twain's text, the behavior of Twain's mother and the behavior of people at dining tables, the Negro youth's imitation of clergymen and the "Voice of God" at the end.

2. How do you know that Twain is being humorous in the first paragraph? Can you distinguish two or three kinds of humor in it? What

does the lightness of tone imply about the manner in which Twain will conduct his argument?

3. Compare the general quality of seriousness in the first and last paragraphs. Which is more typical of the whole essay?

4. Do you see any organizing principle governing the order in which Twain presents his major illustrations? If you do not see one, can you suggest a principle upon which the illustrations might be re-arranged?

5. In the tenth paragraph Twain says, "But as a rule our self-approval has its source in . . . the approval of other people." In the fourteenth paragraph he says the same thing, "Self-approval is acquired mainly from the approval of other people." Has his argument stood still? Can the intervening material be omitted without damaging the discussion in any way?

6. Describe the general principle of organization governing the essay. If you have read the preceding selection by Bernard Shaw, compare the distinctness with which the two men separate the elements of their organizational patterns. What sort of rationale can you offer for Twain's organizing the essay the way he has, rather than, say, employing an investigative pattern?

7. In the course of his discussion Twain says that most people don't listen to reason. Do you think he is addressing the few people who listen to reason or the majority who don't? Why do you think so?

8. How novel do you think Twain's general viewpoint is? For what reasons unmentioned by Twain might a woman buy a hoopskirt—or refuse to? Is he dishonest in neglecting to mention such reasons?

9. It might be inferred from the essay that Twain is irreligious, cynical, and anti-democratic. Point out the evidence, and then point out other evidence—if there is any—to the contrary.

Death in the Afternoon

ERNEST HEMINGWAY

Ernest Hemingway (1898-1961) was one of the two or three most influential writers of fiction of his time. In a style terse and at times ironic, he fashioned his work from his own large and varied experiences, which in turn reflected some of the principal cultural shocks of the century—*A Farewell to Arms* derives from his experiences during the First World War; *The Sun Also Rises* from what he saw as an American expatriate in post-war Paris; *For Whom the Bell Tolls* from the strife he witnessed as a newspaperman during the Spanish Civil War. He received the Nobel Prize in 1954, two years after the publication of *The Old Man and the Sea*, a moving short novel which celebrates man's powers of endurance. His one play and some of his many short stories have been collected in *The Fifth Column and the First Forty-Nine Stories;* his non-fiction includes *Green Hills of Africa*, on big-game hunting, and *Death in the Afternoon*, on bullfighting.

In the modern formal bullfight or corrida de toros there are usually six bulls that are killed by three different men. Each man kills two bulls. The bulls by law are required to be from four to five years old, free from physical defects, and well armed with sharp-pointed horns. They are inspected by a municipal veterinary surgeon before the fight. The veterinary is supposed to reject bulls that are under age, insufficiently armed or with anything wrong with their eyes, their horns or any apparent disease or visible bodily defect such as lameness.

The men who are to kill them are called matadors and which of the six bulls they are to kill is determined by lot. Each matador or killer, has a cuadrilla, or team, of from five to six men who are paid by him and work under his orders. Three of these men who aid him on foot with capes, and, at his orders place the banderillas, three-foot wooden shafts with harpoon points, are called peones or banderilleros. The other two, who are mounted on horses when they appear in the ring, are called picadors.

No one is called a toreador in Spain. That is an obsolete word which was applied to those members of the nobility who, in the days before professional bullfighting, killed bulls from horseback for sport. Anyone who fights bulls for money, whether as a matador, banderillero or a picador is called a torero. A man who kills them on horseback with a javelin, using trained thoroughbred horses, is called a rejoneador or a caballero en plaza. A bullfight in Spanish is called a corrida de toros or a running of bulls. A bull ring is called a plaza de toros.

In the morning before the bullfight the representatives of each matador, usually their oldest or most trusted banderilleros, meet at the corrals of the plaza de toros where the bulls that are to be fought that afternoon are quartered. They look over the bulls, compare their size, weight, height, the length of their horns, width of horns, sharpness of horns, and the condition of their coats. This last is as good an indication as any of their physical condition and probable bravery. There is no sure sign by which bravery may be determined although there are many indications of probable cowardice. The confidential banderilleros question the herder or vaquero who has travelled from the ranch with the bulls and who, while he is in charge of them, is called the mayoral, about the qualities and probable disposition of each bull. The bulls must be divided into three lots of two bulls each by common consent of the representatives assembled and the effort is to have one good bull and one bad bull, good and bad from the bullfighter's standpoint, in each lot. A good bull for the bullfighter is not too big, not too strong, not too much horns, not too much height at shoulder, but above all with good vision, good reaction to color and movement, brave and frank to charge. A bad bull, for the bullfighter, is too big a bull, too old a bull, too powerful a bull, with too wide horns; but above all a bad bull is one with no reaction to color or movement or with defective courage and lack of sustained viciousness, so that the bullfighter cannot tell when, whether or how he will charge. The representatives, usually short men in caps, not yet shaven for the day, with a great variety of accents, but all with the same hard eyes, argue and discuss. They say the number 20 has more horns than the 42, but the 42 weighs two arrobas (fifty pounds) more than the 16. The 46 is as big as a cathedral, one calls to him and he raises his head from where he has been feeding, and the 18 is roan-colored and may be as cowardly as a steer. The lots are made up after much arguing and the numbers of two bulls, those branded on their flanks, are written on three different cigarette papers and the papers rolled up into balls and dropped into a cap. The roan-colored probable coward has been paired with a medium-weight, black bull with not too long horns and a glossy coat. The cathedral-sized 46 is coupled with the 16 which, being just barely big enough to be passed by the veterinaries and without salient characteristics, is the ideal of the half-bull that looks like a bull but lacks the full development of muscle and knowledge of how to use his horns, that all the representatives have hoped to get for their bullfighter. The number 20 with the wide horns with the needle points is balanced by the 42 which is the next smallest to the 16. The man who holds the cap shakes it and each representative puts in a brown hand and draws out a tight-rolled cigarette paper. They unroll them, read them, perhaps take a final look at the two bulls they have drawn and go off to the hotel to find the matador and tell him what he has to kill.

The matador decides in which order he prefers to take his

bulls. He may take the worst one first and hope to rehabilitate himself with the second in case his work with the first turns out badly. Or if he is third in the order to kill he may take the best one first knowing that he will be killing the sixth bull and if it should be getting dark and the crowd wanting to leave he will be pardoned an attempt to finish quickly and in the easiest way possible should this bull turn out to be difficult.

The matadors kill their bulls in turn in the order of their seniority; this dating from their presentation as a matador de toros in the Plaza of Madrid. If any matador is gored so that he is unable to return from the infirmary his bulls were formerly all killed by the senior-ranking matador of those remaining in the ring. Now they are divided between the remaining matadors.

The bullfight usually takes place at five o'clock or five-thirty in the afternoon. At a half-hour past noon of the day of the fight the apartado takes place. This is the sorting out of bulls in the corrals with the aid of steers and, by the use of swinging doors, runways and trap doors, separating them and trapping them into the individual pens or chiqueros where they are to stay and rest until they come out into the ring in the order in which it has been determined they are to be fought. Bulls are not deprived of food and water before fighting as one may read in various guides to Spain nor are they kept in a dark pen for several days. They are in the chiqueros in a dim light for not more than four hours before the bullfight commences. They are not fed there after they leave the corral any more than a boxer would be fed immediately before a fight, but the reason for placing them in the small dimly lighted pens is to have some way of getting them promptly into the ring, and to rest them and keep them quiet before the fight.

Usually only the matadors, their friends and representatives, the bull ring management, the authorities, and a very few spectators attend the apartado. It is usually the first time the matador sees the bulls he is to kill that afternoon. The number of spectators is kept down in most places by putting the price of tickets at five pesetas. The bull ring management wants few people at the sorting in order that the bulls may not have their attention attracted by the spectators who want to see action and so call to the bulls to excite them that they may charge the doors or the walls or each other. If they charge in the corrals they run a risk of injuring their horns or of goring each other and the management would have to replace them in the ring at the expense of a couple of hundred dollars apiece. Many bullfight spectators and hangers-on have a belief that they can talk to the bulls as well or better than the bullfighters. Protected by the high fence or the wall of the corral they try to catch the bull's eye and they utter the guttural "huh!-huh!-huh!" that the herders and toreros use to call the bull's attention. If the bull in the pen below raises his great head with the wide horns, solid-looking as wood and smoothly pointed, and the hump of muscle in his neck and shoulders, heavy and wide in repose, rises in a great swelling crest under the black, hairy sheen of his hide and his nostrils widen and he lifts and jerks his horns as he looks toward the spectator then the amateur speaker of bull talk has had a success. If the bull should really charge, driving his horns into the wood, or tossing his head at the talker it would be a triumph. To hold down the number of successes and avoid triumphs the management puts the tickets at five pesetas on the theory that anyone able to pay five pesetas to see bulls sorted will be too dignified to try to talk to bulls before bullfights.

There is no way they can be sure of this, and at some places in the country where they have bulls only once a year you see men at the apartado who pay five pesetas only in order to have a better opportunity to exercise their powers as talkers to bulls. But in general the five pesetas reduce the amount of sober talking. The bulls pay little attention to a drunk. I have many times seen drunken men shout at bulls and never seen the bulls pay any attention. The five-peseta atmosphere of dignity in a town like Pamplona, where a man can be drunk twice and eat a meal at the horse fair on five pesetas, gives an almost religious hush to the apartado. No one spends five pesetas there to see the bulls sorted unless he is very rich and dignified. But the atmosphere of the sorting can be very different in other places. I have never seen it quite the same in any two towns. After the sorting everybody goes to the café.

The bullfight itself takes place in a sand-covered ring enclosed by a red wooden fence a little over four feet high. This red wooden fence is called a barrera. Behind it is a narrow circular passageway that separates it from the first row of seats in the amphitheatre. This narrow runway is called the callejon. In it stand the sword-handlers with their jugs of water, sponges, piles of folded muletas and heavy leather sword cases, the bull ring servants, the vendors of cold beer and gaseosas, of iced fruits in nets that float in gal-vanized buckets full of ice and water, of pastries in flat baskets, of salted almonds, and of peanuts. In it also are the police, the bullfighters who are not in the ring at the moment, several plain-clothes policemen ready to arrest amateurs who may jump into the ring, the photographers, and on seats built in it and protected by shields of boards, are the doctors, the carpenters who repair the barrera if it is broken, and the delegates of the government. In some rings the photographers are allowed to circulate in the cal-lejon; in others they must work from their seats.

The seats of the bull ring are uncovered except for the boxes or palcos and the first gallery or grada. From the gallery the seats de-scend in circular rows to the edge of the ring. These rows of numbered places are called tendidos. The two rows nearest the ring, the front rows of all the seats, are called barreras and contra-barreras. The third row are known as delanteras de tendidos or the front row of the tendidos. The bull ring for numbering purposes is cut into sections as you would cut a pie, and these sections num-bered tendidos 1, 2, 3, and so on up to 11 and 12 depending on the size of the ring.

If you are going to a bullfight for the first time the best place for you to sit depends on your temperament. From a box or from the first row in the gallery details of sound and smell and those de-tails of sight that make for the perception of danger are lost or minimized, but you see the fight better as a spectacle and the chances are that, if it is a good bullfight, you will enjoy it more. If it is a bad bullfight, that is, not an artistic spectacle, you will be better off the closer you are, since you can then, for lack of a whole to appreciate, learn and see all the details, the whys and the wherefores. The boxes and the gallery are for people who do not want to see things too closely for fear they may upset them, for people who want to see the bullfight as a spectacle or a pageant, and for experts who can see details even though a long way from them and want to be high enough up so they can see everything that happens in any part of the ring in order to be able to judge it as a whole.

The barrera is the best seat if you want to see and hear what happens and to be so close to the bull that you will have the bull-fighter's point of view. From the barrera the action is so near and so detailed that a bullfight that would be soporific from the boxes or the balcony is always interesting. It is from the barrera that you see danger and learn to appreciate it. There too you have an un-interrupted view of the ring. The only other seats, besides the first row in the gallery and the first row in the boxes, where you do not see people between you and the ring, are the sobrepuertas. These are the seats that are built over the doorways through which you enter the various sections of the ring. They are about half-way up to the sides of the bowl and from them you get a good view of the ring and a good perspective, yet you are not as distant as in the boxes or gallery. They cost about half as much as the barreras or the first row of gallery or boxes and they are very good seats.

The west walls of the bull ring building cast a shadow and those seats that are in the shade when the fight commences are called seats of the sombra or shade. Seats that are in the sun when the fight commences but that will be in the shadow as the afternoon advances are called of sol y sombra. Seats are priced according to their desirability and whether they are shaded or not. The cheapest seats are those which are nearest the roof on the far sunny side and have no shade at all at any time. They are the andanadas del sol and on a hot day, close under the roof, they must reach temperatures that are unbelievable in a city like Valencia where it can be 104° Fahrenheit in the shade, but the better seats of the sol are good ones to buy on a cloudy day or in cold weather.

At your first bullfight if you are alone, with no one to instruct you, sit in a delantra de grada or a sobrepuerta. If you cannot get these seats you can always get a seat in a box. They are the most expensive seats and the farthest from the ring, but they give a good panoramic view of the fight. If you are going with someone who really knows bullfighting and want to learn to understand it and have no qualms about details a barrera is the best seat, contra-barrera the next best and sobrepuerta the next.

If you are a woman and think you would like to see a bullfight and are afraid you might be badly affected by it do not sit any closer than the gallery the first time. You might enjoy the fight from there where you will see it as a spectacle and not care for it at all if you sat closer so that the details destroyed the effect of the whole. If you have plenty of money, want not to see but to have seen a bullfight and plan no matter whether you like it or not to leave after the first bull, buy a barrera seat so that someone who has never had enough money to sit in a barrera can make a quick rush from above and occupy your expensive seat as you go out taking your preconceived opinions with you.

That is the way it used to happen at San Sebastian. Due to various grafts of ticket resale and the reliance of the management on the wealthy curiosity trade from Biarritz and the Basque Coast, the barreras, by the time you buy them, cost a hundred pesetas apiece or over. A man could live a week on that in a bullfighters' boarding-house in Madrid, go to the Prado four times a week, buy good seats in the sun for two bullfights, buy the papers afterwards and drink beer and eat shrimps in the Pasaje Alvarez off the Calle de Vitoria, and still have something left to get his shoes shined with. Yet by buying any sort of seat within diving range of the barrera at San Sebastian you could be sure of having a hundred-peseta seat to occupy when the citizens who knew they were mor-ally bound to leave the bull ring after the first bull stand up to make their well-fed, skull and bones-ed, porcelain-ed, beach-tanned, flannelled, Panama-hatted, sport-shod exits. I've seen them go many times when the women with them wanted to stay. They could go to the bullfight, but they had to meet at the Casino after they had seen the first bull killed. If they didn't leave and liked it there was something wrong with them. Maybe they were queer. There was never anything wrong with them. They always left. That was until bullfights became respectable. In nineteen-thirty-one I did not see one leave within range and now it looks as though the good days of the free barreras at San Sebastian are over.

QUESTIONS

1. Hemingway begins with the bull and ends with the audience. What other subjects does he discuss? What does he not discuss that you would expect him to? What in fact is the general scope of the selection?

2. Hemingway uses at least three organizational patterns: chronological, processive, and spatial. Locate them. What other significant pattern, if any, do you see?

3. Describe the overall organization of the selection. What is its rationale?

4. What is the effect of the arrangement of material in the sentence that begins: "A good bull for the bullfighter is not too big" (paragraph four)? What if the sentence began: "A good bull for the bullfighter is brave"? How do you respond to the sentence that begins: "If it is a bad bullfight, that is, not an artistic spectacle" (in the paragraph beginning "If you are going to a bullfight")? What do the two sentences together suggest about Hemingway's attitude towards bullfighting?

5. What would you say is the tone of voice in which Hemingway offers the first three paragraphs? What other tone would be a more obvious one to adopt in discussing bullfighting? Why do you suppose he adopts the particular tone that he does?

6. About two-thirds of the way through the selection Hemingway moves from third person to second. Can you justify his doing so? Has his subject-matter shifted, or his attitude towards his subject?

7. Try to define Hemingway's attitudes towards drunkards at the apartado, "rich and dignified" people at the apartado, women who "want not to see" the bullfight, and men who "had to meet at the Casino after they had seen the first bull killed."

8. Analyze the irony in the last seven sentences of the selection.

The Return Home

ROBERT PENN WARREN

Robert Penn Warren (1905——) has distinguished himself as poet, novelist, literary critic, and teacher. Born in Kentucky, he studied at Vanderbilt University, the University of California, and Oxford, where he was a Rhodes Scholar. He early identified himself with other Southern writers, and though he has made his home away from the South for the past twenty years, that region continues to influence most of his work. His novels include *Night Rider*, *All the King's Men* (which won a Pulitzer Prize), and *World Enough and Time*; and he has written a long narrative poem, *Brother to Dragons*, on the circumstances of the Lewis and Clarke expedition. What follows is the opening portion of a survey Warren made of Southern attitudes on the racial problem.

"I'm glad it's you going," my friend, a Southerner, long resident in New York, said, "and not me." But I went back, for going back this time, like all the other times, was a necessary part of my life. I was going back to look at the landscapes and streets I had known —Kentucky, Tennessee, Arkansas, Mississippi, Louisiana—to look at the faces, to hear the voices, to hear, in fact, the voices in my own blood. A girl from Mississippi had said to me: "I feel it's all happening inside of me, every bit of it. It's all there."

I know what she meant.

To the right, the sun, cold and pale, is westering. Far off, a little yellow plane scuttles down a runway, steps awkwardly into the air, then climbs busily, learning grace. Our big plane trundles ponderously forward, feeling its weight like a fat man, hesitates, shudders with an access of sudden, building power; and with a new roar in my ears, I see the ground slide past, then drop away, like a dream. I had not been aware of the instant we had lost that natural contact.

Memphis is behind me, and I cannot see it, but yonder is the river, glittering coldly, and beyond, the tree-sprigged flats of Arkansas. Still climbing, we tilt eastward now, the land pivoting away below us, the tidy toy farms, white houses, silos the size of a spool of white thread, or smaller, the stock ponds bright like little pieces of gum wrapper dropped in brown grass, but that brown grass is really trees, the toy groves with shadows precise and long in the leveling light.

Arkansas has pivoted away. It is Mississippi I now see down there, the land slipping away in the long light, and in my mind I see, idly, the ruined, gaunt, classic clay hills, with the creek bottoms throttled long since in pink sand, or the white houses of Holly Springs, some of them severe and beautiful, or Highway 61 striking south from Memphis, straight as a knife edge through the sad and baleful beauty of the Delta country, south toward Vicksburg and the Federal cemeteries, toward the fantasia of Natchez.

It seems like a thousand years since I first drove that road, more than twenty-five years ago, a new concrete slab then, dizzily glittering in the August sun-blaze, driving past the rows of tenant shacks, Negro shacks set in the infinite cotton fields, and it seems like a hundred years since I last drove it, last week, in the rain, then toward sunset the sky clearing a little, but clouds solid and low on the west like a black range of mountains frilled upward with an edge of bloody gold light, quickly extinguished. Last week, I noticed that more of the shacks were ruinous, apparently abandoned. More, but not many, had an electric wire running back from the road. But when I caught a glimpse, in the dusk, of the interior of a lighted shack, I usually saw the coal-oil lamp. Most shacks were not lighted. I wondered if it was too early in the evening. Then it was early no longer. Were that many of the shacks abandoned?

Then we would pass in the dark some old truck grudging and clanking down the concrete, and catch, in the split-second flick of our headlamps, a glimpse of the black faces and the staring eyes. Or the figure, sudden in our headlight, would rise from the roadside, dark and shapeless against the soaked blackness of the cotton land: the man humping along with the croker sack on his shoulders (containing what?), the woman with a piece of sacking or paper over her head against the drizzle now, at her bosom a bundle that must be a small child, the big children following with the same slow, mud-lifting stride in the darkness. The light of the car snatches past, and I think of them behind us in the darkness, moving up the track beside the concrete, seeing another car light far yonder toward Memphis, staring at it perhaps, watching it grow, plunge at them, strike them, flick past. They will move on, at their pace. Yes, they are still here.

I see a river below us. It must be the Tennessee. I wonder on which side of us Shiloh is, and guess the right, for we must have swung far enough north for that. I had two grandfathers at Shiloh, that morning of April 6, 1862, young men with the other young men in gray uniforms stepping toward the lethal spring thickets of dogwood and redbud, to the sound of bird song. "One hundred and sixty men we took in the first morning, son. Muster the next night, and it was sixteen answered." They had fallen back on Corinth, into Mississippi.

The man in the seat beside me on the plane is offering me a newspaper. I see the thumb of the hand clutching the paper. The nail is nearly as big as a quarter, split at the edges, grooved and horny, yellowish, with irrevocable coal-black grime deep under the nail and into the cuticle. I look at the man. He is a big man, very

big, bulging over the seat, bulging inside his blue serge. He is
fiftyish, hair graying. His face is large and raw-looking, heavy-
jowled, thick gray eyebrows over small, deep-set, appraising eyes.
His name, which he tells me, sounds Russian or Polish, something
ending in -*ski*.

I begin to read the paper, an article about the riots at the University of Alabama. He notices what I am reading. "Bet you thought
I was from down here," he said. "From the way I talk. But I ain't.
I was born and raised in New York City, but I been in the scrap
business down here ten years. Didn't you think I was from down
here?"

"Yes," I say, for that seems the sociable thing to say.

He twists his bulk in the blue serge and reaches and stabs a
finger at the headline about Alabama. "Folks could be more gen'-
rous and fair-thinking," he says. "Like affable, you might say, and
things would work out. If folks get affable and contig'ous, you might
say, things sort of get worked out in time, but you get folks not
being affable-like and stirring things up and it won't work out.
Folks on both sides the question."

He asks me if I don't agree, and I say, sure, I agree. Sure, if
folks were just affable-like.

I am thinking of what a taxi driver had said to me in Memphis:
"Looks like the Lucy girl wouldn't want to go no place where people throwed eggs at her and sich. But if they'd jist let her alone,
them Goodrich plant fellers and all, it would blow over. What few
niggers come would not have stayed no duration. Not when they
found she couldn't git the social stuff, and all."

And what the school superintendent, in middle Tennessee, had
said: "You take a good many people around here that I know,
segregationists all right, but when they read about a thousand to
one, it sort of makes them sick. It is the unfairness in that way
that gets them."

And an organizer of one of the important segregation groups, a
lawyer, when I asked him if Autherine Lucy wasn't acting under

law, he creaked his swivel chair, moved his shoulders under his coat, and touched a pencil on his desk, before saying: "Yes—yes—but it was just the Federal Court ruled it."

And a taxi driver in Nashville, a back-country man come to the city, a hard, lean, spare face, his lean, strong shoulders humped forward over the wheel so that the clavicles show through the coat: "A black-type person and a white-type person, they ain't alike. Now the black-type person, all they think about is fighting and having a good time and you know what. Now the white-type person is more American-type, he don't mind fighting but he don't fight to kill for fun. It's that cannibal blood you caint git out."

Now, on the plane, my companion observes me scribbling something in a notebook.

"You a writer or something?" he asks. "A newspaper fellow, maybe?"

I say yes.

"You interested in that stuff?" he asks, and points to the article. "Somebody ought to tell 'em not to blame no state, not even Alabam' or Mississippi, for what the bad folks do. Like stuff in New York or Chicago. Folks in Mississippi got good hearts as any place. They always been nice and good-hearted to me, for I go up to a man affable. The folks down here is just in trouble and can't claw out. Don't blame 'em, got good hearts but can't claw out of their trouble. It is hard to claw out from under the past and the past way."

He asks me if I have been talking to a lot of people.

I had been talking to a lot of people.

I had come to the shack at dusk, by the brimming bayou, in the sea of mud where cotton had been. The cold drizzle was still falling. In the shack, on the hickory chair, the yellow girl, thin but well made, wearing a salmon sweater and salmon denim slacks, holds the baby on her knee and leans toward the iron stove. On the table beyond her is an ivory-colored portable radio and a half-full bottle of Castoria. On the other side of the stove are her three other children, the oldest seven. Behind me, in the shadowy background, I know there are faces peering in from the other room of the shack, black faces, the half-grown boys, another girl I had seen on entering. The girl in the salmon sweater is telling how she heard her husband had been killed. "Livin in town then, and my sister, she come that night and tole me he was shot. They had done shot him dead. So I up and taken out fer heah, back to the plantation. Later, my sister got my chillen and brought 'em. I ain't gonna lie, mister. I tell you, I was scairt. No tellin if that man what done it was in jail or no. Even if they had arrest him, they might bon' him out and he come and do it to me. Be mad because they 'rest him. You caint never tell. And they try him and 'quit him, doan know as I kin stay heah. Even they convick him, maybe I leave. Some good folks round heah and they helpin me, and I try to appreciate and be a prayin chile, but you git so bore down on and nigh ruint and sort of brain-washed, you don't know what. Things git to goin round in yore head. I could run out or somethin, but you caint leave yore chillen. But look like I might up and leave. He git 'quitted, that man, and maybe I die, but I die goin."

This is the cliché. It is the thing the uninitiate would expect. It is the cliché of fear. It is the cliché come fresh, and alive.

There is another image. It is morning in Nashville. I walk down Union Street, past the Negro barber shops, past the ruinous buildings plastered over with placards of old circuses and rodeos, buildings being wrecked now to make way for progress, going into the square where the big white stone boxlike, ugly and expensive Davidson County Court House now stands on the spot where the old brawling market once was. Otherwise, the square hasn't changed much, the same buildings, wholesale houses, liquor stores, pawn shops, quick lunches, and the same kind of people stand on the corners, countrymen, in khaki pants and mackinaw coats, weathered faces and hard, withdrawn eyes, usually pale eyes, lean-hipped men ("narrow-assted" in the country phrase) like the men who rode with Forrest, the farm wives, young with a baby in arms, or middle-aged and work-worn, with colored cloths over the head, glasses, false teeth, always the shopping bag.

I walk down toward the river, past the Darling Display Distribution show window, where a wax figure stands in skirt and silk blouse, the fingers spread on one uplifted hand, the thin face lifted with lips lightly parted as though in eternal, tubercular expectation of a kiss. I see the power pylons rising above the river mist. A tug is hooting up-river in the mist.

I go on down to the right, First Street, to the replica of Fort Nashborough, the original settlement, which stands on the river bank under the shadow of warehouses. The stockade looks so child-flimsy and jerry-built jammed against the massive, soot-stained warehouses. How could the settlers have ever taken such protection seriously? But it was enough, that and their will and the long rifles and the hunting knives and the bear-dogs they unleashed to help them when they broke the Indians at the Battle of the Bluffs. They took the land, and remain.

I am standing in the middle of the empty stockade when a boy enters and approaches me. He is about fifteen, strongly built, wearing a scruffed and tattered brown leather jacket, blue jeans, a faded blue stocking cap on the back of his head, with a mop of yellow hair hanging over his forehead. He is a fine-looking boy, erect, manly in the face, with a direct, blue-eyed glance. "Mister," he said to me, "is this foh't the way it was, or they done remodeled it?"

I tell him it is a replica, smaller than the original and not on the right spot, exactly.

"I'm glad I seen it, anyway," he says. "I like to go round seeing things that got history, and such. It gives you something to think about. Helps you in a quiz sometimes, too."

I ask him where he goes to school.

"Atlanta," he says. "Just come hitch-hiking up this a-way, looking at things for interest. Like this here foh't."

"You all been having a little trouble down your way," I ask, "haven't you?"

He looks sharply at me, hesitates, then says: "Niggers—you mean niggers?"

"Yes."

"I hate them bastards," he says, with a shuddering, automatic violence, and averts his face and spits through his teeth, a quick, viperish, cut-off expectoration.

I say nothing, and he looks at me, stares into my face with a dawning belligerence, sullen and challenging, and suddenly demands: "Don't you?"

"I can't say that I do," I reply. "I like some and I don't like some others."

He utters the sudden obscenity, and removes himself a couple of paces from me. He stops and looks back over his shoulder. "I'm hitching on back to Atlanta," he declares in a flat voice, "this afternoon," and goes on out of the fort.

This, too, is a cliché. The boy, standing on the ground of history and heroism, his intellect and imagination stirred by the fact, shudders with that other, automatic emotion which my question had evoked. The cliché had come true: the cliché of hate. And somehow the hallowedness of the ground he stood on had vindicated, as it were, that hate.

QUESTIONS

1. The second section of the sketch closes with mention of Warren's grandfathers at Shiloh. What phrase in the first section does his mention of them recall? State the broad meaning of that phrase.

2. In the second section Warren describes the plane take-off and the look of Highway 61. These things have nothing directly to do with the subject of segregation. What justifies their inclusion?

3. Analyze Warren's use of chronology and geography as organizing patterns in the second section.

4. How sympathetic is Warren to the man who sits beside him on the plane? What does Warren achieve—apart from unity—by using his conversation with the man as a frame for the viewpoints of four other people? Can you see any basis for the order of the viewpoints?

5. Does the final sentence in the first section add further meaning to the section? Distinguish that meaning or justify the sentence in another way. What is the particular quality of the sentence that closes the third section?

6. Is there any reason for believing that Warren presents the two episodes in the fourth section in chronological order? In what respect does the ordering of the two episodes parallel the ordering of material in the third section?

7. The four sections of the sketch do not constitute an independent unit of Warren's book, but do display a certain development appropriate to their position as opening sections of it. What is that development? (Your answer should imply a rationale.)

8. What does Warren mean by the "cliché of fear" and the "cliché of hate"? What does he mean when he says that the hallowedness of the ground vindicated the boy's hate?

9. Distinguish in at least two respects the function of the comparison in the fourth section from that of the comparisons in the third section. Does Warren's attitude towards the people he talks to shift from one section to the other?

10. In some respects Warren is objective and dispassionate in his sketch; in other respects he is subjective. Point out the clearest illustration of each attitude. Why does he try to maintain both attitudes?

Marrakech

GEORGE ORWELL

George Orwell, in real life Eric Blair (1903-1950), was born in Bengal, of English parents. Sent to England for his education, he returned to India before he was twenty, served for five years with the Imperial Police in Burma, and then lived a vagrant's existence in Europe. His experiences (recounted in *Down and Out in Paris and London*) sharpened his awareness of social injustice, and convinced him of the efficacy of socialism. He subsequently fought in the Spanish Civil War, on the side of the anti-Fascists, and was severely wounded. He settled finally in England, where he wrote his best-known books, *Animal Farm*, a satire on Soviet history, and *1984*, a frighteningly vivid picture of life in a totalitarian society. The essay that follows was written in 1939, on the eve of the Second World War. (Further headnote information on Orwell appears on pp. 175, 393.)

As the corpse went past the flies left the restaurant table in a cloud and rushed after it, but they came back a few minutes later.

The little crowd of mourners—all men and boys, no women—threaded their way across the market-place between the piles of pomegranates and the taxis and the camels, wailing a short chant over and over again. What really appeals to the flies is that the corpses here are never put into coffins, they are merely wrapped in a piece of rag and carried on a rough wooden bier on the shoulders of four friends. When the friends get to the burying-ground they hack an oblong hole a foot or two deep, dump the body in it and fling over it a little of the dried-up, lumpy earth, which is like broken brick. No gravestone, no name, no identifying mark of any kind. The burying-ground is merely a huge waste of hummocky earth, like a derelict building-lot. After a month or two no one can even be certain where his own relatives are buried.

When you walk through a town like this—two hundred thousand inhabitants, of whom at least twenty thousand own literally nothing except the rags they stand up in—when you see how the people live, and still more how easily they die, it is always difficult to believe that you are walking among human beings. All colonial empires are in reality founded upon that fact. The people have brown faces—besides, there are so many of them! Are they really the same flesh as yourself? Do they even have names? Or are they merely a kind of undifferentiated brown stuff, about as individual as bees or coral insects? They rise out of the earth, they sweat and starve for a few years, and then they sink back into the nameless mounds of the graveyard and nobody notices that they are gone. And even the graves themselves soon fade back into the soil. Sometimes, out for a walk, as you break your way through the prickly pear, you notice that it is rather bumpy underfoot, and only a certain regularity in the bumps tells you that you are walking over skeletons.

I was feeding one of the gazelles in the public gardens.

Gazelles are almost the only animals that look good to eat when they are still alive, in fact, one can hardly look at their hind-quarters without thinking of mint sauce. The gazelle I was feeding seemed to know that this thought was in my mind, for though it took the piece of bread I was holding out it obviously did not like me. It nibbled rapidly at the bread, then lowered its head and tried to butt me, then took another nibble and then butted again. Probably its idea was that if it could drive me away the bread would somehow remain hanging in mid-air.

An Arab navvy working on the path nearby lowered his heavy hoe and sidled slowly towards us. He looked from the gazelle to the bread and from the bread to the gazelle, with a sort of quiet amazement, as though he had never seen anything quite like this before. Finally he said shyly in French:

"*I* could eat some of that bread."

I tore off a piece and he stowed it gratefully in some secret place under his rags. This man is an employee of the Municipality.

When you go through the Jewish quarters you gather some idea of what the medieval ghettoes were probably like. Under their Moorish rulers the Jews were only allowed to own land in certain restricted areas, and after centuries of this kind of treatment they have ceased to bother about overcrowding. Many of the streets are a good deal less than six feet wide, the houses are completely windowless, and sore-eyed children cluster everywhere in unbelievable numbers, like clouds of flies. Down the centre of the street there is generally running a little river of urine. .

In the bazaar huge families of Jews, all dressed in the long black robe and little black skull-cap, are working in dark fly-infested booths that look like caves. A carpenter sits crosslegged at a prehistoric lathe, turning chair-legs at lightning speed. He works the lathe with a bow in his right hand and guides the chisel with his left foot, and thanks to a lifetime of sitting in this position his left leg is warped out of shape. At his side his grandson, aged six, is already starting on the simpler parts of the job.

I was just passing the coppersmiths' booths when somebody noticed that I was lighting a cigarette. Instantly, from the dark holes all round, there was a frenzied rush of Jews, many of them old grandfathers with flowing grey beards, all clamouring for a cigarette. Even a blind man somewhere at the back of one of the booths heard a rumour of cigarettes and came crawling out, groping in the air with his hand. In about a minute I had used up the whole packet. None of these people, I suppose, works less than twelve hours a day, and every one of them looks on a cigarette as a more or less impossible luxury.

As the Jews live in self-contained communities they follow the same trades as the Arabs, except for agriculture. Fruit-sellers, potters, silversmiths, blacksmiths, butchers, leatherworkers, tailors, water-carriers, beggars, porters—whichever way you look you see nothing but Jews. As a matter of fact there are thirteen thousand of them, all living in the space of a few acres. A good job Hitler wasn't here. Perhaps he was on his way, however. You hear the usual dark rumours about the Jews, not only from the Arabs but from the poorer Europeans.

"Yes, mon vieux, they took my job away from me and gave it to a Jew. The Jews! They're the real rulers of this country, you know. They've got all the money. They control the banks, finance —everything."

"But," I said, "isn't it a fact that the average Jew is a labourer working for about a penny an hour?"

"Ah, that's only for show! They're all moneylenders really. They're cunning, the Jews."

In just the same way, a couple of hundred years ago, poor old women used to be burned for witchcraft when they could not even work enough magic to get themselves a square meal.

All people who work with their hands are partly invisible, and the more important the work they do, the less visible they are. Still, a white skin is always fairly conspicuous. In northern Europe, when you see a labourer ploughing a field, you probably give him a second glance. In a hot country, anywhere south of Gibraltar or east of Suez, the chances are that you don't even see him. I have noticed this again and again. In a tropical landscape one's eye takes in everything except the human beings. It takes in the dried-up soil, the prickly pear, the palm tree and the distant mountain, but it always misses the peasant hoeing at his patch. He is the same colour as the earth, and a great deal less interesting to look at.

It is only because of this that the starved countries of Asia and

Africa are accepted as tourist resorts. No one would think of running cheap trips to the Distressed Areas. But where the human beings have brown skins their poverty is simply not noticed. What does Morocco mean to a Frenchman? An orange-grove or a job in Government service. Or to an Englishman? Camels, castles, palm trees, Foreign Legionnaires, brass trays, and bandits. One could probably live there for years without noticing that for nine-tenths of the people the reality of life is an endless, back-breaking struggle to wring a little food out of an eroded soil.

Most of Morocco is so desolate that no wild animal bigger than a hare can live on it. Huge areas which were once covered with forest have turned into a treeless waste where the soil is exactly like broken-up brick. Nevertheless a good deal of it is cultivated, with frightful labour. Everything is done by hand. Long lines of women, bent double like inverted capital L's, work their way slowly across the fields, tearing up the prickly weeds with their hands, and the peasant gathering lucerne for fodder pulls it up stalk by stalk instead of reaping it, thus saving an inch or two on each stalk. The plough is a wretched wooden thing, so frail that one can easily carry it on one's shoulder, and fitted underneath with a rough iron spike which stirs the soil to a depth of about four inches. This is as much as the strength of the animals is equal to. It is usual to plough with a cow and a donkey yoked together. Two donkeys would not be quite strong enough, but on the other hand two cows would cost a little more to feed. The peasants possess no harrows, they merely plough the soil several times over in different directions, finally leaving it in rough furrows, after which the whole field has to be shaped with hoes into small oblong patches to conserve water. Except for a day or two after the rare rainstorms there is never enough water. Along the edges of the fields channels are hacked out to a depth of thirty or forty feet to get at the tiny trickles which run through the subsoil.

Every afternoon a file of very old women passes down the road outside my house, each carrying a load of firewood. All of them are mummified with age and the sun, and all of them are tiny. It seems to be generally the case in primitive communities that the women, when they get beyond a certain age, shrink to the size of children. One day a poor old creature who could not have been more than four feet tall crept past me under a vast load of wood. I stopped her and put a five-sou piece (a little more than a farthing) into her hand. She answered with a shrill wail, almost a scream, which was partly gratitude but mainly surprise. I suppose that from her point of view, by taking any notice of her, I seemed almost to be violating a law of nature. She accepted her status as an old woman, that is to say as a beast of burden. When a family is travelling it is quite usual to see a father and a grown-up son riding ahead on donkeys, and an old woman following on foot, carrying the baggage.

But what is strange about these people is their invisibility. For several weeks, always at about the same time of day, the file of old women had hobbled past the house with their firewood, and though they had registered themselves on my eyeballs I cannot truly say that I had seen them. Firewood was passing—that was how I saw it. It was only that one day I happened to be walking behind them, and the curious up-and-down motion of a load of wood drew my attention to the human being beneath it. Then for the first time I noticed the poor old earth-coloured bodies, bodies reduced to bones and leathery skin, bent double under the crushing weight. Yet I suppose I had not been five minutes on Moroccan soil before I noticed the overloading of the donkeys and was infuriated by it. There is no question that the donkeys are damnably treated. The Moroccan donkey is hardly bigger than a St. Bernard dog, it carries a load which in the British Army would be considered too much for a fifteen-hands mule, and very often its pack-saddle is not taken off its back for weeks together. But what is peculiarly pitiful is that it is the most willing creature on earth, it follows its master like a dog and does not need either bridle or halter. After a dozen years of devoted work it suddenly drops dead, whereupon its master tips it into the ditch and the village dogs have torn its guts out before it is cold.

This kind of thing makes one's blood boil, whereas—on the whole —the plight of the human beings does not. I am not commenting, merely pointing to a fact. People with brown skins are next door to invisible. Anyone can be sorry for the donkey with its galled back, but it is generally owing to some kind of accident if one even notices the old woman under her load of sticks.

As the storks flew northward the Negroes were marching southward—a long, dusty column, infantry, screw-gun batteries, and then more infantry, four or five thousand men in all, winding up the road with a clumping of boots and a clatter of iron wheels.

They were Senegalese, the blackest Negroes in Africa, so black that sometimes it is difficult to see whereabouts on their necks the hair begins. Their splendid bodies were hidden in reach-me-down khaki uniforms, their feet squashed into boots that looked like blocks of wood, and every tin hat seemed to be a couple of sizes too small. It was very hot and the men had marched a long way. They slumped under the weight of their packs and the curiously sensitive black faces were glistening with sweat.

As they went past a tall, very young Negro turned and caught my eye. But the look he gave me was not in the least the kind of look you might expect. Not hostile, not contemptuous, not sullen, not even inquisitive. It was the shy, wide-eyed Negro look, which actually is a look of profound respect. I saw how it was. This wretched boy, who is a French citizen and has therefore been dragged from the forest to scrub floors and catch syphilis in garrison towns, actually has feelings of reverence before a white skin. He has been taught that the white race are his masters, and he still believes it.

But there is one thought which every white man (and in this connection it doesn't matter twopence if he calls himself a socialist) thinks when he sees a black army marching past. "How much longer can we go on kidding these people? How long before they turn their guns in the other direction?"

It was curious, really. Every white man there had this thought stowed somewhere or other in his mind. I had it, so had the other onlookers, so had the officers on their sweating chargers and the white N.C.O.'s marching in the ranks. It was a kind of secret which we all knew and were too clever to tell; only the Negroes didn't know it. And really it was like watching a flock of cattle to see the long column, a mile or two miles of armed men, flowing peacefully up the road, while the great white birds drifted over them in the opposite direction, glittering like scraps of paper.

QUESTIONS

1. The objects of Orwell's attention are corpses, a gazelle, a hungry Arab, Jews, laborers, etc. In what single respect is Orwell interested in them? What, then, is the subject of the essay? In what passage or passages do you find the subject most explicitly stated? Of what relevance to the subject is Orwell's juxtaposition of skeletons in a field and the gazelle in the public gardens, his juxtaposition of the hungry Arab and Jews?

2. In context, what does the word "invisible" mean (first sentence, second section)? What sort of work is "important" work (same sentence)?

3. If you were reading the essay aloud, what would be the difference in tone with which you would read "Are they really the same flesh as yourself?" (paragraph three) and "How much longer can we go on kidding these people?" (next-to-last paragraph)? What is the significance of the difference?

4. In terms of Orwell's subject, what is the difference in implication of the processions with which he begins and ends the essay?

5. What parts of the first section of the essay are direct observation? What parts are reflection? Why is there so little reflection in the gazelle-Arab episode? Does observation or reflection predominate in the other sections of the essay?

6. Is it important to the organization of the essay that Orwell is walking through Marrakech? Is there any evidence that he is describing

more than one walk? At what point does he clearly abandon the walk? Does he resume it?

7. What is the distinguishing characteristic of the material in each of the three sections? Can the order of the sections be shifted? Can you suggest an organizing principle that governs their present order? What would be its rationale?

8. Orwell remarks at one juncture that he is "not commenting, merely pointing to a fact." Where in the essay does his pointing seem equivalent to commenting? Does the apparent casualness of the organization seem to suggest pointing or commenting? By what means does Orwell achieve the effect of casualness in organization?

9. Can you distinguish the dramatic quality of the opening two paragraphs of the essay from that of the third section? How much dramatic tension does the second section have? How would you describe the overall dramatic pattern?

On Certain Modern Writers and the Institution of the Family

G. K. CHESTERTON

Born in London, into comfortable middle-class family, G. K. Chesterton (1874-1936) studied painting as a youth, but soon found his abilities better employed at writing. Through a long career he wrote voluminously and in virtually every form —novels, biographies, histories, poetry, essays by the hundreds, mystery stories (whose hero-detective is Father Brown) —and for a time even edited his own newspaper, *G. K.'s Weekly*, the better to protest the coldness and secularization of modern life, the largeness of modern business, the socialism of his arch-opponent George Bernard Shaw. Chesterton's work is often uneven, much of it journalistic ephemera, but at its best it expresses the energy and wit of a resourceful and imaginative controversialist.

The family may fairly be considered, one would think, an ultimate human institution. Every one would admit that it has been the main cell and central unit of almost all societies hitherto, except, indeed, such societies as that of Lacedaemon, which went in for "efficiency," and has, therefore, perished, and left not a trace behind. Christianity, even enormous as was its revolution, did not alter this ancient and savage sanctity, it merely reversed it. It did not deny the trinity of father, mother, and child. It merely read it backwards, making it run child, mother, father. This it called,

From *Heretics* by G. K. Chesterton. Reprinted by permission of The Bodley Head Ltd.

not the family, but the Holy Family, for many things are made holy by being turned upside down. But some sages of our decadence have made a serious attack on the family. They have impugned it, as I think, wrongly; and its defenders have defended it, and defended it wrongly. The common defence of the family is that, amid the stress and fickleness of life, it is peaceful, pleasant, and at one. But there is another defence of the family which is possible, and to me evident; this defence is that the family is not peaceful and not pleasant and not at one.

It is not fashionable to say much nowadays of the advantages of the small community. We are told that we must go in for large empires and large ideas. There is one advantage, however, in the small state, the city, or the village, which only the wilfully blind can overlook. The man who lives in a small community lives in a much larger world. He knows much more of the fierce varieties and uncompromising divergences of men. The reason is obvious. In a large community we can choose our companions. In a small community our companions are chosen for us. Thus in all extensive and highly civilized societies groups come into existence founded upon what is called sympathy, and shut out the real world more sharply than the gates of a monastery. There is nothing really narrow about the clan; the thing which is really narrow is the clique. The men of the clan live together because they all wear the same tartan or are all descended from the same sacred cow; but in their souls, by the divine luck of things, there will always be more colours than in any tartan. But the men of the clique live together because they have the same kind of soul, and their narrowness is a narrowness of spiritual coherence and contentment, like that which exists in hell. A big society exists in order to form cliques. A big society is a society for the promotion of narrowness. It is a machinery for the purpose of guarding the solitary and sensitive individual from all experience of the bitter and bracing human compromises. It is, in the most literal sense of the words, a society for the prevention of Christian knowledge.

We can see this change, for instance, in the modern transformation of the thing called a club. When London was smaller, and the parts of London more self-contained and parochial, the club was what it still is in villages, the opposite of what it is now in great cities. Then the club was valued as a place where a man could be sociable. Now the club is valued as a place where a man can be unsociable. The more the enlargement and elaboration of our civilization goes on the more the club ceases to be a place where a man can have a noisy argument, and becomes more and more a place where a man can have what is somewhat fantastically called a quiet chop. Its aim is to make a man comfortable, and to make a man comfortable is to make him the opposite of sociable. Sociability, like all good things, is full of discomforts, dangers, and renunciations. The club tends to produce the most degraded of all combinations—the luxurious anchorite, the man who combines the self-indulgence of Lucullus with the insane loneliness of St. Simeon Stylites.

If we were tomorrow morning snowed up in the street in which we live, we should step suddenly into a much larger and much wilder world than we have ever known. And it is the whole effort of the typically modern person to escape from the street in which he lives. First he invents modern hygiene and goes to Margate. Then he invents modern culture and goes to Florence. Then he invents modern imperialism and goes to Timbuctoo. He goes to the fantastic borders of the earth. He pretends to shoot tigers. He almost rides on a camel. And in all this he is still essentially fleeing from the street in which he was born; and of this flight he is always ready with his own explanation. He says he is fleeing from his street because it is dull; he is lying. He is really fleeing from his street because it is a great deal too exciting. It is exciting because it is exacting; it is exacting because it is alive. He can visit Venice because to him the Venetians are only Venetians; the people in his own street are men. He can stare at the Chinese because for him the Chinese are a passive thing to be stared at; if he stares at the old lady in the next garden, she becomes active. He is forced to flee, in short, from the too stimulating society of his equals—of free men, perverse, personal, deliberately different from himself. The street in Brixton is too glowing and overpowering. He has to soothe and quiet himself among tigers and vultures, camels and crocodiles. These creatures are indeed very different from himself. But they do not put their shape or color or custom into a decisive intellectual competition with his own. They do not seek to destroy his principles and assert their own; the stranger monsters of the suburban street do seek to do this. The camel does not contort his features into a fine sneer because Mr. Robinson has not got a hump; the cultured gentleman at No. 5 does exhibit a sneer because Robinson has not got a dado. The vulture will not roar with laughter because a man does not fly; but the major at No. 9 will roar with laughter because a man does not smoke. The complaint we commonly have to make of our neighbours is that they will not, as we express it, mind their own business. We do not really mean that they will not mind their own business. If our neighbours did not mind their own business they would be asked abruptly for their rent, and would rapidly cease to be our neighbours. What we really mean when we say that they cannot mind their own business is something much deeper. We do not dislike them because they have so little force and fire that they cannot be interested in themselves. We dislike them because they have so much force and fire that they can be interested in us as well. What we dread about our neighbours, in short, is not the narrowness of their horizon, but their superb tendency to broaden it. And all aversions to ordinary humanity have this general character. They are not aversions to its feebleness (as is pretended), but to its energy. The misanthropes pretend that they despise humanity for its weakness. As a matter of fact, they hate it for its strength.

Of course, this shrinking from the brutal vivacity and brutal variety of common men is a perfectly reasonable and excusable thing as long as it does not pretend to any point of superiority. It is when it calls itself aristocracy or aestheticism or a superiority to the bourgeoisie that its inherent weakness has in justice to be pointed out. Fastidiousness is the most pardonable of vices; but it is the most unpardonable of virtues. Nietzsche, who represents most prominently this pretentious claim of the fastidious, has a description somewhere—a very powerful description in the purely literary sense—of the disgust and disdain which consume him at the sight of the common people with their common faces, their common voices, and their common minds. As I have said, this attitude is almost beautiful if we may regard it as pathetic. Nietzsche's aristocracy has about it all the sacredness that belongs to the weak. When he makes us feel that he cannot endure the innumerable faces, the incessant voices, the overpowering omnipresence which belongs to the mob, he will have the sympathy of anybody who has ever been sick on a steamer or tired in a crowded omnibus. Every man has hated mankind when he was less than a man. Every man has had humanity in his eyes like a blinding fog, humanity in his nostrils like a suffocating smell. But when Nietzsche has the incredible lack of humour and lack of imagination to ask us to believe that his aristocracy is an aristocracy of strong muscles or an aristocracy of strong wills, it is necessary to point out the truth. It is an aristocracy of weak nerves.

We make our friends; we make our enemies; but God makes our next-door neighbour. Hence he comes to us clad in all the careless terrors of nature; he is as strange as the stars, as reckless and indifferent as the rain. He is Man, the most terrible of the beasts. That is why the old religions and the old scriptural language showed so sharp a wisdom when they spoke, not of one's duty towards humanity, but one's duty towards one's neighbour. The duty towards humanity may often take the form of some choice which is personal or even pleasurable. That duty may be a hobby; it may even be a dissipation. We may work in the East End because we are peculiarly fitted to work in the East End, or because we think we are; we may fight for the cause of international peace because we are very fond of fighting. The most monstrous martyrdom, the most repulsive experience, may be the result of choice or a kind of taste. We may be so made as to be particularly fond of lunatics or specially interested in leprosy. We may love Negroes

because they are black or German Socialists because they are
pedantic. But we have to love our neighbour because he is there—
a much more alarming reason for a much more serious operation.
He is the sample of humanity which is actually given us. Precisely
because he may be anybody he is everybody. He is a symbol because he is an accident.

Doubtless men flee from small environments into lands that are
very deadly. But this is natural enough; for they are not fleeing
from death. They are fleeing from life. And this principle applies to
ring within ring of the social system of humanity. It is perfectly
reasonable that men should seek for some particular variety of the
human type, so long as they are seeking for that variety of the
human type, and not for mere human variety. It is quite proper
that a British diplomatist should seek the society of Japanese generals, if what he wants is Japanese generals. But if what he wants
is people different from himself, he had much better stop at
home and discuss religion with the housemaid. It is quite reasonable
that the village genius should come up to conquer London if what
he wants is to conquer London. But if he wants to conquer something fundamentally and symbolically hostile and also very strong,
he had much better remain where he is and have a row with the
rector. The man in the suburban street is quite right if he goes to
Ramsgate for the sake of Ramsgate—a difficult thing to imagine.
But if, as he expresses it, he goes to Ramsgate "for a change," then
he would have a much more romantic and even melodramatic
change if he jumped over the wall into his neighbour's garden. The
consequences would be bracing in a sense far beyond the possibilities of Ramsgate hygiene.

Now, exactly as this principle applies to the empire, to the
nation within the empire, to the city within the nation, to the street
within the city, so it applies to the home within the street. The institution of the family is to be commended for precisely the same
reasons that the institution of the nation, or the institution of the
city, are in this matter to be commended. It is a good thing for a

man to live in a family for the same reason that it is a good thing
for a man to be besieged in a city. It is a good thing for a man to
live in a family in the same sense that it is a beautiful and delightful thing for a man to be snowed up in a street. They all force
him to realize that life is not a thing from outside but a thing from
inside. Above all, they all insist upon the fact that life, if it be a
truly stimulating and fascinating life, is a thing which, of its nature,
exists in spite of ourselves. The modern writers who have suggested,
in a more or less open manner, that the family is a bad institution, have generally confined themselves to suggesting, with much
sharpness, bitterness, or pathos, that perhaps the family is not always very congenial. Of course the family is a good institution because it is uncongenial. It is wholesome precisely because it contains so many divergencies and varieties. It is, as the sentimentalists
say, like a little kingdom, and, like most other little kingdoms, is
generally in a state of something resembling anarchy. It is exactly
because our brother George is not interested in our religious difficulties, but is interested in the Trocadero Restaurant, that the
family has some of the bracing qualities of the commonwealth. It
is precisely because our uncle Henry does not approve of the theatri-
cal ambitions of our sister Sarah that the family is like humanity.
The men and women who, for good reasons and bad, revolt against
the family, are, for good reasons and bad, simply revolting against
mankind. Aunt Elizabeth is unreasonable, like mankind. Papa is
excitable, like mankind. Our youngest brother is mischievous, like
mankind. Grandpapa is stupid, like the world; he is old, like the
world.

Those who wish, rightly or wrongly, to step out of all this, do
definitely wish to step into a narrower world. They are dismayed
and terrified by the largeness and variety of the family. Sarah
wishes to find a world wholly consisting of private theatricals;
George wishes to think the Trocadero a cosmos. I do not say, for
a moment, that the flight to this narrower life may not be the right
thing for the individual, any more than I say the same thing about

flight into a monastery. But I do say that anything is bad and artificial which tends to make these people succumb to the strange delusion that they are stepping into a world which is actually larger and more varied than their own. The best way that a man could test his readiness to encounter the common variety of mankind would be to climb down a chimney into any house at random, and get on as well as possible with the people inside. And that is essentially what each one of us did on the day that he was born.

This is, indeed, the sublime and special romance of the family. It is romantic because it is a toss-up. It is romantic because it is everything that its enemies call it. It is romantic because it is arbitrary. It is romantic because it is there. So long as you have groups of men chosen rationally, you have some special or sectarian atmosphere. It is when you have groups of men chosen irrationally that you have men. The element of adventure begins to exist; for an adventure is, by its nature, a thing that comes to us. It is a thing that chooses us, not a thing that we choose. Falling in love has been often regarded as the supreme adventure, the supreme romantic accident. In so much as there is in it something outside ourselves, something of a sort of merry fatalism, this is very true. Love does take us and transfigure and torture us. It does break our hearts with an unbearable beauty, like the unbearable beauty of music. But in so far as we have certainly something to do with the matter; in so far as we are in some sense prepared to fall in love and in some sense jump into it; in so far as we do to some extent choose and to some extent even judge—in all this falling in love is not truly romantic, is not truly adventurous at all. In this degree the supreme adventure is not falling in love. The supreme adventure is being born. There we do walk suddenly into a splendid and startling trap. There we do see something of which we have not dreamed before. Our father and mother do lie in wait for us and leap out on us, like brigands from a bush. Our uncle is a surprise. Our aunt is, in the beautiful common expression, a bolt from the blue. When we step into the family, by the act of being born, we do step into a world which is incalculable, into a world which has

its own strange laws, into a world which could do without us, into
a world that we have not made. In other words, when we step
into the family we step into a fairy-tale.

This colour as of a fantastic narrative ought to cling to the family and to our relations with it throughout life. Romance is the
deepest thing in life; romance is deeper even than reality. For even
if reality could be proved to be misleading, it still could not be
proved to be unimportant or unimpressive. Even if the facts are
false, they are still very strange. And this strangeness of life, this
unexpected and even perverse element of things as they fall out,
remains incurably interesting. The circumstances we can regulate
may become tame or pessimistic; but the "circumstances over which
we have no control" remain god-like to those who, like Mr. Micaw-
ber, can call on them and renew their strength. People wonder
why the novel is the most popular form of literature; people wonder why it is read more than books of science or books of metaphysics. The reason is very simple; it is merely that the novel is
more true than they are. Life may sometimes legitimately appear
as a book of science. Life may sometimes appear, and with a much
greater legitimacy, as a book of metaphysics. But life is always a
novel. Our existence may cease to be a song; it may cease even
to be a beautiful lament. Our existence may not be an intelligible
justice, or even a recognizable wrong. But our existence is still a
story. In the fiery alphabet of every sunset is written "to be continued in our next." If we have sufficient intellect, we can finish
a philosophical and exact deduction, and be certain that we are
finishing it right. With the adequate brain-power we could finish any
scientific discovery, and be certain that we were finishing it right.
But not with the most gigantic intellect could we finish the sim-
plest or silliest story, and be certain that we were finishing it right.
That is because a story has behind it, not merely intellect which
is partly mechanical, but will, which is in its essence divine. The
narrative writer can send his hero to the gallows if he likes in the
last chapter but one. He can do it by the same divine caprice
whereby he, the author, can go to the gallows himself, and to hell

afterwards if he chooses. And the same civilization, the chivalric European civilization which asserted freewill in the thirteenth century, produced the thing called "fiction" in the eighteenth. When Thomas Aquinas asserted the spiritual liberty of man, he created all the bad novels in the circulating libraries.

But in order that life should be a story of romance to us, it is necessary that a great part of it, at any rate, should be settled for us without our permission. If we wish life to be a system, this may be a nuisance; but if we wish it to be a drama, it is an essential. It may often happen, no doubt, that a drama may be written by somebody else which we like very little. But we should like it still less if the author came before the curtain every hour or so, and forced on us the whole trouble of inventing the next act. A man has control over many things in his life; he has control over enough things to be the hero of a novel. But if he had control over everything, there would be so much hero that there would be no novel. And the reason why the lives of the rich are at bottom so tame and uneventful is simply that they can choose the events. They are dull because they are omnipotent. They fail to feel adventures because they can make the adventures. The thing which keeps life romantic and full of fiery possibilities is the existence of these great plain limitations which force all of us to meet the things we do not like or do not expect. It is vain for the supercilious moderns to talk of being in uncongenial surroundings. To be in a romance is to be in uncongenial surroundings. To be born into this earth is to be born into uncongenial surroundings, hence to be born into a romance. Of all these great limitations and frameworks which fashion and create the poetry and variety of life, the family is the most definite and important. Hence it is misunderstood by the moderns, who imagine that romance would exist most perfectly in a complete state of what they call liberty. They think that if a man makes a gesture it would be a startling and romantic matter that the sun should fall from the sky. But the startling and romantic thing about the sun is that it does not fall from the sky. They are seeking under every shape and form a world where there are no limitations—that is, a world where there are no outlines; that is, a world where there are no shapes. There is nothing baser than that infinity. They say they wish to be as strong as the universe, but they really wish the whole universe as weak as themselves.

QUESTIONS

1. Where in the first paragraph is the ostensible subject of the essay stated? What is the relationship of the rest of the paragraph to the subject?

2. What makes Chesterton's defense of the family unusual? Explain his distinction between clans and cliques. Why does he think next-door neighbors are more dangerous than vultures?

3. To what extent is the material in the first paragraph arranged chronologically? In what respect is Chesterton offering a chronological survey in the second paragraph? Why in the third paragraph does he focus upon clubs of present and past rather than upon clubs of city and village?

4. In the second paragraph Chesterton says that "the man who lives in a small community lives in a much larger world." What does he mean by "larger"? With what other words in the rest of the paragraph—and in the rest of the essay—does it become equated?

5. Paragraphs two, three, and four form a unit. To what extent is their common subject defined by the phrase "advantages of the small community" (the opening of the second paragraph)? How would you define their subject? On what rough basis are they ordered? What is their relationship to the first paragraph?

6. What is the special function of the fifth paragraph? To what extent do paragraphs six and seven recapitulate earlier views? To what extent do they expand those views?

7. Chesterton comes to the subject of the family in the eighth paragraph. Explain the broad relationship of the preceding material to it, and describe the general ordering of the discussion thus far.

8. How does the broad ordering of material in the eighth paragraph compare with the ordering of material in paragraphs two through four?

In what respect might the ninth paragraph be said to parallel the fifth paragraph, and the tenth paragraph the sixth?

9. Describe the broad ordering of material in paragraphs eight through twelve. Describe the general organization of the essay. (A rationale will probably be implicit in your explanation.)

10. Chesterton relies upon paradox to a considerable extent in his argument ("the man who lives in a small community lives in a much larger world"). Locate some paradoxes in the first four paragraphs and explain their meanings. What is the argumentative advantage of paradox over straightforward assertion?

The Abacus and the Brain

JOSEPH WOOD KRUTCH

Joseph Wood Krutch (1893–) was for many years Professor of English and Dramatic Literature at Columbia University, and also a distinguished drama critic for the *Nation*. He has written several important scholarly studies (*Thoreau, Samuel Johnson*), but is perhaps best known for two sharply contrasting books, published twenty-five years apart. *The Modern Temper* (1929) reflects the despair of modern man in a world of lost values; *The Measure of Man* (1954) resumes the discussion of modern problems, but with some hopefulness. Since 1950, Krutch has lived most of the time in the Southwest and has been studying the natural life of the region (*The Desert Year, Voice of the Desert*).

The statement that man behaves like a machine and that therefore he is one, involves two propositions which many physiologists as well as many psychologists appear to regard as demonstrated. It would seem unreasonable to ask that they clinch the argument by proving its obverse; that they conclude the demonstration by making a machine which behaves like a man. No one would really issue so unfair a challenge but many believe that it has been met already. "I think, therefore I am." The electronic calculator thinks, therefore it *is*. Is what? Is a man. Or at least the most important part of him, namely a brain.

Now to understand just what this means and why the argument is dubious, we should really go back as far as the abacus, though to most of us this ingenious device is only a harmless toy of wire and beads. Sometimes our Chinese laundryman plays with it for a few seconds before announcing, "Two dollars and thirty-five cents." We then go our way unaware of danger.

Nobody seems to know who invented this prophetic gadget but whoever did started more than he knew. Arabic numerals came later into Europe and at first they seemed to relegate the abacus to the past. But it was only biding its time. About three hundred years ago John Napier with his "bones" taught the abacus how to be logarithmic instead of merely arithmetical and thus gave to the engineer the slide rule which can multiply or extract square roots faster than he can. Ever since then the human brain has been competing less and less successfully with the machine in the matter of calculation.

When Marconi or De Forest—it was long a vexed question which—invented the grid radio tube, he had no idea that it would be able to figure. Neither, for that matter, did whoever invented the wheeled vehicle have any idea of using it to make pottery, though the anthropologists now tell us that the potter's wheel comes into every culture only after the cart. In other words, most fundamentally new gadgets turn out to be usable in fantastically disparate ways, and the man who made radio practical hit upon a device scarcely less adaptable than the wheel, the wedge or the lever. As everyone knows, contraptions which look rather like huge radios are now solving in minutes, or at most in weeks, problems either totally unsolvable by the human brain or so laborious that an individual would spend a large part of his lifetime with pencil, paper, and slide rule if he tried to work them out.

As is usual when something like this comes along, the result is to make mechanists very happy and the rest of us uncomfortable. The abacus and the slide rule were merely tools. Man made them. They were a credit to his ingenuity. They proved how smart *he* was, not how smart *they* were; and nobody thought of them as having any significance or even any existence apart from him. But these electronic calculators are, we are now told, something quite different. They do not have the limitations which we commonly associate with mechanical devices because electricity has endowed them with a kind of life. We are assured that they have memories or, as the followers of Korzybski would say, that they are the first inorganic thing which is capable of "time binding." Some people go even so far as to say that they can exercise judgment, that they think for themselves. In the opinion of their most ardent admirers they are less like a machine and more like a human brain than anything man has ever succeeded in making before.

The poor deluded chemists have been working for a long time learning to synthesize the amino acids in the hope that these would lead to synthetic protein and that, in turn, to synthetic protoplasm. But suppose that at last they did succeed. What would they have? An amoeba at best. Your engineer, on the other hand, brushes aside all nonsense about the mysterious nature of life and, firm in his conviction that all is mechanical, creates at one fell swoop life's highest manifestation, namely, thought.

So at least some of them are telling us and we are ill equipped to argue with them. The equations with which they juggle may seem like mumbo jumbo to us but they have proved in many ways that they are not. Mr. Einstein writes "$E = MC^2$" and (after a few merely technological intermediary steps) Hiroshima goes up in smoke. Obviously these mathematicians know what they are talking about and if they tell us that machines are now thinking—just like men only better—perhaps we should marvel and keep silent.

There is, however, a good deal at stake and it is hard not to protest a little, not to hope that at least the metaphysical conclusions of some mathematicians and engineers may not be incontrovertible. It is bad enough to be caught up in a world which whizzes and bangs; bad enough to be, ultimately, not merely blown up but disintegrated. That, however, we are beginning to get used to. Must we also accept the conviction, not only that we are victims of the machine, but also that we are merely machines ourselves? If, as is obvious, contraptions are becoming more and more manlike, does it necessarily follow that man must be assumed to be no more than a contraption himself?

According to the mechanists, the electronic calculator is the best new evidence for their side in a long, long time. So far as I am aware, no one has yet claimed that a calculator can have children, and the power of self-reproduction has long been on the biologist's list of the criteria for life. But biologists and engineers do not always see eye to eye, and the engineer would no doubt be eager to maintain that if a machine can think, that alone is sufficient to prove his point—namely that the so-called higher faculties of man are the result of the operation of physical forces and that the brain is, at most, no more different from a man-made machine than, say, the man-made electronic "valve" is different from the valve we turn on and off at our steam radiator.

You can't see the wheels go round in the brain; but neither can you turn off an electronic valve by hand, though it is a mechanical device nonetheless. The calculator can remember and it can think. The first of these may be one of the lower capacities of the mind, but the second is, by common consent, the highest. Some, indeed, say that among all living things only man and, perhaps, the ape is capable of it. And if that is true, then the calculator is very far up the evolutionary scale, perhaps farther up than man himself. At least it can think better along certain lines than he can.

Unfortunately for those of us who would like to resist this conclusion, it has been prepared for by the whole tendency of thought on such subjects during the last three hundred years. No one can deny that the study of the human body as a machine has been extremely fruitful of results, while theology and metaphysics have often seemed merely to march round and round in their familiar circles. The study of animal and of human *behavior* has led to apparently stable conclusions, while speculations about the soul, or even the mental processes, seemed to get nowhere.

The psychologist, even though he was not clearly a mechanist by conviction, found it more and more advisable to concentrate his attention on instincts and conditioned reflexes. By consequence, we all fell into the habit of assuming that sooner or later all rational need for the consideration of anything else would vanish. What mechanism could not explain was assumed to be a mere residuum growing smaller and smaller. If the body is mostly a machine, then, it seemed, it is probably entirely a machine. And because we had been long prepared, most people were probably relieved to be told that the last objection to mechanism had been removed. Hitherto machines couldn't think. But my new calculator, says the engineer, can. *Quod erat* (for a long time) *demonstrandum.*

If we do not want to accept this demonstration, then it is evident that we cannot resist merely the last steps in the argument, but will have to go a long way back and begin to resist certain premises, long implicit and sometimes concealed. Again we shall have to point out that the very methods which scientists have chosen to use have prejudiced the conclusions; that to observe human or animal behavior *as though* it were merely mechanical, is inevitably to make it seem so; that to begin with the proposition "We cannot conveniently deal with consciousness and therefore we are justified in disregarding it," is simply to invite the confusions which have, in actual fact, arisen. It is to assume that what a given method finds intractable simply does not exist.

Obviously, then, we have to begin by telling the mechanist that, however inconvenient he may find our insistence, we simply will not permit him to disregard any of the facts; not *any* of the facts and, especially, not so tremendous a fact as the fact of consciousness. Descartes, we shall say, was right. That we think—or rather that we are aware—is, of all things, the one which we know most directly and incontrovertibly. It may be a difficult fact to deal with but it is primary. Consciousness is the one thing which incontrovertibly *is*, and if there is one thing which we cannot afford to

leave out of consideration it is that. To refuse to concern ourselves
with it is to make the most monstrous error that could possibly
be made.

Certainly, then, we have a right to ask whether the electronic
calculator is conscious. "Does it," we may also ask, "have ideas
about itself?" Does it, for example, "believe" that mechanistic
theories of life are "true"? These are some of the most important
things that the human brain is capable of. No doubt some of the
machine's admirers will scornfully reply that we can't prove that it
doesn't. But that is hardly enough. If we are going to accept a conclusion so momentous as the conclusion that there is no important
difference between us and a circuit of electronic tubes, then we
may reasonably ask for more than merely negative evidence. The
theory that consciousness is only an epiphenomenon is a theory not
a fact. We have a right to say that awareness is the most important
as well as the most obvious fact about us. Nothing which is not
aware of itself is anything like what we are. It has not been proved
that we are machines until it has been proved that a machine can,
to begin with—and it is only to begin with—say to itself, *"Cogito
ergo sum."* If we are going to deal in mere guesses or probabilities,
then some of us may guess that what goes on in a brain is not
identical with what goes on in an electronic circuit.

If there was no more to be said than this, it would still be
worth saying. To some extent the air would be cleared and we
would know where we stand. Those to whom a man is, first of
all, a mere figuring machine, would be clearly separated from those
to whom consciousness is the essential condition of all those activities which define the human being. But there is more to be said,
and there are conclusions to be drawn.

Let us remember that when Diogenes exhibited a plucked hen in
the market place and called it "Plato's Man," no one supposed that
he meant what he said. He was making it obvious to the meanest intelligence that "a two-legged animal without feathers" is an in-

adequate definition of man. Similarly when the mechanists exhibit a calculating machine as a contraption whose operations are essentially human, what we ought to conclude is precisely what the ancients concluded from Diogenes' demonstration. Obviously the mechanist's definition of the human being is as inadequate as Plato's definition of man. What he has done is not to prove his point but simply to achieve a glorious *reductio ad absurdum*. What we ought to do is to laugh first, and then to re-examine, not merely the definition so comically exposed, but also the whole long series of dubious assumptions and faulty methods which have led to so preposterous a conclusion. Only at the end of a long series of missteps could anyone be brought to the point where he would be compelled to entertain, even for the purpose of refuting it, the proposition that either a plucked hen or a calculating machine is the same thing as a man.

Moreover definitions are, in this case, extremely important because we tend to cherish and to cultivate in the human race whatever traits and capacities enter into the definition of man which we, at the moment, accept. And it is evident enough that in recent centuries we have fixed our attention chiefly on those aspects of the human being which most resemble, rather than those which least resemble, what a machine is capable of. Not only have we thought of man chiefly in terms of his anatomy, his instincts and his conditioned reflexes, but we have also talked as though the fact that he had an anatomy and had instincts was sufficient proof that the sum of these things was the whole of him.

Even when we have gone beyond anatomy and reflexes to consider his mind, even when we have stopped short of the conviction that this mind was merely a refined manifestation of his ability to acquire habits and become conditioned, we have, nevertheless, tended to consider important chiefly the planning and the calculating powers of this mind. "Man," we have said, "is capable of reason"; not, as we might have said, "capable of hope," or of "doubt," or of "delight"—though all these capacities are certainly as important to him in his experience of living as reason; especially when "reason" means no more than the ability to scheme success-fully.

In "mental tests," those most characteristically limited manifesta-tions of our concept of the criteria appropriate to the judgment of the human mind, the stress is chiefly upon the ability to analyze and to scheme, so that we put into the category of the most superior men those most likely to scheme successfully and we usually exhibit not the slightest concern over the question whether these "most superior" men are capable, to even an average extent, of the awarenesses, the emotions or the mental reactions which make men attractive, either to themselves or to others. And so, just as the econ-omists have given us the ideal economic man who does nothing but produce and consume, so the mental testers have given us the ideal intelligent man who does nothing except scheme. Between them they have outlined a utopia in which creatures who are really only very flexible calculating machines do nothing except make goods which they then use up—living to eat and eating to live. For such creatures, living in such a world, most of the forms of consciousness would be not only unnecessary but also a burden. In a sense, there-fore, the definition of man assumed by the tester prepares us for that definition of man in terms of which the calculator is human.

If we stop to think, most of us do not really believe that the Eco-nomic Man is more than a possibly useful methodological fiction, or that the Superior Man of the mental testers is more than simply the man most likely to succeed at tasks requiring the capacities which the tests do actually measure. The fact nevertheless remains that it is to the Economic Man and the I. Q. Man that our attention is di-rected far more often than on the whole man, who is something very different from either, something far less like anything the mechanists seem likely to be able to construct. And that fact has its consequences.

Perhaps it is too soon, perhaps it will always be too soon, to try to formulate an adequate definition of man. Perhaps the fact that he is indefinable by his own mind is an essential fact about him. But we might, at least, consider more frequently than we do those of his characteristics which we have got into the habit of thinking about very seldom. We might, to begin with, ask concerning the calculating machine those questions posed earlier, and then add some more. Is it capable, we might ask, of imagination? Does it have any curiosity? Can it sympathize with anything? Can it be happy or miserable? Was it ever known to laugh, or even to show, by any unwonted flickerings in its tubes, that it considered something amusing? Does it—and this is most important of all—prefer one thing to another, or does it have its being in a universe where nothing has value, where all things are indifferent?

Presumably we shall not get answers, though some of us may think we know what the answers would be if we could get them. But the real reason for asking is not that. The real reason is that even to ask is to be reminded how important is the "Yes" we get if we interrogate, not a machine, but a fellow creature; how defective, therefore, is that so called Science of Man which never really asks the questions at all and thus proves itself to be, not the Science of Man, but only the Science-of-What-Man-Would-Be-If-He-Were-Not-a-Man-But-a-Machine.

In any event, to ask the questions either of the machine or of ourselves is to take the first step back in the direction of that crossroads, passed perhaps three centuries ago, when we first began to diverge from the path of Wisdom into the path of Inadequate Knowledge. If we retrace our course, we shall be surprised to discover how much we have tended to forget about ourselves, how little we have studied, or even considered, the most remarkable of our capacities. We may even conclude that the ability to figure or to scheme is so far from being our only unique ability that it is not even the most important one—as indeed the possibility of making a machine which can do it for us sufficiently indicates. Perhaps man is not, first of all, a Reasoning Animal; perhaps something else that he does with his mind is even more obviously unique than reasoning. But what, then, shall we call this other thing; what is it that it is hardest to imagine a machine's doing for us?

We might, I suppose, call it "wanting." Certainly even the stupidest man is capable of desiring something, and the cleverest of machines, no matter how brilliantly it may solve differential equations, is not. But the word "wanting" has a more refined and subtler cousin called "preference," which might do better. Man is an animal who not only wants something tangible but is capable also, even among things as insubstantial as ideas or beliefs, of *preferring* one thing to another. And when one has said that, one has arrived at the conventional terminology of metaphysics: Man has a Sense of Values. Other animals may or may not be capable of something out of which the Sense of Values develops. But a machine certainly is not. And there is the grandest of all the differences.

When we think without reference to any preferences or "values" we think like a machine. That means also thinking without reference to joy, or laughter, or love. Very often nowadays we are urged by certain sociologists, political propagandists, and even anthropologists to do just that although they prefer to call it "thinking with detachment." But the thing from which we are asked to detach ourselves is, nevertheless, the state of being human, and the result of such thinking would be a world fit for machines, not for men.

Perhaps, then, those wonderful electronic calculators are not, after all, anything like our brains. Perhaps the best of them is only a super-abacus and therefore a triumph of human ingenuity but, no more than the laundryman's convenient device, a real challenge to the human being's uniqueness. To ask which it is—gadget or brain—is at least no academic question.

To answer one way is to take what is perhaps the final step, not merely in the acceptance of mechanism as a philosophical doctrine, but in the direction of a civilization in which men will become more and more machinelike. To answer the other way is to choose instead the working conviction that man, as he was and as he can be, is neither the Economic Man nor the I. Q. Man but "The Animal Which Can Prefer." It is to believe that the most stupendous of his inventions was not the wheel, or the wedge, or the lever, but the values by which he has lived, and that the ability to act on, for example, the assumption that loyalty is better than treachery even when both seem to give a practical answer to a given problem, is more significant than any other ability he has ever manifested. It is also to believe that, in the future as in the past, what becomes of him will depend less on what machines he invents or what governments are imposed upon him than on what values he creates.

Distrust of our mechanical age, fear that men will be destroyed by the engines which they have devised, is so widespread today that it has developed its own cant. But it often happens that men's fate overtakes them in the one way they had not sufficiently feared, and it may be that if we are to be destroyed by the machine it will not be in quite the manner we have been fearfully envisaging. Perhaps we are in no greater danger of being blown up by the atom bomb than we are of being destroyed by a wrong understanding of the abacus.

QUESTIONS

1. On what basis do paragraphs two, three, and four form a unit? To what point in the first paragraph do they most directly refer? What is their relationship to the fifth paragraph?

2. Explain the phrase "poor deluded chemists" that opens the sixth paragraph. From whose standpoint are the chemists deluded? About what are they deluded?

3. Consider the following revision (paragraph seven): Mr. Einstein writes "$E = MC^2$" and (after a few merely technological intermediary steps) we have atomic power. What is the loss in implication? Relate the words "better" and "marvel" in the succeeding sentence to that implication.

4. Is Krutch more interested in disproving the view that men are like machines or the view that machines are like men? (Compare the first and last paragraphs in the first section.) Describe the general movement of Krutch's discussion in the first section.

5. The second section of the essay divides broadly into three parts: paragraphs one and two, three and four, and five through seven. Describe their relationship to each other, and then compare their ordering with the ordering of material in the first section. What is the general organizing principle at work in each section?

6. Supply the mechanist's definition of man that parallels Plato's definition (see paragraph two in the third section). Where in the essay does Krutch first mention the mechanist's definition? What does he mean when he calls it a *reductio ad absurdum?* Explain the relationship of the "I.Q. Man" and the "Economic Man" to the *reductio ad absurdum.*

7. Krutch's final section contains a warning and a plea. State explicitly what they are. Contrast the tone of the warning here with the tone of the warning in the second paragraph of the essay. What is the effect of Krutch's concluding in this way?

8. Once you have seen the general ordering of material in the first two sections, you should be able to describe the general movement of the remainder of the essay. How clearly do the section divisions mark that movement? If you have read the Shaw essay in this section of the text, contrast the organizing principles of the two essays. What would you say is the rationale for Krutch's approach?

9. Does the essay strike you as the thinking of a witty or a solemn person? Examine the first section for evidence to support your opinion.

10. Trace the shifting use to which Krutch puts "I think; therefore I am" in the course of the essay.

Progress

CARL BECKER

Carl Becker (1873-1945) was born in Iowa, and was educated
at Cornell College and the University of Wisconsin. He subsequently taught at Dartmouth and the Universities of Kansas
and Minnesota, and for the last twenty-eight years of his life
was Professor of History at Cornell University (whose origins
he treated in *Cornell University: Founders and the Founding*).
From the first, his concern was with ideas and their role in
history, a concern that may be seen in his best-known books,
The Declaration of Independence and *The Heavenly City
of the Eighteenth Century Philosophers,* both of which study
certain major currents of eighteenth-century thought. Though
never an easy optimist, Becker was sorely tried in the
nineteen-thirties, as the following essay, written towards the
middle of the decade, more than suggests. (Further headnote
information on Becker appears on p. 318.)

"Thought," says Pascal, "makes the greatness of man." The universe
can destroy an individual by a mere breath; but even if the entire
force of the universe were employed to destroy a single man, the
man "would still be more noble than that which destroys him,
since he is aware of his own death and of the advantage which
the universe has over him: of all this the universe knows noth-

ing." This awareness of himself and of the universe is no doubt
what chiefly distinguishes man from all other forms of life. Man
alone is conscious in the sense that he alone can stand outside
of himself, as it were, and watch himself functioning for a brief
span in the universe of which he is part. Man alone can coördi-
nate memory of things past, perception of things present, anticipa-
tion of things to come, sufficiently so at least to know that he, like
generations before him and after him, will live his brief span and
will die. It is in virtue of this awareness, and somewhat in proportion to its intensity, that man alone asks the fundamental questions.
Why and for what purpose this brief and precarious existence in a
universe that endures? What is man's relation to the universe that
is sometimes friendly, sometimes hostile, but in the end always fatal
to him? How may he elude its hostility, win its favor, find compen-
sations for the intolerable certainty of the death which it will inflict
upon him? The answers which men have given to these questions
are to be found in the various myths, religious doctrines, philosophical and ethical interpretations which they have accepted, and in
those unconsciously held preconceptions which in every age so
largely shape their thought and conduct. The modern idea of
progress belongs in this category of answers to necessary but insoluble questions. Like the myths of primitive peoples and the religious
and philosophical beliefs of more advanced societies, it springs
from the nature of man as a conscious creature, who finds existence
intolerable unless he can enlarge and enrich his otherwise futile
activities by relating them to something more enduring and significant than himself.

Although grounded in the nature of man as a conscious creature,
the idea of progress belongs historically to the European tradition,
and its origin may be derived from two sources. One of these is the
classical conception of history as an endless series of cycles; the
other is the Hebraic-Christian doctrine of messianic intervention
and salvation.

In Greek mythology the reign of Cronus was regarded as a
golden age when men lived like gods free from toil and grief. The

present appeared to be a period of degeneration, and improvement or progress could be conceived only in terms of regeneration—a return to the lost golden age. After the myth ceased to be believed, the Greeks continued to look back to the time of great lawgivers, such as Lycurgus and Solon, whose work they idealized, and forward to the time when other great lawgivers would appear and give them better laws again. "Until philosophers become kings . . . ," said Plato, "cities will not cease from ill." Yet however often restoration was accomplished by inspired lawgivers or philosopher-kings, fate and human frailty would again bring degeneration; so that, since "time is the enemy of man," most classical writers regarded human history as an endless series of cycles, a continual repetition of the familiar phenomena of recovery and degeneration. The rational mind, according to Marcus Aurelius, "stretches forth into the infinitude of Time, and comprehends the cyclical Regeneration of all things, and . . . discerns that our children will see nothing fresh, just as our fathers too never saw anything more than we" (*The Communings with Himself of Marcus Aurelius Antoninus*, tr. by C. R. Haines, Loeb Classical Library, London 1916, bk. XI, sect. I). To regenerate the Roman Empire was obviously less easy than to construct a constitution for a small city-state; and Marcus Aurelius, philosopher-king though he was, instead of giving new laws to society recommended that the individual cultivate resignation. The later centuries of the Roman Empire, when resignation became at once more necessary and more difficult, were therefore a suitable time for the hopeless classical doctrine of endless cycles to be replaced by the Hebraic-Christian doctrine of messianic intervention and salvation.

The Jews like the Greeks looked back to a golden age, but it was identified with the creation of the world and with the Garden of Eden, in which the first men lived in innocence. Like the Greeks the Jews regarded the present as a period of degeneration, but they attributed the "fall" to Adam's disobedience to God's commands. God was at once the omniscient creator of the world and the supreme lawgiver, so that regeneration was identified with the com-

ing of a God-inspired king of the house of David. Multiplied reverses and the destruction of the Hebraic state gave to this doctrine
a less political, a more mystical and transcendent character. The
once actual but now vanished kingdom was replaced by an ideal
Israel, symbolized as the "son of man"; and the idea of a God-
inspired king was replaced by the idea of a messiah who would
effect a catastrophic intervention in the affairs of men and pronounce a doomlike judgment on the world. The Christian myth
was but an elaboration of these ideas. Jesus, son of man, son of God,
was the Messiah. But the end was not yet. The death of Jesus was
expiation for the sins of men, faith in Him the means of salvation.
Jesus the man was dead, but Christ the Lord still lived and would
come again; then the earthly city would be destroyed and all
the faithful be gathered with God in the heavenly city, there to
dwell in perfection forever.

The weakness of the classical version of degeneration and recovery was that it offered no ultimate hope; of the Jewish, that its
promise was for the chosen people only. The strength of the Christian version was that, conceiving human history as a cosmic drama
in which all men played their predestined part, it offered to all
the hope of eternal life as a compensation for the frustrations of
temporal existence: by transferring the golden age from the past to
the future it substituted an optimistic for a disillusioned view of human destiny. It is easily to be understood that such a view won wide
assent in the Roman Empire during the centuries (300-500) of declining prosperity and increasing oppression or that it served so
well to make existence tolerable in the relatively anarchic, isolated
and static society of western Europe from the dissolution of the
Roman Empire to the Renaissance of classical learning. But it lost
its hold on the imaginations of men as a result of profound changes
in the outward conditions of life which occurred in western Europe
from the fourteenth to the nineteenth century. Among these
changes were the rise of ordered secular governments, the growth
of towns and industry, the geographical discoveries and the extension of commerce which brought western Europe into direct con-

tact with alien customs and ideas, and above all the rise of an educated middle class whose interests were hampered by a form of society in which both the power and the doctrines of the Christian church supported the autocracy of kings and the privileges of a landed aristocracy. It was in this time of revolt against ecclesiastical and secular authority that the Christian doctrine of salvation was gradually transformed into the modern idea of progress.

So long as Christian philosophy was little questioned, men could afford to ignore the factual experience of mankind since they were so well assured of its ultimate significance. But the declining influence of the church was accompanied by an increasing interest in the worldly activities of men in the past. Italian humanists turned to the study of classical writers; Protestant reformers appealed from current theologians to the beliefs and practises of the primitive church. Thus was born the modern historical approach to problems, and human life came increasingly to be regarded rather as a historical process than as a finished drama to be played out according to a divine plan. Seen in historical perspective, classical civilization emerged for the humanists as a resplendent epoch from which the middle period of ecclesiastical ascendancy was manifestly a degeneration. Until the seventeenth century secular thought and learning turned for inspiration to the past—to the golden ages of Pericles and Augustus; and classical writers were idealized as models to be imitated, to be equaled if possible but hardly to be surpassed. In all this there was nothing that could not be found in the Greek notion of history with its cycles of recovery and degeneration, and but for two general influences modern thought might have been no more than a return to the classical view of human destiny.

One of these influences was Christian philosophy itself. Although it was gradually discredited as an account of events historically verifiable, Christian philosophy had so thoroughly habituated men to the thought of an ultimate happy destiny that they could never be content with a pale imitation of Greek pessimism. The other influence was experimental science which, in proportion as it displaced the Christian notion of a utopian existence after death to be brought about by the miraculous intervention of God, opened up the engaging prospect of indefinite improvement in this life to be effected by the application of human reason to the mastery of the physical and social environment which determines men's lives for good or ill.

In the seventeenth century Galileo and Newton made possible a new attitude toward nature. Nature was now seen to be friendly to man since the universe behaved in a uniform way according to universal natural laws—a behavior capable of being observed and measured and subjected to the uses of men. God was still the supreme lawgiver, the author of the universe; but His will was revealed in the great book of nature which men were to study in order to interpret, and to interpret in order that their ideas and customs might attain an increasing perfection by being brought into greater harmony with the laws of nature and of nature's God. God's revelation to men was thus made not through an inspired book or a divinely established church but through His works, and man had been endowed with reason precisely that he might learn through the course of the centuries what that revelation was. It was therefore no longer so necessary to think of the golden age of Greece and Rome as unsurpassable. "Those whom we call the ancients were really those who lived in the youth of the world," said Pascal, and "as we have added the experience of the ages between us and them to what they knew, it is in ourselves that is to be found that antiquity which we venerate in others." In the ascription of antiquity to the race there is still the implication of degeneration; but if a continuously richer experience made the moderns wiser than the ancients, it was not difficult to hit upon the idea that future generations would, in virtue of the same advantages, surpass the moderns. "We have admired our ancestors less," said Chastellux, "but we have loved our contemporaries better, and have expected more of our descendants" (*De la félicité publique*, 2 vols., new ed. Paris 1822, vol. ii, p. 71). Thus in the eighteenth century the modern idea of progress was born. Under the pressure of social discontents the dream of perfection, that necessary compensation for the limitations of the present state, having long been identified with the golden age or the Garden of Eden or life eternal in the heavenly city of God, was at last projected into the temporal life of man on earth and identified with the desired and hoped for regeneration of society.

As formulated by the *philosophes* the doctrine of progress was but a modification, however important, of the Christian doctrine of redemption; what was new in it was faith in the goodness of man and the efficacy of conscious reason to create an earthly utopia. The French Revolution was the outward expression of this faith. In the nineteenth century the doctrine of progress still reigned and won even a wider popular support, but it was somewhat differently conceived. After the disillusionment occasioned by the revolution and the Napoleonic conquests the prevailing desire was for social stability and national independence. The rationalization of this desire was provided by the historians and jurists who formulated the notion of historical continuity and deprecated the attempt to transform institutions according to a rational plan. Change was considered necessary but was thought to be beneficial only when it issued spontaneously from national tradition; the concept of natural law was not abandoned, but it was regarded as implicit in historical evolution rather than as a conclusion from abstract reason. Law is not made by the legislator, said Savigny, any more than language is made by the grammarian. Ranke, who influenced three generations of historians, viewed progress as something to be discovered by tracing the history of each nation just as it had occurred and by noting the peculiar contribution which each nation at the appropriate moment had made to European civilization. Hegel formulated the point of view of early nineteenth century jurists and historians in his *Philosophie der Geschichte*. A reason of nature working over the heads of men, a transcendent *Vernunft* reconciling within its cloudy recesses innumerable and conflicting *Verstände*, progressively realized itself in the actual events of history.

After the middle of the century natural science invested the doctrine of progress with a more materialistic implication. Progress was still regarded as the result of a force external to man; but the force was to be found not above but inherent in the phenomenal world. This view found support in the Darwinian theory of struggle for existence and survival of the fittest and in Schopenhauer's doctrine of the will as an aspect of a universal blind force. Guided by these preconceptions thinkers abandoned the effort to hasten progress by describing utopias and turned to the search for the inevitable law by which progress had been and would be achieved. Of the many efforts of this sort the most important were those of Auguste Comte and Karl Marx. Comte looked upon history as the result of the instinctive effort of men to ameliorate their condition—an effort which could be observed to fall into three stages of culture, the theological, the metaphysical and the positive, or scientific. Marx, interpreting the historic process in terms of Hegel's famous dialectic, found the determining force in the economic class conflict which, having substituted the nineteenth century capitalist competitive society for the aristocratic landed society of the Middle Ages and early modern times, would in turn replace the capitalist competitive society of the nineteenth century by the proletarian communist society of the future.

Of the many theories of progress formulated in the nineteenth century the only one that had much influence on the thought of common men was that of Marx. Yet the idea of progress, vaguely conceived as a rapid improvement in general prosperity and happiness, became a living force. The chief reason for this was no doubt the rapid changes in the outward conditions of life consequent upon the technological revolution. The common man, before whose eyes the marvels of science and invention were constantly displayed, noted the unprecedented increase in wealth, the growth of cities, the new and improved methods of transportation and communication, the greater security from disease and death and all the conveniences of domestic life unknown to previous generations, and accepted the doctrine of progress without question: the world was obviously better than it had been, obviously would be better than it was. The precise objective toward which the world was progressing remained, however, for the common man and for the intellectual, somewhat vague.

Thus the nineteenth century doctrine of progress differed somewhat from that of the eighteenth. The difference may be expressed, with some exaggeration in the contrast, by saying that whereas the eighteenth century held that man can by taking thought add a cubit to his stature, the nineteenth century held that a cubit would be added to his stature whether he took thought or not. This latter faith that the stars were carrying men on to better things received a rude shock during the World War and subsequently; and there may be noted two significant changes in the present attitude toward the doctrine of progress. Certain thinkers, notably Spengler, are returning to the Greek notion of cycles, now formulated in terms of the rise, flourishing and decline of "cultures." Others are reverting to the eighteenth century idea that by deliberate purpose and the rational use of knowledge man can reconstruct society according to a more just and intelligible design. To this class belong those who have faith in communism, fascism and the planned capitalist society.

The doctrine of progress is peculiarly suited to western society in modern times; that is, a highly dynamic society capable of seeing its achievements against a long historical background. From the practical and from the rational point of view there is no reason to suppose that it will have a more enduring virtue than other doctrines which it has supplanted. If, as may well happen, the possibilities of scientific discovery and of technological invention should some time be exhausted, the outward conditions of life might become sufficiently stabilized so that the idea of progress would cease to be relevant. Rationally considered, the idea of progress is always at war with its premises. It rests upon the notion of a universe in perpetual flux; yet the idea of progress has always carried the implication of finality, for it seems to be meaningless unless there is movement toward some ultimate objective. The formal theories of progress are all vitiated by this radical inconsistency. In Hegel's scheme the objective was freedom, already realized in the Prussian state. In Comte's theory the objective was the final positive stage into which Europe had already entered. Marx criticized Hegel for explaining history by a process which would not explain the future, but he is himself open to the criticism of having explained history in terms of a class conflict which would end with the establishment of a classless society. It is easy to picture history as a process working toward an ultimate good if the world is to come to an end when that good is attained; but if the universe as presented by modern science is to be accepted—a universe in perpetual flux —then a law of history which at some determinate time ceases to apply leaves much to be desired.

Thus the final good, absolute standards of value, are sought in vain; there is merely a universe in which the ideas of things as well as the things themselves arise out of temporary conditions and are transformed with the modification of the conditions out of which they arose. On this assumption we must dispense with the notion of finality, must suppose that the idea of progress and all of its special formulations are but temporary insights useful for the brief moment in which they flourish. "In escaping from the illusion of finality, is it legitimate to exempt that dogma itself? Must not it, too, submit to its own negation of finality? Will not that process of change, for which Progress is the optimistic name, compel 'Progress' too to fall from the commanding position in which it is now, with apparent security, enthroned?" (Bury, J.B., *The Idea of Progress*, p. 352). The price we pay for escaping from the illusion of finality is the recognition that nothing, not even the belief that we have escaped that illusion, is likely to endure. All philosophies based upon the absolute and the unconditioned have their defects; but all philosophies based upon the universal relativity of things have their defects also, a minor one being that they must be prepared, at the appropriate moment, to commit hara-kiri in deference to the ceaseless change which they postulate.

Belief in progress as a fact depends upon the standard of value chosen for measuring it and upon the time perspective in which it is measured. If we look back a hundred years, it is obvious that there has been progress in the mastery of physical forces. If we look back two thousand years, it is uncertain whether there has been much if any progress in intelligence and the art of living. If we look back two hundred and fifty thousand years, it is apparent that there has been progress in all those aspects of life which civilized men regard as valuable. All these judgments are based on standards of value appreciable by the mind of civilized man. But if we take a still longer perspective and estimate the universe as a whole, as an omniscient intelligence indifferent to human values might estimate it, in terms of cosmic energy, then progress and the very existence of man himself become negligible and meaningless. In such a perspective we should see the whole life of man on the earth as a mere momentary ripple on the surface of one of the minor planets in one of the minor stellar systems.

QUESTIONS

1. "Thought" and "greatness" are the key words in the first sentence of the opening paragraph of Becker's essay. What succeeding words, phrases, and sentences are equivalents and instances of each term?

2. What is the function of paragraph two? What pattern of organization is Becker invoking in it: classification, chronology, or comparison? To what extent does each of these patterns operate in the succeeding paragraphs? What key words and phrases mark the chronological progression in the essay?

3. Where is the topic sentence or phrase for paragraph seven? What are the topic sentences or phrases for the next three paragraphs? (There may be more than one to a paragraph.)

4. In which sentence does Becker pass judgment on the usefulness of each of the three conceptions of history? In which does he pass judgment on their validity? If he thinks none of the conceptions can be absolutely valid, which one does he think is most nearly valid and which one least?

5. Would the meaning of the essay be altered by the omission of the first paragraph? Can you relate Becker's mood in the final paragraph to his assertion in the first that the notion of progress is an answer to an insoluble question?

6. To the extent that the essay is organized chronologically, what is the rationale for its organization?

7. Becker's evidence for the variant forms of the conception of progress consists mainly of references to leading thinkers of the past three centuries. What other kinds of evidence does he supply?

8. What is the irony in the phrase "engaging prospect" in paragraph seven? Is there a clear indication in Becker's later discussion that he is being ironical here? Can you know from his earlier discussion that he is being ironical? By what modification can you eliminate the irony?

The Last Parade

E. M. FORSTER

E. M. Forster (1879—) is highly esteemed both as novelist and essayist. Born in London, the son of an architect, he read classics and history at Cambridge, spent some time travelling in Italy and Greece, and on his return to England began writing in earnest. His first novel, *Where Angels Fear to Tread*, appeared when he was twenty-six; three more (most notably *Howards End*) appeared within the next five years. After a lapse of fourteen years he published his last and best novel, *A Passage to India*, based on two short stays in India. His essays, written over a long period and on many subjects, have been collected in *Abinger Harvest* and *Two Cheers for Democracy*; his short stories appear in two volumes, *The Celestial Omnibus and Other Stories* and *The Eternal Moment*. (Further headnote information on Forster appears on pp. 151, 275.)

Paris Exhibition, 1937: Palace of Discovery, Astronomical Section: model of the Earth in space. Yes, here is a model of this intimate object. It is a tidy size—so large that Europe or even France should be visible on it—and it revolves at a suitable rate. It does not take twenty-four hours to go round as in fact, nor does it whizz as in poetry. It considers the convenience of the observer, as an exhibit should. Staged in a solemn alcove, against a background of lamp-super-black, it preens its contours eternally, that is to say from opening to closing time, and allows us to see our home as others would see it, were there others who could see. Its colouring, its general appearance, accord with the latest deductions. The result is surprising. For not France, not even Europe, is visible. There are great marks on the surface of the model, but they represent clouds and snows, not continents and seas. No doubt the skilled observer could detect some underlying fussiness, and infer our civilisation, but the average voyager through space would only notice our clouds and our snows; they strike the eye best. Natural boundaries, guns in action, beautiful women, pipe-lines—at a little distance they all wear the same veil. Sir Malcolm Campbell beats his own records till he sees his own back, Mr. Jack Hulbert cracks still cleaner jokes, forty thousand monkeys are born in Brazil and fifty thousand Italians in Abyssinia, the Palace of the Soviets rises even higher than had been planned, Lord Baden-Powell holds a yet larger jamboree, but all these exercises and the areas where they occur remain hidden away under an external shimmer. The moon—she shows her face. Throned in an adjacent room, the moon exhibits her pockmarks nakedly. But the Earth, because she still has atmosphere and life, is a blur.

Paris Exhibition: the Spanish Pavilion, the Italian Pavilion. The other pavilions. The Palaces of Glass and of Peace. The Eiffel Tower. The last named occasionally sings. Moved by an emission of Roman Candles from its flanks, it will break of an evening into a dulcet and commanding melody. When this happens the pavilions fold their hands to listen, and are steeped for a little in shadow, so that the aniline fountains may play more brightly in the Seine. The melody swells, inciting the fireworks as they the melody, and both of them swell the crowd. O synchronisation! O splendour unequalled! Splendour ever to be surpassed? Probably never to be surpassed. The German and Russian Pavilions, the Chinese and Japanese Pavilions, the British and Italian Pavilions, any and all of the pavilions, will see to that. The Eiffel Tower sings louder, a scientific swan. Rosy chemicals stimulate her spine, she can scarcely bear the voltage, the joy, the pain. . . . The emotion goes to her tiny head, it turns crimson and vomits fiery serpents. All Paris sees them. They astonish the Pantheon and Montmartre. Even the Institut de France notices, heavy browed, dreaming of cardinals, laurels, and réclame in the past. O inspired giraffe! Whatever will the old thing turn into next? Listen and see. The crisis is coming. The melody rises by slight and sure gradations, à la César Franck, spiralling easily upward upon the celestial roundabout. Bell pop popple crack, is the crisis, bell pop popple crack, the senses reel, music and light, lusic and might, the Eiffel Tower becomes a plesiosauros, flings out her arms in flame, and brings them back smartly to her vibrating sides, as one who should say "là!" Bell pop crack pop popple bell. The carillon dies away, the rockets fall, the senses disentangle. There is silence, there are various types of silences, and during one of them the Angel of the Laboratory speaks. "Au revoir, mes enfants," she says. "I hope you have enjoyed yourselves. We shall meet again shortly, and in different conditions." The children applaud these well-chosen words. The German Pavilion, the Russian Pavilion, confront one another again, and a small star shines out on the top of the Column of Peace.

Paris Exhibition: Van Gogh. When the day breaks, Van Gogh can be found if wanted. He is housed in the corner of another palace between maps of Paris and intellectual hopes for the future, and the space suffices him. Well content with his half-dozen rooms, he displays his oddness and his misery to tired feet. "Sorrow is better than joy," he writes up upon the white walls of his cell. Here are pictures of potatoes and of miners who have eaten potatoes until their faces are tuberous and dented and their skins grimed and unpeeled. They are hopeless and humble, so he loves them. He has his little say, and he understands what he is saying, and he cuts off his own ear with a knife. The gaily painted boats of Saintes Maries sail away into the Mediterranean at last, and the Alpilles rise over St. Rémy for ever, but nevertheless "Sorrow is better than joy," for Van Gogh. What would the Eiffel Tower make of such a conclusion? Spinning in its alcove for millions of years, the earth brings a great artist to this. Is he just dotty, or is he failing to put across what is in his mind? Neither, if we may accept historical parallels. Every now and then people have preferred sorrow to joy, and asserted that wisdom and creation can only result from suffering. Half a mile off, Picasso has done a terrifying fresco in the Spanish Pavilion, a huge black and white thing called "Guernica." Bombs split bull's skull, woman's trunk, man's shins. The fresco is indignant, and so it is less disquieting than the potato-feeders of Van Gogh. Picasso is grotesquely angry, and those who are angry still hope. He is not yet wise, and perhaps he is not yet a creator. Nevertheless, he too succeeds in saying something about injustice and pain. Can one look through pain or get round it? And can anything be done against money? On the subject of money, Van Gogh becomes comprehensible and sound. He has got round money because he has sought suffering and renounced happiness. In the sizzle surrounding him, his voice stays uncommercial, unscientific, pure. He sees the colour "blue," observes that the colour "yellow" always occurs in it, and writes this preposterous postulate up upon the white walls. He has a home beyond comfort and common sense with the saints, and perhaps he sees God.

The Soviet Pavilion. This, bold and gleaming, hopes to solve such problems for the ordinary man. And for the ordinary woman too, who, of enormous size, leans forward on the roof beside her gigantic mate. Seen from the side, they and the building upon which they stand describe a hyperbola. They shoot into space, following their hammer and sickle, and followed by the worker's world state. The conception is satisfying, but a hyperbola is a mathematical line, not necessarily an esthetic one, and the solid and ardent pair do not group well when viewed from the banks of

the bourgeois Seine. Challenging injustice, they ignore good taste,
indeed they declare in their sterner moments that injustice and
good taste are inseparable. Their aims are moral, their methods dis-
ciplinary. Passing beneath their sealed-up petticoats and trousers,
we enter a realm which is earnest, cheerful, instructive, constructive
and consistent, but which has had to blunt some of the vagrant sen-
sibilities of mankind and is consequently not wholly alive. Statistics,
maps and graphs preach a numerical triumph, but the art-stuff on
the walls might as well hang on the walls of the German Pavilion
opposite: the incidents and the uniforms in the pictures are different
but the mentality of the artists is the same, and is as tame. Only
after a little thinking does one get over one's disappointment and
see the matter in perspective. For the Soviet Pavilion is a nudge to
the blind. It is trying, like Van Gogh, to dodge money and to wipe
away the film of coins and notes which keeps forming on the human retina. One of the evils of money is that it tempts us to look at
it rather than at the things that it buys. They are dimmed because
of the metal and the paper through which we receive them. That is
the fundamental deceitfulness of riches, which kept worrying Christ.
That is the treachery of the purse, the wallet and the bank-balance,
even from the capitalist point of view. They were invented as a
convenience to the flesh, they have become a chain for the spirit.
Surely they can be cut out, like some sorts of pain. Though deprived of them the human mind might surely still keep its delicacy
unimpaired, and the human body eat, drink and make love. And
that is why every bourgeois ought to reverence the Soviet Pavilion.
Even if he is scared at Marxism he ought to realise that Russia has
tried to put men into touch with things. She has come along with a
handkerchief and wiped. And she has wiped close to the exhibition
turnstiles and amid the chaos and carnage of international finance.

Park of Attractions. I did enjoy myself here, I must say. That is
the difficulty of considering the Exhibition: it is in so many pieces
and so is oneself. After seeing the German Pavilion, which presents

Valhalla as a telephone box, and the Belgian Pavilion, which is very lovely, and many other sacred and serious objects, I sought the Park of Attractions and went up to space in a pretence-balloon. A crane lifted me into the void while another crane lowered another balloon which filled with people when my balloon was up. Then my balloon came down and the other balloon went up. So I got out and walked over the surface of the earth to the Dervish Theatre. Then I watched other people play a game called "Deshabillez vos vedettes." I thought a vedette was a boat. Here it was a tin lady, naked except for a cincture of green feathers which the entrants tried to shoot off. Then I went to a booth advertising "Perversités. Images Troublantes." The entrance fee was a franc, which helped me to keep my head. Inside were some distorting mirrors, a little black savage who kept lashing herself or himself with a bunch of bootlaces, and some holes through which improper photographs should have been seen, but I got muddled and missed them. Oh, the French, the French! Well pleased, I came out. It was a lovely evening. The moon, which had been trying various styles from Neon to Pantheon, now imitated a pretence-balloon. The Park of Attractions, which is extremely clever and pretty, was girt with a scenic railway, and at intervals the shrieks of voyagers through space rent the night. There was plenty to spend money on. Money, money, money! The crowd was what journalists call "good humoured"; and I, a journalist, was part of it. Tunisians and Moroccans strolled about and sometimes kissed one another. Oh, the French! Why are they so good at organizing these lighter happinesses? The English admire them, and themselves produce the suety dreariness, the puffed pretentiousness, of Wembley.

Satan. Unexpected but unmistakable, he appears in the great entrance court of the Italian Pavilion, amongst the fragments of the lovely Italian past. These fragments are bent to his service—Garibaldi, St. Francis, Ravenna mosaics, Pompeian doves. He is to the left as one comes in, clothed all in black, and he dominates a

large feeble picture of carnage. He is weakness triumphant—that is
his rôle in the modern world. He presses a button and a bull bursts.
He sprays savages with scent. He tilts his head back till his chin
sticks out like a tongue and his eyeballs stare into his brain. Decent
people take no notice of him or make fun of him, but presently
something goes wrong with their lives; certain islands are inac-
cessible, a letter is unanswered, bonds confiscated, a friend takes a
trip over the frontier and never returns. Elsewhere in this same
pavilion are his instruments: things easily let off. He has only one remark to make: "I, I, I." He uses the symbols of the sacred and
solemn past, but they only mean "I." Here, among superficial splen-
dours of marble, he holds his court, and no one can withstand him
except Van Gogh, and Van Gogh has nothing to lose. The rest of us
are vulnerable, science is doing us in, the Angel of the Laboratory
switches off the fireworks, and burns up the crowd without flame.

Meanwhile, and all the while, the Earth revolves in her alcove,
veiled in wool. She has sent samples of her hopes and lusts to Paris;
that they will again be collected there, or anywhere, is unlikely, but
she herself will look much the same as soon as one stands a little
back in space. Even if the Mediterranean empties into the Sahara it
will not make much difference. It is our clouds and our snows
that show.

QUESTIONS

1. Which items in the two series in the opening section of the essay,
"Natural boundaries . . ." and "Sir Malcolm Campbell . . . ," are referred to—directly and indirectly—in later sections of the essay? To
which other section is the main body of the first section most closely
linked?

2. Identify the several direct and indirect references to peace and war
in the second section. Which theme dominates the section? How do
you know?

3. Of what relevance are the first and second sections to the implication of Forster's statement in the opening of the third section, "Van

Gogh can be found if wanted"? How would you describe the thematic movement (or organizational movement) of the first three sections?

4. What themes run through both sections three and four? What differences does Forster see between Van Gogh and the Soviet citizens? With whom does he side? How do you know?

5. Identify four themes that Forster touches upon in both sections four and five. In what ways do the themes in section five clarify or modify the themes in section four? What reverberation from an earlier section does Forster achieve with his phrase "shrieks of voyagers through space"?

6. At what points in the sixth section is Forster describing a physical image of Satan and at what points imagining things about him? Which of Satan's attributes has Forster alluded to earlier in the essay?

7. On the basis of your examination of the previous questions, answer the following ones. What are the major themes of the essay? What is the relationship of the first section to them? What is the relationship of Satan to them? Why does the section on Van Gogh follow the description of the Eiffel Tower rather than precede it? Why are Van Gogh and the Russian Pavilion juxtaposed? Why are the Park of Attractions and Satan juxtaposed? Why would it be undesirable to follow the section on the Eiffel Tower with the section on Satan? What would you say is the organizing principle—or principles—governing the essay? (Your answer should imply a rationale.)

8. What advantages does Forster derive from the fragmentary and disjointed way in which he presents his material? What are the implications of his title?

9. Explain the meanings of the following phrases that appear in the first section: "intimate object," "tidy size," "whizz as in poetry," "detect some underlying fussiness and infer our civilization," "the earth, because she still has atmosphere and life, is a blur." What quality do they have in common? What color do they give to the writing?

10. Identify the several ironic juxtapositions (such as "maps of Paris and intellectual hopes for the future") and apparent *non sequiturs* (such as "they are hopeless and humble, so he loves them") in the third paragraph. Explain their meanings. Try to define the quality that they lend to the writing.

SECTION III

Strategy

Strategy

By and large, the discussion of organization and development assumed that writers have processes to describe, five causes of the Civil War to explain, and three days at college to account for—as though all the parts of an essay were of equal importance and the writer needed only to arrange them in a sensible order suitable to his purpose. But suppose the writer believes that there are six causes of the Civil War and that the sixth—Charles Sumner—is the only true cause, the others being causes trumped up by Northern historians. He is faced not so much with finding a rationale for organizing his material as with developing a strategy of argument. Should he make a frontal assault on his opponents? Should he ignore the one false cause that is not susceptible to easy attack and allow the true cause to emerge from a disinterested examination of the others? How can he show the true cause to best advantage? Very possibly he will break or abandon customary patterns of organization to accommodate his strategy.

To put the matter differently, we could say that the discussion of organization assumed that the act of writing involves a writer with materials: gathering, weighing, sorting, and arranging; whereas the present discussion assumes that the writer is equally involved with his audience. By "audience" we mean the actual or hypothetical person or group to whom a writer addresses his remarks. The student who writes around a subject, hoping to bemuse his teacher into believing that he has written on it, has his eye on both materials and audience. His predicament may be unusual, but his attitude is inescapable: every writer has an audience in the front or at the back of his mind (an audience that he may consider to be friendly or hostile, knowledgeable or ignorant), and he adapts his material according to his needs and desires regarding that audience. Does he want to dazzle, persuade, cajole, or deceive his audience? He selects and arranges his material—or deranges it —to suit the case.

To put the matter still differently, we might say that every piece of writing is a kind of argument. If we consider that the ultimate justification for a piece of writing is that it says something that has not been said before—presents a unique view of London on the morning of January 1, 1962, or offers the unique feelings of the person seeing London that morning—then we recognize a kind of argument: the piece of writing must convince the reader that the view or the feeling is unique rather than a repetition of things said before. Such a conception of "argument" leads to point of view and tone and style (considered in the next two sections of the text). It refers to the desire of the writer to engage and hold the attention of—to speak to—other men.

In the present discussion, strategy is to be thought of as occupying the middle ground of a writer's concerns, between the extremes of unity, coherence, and development on the one side, and tone and style on the other. None of these elements is truly distinct from the others: the sorts of transitions that a writer employs help to define his style; strategy itself can be regarded as a special case of rationale. But for pedagogical purposes we make the distinctions, and we say—inexactly—that at the one extreme of unity, coherence, and development the writer is absorbed in his materials, building paragraphs out of them; and that at the other extreme of tone and style he is preoccupied (consciously and unconsciously) with himself as a person writing, and with the attitudes and character he is displaying to his audience. The middle ground of strategy concerns materials handled with an audience in mind. The basic question about each of the essays in the present section will be: what influence upon the choice and arrangement of subject-matter has been exerted by the writer's presumed needs and desires with regard to his audience? To answer that question it will usually be necessary to infer—from, say, the kind of language employed—the sort of audience that the writer is addressing.

In the previous section of the text we saw George Bernard Shaw attacking capitalism. He himself said that he chose the manufacture of pins as his instrument of attack because his audience was female; and we inferred that he talked about pins instead of clothes (except for a brief paragraph) because pins offered a simpler, more lucid, and humorous argument for his audience than clothes might have. In another essay G. K. Chesterton defended the institution of the family, and we observed that he devoted most of his attention to other institutions such as pubs, neighborhoods, small towns, small cities, and small countries. Shaw's broad strategy goes under the name of argument by example, Chesterton's under the name of argument by analogy. Each strategy reflects the fact that a writer often begins with a point that he wishes to establish rather than a mass of material that he must organize; each strategy illustrates the fact that a writer often says to himself: I shall use this sort of material because my audience . . .

And then—with his audience still in mind—he must decide how to use his material; he must devise a strategy of arrangement, determine upon a focus. Shaw uses pins, and he begins with pins; he uses clothes too, but he uses them second; he puts first things first; he is forthright, direct. (He is Saint George, slaying the dragon of capitalism with pins. And he very nearly succeeds, so devastating is his strategy.) Chesterton, on the other hand, puts first things last. He approaches the family circumspectly. Moreover, he arrives without fuss, and he stays a short time. His focus, that is to say, rests as much and as long upon his analogies as upon his presumed subject; his strategy is to rely upon the strength of his analogies. If the reader re-examines the essay he may find that the least convincing part is the direct analysis of family life. For writing directly about "the sublime and special romance of the family" is difficult: sublimity has to refer to quarrels about private theatricals and the Trocadero; sublimity too easily becomes sentimentality. Better to bemuse the audience with analogies.

Trying to infer the strategy of a writer has its hazards. Shaw is thoughtful enough to mention his strategy, but usually writers are as secretive as generals; and the reader is the enemy. It may be, for instance, that Chesterton's strategy is to bemuse the reader into thinking that the subject is the family and thus to take him un-awares and plant the flag of Christian knowledge in heathendom. (He is Saint Gilbert.) The reader cannot be certain about Chesterton's strategy; but he can learn from it for his own purposes.

Not Listening to Music

E. M. FORSTER

Witty, gentle, intimate, Forster's style lends itself admirably
to the informal essay, of which he is an established master. As
in the following selection, he can treat a subject that he finds
personally meaningful, and yet retain a whimsical distance.
His interest in the arts, reflected below, weaves in and out of
many of his essays, and receives most extensive expression in
his classic of criticism, *Aspects of the Novel*, originally a series
of lectures he delivered at Cambridge, where he has since
become an honorary Fellow of King's College. (Further headnote information on Forster appears on pp. 137, 275.)

Listening to music is such a muddle that one scarcely knows how to
start describing it. The first point to get clear in my own case is
that during the greater part of every performance I do not attend.
The nice sounds make me think of something else. I wool-gather
most of the time, and am surprised that others don't. Professional
critics can listen to a piece as consistently and as steadily as if they
were reading a chapter in a novel. This seems to me an amazing
feat, and probably they only achieve it through intellectual training;
that is to say, they find in the music the equivalent of a plot; they
are following the ground bass or expecting the theme to re-enter in
the dominant, and so on, and this keeps them on the rails. But I fly

From *Two Cheers for Democracy*, copyright, 1951, by E. M. Forster. Reprinted
by permission of Harcourt, Brace & World, Inc., and Edward Arnold (Pub-
lishers) Ltd.

off every minute: after a bar or two I think how musical I am, or of something smart I might have said in conversation; or I wonder what the composer—dead a couple of centuries—can be feeling as the flames on the altar still flicker up; or how soon an H.E. bomb would extinguish them. Not to mention more obvious distractions: the tilt of the soprano's chin or chins; the antics of the conductor, that impassioned beetle, especially when it is night time and he waves his shards; the affectation of the pianist when he takes a top note with difficulty, as if he too were a soprano; the backs of the chairs; the bumps on the ceiling; the extreme physical ugliness of the audience. A classical audience is surely the plainest collection of people anywhere assembled for any common purpose; contributing my quota, I have the right to point this out. Compare us with a gang of navvies or with an office staff, and you will be appalled. This, too, distracts me.

What do I hear during the intervals when I do attend? Two sorts of music. They melt into each other all the time, and are not easy to christen, but I will call one of them "music that reminds me of something," and the other "music itself." I used to be very fond of music that reminded me of something, and especially fond of Wagner. With Wagner I always knew where I was; he never let the fancy roam; he ordained that one phrase should recall the ring, another the sword, another the blameless fool and so on; he was as precise in his indications as an oriental dancer. Since he is a great poet, that did not matter, but I accepted his leitmotiv system much too reverently and forced it on to other composers whom it did not suit, such as Beethoven and Franck. I thought that music must be the better for having a meaning. I think so still, but am less clear as to what "a meaning" is. In those days it was either a non-musical object, such as a sword or a blameless fool, or a non-musical emotion, such as fear, lust, or resignation. When music reminded me of something which was not music, I supposed it was getting me somewhere. "How like Monet!" I thought when listening to Debussy, and "How like Debussy!" when looking at Monet. I

translated sounds into colours, saw the piccolo as apple-green, and
the trumpets as scarlet. The arts were to be enriched by taking in one
another's washing.

I still listen to some music this way. For instance, the slow start of
Beethoven's Seventh Symphony invokes a grey-green tapestry of
hunting scenes, and the slow movement of his Fourth Piano Concerto (the dialogue between piano and orchestra) reminds me of
the dialogue between Orpheus and the Furies in Gluck. The
climax of the first movement of the Appassionata (the "più al-
legro") seems to me sexual, although I can detect no sex in the
Kreutzer, nor have I come across anyone who could, except Tolstoy.
That disappointing work, Brahms' Violin Concerto, promises me
clear skies at the opening, and only when the violin has squealed up
in the air for page after page is the promise falsified. Wolf's "Gan-
ymed" does give me sky—stratosphere beyond stratosphere. In
these cases and in many others music reminds me of something non-
musical, and I fancy that to do so is part of its job. Only a purist
would condemn all visual parallels, all emotional labellings, all
programmes.

Yet there is a danger. Music that reminds does open the door to
that imp of the concert hall, inattention. To think of a grey-green
tapestry is not very different from thinking of the backs of the
chairs. We gather a superior wool from it, still we do wool-gather,
and the sounds slip by blurred. The sounds! It is for them that we
come, and the closer we can get up against them the better. So I
do prefer "music itself" and listen to it and for it as far as possible.
In this connection, I will try to analyse a mishap that has recently
overtaken the Coriolanus Overture. I used to listen to the Coriolanus for "itself," conscious when it passed of something important
and agitating, but not defining further. Now I learn that Wagner,
endorsed by Sir Donald Tovey, has provided it with a Programme:
the opening bars indicate the hero's decision to destroy the Vol-
scii, then a sweet tune for female influence, then the dotted-
quaver-restlessness of indecision. This seems indisputable, and

there is no doubt that this was, or was almost, Beethoven's intention. All the same, I have lost my Coriolanus. Its largeness and
freedom have gone. The exquisite sounds have been hardened like
a road that has been tarred for traffic. One has to go somewhere
down them, and to pass through the same domestic crisis to the
same military impasse, each time the overture is played.

Music is so very queer that an amateur is bound to get muddled
when writing about it. It seems to be more "real" than anything, and
to survive when the rest of civilisation decays. In these days I am
always thinking of it with relief. It can never be ruined or national-
ised. So that the music which is untrammelled and untainted by
reference is obviously the best sort of music to listen to; we get
nearer the centre of reality. Yet though it is untainted, it is never
abstract; it is not like mathematics, even when it uses them. The
Goldberg Variations, the last Beethoven Sonata, the Franck Quar-
tet, the Schumann Piano Quintet and the Fourth Symphonies of
Tchaikovsky and of Brahms certainly have a message. Though what
on earth is it? I shall get tied up trying to say. There's an insistence
in music—expressed largely through rhythm; there's a sense that it
is trying to push across at us something which is neither an esthetic
pattern nor a sermon. That's what I listen for specially.

So music that is itself seems on the whole better than music that
reminds. And now to end with an important point: my own per-
formances upon the piano. These grow worse yearly, but never will
I give them up. For one thing, they compel me to attend—no
wool-gathering or thinking myself clever here—and they drain off
all non-musical matter. For another thing, they teach me a little
about construction. I see what becomes of a phrase, how it is transformed or returned, sometimes bottom upward, and get some notion
of the relation of keys. Playing Beethoven, as I generally do, I grow
familiar with his tricks, his impatience, his sudden softnesses, his
dropping of a tragic theme one semitone, his love, when tragic, for
the key of C minor, and his aversion to the key of B major. This
gives me a physical approach to Beethoven which cannot be gained

through the slough of "appreciation." Even when people play as badly as I do, they should continue: it will help them to listen.

QUESTIONS

1. Forster's essay divides into three parts: not listening to music, listening to "music that reminds me of something," and listening to "music itself." Insofar as these parts are material that he has organized, what is the principle of organization?

2. Again considering the three parts as material that Forster has organized, which part would you say is most important to him? Which part could be omitted without significant damage to the most important part? Which part does he give the most space to?

3. What is the effect of Forster's using such terms as "muddle," "wool-gather," and "on the rails" in the first paragraph? Where else in the essay do you find similar language?

4. Would you say that Forster is addressing his essay to both the professional critic and the amateur listener or to only one of them? How can you tell? With what particular authority does he speak? What relationship does he establish with his audience?

5. What is the subject of the second paragraph? How carefully and systematically does Forster develop it? Does the paragraph seem more, or less, carefully developed than most of the other paragraphs?

6. Forster is quite confident that Wagner is "a great poet" and that Brahms' Violin Concerto is a "disappointing work." To what extent would you say that this dogmatism pervades the essay? Examine the degree of dogmatism in the fifth paragraph.

7. In the fourth paragraph Forster says, "The sounds! It is for them that we come, and the closer we can get up against them the better." To what extent does he seem to be getting up against sounds in his description of "my Coriolanus" and in his discussion in the next paragraph? What about in the final paragraph? Do you conclude that his discussion is muddled?

8. On the basis of your answers to the previous questions you should be able to explain the strategic reason for the presence of the first para-

graph in the essay (or the reason for Forster's placing it first) and the strategic reason for his discussing "music that reminds me of something" prior to discussing "music itself." (Phrase your explanations in terms of Forster's presumed needs and desires with regard to his audience.)

9. What is the appropriateness of Forster's title?

The Patron and the Crocus

VIRGINIA WOOLF

The daughter of Sir Leslie Stephen, himself a notable essayist, critic, and editor, Virginia Woolf was brought up in an atmosphere flavored largely by literary matters. Educated informally at home, given the freedom of her father's books, she early began to write, did many reviews for magazines and newspapers when still in her twenties, and later, with her husband Leonard Woolf, established the Hogarth Press. Under their supervision, the Press grew in size and prestige: it published the works of such distinguished authors as E. M. Forster, T. S. Eliot, and Katherine Mansfield. "The Patron and the Crocus" is but one expression of Virginia Woolf's life-long concern with the nature of art, of the artist, and of his relationship to his audience. (Further headnote information on Virginia Woolf appears on p. 38.)

Young men and women beginning to write are generally given the plausible but utterly impracticable advice to write what they have to write as shortly as possible, as clearly as possible, and without other thought in their minds except to say exactly what is in them. Nobody ever adds on these occasions the one thing needful: "And be sure you choose your patron wisely," though that is the gist of the whole matter. For a book is always written for somebody to read, and, since the patron is not merely the paymaster, but also in a very subtle and insidious way the instigator and inspirer of what is written, it is of the utmost importance that he should be a desirable man.

But who, then, is the desirable man—the patron who will cajole the best out of the writer's brain and bring to birth the most varied and vigorous progeny of which he is capable? Different ages have answered the question differently. The Elizabethans, to speak roughly, chose the aristocracy to write for and the playhouse public. The eighteenth-century patron was a combination of coffee-house wit and Grub Street bookseller. In the nineteenth century the great writers wrote for the half-crown magazines and the leisured classes. And looking back and applauding the splendid results of these different alliances, it all seems enviably simple, and plain as a pike-staff compared with our own predicament—for whom should we write? For the present supply of patrons is of unexampled and bewildering variety. There is the daily Press, the weekly Press, the monthly Press; the English public and the American public; the best-seller public and the worst-seller public; the high-brow public and the red-blood public; all now organised self-conscious entities capable through their various mouthpieces of making their needs known and their approval or displeasure felt. Thus the writer who has been moved by the sight of the first crocus in Kensington Gardens has, before he sets pen to paper, to choose from a crowd of competitors the particular patron who suits him best. It is futile to say, "Dismiss them all; think only of your crocus," because writing is a method of communication; and the crocus is an imperfect crocus until it has been shared. The first man or the last may write for himself alone, but he is an exception and an unenviable one at that, and the gulls are welcome to his works if the gulls can read them.

Granted, then, that every writer has some public or other at the end of his pen, the high-minded will say that it should be a submissive public, accepting obediently whatever he likes to give it. Plausible as the theory sounds, great risks are attached to it. For in that case the writer remains conscious of his public, yet is superior to it—an uncomfortable and unfortunate combination, as the works of Samuel Butler, George Meredith, and Henry James may be taken to prove. Each despised the public; each desired a public; each failed to attain a public; and each wreaked his failure upon the public by a succession, gradually increasing in intensity, of angularities, obscurities, and affectations which no writer whose patron was his equal and friend would have thought it necessary to inflict. Their crocuses, in consequence, are tortured plants, beautiful and bright, but with something wry-necked about them, malformed, shrivelled on the one side, overblown on the other. A touch of the sun would have done them a world of good. Shall we then rush to the opposite extreme and accept (if in fancy alone) the flattering proposals which the editors of the *Times* and the *Daily News* may be supposed to make us—"Twenty pounds down for your crocus in precisely fifteen hundred words, which shall blossom upon every breakfast table from John o' Groats to the Land's End before nine o'clock to-morrow morning with the writer's name attached"?

But will one crocus be enough, and must it not be a very brilliant yellow to shine so far, to cost so much, and to have one's name attached to it? The Press is undoubtedly a great multiplier of crocuses. But if we look at some of these plants, we shall find that they are only very distantly related to the original little yellow or purple flower which pokes up through the grass in Kensington Gardens early in March every year. The newspaper crocus is an amazing but still a very different plant. It fills precisely the space allotted to it. It radiates a golden glow. It is genial, affable, warm-hearted. It is beautifully finished, too, for let nobody think that the art of "our dramatic critic" of the *Times* or of Mr. Lynd of the *Daily News* is an easy one. It is no despicable feat to start a million brains running at nine o'clock in the morning, to give two million eyes something bright and brisk and amusing to look at. But the night comes and these flowers fade. So little bits of glass lose their lustre if you take them out of the sea; great prima donnas howl like hyenas if you shut them up in telephone boxes; and the most brilliant of articles when removed from its element is dust and sand and the husks of straw. Journalism embalmed in a book is unreadable.

The patron we want, then, is one who will help us to preserve our flowers from decay. But as his qualities change from age to age, and it needs considerable integrity and conviction not to be dazzled by the pretensions or bamboozled by the persuasions of the competing crowd, this business of patron-finding is one of the tests and trials of authorship. To know whom to write for is to know how to write. Some of the modern patron's qualities are, however, fairly plain. The writer will require at this moment, it is obvious, a patron with the book-reading habit rather than the play-going habit. Nowadays, too, he must be instructed in the literature of other times and races. But there are other qualities which our special weaknesses and tendencies demand in him. There is the question of indecency, for instance, which plagues us and puzzles us much more than it did the Elizabethans. The twentieth-century patron must be immune from shock. He must distinguish infallibly between the little clod of manure which sticks to the crocus of necessity, and that which is plastered to it out of bravado. He must be a judge, too, of those social influences which inevitably play so large a part in modern literature, and able to say which matures and for-tifies, which inhibits and makes sterile. Further, there is emotion for him to pronounce on, and in no department can he do more use-ful work than in bracing a writer against sentimentality on the one hand and a craven fear of expressing his feeling on the other. It is worse, he will say, and perhaps more common, to be afraid of feel-ing than to feel too much. He will add, perhaps, something about language, and point out how many words Shakespeare used and how much grammar Shakespeare violated, while we, though we keep our fingers so demurely to the black notes on the piano, have not appreciably improved upon *Antony and Cleopatra*. And if you can forget your sex altogether, he will say, so much the better; a writer has none. But all this is by the way—elementary and dis-putable. The patron's prime quality is something different, only to be expressed perhaps by the use of that convenient word which cloaks so much—atmosphere. It is necessary that the patron should shed and envelop the crocus in an atmosphere which makes it appear a plant of the very highest importance, so that to misrepresent it is the one outrage not to be forgiven this side of the grave. He must make us feel that a single crocus, if it be a real crocus, is enough for him; that he does not want to be lectured, elevated, instructed, or improved; that he is sorry that he bullied Carlyle into vociferation, Tennyson into idyllics, and Ruskin into insanity; that he is now ready to efface himself or assert himself as his writers require; that he is bound to them by a more than maternal tie; that they are twins indeed, one dying if the other dies, one flourishing if the other flourishes; that the fate of literature depends upon their happy alliance—all of which proves, as we began by saying, that the choice of a patron is of the highest importance. But how to choose rightly? How to write well? Those are the questions.

QUESTIONS

1. What words and phrases in the first paragraph suggest that Mrs. Woolf will consider patrons in an unusual sense? What distinction do you see between the "submissive public" that Mrs. Woolf says Henry James wanted (paragraph three) and her ideal patron who is "ready to efface himself or assert himself as his writers require" (paragraph five)? Does your answer suggest a reason for Mrs. Woolf's ending her essay with two questions? Who (or what) does the patron seem to be in the last lines of the essay? (Consider the relationship between the two questions at the end and the third sentence at the beginning of the paragraph.)

2. What special qualities does Mrs. Woolf want to attribute to art by calling it a crocus rather than, say, a mirror? What, then, is the effect that she achieves when she has the editor of the *Daily News* say, "Twenty pounds down for your crocus"? Examine the aspects of the image of the crocus in the last three sentences of the third paragraph.

3. What groups of people do you suppose Mrs. Woolf has automatically excluded from her intended audience? Point out passages that imply

such exclusion or that would merely irritate such groups. Suppose that Mrs. Woolf wanted to write an essay for these groups: what instead of a crocus would be her metaphor for art? How crucial is the choice of the crocus to her persuasiveness?

4. To whom do you think Mrs. Woolf is most specifically addressing her essay? (It will help you in answering this question to re-examine the last part of Question 1.)

5. Mrs. Woolf organizes her essay in a quasi-logical pattern. She sets up a question (how to choose a patron) and answers it by a process of elimination. Assuming that she is not really interested in logic, explain the selection and arrangement of material according to her presumed needs and desires with regard to her audience: why does she choose to discuss journalism if both she and her audience know that it is unimportant? why doesn't she discuss the actual qualities of the audience that did read James and that does read the *Times* and the *Daily News?* why does she interpose the discussion of journalism between that of the submissive patron and the ideal patron rather than put it first?

6. Mrs. Woolf's metaphor of the crocus is at once concrete and suggestive. She elaborates it skillfully and with good humor. Argue the view that these merits are a means by which she avoids or obscures thought. (Paragraph four is perhaps most useful to examine. The last three sentences offer a clear illustration of the use to which she puts metaphor in argument.)

7. Would you say that the crocus is inherently a more suggestive metaphor than the patron? What is the difference in relationship between patron-audience and crocus-artwork? Would you say that the two metaphors go well together? If you think that they do not, can you make an appropriate substitution for either one?

Conclusion to The Renaissance

WALTER PATER

Walter Pater (1839-1894) was born in London and educated at Oxford, where he remained the better part of his life, devoting himself to the study of art, literature, and philosophy. Shy, preferring a life of seclusion, he shocked many by the apparent hedonism of his *Studies in the History of the Renaissance,* and was even termed by some a corrupter of youth. He subsequently clarified and developed his philosophy in a number of essays on the art and thought of the ancient Greeks, and particularly in *Marius the Epicurean,* a work of fiction set in second-century Rome and marked by a style delicately ornate. Contrary to his wishes, he became the symbolic head of a late nineteenth-century aesthetic movement, whose tendencies and sentiments have been roughly summarized by the term "art for art's sake."

To regard all things and principles of things as inconstant modes or fashions has more and more become the tendency of modern thought. Let us begin with that which is without—our physical life. Fix upon it in one of its more exquisite intervals, the moment, for instance, of delicious recoil from the flood of water in summer heat. What is the whole physical life in that moment but a combination of natural elements to which science gives their names? But those elements, phosphorus and lime and delicate fibres, are present not in the human body alone: we detect them in places most remote from it. Our physical life is a perpetual motion of them—the passage of the blood, the waste and repairing of the lenses of the eye, the modification of the tissues of the brain under every ray of light and sound—processes which science reduces to simpler and more elementary forces. Like the elements of which we are composed, the action of these forces extends beyond us: it rusts iron and ripens corn. Far out on every side of us those elements are broadcast, driven in many currents; and birth and gesture and death and the springing of violets from the grave are but a few out of ten thousand resultant combinations. That clear, perpetual outline of face and limb is but an image of ours, under which we group them—a design in a web, the actual threads of which pass out beyond it. This at least of flame-like our life has, that it is but the concurrence, renewed from moment to moment, of forces parting sooner or later on their ways.

Or, if we begin with the inward world of thought and feeling, the whirlpool is still more rapid, the flame more eager and devouring. There it is no longer the gradual darkening of the eye, the gradual fading of colour from the wall—movements of the shore-side, where the water flows down indeed, though in apparent rest—but the race of the mid-stream, a drift of momentary acts of sight and passion and thought. At first sight experience seems to bury us under a flood of external objects, pressing upon us with a sharp and importunate reality, calling us out of ourselves in a thousand forms of action. But when reflexion begins to play upon those objects they are dissipated under its influence; the cohesive force seems suspended like some trick of magic; each object is loosed into a group of impressions—colour, odour, texture—in the mind of the observer. And if we continue to dwell in thought on this world, not of objects in the solidity with which language invests them, but of impressions, unstable, flickering, inconsistent, which burn and are extinguished with our consciousness of them, it contracts still further: the whole scope of observation is dwarfed into the narrow chamber of the individual mind. Experience, already reduced to a group of impressions, is ringed round for each one of us by that thick wall of personality through which no real voice has ever pierced on its way to us, or from us to that which we can only conjecture to be without. Every one of those impressions is the impression of the individual in his isolation, each mind keeping as a solitary prisoner its own dream of a world. Analysis goes a step farther still, and assures us that those impressions of the individual mind to which, for each one of us, experience dwindles down, are in perpetual flight; that each of them is limited by time, and that as time is infinitely divisible, each of them is infinitely divisible also; all that is actual in it being a single moment, gone while we try to apprehend it, of which it may ever be more truly said that it has ceased to be than that it is. To such a tremulous wisp constantly reforming itself on the stream, to a single sharp impression, with a sense in it, a relic more or less fleeting, of such moments gone by, what is real in our life fines itself down. It is with this movement, with the passage and dissolution of impressions, images, sensations, that analysis leaves off—that continual vanishing away, that strange, perpetual weaving and unweaving of ourselves.

Philosophiren, says Novalis, *ist dephlegmatisiren, vivificiren.* The service of philosophy, or speculative culture, towards the human spirit, is to rouse, to startle it to a life of constant and eager observation. Every moment some form grows perfect in hand or face; some tone on the hills or the sea is choicer than the rest; some mood of passion or insight or intellectual excitement is irresistibly real and attractive to us,—for that moment only. Not the fruit of experience, but experience itself, is the end. A counted number of pulses only is given to us of a variegated, dramatic life. How may we see in them all that is to be seen in them by the finest senses? How shall we pass most swiftly from point to point, and be present always at the focus where the greatest number of vital forces unite in their purest energy?

To burn always with this hard, gem-like flame, to maintain this ecstasy, is success in life. In a sense it might even be said that our failure is to form habits: for, after all, habit is relative to a stereo-typed world, and meantime it is only the roughness of the eye that makes any two persons, things, situations, seem alike. While all melts under our feet, we may well grasp at any exquisite passion, or any contribution to knowledge that seems by a lifted horizon to set the spirit free for a moment, or any stirring of the senses, strange dyes, strange colours, and curious odours, or work of the artist's hands, or the face of one's friend. Not to discriminate every moment some passionate attitude in those about us, and in the very brilliancy of their gifts some tragic dividing of forces on their ways, is, on this short day of frost and sun, to sleep before evening. With this sense of the splendour of our experience and of its awful brevity, gathering all we are into one desperate effort to see and touch, we shall hardly have time to make theories about the things we see and touch. What we have to do is to be for ever curiously testing new opinions and courting new impressions, never acquiescing in a facile orthodoxy of Comte, or of Hegel, or of our own. Philosophical theories or ideas, as points of view, instruments of criticism, may help us to gather up what might otherwise pass unregarded by us. "Philosophy is the microscope of thought." The theory or idea or system which requires of us the sacrifice of any part of this experience, in consideration of some interest into which we cannot enter, or some abstract theory we have not identified with ourselves, or of what is only conventional, has no real claim upon us.

One of the most beautiful passages of Rousseau is that in the sixth book of the *Confessions*, where he describes the awakening in him of the literary sense. An undefinable taint of death had clung always about him, and now in early manhood he believed himself smitten by mortal disease. He asked himself how he might make as much as possible of the interval that remained; and he was not biassed by anything in his previous life when he decided that it must be by intellectual excitement, which he found just then in the clear, fresh writings of Voltaire. Well! we are all *condamnés* as Victor Hugo says: we are all under sentence of death but with a sort of indefinite reprieve—*les hommes sont tous condamnés à mort avec des sursis indéfinis:* we have an interval, and then our place knows us no more. Some spend this interval in listlessness, some in high passions, the wisest, at least among "the children of this world," in art and song. For our one chance lies in expanding that interval, in getting as many pulsations as possible into the given time. Great passions may give us this quickened sense of life, ecstasy and sorrow of love, the various forms of enthusiastic activity, disinterested or otherwise, which come naturally to many of us. Only be sure it is passion—that it does yield you this fruit of a quickened, multiplied consciousness. Of such wisdom, the poetic passion, the desire of beauty, the love of art for its own sake, has most. For art comes to you proposing frankly to give nothing but the highest quality to your moments as they pass, and simply for those moments' sake.

QUESTIONS

1. What signs are there in the first paragraph that Pater is particularly aware of his audience? How would you characterize his attitude towards his audience? What does the presence of the quotations from Novalis and Hugo suggest about the sort of audience that he is addressing? What corollary evidence suggests the same sort of audience?

2. Would you say that Pater is primarily addressing scientists, philosophers, artists, or some other group? On the basis of your answer to this question and Question 1, explain the absence of evidence that there is little time for theorizing when we live well (paragraph four) and the absence of an extended example of a great passion (paragraph five).

3. What is the subject of the first two paragraphs? Could the two paragraphs easily be reversed? In terms of the organization of materials, what justifies their present order? What effect, if any, would you say Pater's presumed audience had upon his arrangement?

4. Structurally, the essay separates into three parts: the first two paragraphs, the next two, and the last. Considering the relationships between the central ideas in each part, can you see the strategic value in Pater's having ordered his material in this way? What would you say he has been seeking to prove or establish?

5. It would be easy for another writer to begin with Pater's first two paragraphs and then in the third and fourth paragraphs write: to

transform that flame into a gem, to create from evanescent reality the enduring structures of science, philosophy, and art, is success in life. To what extent does this alternative undermine Pater's position in the next two paragraphs? Does it necessarily weaken the conclusions he reaches in the last paragraph?

6. Note the pairing of words and phrases in the first sentence of the second paragraph: thought and feeling, whirlpool and flame, eager and devouring. What quality would you say this stylistic characteristic lends to the essay?

7. Examine the phrase "to burn always with this hard, gem-like flame" at the beginning of the fourth paragraph. Why does Pater call the flame a hard flame? Why a gem-like flame? Is the meaning of the image of burning in the first two paragraphs the same as it is here? What is the effect of Pater's renewing the image in the fourth paragraph after not having used it in the third?

8. Would you say that Pater's style burns with a hard, gem-like flame? (Consider broadly his sentence rhythms, the degree of precision of the images he creates—such as those in the first paragraph, his use of repetition.) What is the overall feeling they evoke? Is that feeling consistent with any aspect of Pater's outlook on life?

Imagination

GEORGE SANTAYANA

Born in Madrid, of Spanish parents, George Santayana (1863-1952) was brought to the United States at the age of nine, attended public schools in Boston, and then studied at Harvard, where he subsequently taught philosophy for twenty-two years, until his resignation in 1912. From then until his death, he lived in different parts of Europe, much of the time in Rome, lecturing and writing on literature, aesthetics, metaphysics, religion, and politics. Among his better-known works are *The Sense of Beauty*, *The Life of Reason* (in five volumes), and *Persons and Places*, a series of autobiographical essays. He also wrote several volumes of poetry, one long novel, *The Last Puritan*, and a number of translations. (Further headnote information on Santayana appears on p. 306.)

Men are ruled by imagination: imagination makes them into men, capable of madness and of immense labors. We work dreaming. Consider what dreams must have dominated the builders of the Pyramids—dreams geometrical, dreams funereal, dreams of resurrection, dreams of outdoing the pyramid of some other Pharaoh! What dreams occupy that fat man in the street, toddling by under his shabby hat and bedraggled rain-coat? Perhaps he is in love; perhaps he is a Catholic, and imagines that early this morning he has partaken of the body and blood of Christ; perhaps he is a

From *Soliloquies in England* by George Santayana. Reprinted by permission of Constable & Co., Ltd.

revolutionist, with the millennium in his heart and a bomb in his pocket. The spirit bloweth where it listeth; the wind of inspiration carries our dreams before it and constantly refashions them like clouds. Nothing could be madder, more irresponsible, more dangerous than this guidance of men by dreams. What saves us is the fact that our imaginations, groundless and chimerical as they may seem, are secretly suggested and controlled by shrewd old instincts of our animal nature, and by continual contact with things. The shock of sense, breaking in upon us with a fresh irresistible image, checks wayward imagination and sends it rebounding in a new direction, perhaps more relevant to what is happening in a world outside.

When I speak of being governed by imagination, of course I am indulging in a figure of speech, in an ellipsis; in reality we are governed by that perpetual latent process within us by which imagination itself is created. Actual imaginings—the cloud-like thoughts drifting by—are not masters over themselves nor over anything else. They are like the sound of chimes in the night; they know nothing of whence they came, how they will fall out, or how long they will ring. There is a mechanism in the church tower; there was a theme in the composer's head; there is a beadle who has been winding the thing up. The sound wafted to us, muffled by distance and a thousand obstacles, is but the last lost emanation of this magical bell-ringing. Yet in our dream it is all in all; it is what first entertains and absorbs the mind. Imagination, when it chimes within us, apparently of itself, is no less elaborately grounded; it is a last symptom, a rolling echo, by which we detect and name the obscure operation that occasions it; and not this echo in its aesthetic impotence, but the whole operation whose last witness it is, receives in science the name of imagination, and may be truly said to rule the human world.

This extension of names is inevitable although unfortunate, because language and perception are poetical before they become scientific, if they ever do; as Aristotle observes that the word anger is used indifferently for two different things: dialectically, or as I call it, imaginatively, for the desire for revenge, but physically for a boiling of the humours. And utterly different as these two things are in quality, no great inconvenience results from giving them the same name, because historically they are parts of the same event. Nature has many dimensions at once, and whenever we see anything happen, much else is happening there which we cannot see. Whilst dreams entertain us, the balance of our character is shifting beneath: we are growing while we sleep. The young think in one way, the drunken in another, and the dead not at all; and I imagine—for I have imagination myself—that they do not die because they stop thinking, but they stop thinking because they die. How much veering and luffing before they make that port! The brain of man, William James used to say, has a hair-trigger organization. His life is terribly experimental. He is perilously dependent on the oscillations of a living needle, imagination, that never points to the true north.

There are books in which the footnotes, or the comments scrawled by some reader's hand in the margin, are more interesting than the text. The world is one of these books. The reciprocal interference of magnetic fields (which I understand is the latest conception of matter) may compose a marvellous moving pattern; but the chief interest to us of matter lies in its fertility in producing minds and presenting recognizable phenomena to the senses; and the chief interest of any scientific notion of its intrinsic nature lies in the fact that, if not literally true, it may liberate us from more misleading conceptions. Did we have nothing but electrical physics to think of, the nightmare would soon become intolerable. But a hint of that kind, like a hasty glance into the crater of a volcano, sends a wholesome shudder through our nerves; we realize how thin is the crust we build on, how mythical and remote from the minute and gigantic scale of nature are the bright images we seem to move among, all cut out and fitted to our human stature. Yet these bright images are our natural companions, and if we do not worship them idolatrously nor petrify them into substances, forget-

ting the nimble use of them in mental discourse, which is where
they belong, they need not be more misleading to us, even for
scientific purposes, than are words or any other symbols.

It is fortunate that the material world, whatever may be its intrinsic structure or substance, falls to our apprehension into such
charming units. There is the blue vault of heaven, there are the
twinkling constellations, there are the mountains, trees, and rivers,
and above all those fascinating unstable unities which we call animals and persons; magnetic fields I am quite ready to believe them,
for such in a vast vague way I feel them to be, but individual bodies
they will remain to my sensuous imagination, and dramatic personages to my moral sense. They, too, are animate: they, too, compose a running commentary on things and on one another, adding
their salacious footnotes to the dull black letter of the world. Many
of them are hardly aware of their own wit; knowing they are but
commentators, they are intent on fidelity and unconscious of invention. Yet against their will they gloss everything, willy-nilly
we are all scholiasts together. Heaven forbid that I should de-
preciate this prodigious tome of nature, or question in one jot or
tittle the absolute authority of its Author; but it is like an ency-
clopaedia in an infinite number of volumes, or a directory with the
addresses of everybody that ever lived. We may dip into it on occasion in search of some pertinent fact, but it is not a book to read;
its wealth is infinite, but so is its monotony; it is not composed in
our style nor in our language, we could not have written one line of
it. Yet the briefest text invites reflection, and we may spin a little
homily out of it in the vernacular for our own edification.

In the *Mahabharata*, a learned friend tells me, a young champion armed for the combat and about to rush forward between the
two armies drawn up in battle array, stops for a moment to receive
a word of counsel from his spiritual adviser—and that word oc-
cupies the next eighteen books of the epic; after which the battle is
allowed to proceed. These Indian poets had spiritual minds, they
measured things by their importance to the spirit, not to the eye.
They despised verisimilitude and aesthetic proportion; they despised

existence, the beauties of which they felt exquisitely nevertheless, and to which their imagination made such stupendous additions. I honor their courage in bidding the sun stand still, not that they might thoroughly vanquish an earthly enemy, but that they might wholly clarify their own soul. For this better purpose the sun need not stand still materially. For the spirit, time is an elastic thing. Fancy is quick and brings the widest vistas to a focus in a single instant. After the longest interval of oblivion and death, it can light up the same image in all the greenness of youth; and if cut short, as it were at Pompeii, in the midst of a word, it can, ages after, without feeling the break, add the last syllable. Imagination changes the scale of everything, and makes a thousand patterns of the woof of nature, without disturbing a single thread. Or rather— since it is nature itself that imagines—it turns to music what was only strain; as if the universal vibration, suddenly ashamed of having been so long silent and useless, had burst into tears and laughter at its own folly, and in so doing had become wise.

QUESTIONS

1. What is the relationship between imagination, dreams, and wind of inspiration in the first paragraph?

2. Under what circumstances does "electrical physics" become "intoler-able"? What can prevent it from so being? What, in sum, is Santayana's attitude towards imagination?

3. Santayana discusses two sorts of imagination, non-sensuous and sen-suous (only the latter term is his; see the fifth paragraph). Distinguish between them. In what similar respect does he discuss each of them? Describe the general progression of his discussion of them from para-graph to paragraph in the first five paragraphs. Which of the two is he more preoccupied with? Is the final paragraph in the essay concerned with both of them?

4. What sort of audience does Santayana seem to have in mind: one that he must convince or one that is already persuaded? one that wants argument or one that wants discussion? one that wants enlightenment

or illumination? reflection or divertissement? Examine the variety of sources of his examples and illustrations. What does their presence and the manner in which he offers them suggest about his audience? To what sort of audience would you expect him to say, "we are all scholiasts together" (paragraph five)? Would you say he is addressing himself primarily to the scientist, the philosopher, the religious man, the artist, or some other person?

5. With the presumed audience in mind, suggest a reason for Santayana's not beginning his essay with a discussion of the reciprocal interference of magnetic fields and for his not developing the discussion of it further. Can you similarly explain why he begins with paragraph one rather than with paragraph two? (Note that with their present order he is forced to back-track a little at the opening of the second paragraph.)

6. Justify the presence of the final paragraph in the essay in terms of the audience. (Ask yourself beforehand to what extent the paragraph introduces a new idea or sums up the previous discussion.)

7. Compare the first three sentences in the essay with the last two. What differences do you observe in the way in which Santayana presents his paradoxes and irony (in part, ironic juxtaposition) in the two passages? Do the paradoxes and irony have the same degree of humor in both passages? Is there any other aspect of either passage that more definitely controls their mood?

8. Examine the metaphor of the world as a book and the activity of the imagination as marginalia. Do the recurrent references to the image merely re-state the original meaning or do they develop new meanings? Would you say, then, that the metaphor is used mainly as an instrument of argument or of illumination? (If you have read Virginia Woolf's essay in this section, you may find it helpful to compare her use of the crocus in the fourth paragraph of her essay with Santayana's use of the book.)

9. Give the literal meaning that Santayana states metaphorically in the final sentence of the essay. Relate the metaphor point by point to the metaphor of the world as a book.

10. If you have read Walter Pater's essay in this section, compare his outlook on the "real" world with Santayana's.

The Art of Donald McGill

GEORGE ORWELL

Although George Orwell wrote novels, several autobiographical accounts, and a sociological study (*The Road to Wigan
Pier*), his best work is probably in the essay form, whose size
and relative openness he found particularly suitable to his perceptions on society. His subjects vary—from an analysis of
gangster fiction to a study of Dickens to reflections on Gandhi
—but characteristically they reveal his concern with the social
and political order, and with the many forms of popular culture. Both interests are reflected in the piece which follows.
His essays have been gathered in *Dickens, Dali, and Others,
Shooting an Elephant,* and *Such, Such were the Joys.* (Further headnote information on Orwell appears on pp. 92, 393.)

Who does not know the "comics" of the cheap stationers' windows, the penny or twopenny coloured post cards with their endless succession of fat women in tight bathing-dresses and their crude
drawing and unbearable colours, chiefly hedge-sparrow's egg tint
and Post Office red?

This question ought to be rhetorical, but it is a curious fact that
many people seem to be unaware of the existence of these things,
or else to have a vague notion that they are something to be
found only at the seaside, like Negro minstrels or peppermint rock.

Actually they are on sale everywhere—they can be bought at nearly any Woolworth's, for example—and they are evidently produced in enormous numbers, new series constantly appearing. They are not to be confused with the various other types of comic illustrated post card, such as the sentimental ones dealing with puppies and kittens or the Wendyish, subpornographic ones which exploit the love-affairs of children. They are a *genre* of their own, specialising in very "low" humour, the mother-in-law, baby's nappy, policemen's boots type of joke, and distinguishable from all the other kinds by having no artistic pretensions. Some half-dozen publishing houses issue them, though the people who draw them seem not to be numerous at any one time.

I have associated them especially with the name of Donald McGill because he is not only the most prolific and by far the best of contemporary post card artists, but also the most representative, the most perfect in the tradition. Who Donald McGill is, I do not know. He is apparently a trade name, for at least one series of post cards is issued simply as "The Donald McGill Comics," but he is also unquestionably a real person with a style of drawing which is recognisable at a glance. Anyone who examines his post cards in bulk will notice that many of them are not despicable even as drawings, but it would be mere dilettantism to pretend that they have any direct aesthetic value. A comic post card is simply an illustration to a joke, invariably a "low" joke, and it stands or falls by its ability to raise a laugh. Beyond that it has only "ideological" interest. McGill is a clever draughtsman with a real caricaturist's touch in the drawing of faces, but the special value of his post cards is that they are so completely typical. They represent, as it were, the norm of the comic post card. Without being in the least imitative, they are exactly what comic post cards have been any time these last forty years, and from them the meaning and purpose of the whole *genre* can be inferred.

Get hold of a dozen of these things, preferably McGill's—if you pick out from a pile the ones that seem to you funniest, you will probably find that most of them are McGill's—and spread them out on a table. What do you see?

Your first impression is of overpowering vulgarity. This is quite apart from the ever-present obscenity, and apart also from the hideousness of the colours. They have an utter lowness of mental atmosphere which comes out not only in the nature of the jokes but, even more, in the grotesque, staring, blatant quality of the drawings. The designs, like those of a child, are full of heavy lines and empty spaces, and all the figures in them, every gesture and attitude, are deliberately ugly, the faces grinning and vacuous, the women monstrously parodied, with bottoms like Hottentots. Your second impression, however, is of indefinable familiarity. What do these things remind you of? What are they so like? In the first place, of course, they remind you of the barely different post cards which you probably gazed at in your childhood. But more than this, what you are really looking at is something as traditional as Greek tragedy, a sort of subworld of smacked bottoms and scrawny mothers-in-law which is a part of Western European consciousness. Not that the jokes, taken one by one, are necessarily stale. Not being debarred from smuttiness, comic post cards repeat themselves less often than the joke columns in reputable magazines, but their basic subject-matter, the *kind* of joke they are aiming at, never varies. A few are genuinely witty, in a Max Millerish style. Examples:

"I like seeing experienced girls home."
"But I'm not experienced!"
"You're not home yet!"

"I've been struggling for years to get a fur coat. How did you get yours?"
"I left off struggling."

JUDGE: *"You are prevaricating, sir. Did you or did you not sleep with this woman?"*
CO-RESPONDENT: *"Not a wink, my lord!"*

In general, however, they are not witty but humorous, and it must be said for McGill's post cards, in particular, that the drawing is often a good deal funnier than the joke beneath it. Obviously the outstanding characteristic of comic post cards is their obscenity, and I must discuss that more fully later. But I give here a rough analysis of their habitual subject-matter, with such explanatory remarks as seem to be needed:

Sex.—More than half, perhaps three-quarters, of the jokes are sex jokes, ranging from the harmless to the all but unprintable. First favourite is probably the illegitimate baby. Typical captions: "Could you exchange this lucky charm for a baby's feeding-bottle?" "She didn't ask me to the christening, so I'm not going to the wedding." Also newlyweds, old maids, nude statues and women in bathing-dresses. All of these are *ipso facto* funny, mere mention of them being enough to raise a laugh. The cuckoldry joke is very seldom exploited, and there are no references to homosexuality.

Conventions of the sex joke:
  (i) Marriage only benefits the women. Every man is plotting seduction and every woman is plotting marriage. No woman ever remains unmarried voluntarily.
  (ii) Sex-appeal vanishes at about the age of twenty-five. Well-preserved and good-looking people beyond their first youth are never represented. The amorous honey-mooning couple reappear as the grim-visaged wife and shapeless moustachioed, red-nosed husband, no intermediate state being allowed for.

Home life.—Next to sex, the henpecked husband is the favourite joke. Typical caption: "Did they get an X-ray of your wife's jaw at the hospital?"—"No, they got a moving picture instead."

Conventions:
  (i) There is no such thing as a happy marriage.
  (ii) No man ever gets the better of a woman in argument.

Drunkenness.—Both drunkenness and teetotalism are *ipso facto* funny.

Conventions:
(i) All drunken men have optical illusions.
(ii) Drunkenness is something peculiar to middle-aged men. Drunken youths or women are never represented.

W. C. jokes.—There is not a large number of these. Chamberpots are *ipso facto* funny, and so are public lavatories. A typical post card, captioned "A Friend in Need," shows a man's hat blown off his head and disappearing down the steps of a ladies' lavatory.

Inter-working-class snobbery.—Much in these post cards suggests that they are aimed at the better-off working class and poorer middle class. There are many jokes turning on malapropisms, illiteracy, dropped aitches and the rough manners of slum-dwellers. Countless post cards show draggled hags of the stage-charwoman type exchanging "unladylike" abuse. Typical repartee: "I wish you were a statue and I was a pigeon!" A certain number produced since the war treat evacuation from the anti-evacuee angle. There are the usual jokes about tramps, beggars and criminals, and the comic maidservant appears fairly frequently. Also the comic navvy, bargee, etc.; but there are no anti-trade union jokes. Broadly speaking, everyone with much over or much under £5 a week is regarded as laughable. The "swell" is almost as automatically a figure of fun as the slum-dweller.

Stock figures.—Foreigners seldom or never appear. The chief locality joke is the Scotsman, who is almost inexhaustible. The lawyer is always a swindler, the clergyman always a nervous idiot who says the wrong thing. The "knut" or "smasher" still appears, almost as in Edwardian days, in out-of-date-looking evening-clothes and an opera hat, or even with spats and a knobby cane. Another survival is the Suffragette, one of the big jokes of the pre-1914 period and too valuable to be relinquished. She has reappeared, unchanged in physical appearance, as the Feminist lecturer or

Temperance fanatic. A feature of the last few years is the complete absence of anti-Jew post cards. The "Jew joke," always somewhat more ill-natured than the "Scotch joke," disappeared abruptly soon after the rise of Hitler.

Politics.—Any contemporary event, cult or activity which has comic possibilities (for example, "free love," feminism, A.R.P., nudism) rapidly finds its way into the picture post cards, but their general atmosphere is extremely old-fashioned. The implied political outlook is a Radicalism appropriate to about the year 1900. At normal times they are not only not patriotic, but go in for a mild guying of patriotism, with jokes about "God save the King," the Union Jack, etc. The European situation only began to reflect itself in them at some time in 1939, and first did so through the comic aspects of A.R.P. Even at this date few post cards mention the war except in A.R.P. jokes (fat woman stuck in the mouth of Anderson shelter: wardens neglecting their duty while young woman undresses at window she has forgotten to black out, etc. etc.). A few express anti-Hitler sentiments of a not very vindictive kind. One, not McGill's, shows Hitler, with the usual hypertrophied backside, bending down to pick a flower. Caption: "What would *you* do, chums?" This is about as high a flight of patriotism as any post card is likely to attain. Unlike the twopenny weekly papers, comic post cards are not the product of any great monopoly company, and evidently they are not regarded as having any importance in forming public opinion. There is no sign in them of any attempt to induce an outlook acceptable to the ruling class.

Here one comes back to the outstanding, all-important feature of comic post cards—their obscenity. It is by this that everyone remembers them, and it is also central to their purpose, though not in a way that is immediately obvious.

A recurrent, almost dominant motif in comic post cards is the woman with the stuck-out behind. In perhaps half of them, or more than half, even when the point of the joke has nothing to do with sex, the same female figure appears, a plump "voluptuous" figure with the dress clinging to it as tightly as another skin and with breasts or buttocks grossly over-emphasised, according to which way it is turned. There can be no doubt that these pictures lift the lid off a very widespread repression, natural enough in a country whose women when young tend to be slim to the point of skimpiness. But at the same time the McGill post card—and this applies to all other post cards in this *genre*—is not intended as pornography but, a subtler thing, as a skit on pornography. The Hottentot figures of the women are caricatures of the Englishman's secret ideal, not portraits of it. When one examines McGill's post cards more closely, one notices that his brand of humour only has meaning in relation to a fairly strict moral code. Whereas in papers like *Esquire*, for instance, or *La Vie Parisienne*, the imaginary background of the jokes is always promiscuity, the utter breakdown of all standards, the background of the McGill post card is marriage. The four leading jokes are nakedness, illegitimate babies, old maids and newly married couples, none of which would seem funny in a really dissolute or even "sophisticated" society. The post cards dealing with honeymoon couples always have the enthusiastic indecency of those village weddings where it is still considered screamingly funny to sew bells to the bridal bed. In one, for example, a young bridegroom is shown getting out of bed the morning after his wedding night. "The first morning in our own little home, darling!" he is saying; "I'll go and get the milk and paper and bring you up a cup of tea." Inset is a picture of the front doorstep; on it are four newspapers and four bottles of milk. This is obscene, if you like, but it is not immoral. Its implication—and this is just the implication the *Esquire* or the *New Yorker* would avoid at all costs—is that marriage is something profoundly exciting and important, the biggest event in the average human being's life. So also with jokes about nagging wives and tyrannous mothers-in-law. They do at least imply a stable society in which marriage is indissoluble and family loyalty taken for granted. And bound up with this is something I noted earlier, the fact that there are no pictures, or hardly any, of good-looking people beyond their first youth. There is the "spooning" couple and the middle-aged, cat-and-dog couple, but nothing in between. The liaison, the illicit but more or less decorous love-affair which used to be the stock joke of French comic papers, is not a post card subject. And this reflects, on a comic level, the working-class outlook which takes it as a matter of course that youth and adventure—almost, indeed, individual life—end with marriage. One of the few authentic class-differences, as opposed to class-distinctions, still existing in England is that the working classes age very much earlier. They do not live less long, provided that they survive their childhood, nor do they lose their physical activity earlier, but they do lose very early their youthful appearance. This fact is observable everywhere, but can be most easily verified by watching one of the higher age groups registering for military service; the middle-and upper-class members look, on average, ten years younger than the others. It is usual to attribute this to the harder lives that the working classes have to live, but it is doubtful whether any such difference now exists as would account for it. More probably the truth is that the working classes reach middle age earlier because they accept it earlier. For to look young after, say, thirty is largely a matter of wanting to do so. This generalisation is less true of the better-paid workers, especially those who live in council houses and labour-saving flats, but it is true enough even of them to point to a difference of outlook. And in this, as usual, they are more traditional, more in accord with the Christian past than the well-to-do women who try to stay young at forty by means of physical jerks, cosmetics and avoidance of child-bearing. The impulse to cling to youth at all costs, to attempt to preserve your sexual attraction, to see even in middle age a future for yourself and not merely for your children, is a thing of recent growth and has only precariously established itself. It will probably disappear again when our standard of living drops and our birth-rate rises. "Youth's a stuff will not endure" expresses the normal, traditional attitude. It is this ancient wisdom that McGill and his colleagues are reflecting, no doubt unconsciously, when they allow for no transition stage between the honeymoon couple and those glamourless figures, Mum and Dad.

I have said that at least half McGill's post cards are sex jokes, and a proportion, perhaps ten per cent., are far more obscene than anything else that is now printed in England. Newsagents are occasionally prosecuted for selling them, and there would be many more prosecutions if the broadest jokes were not invariably protected by double meanings. A single example will be enough to show how this is done. In one post card, captioned "They didn't believe her," a young woman is demonstrating, with her hands held apart, something about two feet long to a couple of open-mouthed acquaintances. Behind her on the wall is a stuffed fish in a glass case, and beside that is a photograph of a nearly naked athlete. Obviously it is not the fish that she is referring to, but this could never be proved. Now, it is doubtful whether there is any paper in England that would print a joke of this kind, and certainly there is no paper that does so habitually. There is an immense amount of pornography of a mild sort, countless illustrated papers cashing in on women's legs, but there is no popular literature specialising in the "vulgar," farcical aspect of sex. On the other hand, jokes exactly like McGill's are the ordinary small change of the revue and music-hall stage, and are also to be heard on the radio, at moments when the censor happens to be nodding. In England the gap between what can be said and what can be printed is rather exceptionally wide. Remarks and gestures which hardly anyone objects to on the stage would raise a public outcry if any attempt were made to reproduce them on paper. (Compare Max Miller's stage patter with his weekly column in the *Sunday Dispatch*.) The comic post cards are the only existing exception to this rule, the only medium in which really "low" humour is considered to be printable. Only in post cards and on the variety stage can the stuck-out behind, dog and lamp-post, baby's nappy type of joke be freely exploited. Remembering that, one sees what function these post cards, in their humble way, are performing.

What they are doing is to give expression to the Sancho Panza view of life, the attitude to life that Miss Rebecca West once summed up as "extracting as much fun as possible from smacking behinds in basement kitchens." The Don Quixote-Sancho Panza combination, which of course is simply the ancient dualism of body and soul in fiction form, recurs more frequently in the literature of the last four hundred years than can be explained by mere imitation. It comes up again and again, in endless variations, Bouvard and Pécuchet, Jeeves and Wooster, Bloom and Dedalus, Holmes and Watson (the Holmes-Watson variant is an exceptionally subtle one, because the usual physical characteristics of the two partners have been transposed). Evidently it corresponds to something enduring in our civilisation, not in the sense that either character is to be found in a "pure" state in real life, but in the sense that the two principles, noble folly and base wisdom, exist side by side in nearly every human being. If you look into your own mind, which are you, Don Quixote or Sancho Panza? Almost certainly you are both. There is one part of you that wishes to be a hero or a saint, but another part of you is a little fat man who sees very clearly the advantages of staying alive with a whole skin. He is your unofficial self, the voice of the belly protesting against the soul. His tastes lie towards safety, soft beds, no work, pots of beer and women with "voluptuous" figures. He it is who punctures your fine attitudes and urges you to look after Number One, to be unfaithful to your wife, to bilk your debts, and so on and so forth. Whether you allow yourself to be influenced by him is a different question. But it is simply a lie to say that he is not part of you, just as it is a lie to say that Don Quixote is not part of you either, though most of what is said and written consists of one lie or the other, usually the first.

But though in varying forms he is one of the stock figures of literature, in real life, especially in the way society is ordered, his point of view never gets a fair hearing. There is a constant world-wide conspiracy to pretend that he is not there, or at least that he doesn't matter. Codes of law and morals, or religious systems, never have much room in them for a humorous view of life. Whatever is funny is subversive, every joke is ultimately a custard pie, and the reason why so large a proportion of jokes centre round obscenity is simply that all societies, as the price of survival, have to insist on a fairly high standard of sexual morality. A dirty joke is not, of course, a serious attack upon morality, but it is a sort of mental rebellion, a momentary wish that things were otherwise. So also with all other jokes, which always centre round cowardice, laziness, dishonesty or some other quality which society cannot afford to encourage. Society has always to demand a little more from human beings than it will get in practice. It has to demand faultless discipline and self-sacrifice, it must expect its subjects to work hard, pay their taxes, and be faithful to their wives, it must assume that men think it glorious to die on the battlefield and women want to wear themselves out with child-bearing. The whole of what one may call official literature is founded on such assumptions. I never read the proclamations of generals before battle, the speeches of führers and prime ministers, the solidarity songs of public schools and Left Wing political parties, national anthems, Temperance tracts, papal encyclicals and sermons against gambling and contraception, without seeming to hear in the background a chorus of raspberries from all the millions of common men to whom these high sentiments make no appeal. Nevertheless the high sentiments always win in the end, leaders who offer blood, toil, tears and sweat always get more out of their followers than those who offer safety and a good time. When it comes to the pinch, human beings are heroic. Women face childbed and the scrubbing brush, revolutionaries keep their mouths shut in the torture chamber, battleships go down with their guns still firing when their decks are awash. It is only that the other element in man, the lazy, cowardly, debt-bilking adulterer who is inside all of us, can never be suppressed altogether and needs a hearing occasionally.

The comic post cards are one expression of his point of view, a humble one, less important than the music halls, but still worthy of attention. In a society which is still basically Christian they naturally concentrate on sex jokes; in a totalitarian society, if they had any freedom of expression at all, they would probably concentrate on laziness or cowardice, but at any rate on the unheroic in one form or another. It will not do to condemn them on the ground that they are vulgar and ugly. That is exactly what they are meant to be. Their whole meaning and virtue is in their unredeemed lowness, not only in the sense of obscenity, but lowness of outlook in every direction whatever. The slightest hint of "higher" influences would ruin them utterly. They stand for the worm's-eye view of life, for the music-hall world where marriage is a dirty joke or a comic dis-- aster, where the rent is always behind and the clothes are always up the spout, where the lawyer is always a crook and the Scotsman always a miser, where the newlyweds make fools of themselves on the hideous beds of seaside lodging-houses and the drunken, red-nosed husbands roll home at four in the morning to meet the linen-nightgowned wives who wait for them behind the front door, poker in hand. Their existence, the fact that people want them, is symp-tomatically important. Like the music halls, they are a sort of satur-nalia, a harmless rebellion against virtue. They express only one tendency in the human mind, but a tendency which is always there and will find its own outlet, like water. On the whole, human beings want to be good, but not too good, and not quite all the time. For:

"there is a just man that perishes in his righteousness, and there is a wicked man that prolongeth his life in his wickedness. Be not righteous over much; neither make thyself over wise; why shouldst thou destroy thyself? Be not overmuch wicked, neither be thou foolish: why shouldst thou die before thy time?"

In the past the mood of the comic post card could enter into the central stream of literature, and jokes barely different from McGill's could casually be uttered between the murders in Shakespeare's tragedies. That is no longer possible, and a whole category of humour, integral to our literature till 1800 or thereabouts, has dwindled down to these ill-drawn post cards, leading a barely legal existence in cheap stationers' windows. The corner of the human heart that they speak for might easily manifest itself in worse forms, and I for one should be sorry to see them vanish.

QUESTIONS

1. What sort of reader does Orwell seem to be addressing in the first two paragraphs? What sort of tastes does he assume his reader to have? To what group is the essay definitely not addressed? Given the particular sort of reader he is addressing, what material does Orwell include in the essay that he might otherwise exclude?

2. Broadly speaking, Orwell treats in order the characteristics, subject-matter, and function of the comic postcards. What organizational pattern governs the order? In what major respect does Orwell abandon his order and hence his pattern? To what extent does he employ the rhetorical form of the opening sentence to mark the stages of his organization?

3. What two different reactions by the reader to the postcards is Orwell aiming at in his discussion of the first two impressions that the cards make (paragraph five)? How does his language differ in the two discussions? What contrasting reaction on the part of the reader is he aiming at in his discussion of the subject-matter of the cards? How does his manner of presentation here serve that purpose? What progression of reaction, if any, do you see Orwell intending thus far?

4. Contrast the degrees of severity with which Orwell intends his reader to regard the vulgarity of the cards and their obscenity. On what basis does he himself excuse one quality more than the other? Relate both of your answers to the contrasting judgments that he expresses in the first and last paragraphs of the essay.

5. Which judgment upon the cards, that of the first or that of the last paragraph, is presumably more familiar (or more readily acceptable) to the sort of reader Orwell is addressing? Which judgment is he more interested in advancing in the essay? Strategically, why wouldn't he reverse the order in which he presents the two judgments? Can you justify Orwell's choice of organizational pattern (Question 2) in terms of his strategy? Can you explain his strategic purpose in breaking that pattern (Question 2)?

6. What material in paragraph three might give you reason to doubt Orwell's authority on the subject of comic postcards? To the extent that he is an authority, would you say he expresses his views modestly

or dogmatically? Where is he most modest? Where is he most dogmatic? Are his organizational pattern and organizational strategy evidences of modesty, dogmatism, or both?

7. What bearing might the following assertions have upon the validity of Orwell's argument: caricature is essential to pornography (see the paragraph beginning "A recurrent, almost dominant motif"); the middle class has no equivalent of the comic postcard (see the next to last paragraph); Shakespeare's age was an age of violence in English society (see the final paragraph)?

8. What suggestiveness does Orwell's title have? Discuss its suggestiveness for the sort of reader that Orwell seems to be addressing, and also in terms of the judgment that he makes upon the postcards.

The Morality of Inertia

LIONEL TRILLING

Lionel Trilling (1905—) was born in New York City and educated at Columbia University, where he has taught English
since 1932. Though his sole novel, *The Middle of the Journey*,
and several short stories have been well received, he has exercised most influence as a critic. His many reviews and essays
(collected in *The Liberal Imagination, The Opposing Self,* and
A Gathering of Fugitives) show how deftly the criticism of
literature can encompass any variety of social and cultural issues. He has also written full-length studies of Matthew Arnold
and E. M. Forster.

A theological seminary in New York planned a series of lectures on
"The Literary Presentations of Great Moral Issues," and invited
me to give one of the talks. Since I have a weakness for the general subject, I was disposed to accept the invitation. But I hesitated
over the particular instance, for I was asked to discuss the moral
issues in *Ethan Frome*. I had not read Edith Wharton's little novel
in a good many years, and I remembered it with no pleasure or
admiration. I recalled it as not at all the sort of book that deserved
to stand in a list which included *The Brothers Karamazov* and
Billy Budd, Foretopman. If it presented a moral issue at all, I could
not bring to mind what that issue was. And so I postponed my

"The Morality of Inertia" from *A Gathering of Fugitives* by Lionel Trilling.
Reprinted by permission of The Beacon Press and Martin Secker & Warburg,
Ltd.

acceptance of the invitation and made it conditional upon my being able to come to terms with the subject assigned to me.

Ethan Frome, when I read it again, turned out to be pretty much as I had recalled it, not a great book or even a fine book, but a factitious book, perhaps even a cruel book. I was puzzled to understand how it ever came to be put on the list, why anyone should want to have it discussed as an example of moral perception. Then I remembered its reputation, which, in America, is very considerable. It is sometimes spoken of as an American classic. It is often assigned to high-school and college students as a text for study.

But the high and solemn repute in which it stands is, I am sure, in large part a mere accident of American culture. *Ethan Frome* appeared in 1911, at a time when, to a degree that we can now only wonder at, American literature was committed to optimism, cheerfulness, and gentility. What William Dean Howells called the "smiling aspects of life" had an importance in the literature of America some fifty years ago which is unmatched in the literature of any other time and place. It was inevitable that those who were critical of the prevailing culture and who wished to foster in America higher and more serious literature should put a heavy stress upon the grimmer aspects of life, that they should equate the smiling aspects with falsehood, the grimmer aspects with truth. For these devoted people, sickened as they were by cheerfulness and hope, the word "stark" seemed to carry the highest possible praise a critical review or a blurb could bestow, with "relentless" and "inevitable" as its proper variants. *Ethan Frome* was admired because it was "stark"— its action, we note, takes place in the New England village of Starkville—and because the fate it describes is *relentless* and *inevitable*.

No one would wish to question any high valuation that may be given to the literary representation of unhappy events—except, perhaps, as the high valuation may be a mere cliché of an intellectual class, except as it is supposed to seem the hallmark of the superior sensibility and intelligence of that class. When it is only this, we have the right, and the duty, to look sniffishly at starkness, and relentlessness, and inevitability, to cock a skeptical eye at grimness. And I am quite unable to overcome my belief that *Ethan Frome* enjoys its high reputation because it still satisfies our modern snobbishness about tragedy and pain.

We can never speak of Edith Wharton without some degree of respect. She brought to her novels a strong if limited intelligence, notable powers of observation, and a genuine desire to tell the truth, a desire which in some part she satisfied. But she was a woman in whom we cannot fail to see a limitation of heart, and this limitation makes itself manifest as a literary and moral deficiency of her work, and of *Ethan Frome* especially. It appears in the deadness of her prose, and more flagrantly in the suffering of her characters. Whenever the characters of a story suffer, they do so at the behest of their author—the author is responsible for their suffering and must justify his cruelty by the seriousness of his moral intention. The author of *Ethan Frome*, it seemed to me as I read the book again to test my memory of it, could not lay claim to any such justification. Her intention in writing the story was not adequate to the dreadful fate she contrived for her characters. She indulges herself by what she contrives—she is, as the phrase goes, "merely literary." This is not to say that the merely literary intention does not make its very considerable effects. There is in *Ethan Frome* an image of life-in-death, of hell-on-earth, which is not easily forgotten: the crippled Ethan, and Zeena, his dreadful wife, and Matty, the once charming girl he had loved, now bedridden and querulous with pain, all living out their death in the kitchen of the desolate Frome farm— a perpetuity of suffering memorializes a moment of passion. It is terrible to contemplate, it is unforgettable, but the mind can do nothing with it, can only endure it.

My new reading of the book, then, did not lead me to suppose that it justified its reputation, but only confirmed my recollection that *Ethan Frome* was a dead book, the product of mere will, of the cold hard literary will. What is more, it seemed to me quite unavailable for any moral discourse. In the context of morality, there is nothing to say about *Ethan Frome*. It presents no moral issue at all.

For consider the story it tells. A young man of good and gentle character is the only son of a New England farm couple. He has some intellectual gifts and some desire to know the world, and for a year he is happy attending a technical school. But his father is incapacitated by a farm accident, and Ethan dutifully returns to manage the failing farm and sawmill. His father dies; his mother loses her mental faculties, and during her last illness she is nursed by a female relative whom young Ethan marries, for no other reason than that he is bemused by loneliness. The new wife, Zeena, immediately becomes a shrew, a harridan and a valetudinarian—she lives only to be ill. Because Zeena now must spare herself, the Fromes take into their home a gentle and charming young girl, a destitute cousin of the wife. Ethan and Matty fall in love, innocently but deeply. The wife, perceiving this, plans to send the girl away, her place to be taken by a servant whose wages the husband cannot possibly afford. In despair at the thought of separation Matty and Ethan attempt suicide. They mean to die by sledding down a steep hill and crashing into a great elm at the bottom. Their plan fails: both survive the crash, Ethan to be sorely crippled, Matty to be bedridden in perpetual pain. Now the wife Zeena surrenders her claim to a mysterious pathology and becomes the devoted nurse and jailer of the lovers. The terrible tableau to which I have referred is ready for inspection.

It seemed to me that it was quite impossible to talk about this story. This is not to say that the story is without interest as a story, but what interest it may have does not yield discourse, or at least not moral discourse.

But as I began to explain to the lecture committee why I could not accept the invitation to lecture about the book, it suddenly came over me how very strange a phenomenon the book made— how remarkable it was that a story should place before us the dreadful image of three ruined and tortured lives, showing how

their ruin came about, and yet propose no moral issue of any kind.
And if *issue* seems to imply something more precisely formulated
than we have a right to demand of a story, then it seemed to me no
less remarkable that the book had scarcely any moral reverberation,
that strange and often beautiful sound we seem to hear generated
in the air by a tale of suffering, a sound which is not always music,
which does not always have a "meaning," but which yet entrances
us, like the random notes of an Aeolian harp, or merely the sound
of the wind in the chimney. The moral sound that *Ethan Frome*
makes is a dull thud. And this seemed to me so remarkable, indeed,
that in the very act of saying why I could not possibly discuss *Ethan
Frome*, I found the reason why it must be discussed.

It is, as I have suggested, a very great fault in *Ethan Frome* that
it presents no moral issue, sets off no moral reverberation. A certain
propriety controls the literary representation of human suffering.
This propriety dictates that the representation of pain may not be,
as it were, gratuitous; it must not be an end in itself. The naked
act of representing, or contemplating, human suffering is a self-
indulgence, and it may be a cruelty. Between a tragedy and a
spectacle in the Roman circus there is at least this much similarity,
that the pleasure both afford derives from observing the pain of
others. A tragedy is always on the verge of cruelty. What saves it
from the actuality of cruelty is that it has an intention beyond itself.
This intention may be so simple a one as that of getting us to do
something practical about the cause of the suffering or to help
actual sufferers, or at least to feel that we should; or it may lead us
to look beyond apparent causes to those which the author wishes
us to think of as more real, such as Fate, or the will of the gods,
or the will of God; or it may challenge our fortitude or intelligence
or piety.

A sense of the necessity of some such intention animates all considerations of the strange paradox of tragedy. Aristotle is concerned
to solve the riddle of how the contemplation of human suffering
can possibly be pleasurable, of why its pleasure is permissible. He
wanted to know what literary conditions were needed to keep a

tragedy from being a display of horror. Here it is well to remember that the Greeks were not so concerned as we have been led to believe to keep all dreadful things off the stage—in the presentation of Aristotle's favorite tragedy, the audience saw Jocasta hanging from a beam, it saw the representation of Oedipus's bloody eyesockets. And so Aristotle discovered, or pretended to discover, that tragedy did certain things to protect itself from being merely cruel. It chose, Aristotle said, a certain kind of hero; he was of a certain social and moral stature; he had a certain degree of possibility of free choice; he must justify his fate, or seem to justify it, by his moral condition, being neither wholly good nor wholly bad, having a particular fault that collaborates with destiny to bring about his ruin. The purpose of all these specifications for the tragic hero is to assure us that we observe something more than mere passivity when we witness the hero's suffering, that the suffering has, as we say, some meaning, some show of rationality.

Aristotle's theory of tragedy has had its way with the world to an extent which is perhaps out of proportion to its comprehensiveness and accuracy. Its success is largely due to its having dealt so openly with the paradox of tragedy. It serves to explain away any guilty feelings that we may have at deriving pleasure from suffering.

But at the same time that the world has accepted Aristotle's theory of tragedy, it has also been a little uneasy about some of its implications. The element of the theory that causes uneasiness in modern times is the matter of the stature of the hero. To a society based in egalitarian sentiments, the requirement that the hero be a man of rank seems to deny the presumed dignity of tragedy to men of lesser status. And to a culture which questions the freedom of the will, Aristotle's hero seems to be a little beside the point. Aristotle's prescription for the tragic hero is clearly connected with his definition, in his *Ethics*, of the nature of an ethical action. He tells us that a truly ethical action must be a free choice between two alternatives. This definition is then wonderfully complicated by a further requirement—that the moral man must be so trained in making the right choice that he makes it as a matter of habit, makes it, as it were, instinctively. Yet it *is* a choice, and reason plays a part in its making. But we, of course, don't give to reason the same place in the moral life that Aristotle gave it. And in general, over the last hundred and fifty years, dramatists and novelists have tried their hand at the representation of human suffering without the particular safeguards against cruelty which Aristotle perceived, or contrived. A very large part of the literature of Western Europe may be understood in terms of an attempt to invert or criticize the heroic prescription of the hero, by burlesque and comedy, or by the insistence on the commonplace, the lowering of the hero's social status and the diminution of his power of reasoned choice. The work of Fielding may serve as an example of how the mind of Europe has been haunted by the great image of classical tragedy, and how it has tried to lay that famous ghost. When Fielding calls his hero Tom Jones, he means that his young man is not Orestes or Achilles; when he calls him a foundling, he is suggesting that Tom Jones is not, all appearances to the contrary notwithstanding, Oedipus.

Edith Wharton was following where others led. Her impulse in conceiving the story of Ethan Frome was not, however, that of moral experimentation. It was, as I have said, a purely literary impulse, in the bad sense of the word "literary." Her aim is not that of Wordsworth in any of his stories of the suffering poor, to require of us that we open our minds to a realization of the kinds of people whom suffering touches. Nor is it that of Flaubert in *Madame Bovary*, to wring from solid circumstances all the pity and terror of an ancient tragic fable. Nor is it that of Dickens or Zola, to shake us with the perception of social injustice, to instruct us in the true nature of social life and to dispose us to indignant opinion and action. These are not essentially literary intentions; they are moral intentions. But all that Edith Wharton has in mind is to achieve that grim tableau of which I have spoken, of pain and imprisonment, of life-in-death. About the events that lead up to this tableau, there is nothing she finds to say, nothing whatever. The best we can conclude of the meaning of her story is that it might perhaps be a subject of discourse in the context of rural sociology—it might be understood to exemplify the thesis that love and joy do not flourish on poverty-stricken New England farms. If we try to bring it into the context of morality, its meaning goes no further than certain cultural considerations—that is, to people who like their literature to show the "smiling aspects of life," it may be thought to say, "This is the aspect that life really has, as grim as this"; while to people who repudiate a literature that represents only the smiling aspects of life it says, "How intelligent and how brave you are to be able to understand that life is as grim as this." It is really not very much to say.

And yet there is in *Ethan Frome* an idea of considerable importance. It is there by reason of the author's deficiencies, not by reason of her powers—because it suits Edith Wharton's rather dull intention to be content with telling a story about people who do not make moral decisions, whose fate cannot have moral reverberations. The idea is this: that moral inertia, the *not* making of moral decisions, constitutes a large part of the moral life of humanity.

This isn't an idea that literature likes to deal with. Literature is charmed by energy and dislikes inertia. It characteristically represents morality as positive action. The same is true of the moral philosophy of the West—has been true ever since Aristotle defined a truly moral act by its energy of reason, of choice. A later development of this tendency said that an act was really moral only if it went against the inclination of the person performing the act: the idea was parodied as saying that one could not possibly act morally to one's friends, only to one's enemies.

Yet the dull daily world sees something below this delightful preoccupation of literature and moral philosophy. It is aware of the morality of inertia, and of its function as a social base, as a social cement. It knows that duties are done for no other reason than that they are said to be duties; for no other reason, sometimes, than that the doer has not really been able to conceive of any other course, has, perhaps, been afraid to think of any other course. Hobbes said of the Capitol geese that saved Rome by their cackling

that they were the salvation of the city, not because they were they
but there. How often the moral act is performed not because we
are we but because we are there! This is the morality of habit, or
the morality of biology. This is Ethan Frome's morality, simple, unquestioning, passive, even masochistic. His duties as a son are discharged because he is a son; his duties as a husband are discharged
because he is a husband. He does nothing by moral election. At one
point in his story he is brought to moral crisis—he must choose
between his habituated duty to his wife and his duty and inclination
to the girl he loves. It is quite impossible for him to deal with the
dilemma in the high way that literature and moral philosophy pre-
scribe, by reason and choice. Choice is incompatible with his idea
of his existence; he can only elect to die.

Literature, of course, is not wholly indifferent to what I have
called the morality of habit and biology, the morality of inertia.
But literature, when it deals with this morality, is tempted to qualify its dullness by endowing it with a certain high grace. There is
never any real moral choice for the Félicité of Flaubert's story "A
Simple Heart." She is all pious habit of virtue, and of blind, unthinking, unquestioning love. There are, of course, actually such people
as Félicité, simple, good, loving—quite stupid in their love, not
choosing where to bestow it. We meet such people frequently in
literature, in the pages of Balzac, Dickens, Dostoievski, Joyce,
Faulkner, Hemingway. They are of a quite different order of
being from those who try the world with their passion and their
reason; they are by way of being saints, of the less complicated
kind. They do not really exemplify what I mean by the morality
of inertia. Literature is uncomfortable in the representation of the
morality of inertia or of biology, and overcomes its discomfort by
representing it with the added grace of that extravagance which we
denominate saintliness.

But the morality of inertia is to be found in very precise exempli-
fication in one of Wordsworth's poems. Wordsworth is pre-eminent
among the writers who experimented in the representation of new
kinds and bases of moral action—he has a genius for imputing

moral existence to people who, according to the classical morality, should have no moral life at all. And he has the courage to make this imputation without at the same time imputing the special grace and interest of saintliness. The poem I have in mind is ostensibly about a flower, but the transition from the symbol to the human fact is clearly, if awkwardly, made. The flower is a small celandine, and the poet observes that it has not, in the natural way of flowers, folded itself against rough weather:

> *But lately, one rough day, this Flower I passed*
> *And recognized it, though in altered form,*
> *Now standing as an offering to the blast,*
> *And buffeted at will by rain and storm.*

> *I stopped, and said with inly-muttered voice,*
> *It doth not love the shower nor seek the cold;*
> *This neither is its courage nor its choice,*
> *But its necessity in being old.*

Neither courage nor choice, but necessity: it cannot do otherwise. Yet it acts as if by courage and choice. This is the morality imposed by brute circumstance, by biology, by habit, by the unspoken social demand which we have not the strength to refuse, or, often, to imagine refusing. People are scarcely ever praised for living according to this morality—we do not suppose it to be a morality at all until we see it being broken.

This is morality as it is conceived by the great mass of people in the world. And with this conception of morality goes the almost entire negation of any connection between morality and destiny. A superstitious belief in retribution may play its part in the thought of simple people, but essentially they think of catastrophes as fortuitous, without explanation, without reason. They live in the moral universe of the Book of Job. In complex lives, morality does in some part determine destiny; in most lives it does not. Between the moral life of Ethan and Matty and their terrible fate we cannot make any reasonable connection. Only a moral judgment cruel to the point of insanity could speak of it as anything but accidental.

I have not spoken of the morality of inertia in order to praise it but only to recognize it, to suggest that when we keep our minds fixed on what the great invigorating books tell us about the moral life, we obscure the large bulking dull mass of moral fact. Morality is not only the high, torturing dilemmas of Ivan Karamazov and Captain Vere. It is also the deeds performed without thought, without choice, perhaps even without love, as Zeena Frome ministers to Ethan and Matty. The morality of inertia, of the dull, unthinking round of duties, may, and often does, yield the immorality of inertia; the example that will most readily occur to us is that of the good simple people, so true to their family responsibilities, who gave no thought to the concentration camps in whose shadow they lived. No: the morality of inertia is not to be praised, but it must be recognized. And Edith Wharton's little novel must be recognized for bringing to our attention what we, and literature, so easily forget.

QUESTIONS

1. Define "literary" as used by Trilling in paragraphs five and fourteen. What does he mean by "literature" in the last five paragraphs of the essay? Does he include *Ethan Frome* in "literature"?

2. Against what opinion of *Ethan Frome* does Trilling set his own? To what extent does his opinion change in the course of the essay? (Compare, for example, the last paragraph with the second and third paragraphs. In your overall answer consider both aspects of the novel that Trilling discusses, the literary and the moral.)

3. Trilling speaks of Aristotelian tragedy, and, variously throughout, of Dostoievski's *The Brothers Karamazov*, Flaubert's *Madame Bovary*, Fielding's *Tom Jones*, and Dickens and Zola. What is the effect on *Ethan Frome* of his use of such touchstones? Would you say it is essentially the same effect as that created by the historical considerations in the third paragraph?

4. Does Trilling approve of the morality of inertia? Does he seem to think that his audience approves of it? How new or unusual an idea does he seem to think it is? What exactly is the attitude he takes towards it at the end? Does he want his audience to take the same attitude?

5. What sort of audience does Trilling seem to be addressing? When he speaks of "our modern snobbishness about tragedy and pain" (paragraph four), to whom is he not referring? Does the excluded group include himself? Does Trilling generally seem to treat his audience as his cultural equals? What is your evidence?

6. What do you suppose is Trilling's strategic purpose in presenting to his audience the account of his reservations about lecturing on *Ethan Frome*? Explain—according to the same strategy—why the synopsis of the novel comes in the seventh paragraph rather than the second.

7. In paragraphs eleven through thirteen Trilling discusses the Aristotelian theory of tragedy. What is the general importance of this material to his essay? What earlier paragraph would have provided the same sort of introduction to it that the tenth paragraph provides? From the standpoint of the organization of materials, why do you suppose Trilling defers the discussion until paragraph eleven? From the standpoint of a strategy with regard to his audience, why do you suppose he defers it?

8. Answer in terms of strategy: if the morality of inertia is, as the title suggests, the actual subject of the essay, why does Trilling wait so long to discuss it? (Your answers to Questions 3 and 5 will help you here.) Describe the broad organization of the essay in strategic terms.

Education by Poetry:
A Meditative Monologue

ROBERT FROST

Robert Frost (1874—) is probably the best read and certainly
one of the most accomplished of modern American poets. Born
in San Francisco, he was brought as a youth to New England,
where he has lived and worked—as mill-hand, teacher, and
farmer—most of his life. More than a regionalist, he has written deceptively simple poetry that uses the settings and often
the postures of the area he knows best to present emotions
and states of mind common to all men. His honors, which have
been many, include four Pulitzer Prizes for Poetry and several
commendations from Congress; and he is well remembered
both for his poetry readings and for such informal addresses
as the following, delivered at Amherst College and taken down
in shorthand by a member of the audience.

I am going to urge nothing in my talk. I am not an advocate. I am
going to consider a matter, and commit a description. And I am
going to describe other colleges than Amherst. Or, rather say all
that is good can be taken as about Amherst; all that is bad will
be about other colleges.

I know whole colleges where all American poetry is barred—

"Education by Poetry" from *The Amherst Graduates' Quarterly*, February, 1931.
Copyright 1931, by Robert Frost. Reprinted by permission of the Amherst
Alumni News and Holt, Rinehart & Winston, Inc.

whole colleges. I know whole colleges where all contemporary poetry is barred.

I once heard of a minister who turned his daughter—his poetry-writing daughter—out on the street to earn a living, because he said there should be no more books written; God wrote one book, and that was enough. (My friend George Russell, "Æ", has read no literature, he protests, since just before Chaucer.)

That all seems sufficiently safe, and you can say one thing for it. It takes the onus off the poetry of having to be used to teach children anything. It comes pretty hard on poetry, I sometimes think,—what it has to bear in the teaching process.

Then I know whole colleges where, though they let in older poetry, they manage to bar all that is poetical in it by treating it as something other than poetry. It is not so hard to do that. Their reason I have often hunted for. It may be that these people act from a kind of modesty. Who are professors that they should attempt to deal with a thing as high and as fine as poetry? Who are *they?* There is a certain manly modesty in that.

That is the best general way of settling the problem; treat all poetry as if it were something else than poetry, as if it were syntax, language, science. Then you can even come down into the American and into the contemporary without any special risk.

There is another reason they have, and that is that they are, first and foremost in life, markers. They have the marking problem to consider. Now, I stand here a teacher of many years' experience and I have never complained of having had to mark. I had rather mark anyone for anything—for his looks, carriage, his ideas, his correctness, his exactness, anything you please,—I would rather give him a mark in terms of letters, A, B, C, D, than have to use adjectives on him. We are all being marked by each other all the time, classified, ranked, put in our place, and I see no escape from that. I am no sentimentalist. You have got to mark, and you have got to mark, first of all, for accuracy, for correctness. But if I am going to give a mark, that is the least part of my marking. The hard part is the part beyond that, the part where the adventure begins.

One other way to rid the curriculum of the poetry nuisance has been considered. More merciful than the others it would neither abolish nor denature the poetry, but only turn it out to disport itself, with the plays and games—in no wise discredited, though given no credit for. Any one who liked to teach poetically could take his subject, whether English, Latin, Greek or French, out into the nowhere along with the poetry. One side of a sharp line would be left to the rigorous and righteous; the other side would be assigned to the flowery where they would know what could be expected of them. Grade marks where more easily given, of course, in the courses concentrating on correctness and exactness as the only forms of honesty recognized by plain people; a general indefinite mark of X in the courses that scatter brains over taste and opinion. On inquiry I have found no teacher willing to take position on either side of the line, either among the rigors or among the flowers. No one is willing to admit that his discipline is not partly in exactness. No one is willing to admit that his discipline is not partly in taste and enthusiasm.

How shall a man go through college without having been marked for taste and judgment? What will become of him? What will his end be? He will have to take continuation courses for college graduates. He will have to go to night schools. They are having night schools now, you know, for college graduates. Why? Because they have not been educated enough to find their way around in contemporary literature. They don't know what they may safely like in the libraries and galleries. They don't know how to judge an editorial when they see one. They don't know how to judge a political campaign. They don't know when they are being fooled by a metaphor, an analogy, a parable. And metaphor is, of course, what we are talking about. Education by poetry is education by metaphor.

Suppose we stop short of imagination, initiative, enthusiasm, inspiration and originality—dread words. Suppose we don't mark in such things at all. There are still two minimal things, that we have got to take care of, taste and judgment. Americans are supposed to have more judgment than taste, but taste is there to be dealt with.

That is what poetry, the only art in the colleges of arts, is there for. I for my part would not be afraid to go in for enthusiasm. There is the enthusiasm like a blinding light, or the enthusiasm of the deafening shout, the crude enthusiasm that you get uneducated by poetry, outside of poetry. It is exemplified in what I might call "sunset raving." You look westward toward the sunset, or if you get up early enough, eastward toward the sunrise, and you rave. It is oh's and ah's with you and no more.

But the enthusiasm I mean is taken through the prism of the intellect and spread on the screen in a color, all the way from hyperbole at one end—or overstatement, at one end—to understatement at the other end. It is a long strip of dark lines and many colors. Such enthusiasm is one object of all teaching in poetry. I heard wonderful things said about Virgil yesterday, and many of them seemed to me crude enthusiasm, more like a deafening shout, many of them. But one speech had range, something of overstatement, something of statement, and something of understatement. It had all the colors of an enthusiasm passed through an idea.

I would be willing to throw away everything else but that: enthusiasm tamed by metaphor. Let me rest the case there. Enthusiasm tamed to metaphor, tamed to that much of it. I do not think anybody ever knows the discreet use of metaphor, his own and other people's, the discreet handling of metaphor, unless he has been properly educated in poetry.

Poetry begins in trivial metaphors, pretty metaphors, "grace" metaphors, and goes on to the profoundest thinking that we have. Poetry provides the one permissible way of saying one thing and meaning another. People say, "Why don't you say what you mean?" We never do that, do we, being all of us too much poets. We like to talk in parables and in hints and in indirections— whether from diffidence or some other instinct.

I have wanted in late years to go further and further in making metaphor the whole of thinking. I find some one now and then to agree with me that all thinking, except mathematical thinking, is metaphorical, or all thinking except scientific thinking. The mathematical might be difficult for me to bring in, but the scientific is easy enough.

Once on a time all the Greeks were busy telling each other what the All was—or was like unto. All was three elements, air, earth, and water (we once thought it was ninety elements; now we think it is only one). All was substance, said another. All was change, said a third. But best and most fruitful was Pythagoras' comparison of the universe with number. Number of what? Number of feet, pounds, and seconds was the answer, and we had science and all that has followed in science. The metaphor has held and held, breaking down only when it came to the spiritual and psychological or the out of the way places of the physical.

The other day we had a visitor here, a noted scientist, whose latest word to the world has been that the more accurately you know where a thing is, the less accurately you are able to state how fast it is moving. You can see why that would be so, without going back to Zeno's problem of the arrow's flight. In carrying numbers into the realm of space and at the same time into the realm of time you are mixing metaphors, that is all, and you are in trouble. They won't mix. The two don't go together.

Let's take two or three more of the metaphors now in use to live by. I have just spoken of one of the new ones, a charming mixed metaphor right in the realm of higher mathematics and higher physics: that the more accurately you state where a thing is, the less accurately you will be able to tell how fast it is moving. And, of course, everything is moving. Everything is an event now. Another metaphor. A thing, they say, is an event. Do you believe it is? Not quite. I believe it is almost an event. But I like the comparison of a thing with an event.

I notice another from the same quarter. "In the neighborhood of matter space is something like curved." Isn't that a good one! It seems to me that that is simply and utterly charming—to say that space is something like curved in the neighborhood of matter. "Something like."

Another amusing one is from—what is the book?—I can't say it now; but here is the metaphor. Its aim is to restore you to your ideas of free will. It wants to give you back your freedom of will. All right, here it is on a platter. You know that you can't tell by name what persons in a certain class will be dead ten years after graduation, but you can tell actuarially how many will be dead. Now, just so this scientist says of the particles of matter flying at a screen, striking a screen; you can't tell what individual particles will come, but you can say in general that a certain number will strike in a given time. It shows, you see, that the individual particle can come freely. I asked Bohr about that particularly, and he said, "Yes, it is so. It can come when it wills and as it wills; and the action of the individual particle is unpredictable. But it is not so of the action of the mass. There you can predict." He says, "That gives the individual atom its freedom, but the mass its necessity."

Another metaphor that has interested us in our time and has done all our thinking for us is the metaphor of evolution. Never mind going into the Latin word. The metaphor is simply the metaphor of the growing plant or of the growing thing. And somebody very brilliantly, quite a while ago, said that the whole universe, the whole of everything, was like unto a growing thing. That is all. I know the metaphor will break down at some point, but it has not failed everywhere. It is a very brilliant metaphor, I acknowledge, though I myself get too tired of the kind of essay that talks about the evolution of candy, we will say, or the evolution of elevators— the evolution of this, that, and the other. Everything is evolution. I emancipate myself by simply saying that I didn't get up the metaphor and so am not much interested in it.

What I am pointing out is that unless you are at home in the metaphor, unless you have had your proper poetical education in the metaphor, you are not safe anywhere. Because you are not at ease with figurative values: you don't know the metaphor in its strength and its weakness. You don't know how far you may expect to ride it and when it may break down with you. You are not safe in science; you are not safe in history. In history, for instance— to show that is the same in history as elsewhere—I heard somebody say yesterday that Aeneas was to be likened unto (those words, "likened unto"!) George Washington. He was that type of national hero, the middle-class man, not thinking of being a hero at all, bent on building the future, bent on his children, his descendants. A good metaphor, as far as it goes, and you must know how far. And then he added that Odysseus should be likened unto Theodore Roosevelt. I don't think that is so good. Someone visiting Gibbon at the point of death, said he was the same Gibbon as of old, still at his parallels.

Take the way we have been led into our present position morally, the world over. It is by a sort of metaphorical gradient. There is a kind of thinking—to speak metaphorically—there is a kind of thinking you might say was endemic in the brothel. It is always there. And every now and then in some mysterious way it becomes epidemic in the world. And how does it do so? By using all the good words that virtue has invented to maintain virtue. It uses honesty, first,—frankness, sincerity—those words; picks them up, uses them. "In the name of honesty, let us see what we are." You know. And then it picks up the word joy. "Let us in the name of joy, which is the enemy of our ancestors, the Puritans . . . Let us in the name of joy, which is the enemy of the kill-joy Puritan . . ." You see. "Let us," and so on. And then, "In the name of health . . ." Health is another good word. And that is the metaphor Freudianism trades on, mental health. And the first thing we know, it has us all in up to the top knot. I suppose we may blame the artists a good deal, because they are great people to spread by metaphor. The stage too —the stage is always a good intermediary between the two worlds, the under and the upper,—if I may say so without personal prejudice to the stage.

In all this I have only been saying that the devil can quote Scripture, which simply means that the good words you have lying around the devil can use for his purposes as well as anybody else. Never mind about my morality. I am not here to urge anything. I don't care whether the world is good or bad—not on any particular day.

Let me ask you to watch a metaphor breaking down here before you.

Somebody said to me a little while ago, "It is easy enough for me to think of the universe as a machine, as a mechanism."

I said, "You mean the universe is like a machine?"

He said, "No. I think it is one . . . Well, it is like . . ."

"I think you mean the universe is like a machine."

"All right. Let it go at that."

I asked him, "Did you ever see a machine without a pedal for the foot, or a lever for the hand, or a button for the finger?"

He said, "No—no."

I said, "All right. Is the universe like that?"

And he said, "No. I mean it is like a machine, only . . ."

". . . it is different from a machine," I said.

He wanted to go just that far with that metaphor and no further. And so do we all. All metaphor breaks down somewhere. That is the beauty of it. It is touch and go with the metaphor, and until you have lived with it long enough you don't know when it is going. You don't know how much you can get out of it and when it will cease to yield. It is a very living thing. It is as life itself.

I have heard this ever since I can remember, and ever since I have taught: the teacher must teach the pupil to think. I saw a teacher once going around in a great school and snapping pupils' heads with thumb and finger and saying, "Think." That was when thinking was becoming the fashion. The fashion hasn't yet quite gone out.

We still ask boys in college to think, as in the nineties, but we seldom tell them what thinking means; we seldom tell them it is just putting this and that together; it is just saying one thing in terms of another. To tell them is to set their feet on the first rung of a ladder the top of which sticks through the sky.

Greatest of all attempts to say one thing in terms of another is the philosophical attempt to say matter in terms of spirit, or spirit in terms of matter, to make the final unity. That is the greatest attempt that ever failed. We stop just short there. But it is the height

of poetry, the height of all thinking, the height of all poetic thinking, that attempt to say matter in terms of spirit and spirit in terms
of matter. It is wrong to call anybody a materialist simply because
he tries to say spirit in terms of matter, as if that were a sin. Ma-
terialism is not the attempt to say all in terms of matter. The only
materialist—be he poet, teacher, scientist, politician, or statesman
—is the man who gets lost in his material without a gathering
metaphor to throw it into shape and order. He is the lost soul.

We ask people to think, and we don't show them what thinking
is. Somebody says we don't need to show them how to think; bye
and bye they will think. We will give them the forms of sentences
and, if they have any ideas, then they will know how to write them.
But that is preposterous. All there is to writing is having ideas. To
learn to write is to learn to have ideas.

The first little metaphor . . . Take some of the trivial ones. I
would rather have trivial ones of my own to live by than the big
ones of other people.

I remember a boy saying, "He is the kind of person that wounds
with his shield." That may be a slender one, of course. It goes a
good way in character description. It has poetic grace. "He is the
kind that wounds with his shield."

The shield reminds me—just to linger a minute—the shield reminds me of the inverted shield spoken of in one of the books of the
Odyssey, the book that tells about the longest swim on record. I
forget how long it lasted—several days, was it?—but at last as
Odysseus came near the coast of Phoenicia, he saw it on the horizon
"like an inverted shield."

There is a better metaphor in the same book. In the end Odysseus comes ashore and crawls up the beach to spend the night under a double olive tree, and it says, as in a lonely farmhouse where
it is hard to get fire—I am not quoting exactly—where it is hard
to start the fire again if it goes out, they cover the seeds of fire with
ashes to preserve it for the night, so Odysseus covered himself with
the leaves around him and went to sleep. There you have something
that gives you character, something of Odysseus himself. "Seeds of

fire." So Odysseus covered the seeds of fire in himself. You get the greatness of his nature.

But these are slighter metaphors than the ones we live by. They have their charm, their passing charm. They are as it were the first steps toward the great thoughts, grave thoughts, thoughts lasting to the end.

The metaphor whose manage we are best taught in poetry—that is all there is of thinking. It may not seem far for the mind to go but it is the mind's furthest. The richest accumulation of the ages is the noble metaphors we have rolled up.

I want to add one thing more that the experience of poetry is to anyone who comes close to poetry. There are two ways of coming close to poetry. One is by writing poetry. And some people think I want people to write poetry, but I don't; that is, I don't necessarily. I only want people to write poetry if they want to write poetry. I have never encouraged anybody to write poetry that did not want to write it, and I have not always encouraged those who did want to write it. That ought to be one's own funeral. It is a hard, hard life, as they say.

(I have just been to a city in the West, a city full of poets, a city they have made safe for poets. The whole city is so lovely that you do not have to write it up to make it poetry; it is ready-made for you. But, I don't know—the poetry written in that city might not seem like poetry if read outside of the city. It would be like the jokes made when you were drunk; you have to get drunk again to appreciate them.)

But as I say, there is another way to come close to poetry, fortunately, and that is in the reading of it, not as linguistics, not as history, not as anything but poetry. It is one of the hard things for a teacher to know how close a man has come in reading poetry. How do I know whether a man has come close to Keats in reading Keats? It is hard for me to know. I have lived with some boys a whole year over some of the poets and I have not felt sure whether they have come near what it was all about. One remark sometimes told me. One remark was their mark for the year; had to be—it

was all I got that told me what I wanted to know. And that is
enough, if it was the right remark, if it came close enough. I think
a man might make twenty fool remarks if he made one good one
some time in the year. His mark would depend on that good remark.

The closeness—everything depends on the closeness with which
you come, and you ought to be marked for the closeness, for nothing else. And that will have to be estimated by chance remarks,
not by question and answer. It is only by accident that you know
some day how near a person has come.

The person who gets close enough to poetry, he is going to know
more about the word *belief* than anybody else knows, even in religion nowadays. There are two or three places where we know
belief outside of religion. One of them is at the age of fifteen to
twenty, in our self-belief. A young man knows more about himself
than he is able to prove to anyone. He has no knowledge that anybody else will accept as knowledge. In his foreknowledge he has
something that is going to believe itself into fulfilment, into acceptance.

There is another belief like that, the belief in someone else, a
relationship of two that is going to be believed into fulfilment. That
is what we are talking about in our novels, the belief of love. And
the disillusionment that the novels are full of is simply the disillusionment from disappointment in that belief. That belief can fail,
of course.

Then there is a literary belief. Every time a poem is written,
every time a short story is written, it is written not by cunning,
but by belief. The beauty, the something, the little charm of the
thing to be, is more felt than known. There is a common jest, one
that always annoys me, on the writers, that they write the last end
first, and then work up to it; that they lay a train toward one
sentence that they think is pretty nice and have all fixed up to set
like a trap to close with. No, it should not be that way at all. No
one who has ever come close to the arts has failed to see the difference between things written that way, with cunning and device,

and the kind that are believed into existence, that begin in something more felt than known. This you can realize quite as well—not quite as well, perhaps, but nearly as well—in reading as you can in writing. I would undertake to separate short stories on that principle; stories that have been believed into existence and stories that have been cunningly devised. And I could separate the poems still more easily.

Now I think—I happen to think—that those three beliefs that I speak of, the self-belief, the love-belief, and the art-belief, are all closely related to the God-belief, that the belief in God is a relationship you enter into with Him to bring about the future.

There is a national belief like that, too. One feels it. I have been where I came near getting up and walking out on the people who thought that they had to talk against nations, against nationalism, in order to curry favor with internationalism. Their metaphors are all mixed up. They think that because a Frenchman and an American and an Englishman can all sit down on the same platform and receive honors together, it must be that there is no such thing as nations. That kind of bad thinking springs from a source we all know. I should want to say to anyone like that: "Look! First I want to be a person. And I want you to be a person, and then we can be as interpersonal as you please. We can pull each other's noses—do all sorts of things. But, first of all, you have got to have the personality. First of all, you have got to have the nations and then they can be as international as they please with each other."

I should like to use another metaphor on them. I want my palette, if I am a painter, I want my palette on my thumb or on my chair, all clean, pure, separate colors. Then I will do the mixing on the canvas. The canvas is where the work of art is, where we make the conquest. But we want the nations all separate, pure, distinct, things as separate as we can make them; and then in our thoughts, in our arts, and so on, we can do what we please about it.

But I go back. There are four beliefs that I know more about from having lived with poetry. One is the personal belief, which is a knowledge that you don't want to tell other people about be-

cause you cannot prove that you know. You are saying nothing
about it till you see. The love belief, just the same, has that same
shyness. It knows it cannot tell; only the outcome can tell. And
the national belief we enter into socially with each other, all together, party of the first part, party of the second part, we enter
into that to bring the future of the country. We cannot tell some
people what it is we believe, partly, because they are too stupid
to understand and partly because we are too proudly vague to
explain. And anyway it has got to be fulfilled, and we are not
talking until we know more, until we have something to show.
And then the literary one in every work of art, not of cunning and
craft, mind you, but of real art; that believing the thing into existence, saying as you go more than you even hoped you were going to be able to say, and coming with surprise to an end that you
foreknew only with some sort of emotion. And then finally the relationship we enter into with God to believe the future in—to believe the hereafter in.

QUESTIONS

1. What does Frost mean by the term "marking"? (See both paragraphs seven and nine.) What does he mean by "enthusiasm tamed
by metaphor" (paragraph twelve)?

2. Why does Frost disclaim the metaphor of evolution? Does he think
it a poor metaphor? What does he mean when he says, "unless you
have had your proper poetical education in the metaphor, you are not
safe anywhere" (paragraph twenty-one)?

3. The ordinary connection between thinking and belief is clear
enough. Can you explain the relationship that is implicit in Frost's
discussion? (It may be helpful to reflect upon the paragraph beginning "Greatest of all attempts.") Identify the metaphors of belief.
Show that the notion of education by poetry underlies the whole of
Frost's discussion of thinking and belief.

4. Frost is addressing a college audience. Does his criticism of teachers
suggest that he is addressing teachers or students? Does his preoccupa-

tion with scientific metaphor—rather than, say, historical metaphor—suggest that he is primarily addressing scientists? (If not, you might try to explain the preoccupation on other grounds.) Do you think that the audience is conglomerate? How interested in poetry would you imagine a college audience to be?

5. What is the general relationship of the first eight paragraphs to the subject of education by poetry? In terms of the organization of materials explain why these paragraphs precede the discussion of thinking and belief. You will observe that Frost could easily have begun the essay with the ninth paragraph. Justify the presence of the first eight paragraphs in terms of a strategy with regard to his audience.

6. To what extent does Frost proceed by subject (science, etc.) in his series of examples of metaphorical thinking, from the Greek metaphor of "the All" to the Greek metaphor describing Odysseus? To the extent that he does arrange the examples according to subject, what strategy do you suppose governs his treating science at the beginning and poetry last?

7. In the earlier examples of metaphorical thinking, Frost is preoccupied, in part, with showing how metaphors break down; in the examples from Homer he is showing the value of metaphors. Where in the earlier discussion do you find acknowledgment of the value of metaphors that break down? From the strategic standpoint, why should he discuss the breakdown of metaphor first?

8. The essay divides into three or four main parts. Try to describe their ordering in terms of the organization of materials. Try to describe it in terms of a strategy. Which seems more satisfactory?

9. Examine the repetition that Frost employs in the first paragraph and in the first sentence of the second paragraph. What effects does he achieve by it? Examine the third and fourth paragraphs for similar qualities. Relate these qualities and effects to the sub-title of the essay.

10. In what differing tones of voice does Frost say, "But I like the comparison of a thing with an event" (paragraph seventeen), "It seems to me that that is simply and utterly charming" (paragraph eighteen), and "Its aim is to restore you to your ideas of free will" (paragraph nineteen)? How do you know?

11. Frost's mood in the essay is sometimes humorous, sometimes serious. Where does each mood predominate? What is the general

progression of mood in the course of the essay? In what way could it be said that the humor serves the seriousness?

12. A question for science students: What does Frost link Pythagorean doctrine to when he speaks of "number of feet, pounds, and seconds" (paragraph fifteen)? What does he mean, then, when he says, "The metaphor [number of feet, pounds, and seconds] has held and held, breaking down only when it came to . . . the out of the way places of the physical"? Why does it break down when it comes to the spiritual and psychological?

13. A question for mathematicians: Explain the fact that although Frost speaks of "four beliefs" in the final paragraph he actually mentions five.

SECTION IV

Point of View and Assumptions

Point of View and Assumptions

In its most obvious pedagogical aspect, point of view is a term that goes with comma-fault and redundancy. "Don't shift your point of view," the teacher writes in the margin opposite the "you" that has taken over from the "I" in the previous paragraph. If a writer begins an essay in the first person (In my first year in high school, I . . .), he should not shift to another person later on (Suddenly in your sophomore year you realize . . .). This is a rule with exceptions, but it remains a rule for good reasons.

Point of view is the perspective from which an author writes. In the so-called personal essay, he writes from either a real or an assumed personal viewpoint, whose visible mark is the grammatical first person ("In Moulmein, in Lower Burma, I was hated by large numbers of people," writes George Orwell). In formal writing, which attempts or pretends to be objective, the writer usually effaces himself. When Carl Becker analyzes the notion of progress (in Section 2), he removes himself from the essay grammatically. He never says, "I have been led to think," or "You will agree with me." Towards the end of the essay he does say, "If we look back a hundred years . . . ," and the reader knows that Becker is present only as an unidentified person among millions of people ("we") who can look back a hundred years.

The ideally objective piece of writing is the report of a scientific investigation. No one imagines that Newton's first law of motion reads: If you look at something that's standing still, chances are— if you don't pay too close attention—that you'll find it stays that

way unless something comes along and moves it. The recorder of
scientific fact is not a casual bystander with a piece of gum in his
mouth and dirt on his trousers. Nor is he a tall, thin man in a rum-
pled suit, with long hair, bifocal glasses, and marital problems. For
the occasion he is Anyman (a scientific fiction), the epitome of
precision, logic, and disinterestedness. If he does happen to use "I"
in his report, "I" refers to Anyman.

Does Anyman have a personality? Imagine him. Is the image less
clear than that of John Jones, who wrote, "In my first year of
high school, I . . ."? No writing can escape a point of view, a perspective. A scientific writer may strive for impersonality (Darwin
did not), but his very impersonality represents a point of view. If a
writer writes consciously, he takes one point of view or another according to his situation and intentions. Impersonality may minimize
distraction from the substance of a logical or scientific discussion.
Or it may persuade the reader that the discussion is indeed logical
or scientific (an authoritative pose that politicians and English
teachers as well as scientists and philosophers sometimes assume).
The personal point of view, in turn, may give life to the substance
of a discussion. Or it may persuade the reader of the passionate integrity of the writer. (There are, it is clear, other kinds of strategy
than that defined in the preceding section of the text.)

The grammatical person that a writer may employ, or decline to
employ, does little more than begin to define a point of view. A
teacher might ask a student to describe Times Square from three
points of view: a country boy's, a Frenchman's, and a taxi-driver's.
For each of the descriptions the student might well use either the
first or the third person singular; the individuality of the points of
view would emerge from the sort of thing that each of the hypothetical persons chose to remark upon and from his particular attitude towards it. Conjure to mind a semi-literate yokel, a cultured
Parisian, and a Damon Runyon type; or bring to mind some less
obvious representatives. In fictional writing it is customary to define
a character thus indirectly. And although in an essay the aim is usually to describe Times Square rather than to characterize a French-

man, the fact is that one cannot describe Times Square without holding some sort and some degree of point of view. The more consciously understood—and usually the more consistently held—that point of view is, the more likely the writing is to be good.

Consider the difference between the essay that begins, "The first thing I did in high school was to join the football team . . . ," and the essay that begins, "In Moulmein, in Lower Burma, I was hated by large numbers of people. . . ." The reader may find at the end of the first essay that he has a vague notion of the point of view of the boy who wrote it (hardly distinguishable from that of another boy who wrote, "The greatest experience of my first year of high school . . ."); whereas he finds at the end of the second essay that he has a clear impression of the moralistic yet dispassionate point of view that George Orwell holds towards British imperialism in Burma. The boy who writes about the first thing he did in high school need not aspire to write as well as Orwell; but if he aspires to write well as a student, he ought to clarify his point of view. Is it that of an enthusiast, a cynic, a sophisticate, a rowdy? If that point of view controls the description not only of joining the football team but also of going to the Sophomore Hop, his essay will begin to acquire consistency and may begin to acquire merit. Later the same student may attain sufficient perspective to write another essay from two points of view: that of the young man he is, looking back at his past self engaged in high school football.

Point of view is a more complex matter than it might offhand appear to be. The preceding discussion, for instance, has used the term to refer to three separate things: the actual and true outlook of a writer (the moralistic yet dispassionate point of view of George Orwell); the limited, constrained outlook that is determined by the pressure of a particular situation and intention (the impersonality that a scientific writer may strive for); and the artificial outlook that a writer constructs rhetorically (the point of view of a Frenchman adopted by a student). To what extent are these distinctions meaningful? Is it possible for a writer's point of view to be either wholly true or wholly artificial? And if the writer's point of view can be one or the other, how does a reader distinguish between them? These are unsettled and perhaps unsolvable problems. Suffice it to say that both writers and readers should be aware of them. The writer who employs irony deals in them; so does the reader who distinguishes between the integrity of George Orwell's point of view and the sham of many a politician's righteous indignation.

Suppose that a student writes an exemplary essay about his high school football days, when he was a starry-eyed youngster who idealized the coach, idolized the captain of the team, and strove to be a perfect alert, fearless, and self-reliant lineman. His point of view is clear, and something else is, too: his assumptions. He may not include in his essay his father's opinion that the battles of free enterprise are won on the football fields of Central High School. He may not feel it necessary to remark that sports builds character. These things are implicit in the self-reliance, courage, and alertness that he mentions. They are assumptions. He may have been conscious of them; then again he may not have been.

The terms point of view and assumptions are sometimes used interchangeably. To say, "He is writing from the point of view of a Republican," is probably to say, "His assumptions are those of a Republican." Point of view is the broader term; it can always be used to embrace assumptions, but it is not always embraced by the term assumptions. Point of view is commonly used to refer to a person's characteral outlook—real or assumed; it can also be used to refer to his ideational outlook. Assumptions is used to refer to his ideational outlook. According to the sort of essay that one is dealing with—a description, say, or a piece of exposition—one term or the other may be more relevant.

Assumptions is a word that people like to apply to other people's ideas. In the midst of an argument over desegregation in the schools, we realize that the opinion of our opponents is wrong-headed because it is based on assumptions rather than on fact. Our opponents either assume that Negroes are the equals of white people, or assume that they are not; they either assume that democracy means the right to discriminate, or assume that it means the obligation to tolerate. Fortunately in arguments there is opportunity to challenge assumptions; and if we can convince our opponents of the folly of their assumptions, we may then be able to proceed with the argument over desegregation in a right-headed way. In essays the opportunity to recognize and challenge—or recognize and accept—assumptions comes in a different way. The writer himself as he is writing his essay may recognize what he has assumed. He may decide that the assumption is so commonly accepted by his potential audience (that democracy is the best form of government) that he need not even take special notice of it. He may decide that the assumption is sufficiently debatable to necessitate some argument in its defense (that people will obey the dictates of reason). He may decide that the assumption requires investigation on his part before he continues writing (that the concept of race has an exact scientific as well as historical meaning). He may have to re-write the whole essay and come to a different conclusion from the one he originally intended. Regardless of what he does, the writer ultimately surrenders his essay to the reader. This surrender has its hazards. Since the reader comes from a background different from that of the writer, he will have a vantage point for recognizing assumptions that the writer was unaware of, for questioning assumptions that the writer thought would be acceptable, and for rejecting others that the writer argued briefly. Then again, he may accept the writer's assumptions, or he may be taken in by them.

The value of being able to recognize assumptions is obvious. A Northern politician should know that what he assumes when he talks about segregation to the average Northern audience will have to be argued if he goes to the South to address either white or Negro groups. More importantly, recognizing assumptions is a process by which to move from writing jejune essays to writing mature ones. If instead of "knowing" that sports builds character, the student had been aware of what he was assuming, he might then have asked himself: does sports build character? Did the captain of the

team become an egotist? Did one of the other linemen develop into
a bully? Did the coach ever recommend excessive roughing? The
answer might emerge: yes, sports builds character, but not always
enviable character. At this point the student may be ready to write
that more sophisticated essay in which he looks back—indulgently?
cynically?—upon a starry-eyed youngster.

If sports does build character (good and bad), the assumption
becomes fact. Fact implies truth, whereas assumption implies ques-
tionableness. Some assumptions may be valid, others invalid, others
radically indeterminable. What we today call an assumption may
once have been considered fact (that mankind is always progressing), and vice versa (that there are atomic particles). In the scep-
ticism that characterizes the modern world, the tendency is to believe that all assertions are assumptions that are based upon more
or less adequate evidence. One must always make the inductive leap
from evidence to inference. Does sports build good and bad character? Or is character already formed in the formative years—pre-
school? Or is it formed in the cradle? Or is it pre-fabricated in the
genes? Or is it formed in prayer? Our age is not so sceptical that the
Freudian psychologist is likely to admit that his views are as half-
baked as he thinks the sociologist's are; but it is sceptical enough
so that the reader who doesn't have a vested interest in psycho-
analysis or sociology will want to understand the assumptions about
free will and determinism that underlie both systems.

From Naples

GEORGE GISSING

Born in Wakefield, England, the son of an apothecary, George
Gissing (1857-1903) suffered much of his life from poverty
and ill health. He supported himself as he could, largely by
clerical work, tutoring, journalism, and the writing of fiction,
but not until his last years did he find relief from a life of op-
pressive drudgery. In all, he published some twenty novels,
most of them realistic studies of the very poor and the shabby
genteel; among the better known are *The Nether World,*
Demos, and *New Grub Street.* The somewhat autobiographical
Private Papers of Henry Ryecroft is cast as a series of reflections on many varied matters. What follows was written not
long before Gissing's death, of pneumonia, in Southern France.

This is the third day of sirocco, heavy-clouded, sunless. All the
colour has gone out of Naples; the streets are dusty and stifling. I
long for the mountains and the sea.

To-morrow I shall leave by the Messina boat, which calls at Paola.
It is now more than a twelve-month since I began to think of Paola,
and an image of the place has grown in my mind. I picture a little
marina; a yellowish little town just above; and behind, rising
grandly, the long range of mountains which guard the shore of
Calabria. Paola has no special interest that I know of, but it is the
nearest point on the coast to Cosenza, which has interest in abun-

From *By the Ionian Sea* by George Gissing. Reprinted by permission of Chap-
man & Hall, Ltd.

dance; by landing here I make a modestly adventurous beginning of
my ramble in the South. At Paola foreigners are rare; one may
count upon new impressions, and the journey over the hills will be
delightful.

Were I to lend ear to the people with whom I am staying, here in
the Chiatamone, I should either abandon my project altogether or
set forth with dire misgivings. They are Neapolitans of the better
class; that is to say, they have known losses, and talk of their former
happiness, when they lived on the Chiaia and had everything handsome about them. The head of the family strikes me as a typical
figure; he is an elderly man, with a fine head, a dignified presence,
and a coldly courteous demeanour. By preference he speaks French,
and his favourite subject is Paris. One observes in him something
like disdain for his own country, which in his mind is associated
only with falling fortunes and loss of self-respect. The cordial Italian
note never sounds in his talk. The *signora* (also a little ashamed of
her own language) excites herself about taxation—as well she may
—and dwells with doleful vivacity on family troubles. Both are astonished at my eccentricity and hardiness in undertaking a solitary
journey through the wild South. Their geographical notions are
vague; they have barely heard of Cosenza or of Cotrone, and of
Paola not at all; it would as soon occur to them to set out for
Morocco as for Calabria. How shall I get along with people whose
language is a barbarous dialect? Am I aware that the country is in
great part pestilential?—*la febbre!* Has no one informed me that in
autumn snows descend, and bury everything for months? It is useless to explain that I only intend to visit places easily accessible,
that I shall travel mostly by railway, and that if disagreeable
weather sets in I shall quickly return northwards. They look at me
dubiously, and ask themselves (I am sure) whether I have not some
more tangible motive than a love of classical antiquity. It ends with
a compliment to the enterprising spirit of the English race.

I have purchases to make, business to settle, and must go hither
and thither about the town. Sirocco, of course, dusks everything to
cheerless grey, but under any sky it is dispiriting to note the

changes in Naples. *Lo sventramento* (the disembowelling) goes on, and regions are transformed. It is a good thing, I suppose, that the broad Corso Umberto I. should cut a way through the old Pendino; but what a contrast between that native picturesqueness and the cosmopolitan vulgarity which has usurped its place! *"Napoli se ne va!"* I pass the Santa Lucia with downcast eyes, my memories of ten years ago striving against the dulness of to-day. The harbour, whence one used to start for Capri, is filled up; the sea has been driven to a hopeless distance beyond a wilderness of dustheaps. They are going to make a long, straight embankment from the Castel dell' Ovo to the Great Port, and before long the Santa Lucia will be an ordinary street, shut in among huge houses, with no view at all. Ah, the nights that one lingered here, watching the crimson glow upon Vesuvius, tracing the dark line of the Sorrento promontory, or waiting for moonlight to cast its magic upon floating Capri! The odours remain; the stalls of sea-fruit are as yet undisturbed, and the jars of the water-sellers; women still comb and bind each other's hair by the wayside, and meals are cooked and eaten *al fresco* as of old. But one can see these things elsewhere, and Santa Lucia was unique. It has become squalid. In the grey light of this sad billowy sky, only its ancient foulness is manifest; there needs the golden sunlight to bring out a suggestion of its ancient charm.

Has Naples grown less noisy, or does it only seem so to me? The men with bullock carts are strangely quiet; their shouts have nothing like the frequency and spirit of former days. In the narrow and thronged Strada di Chiaia I find little tumult; it used to be deafening. Ten years ago a foreigner could not walk here without being assailed by the clamour of *cocchieri;* nay, he was pursued from street to street, until the driver had spent every phrase of importunate invitation; now, one may saunter as one will, with little disturbance. Down on the Piliero, whither I have been to take my passage for Paola, I catch but an echo of the jubilant uproar which used to amaze me. Is Naples really so much quieter? If I had time I would go out to Fuorigrotta, once, it seemed to me, the noisiest village on earth, and see if there also I observed a change. It would not be surprising if the modernization of the city, together with the state of things throughout Italy, had a subduing effect upon Neapolitan manners. In one respect the streets are assuredly less gay. When I first knew Naples one was never, literally never, out of hearing of a hand-organ; and these organs, which in general had a peculiarly dulcet note, played the brightest of melodies; trivial, vulgar if you will, but none the less melodious, and dear to Naples. Now the sound of street music is rare, and I understand that some police provision long since interfered with the soft-tongued instruments. I miss them; for, in the matter of music, it is with me as with Sir Thomas Browne. For Italy the change is significant enough; in a few more years spontaneous melody will be as rare at Naples or Venice as on the banks of the Thames.

Happily, the musicians errant still strum their mandoline as you dine. The old trattoria in the Toledo is as good as ever, as bright, as comfortable. I have found my old corner in one of the little rooms, and something of the old gusto for *zuppa di vongole*. The homely wine of Posillipo smacks as in days gone by, and is commended to one's lips by a song of the South.

Last night the wind changed and the sky began to clear; this morning I awoke in sunshine, and with a feeling of eagerness for my journey. I shall look upon the Ionian Sea, not merely from a train or a steamboat as before, but at long leisure: I shall see the shores where once were Tarentum and Sybaris, Croton and Locri. Every man has his intellectual desire; mine is to escape life as I know it and dream myself into that old world which was the imaginative delight of my boyhood. The names of Greece and Italy draw me as no others; they make me young again, and restore the keen impressions of that time when every new page of Greek or Latin was a new perception of things beautiful. The world of the Greeks and Romans is my land of romance; a quotation in either language thrills me strangely, and there are passages of Greek and Latin verse which I cannot read without a dimming of the eyes, which I cannot repeat aloud because my voice fails me. In Magna Græcia the waters of two fountains mingle and flow together; how exquisite will be the draught!

I drove with my luggage to the Immacolatella, and a boatman put me on board the steamer. Luggage, I say advisedly; it is a rather heavy portmanteau, and I know it will be a nuisance. But the length of my wanderings is so uncertain, its conditions are so vaguely anticipated. I must have books if only for rainy days; I must have clothing against a change of season. At one time I thought of taking a mere wallet, and now I am half sorry that I altered my mind. But——

We were not more than an hour after time in starting. Perfect weather. I sang to myself with joy upon the sunny deck as we steamed along the Bay, past Portici, and Torre del Greco, and into the harbour of Torre Annunziata, where we had to take in cargo. I was the only cabin passenger, and solitude suits me. All through the warm and cloudless afternoon I sat looking at the mountains, trying not to see that cluster of factory chimneys which rolled black fumes above the many-coloured houses. They reminded me of the same abomination on a shore more sacred; from the harbour of Piræus one looks to Athens through trails of coal-smoke. By a contrast pleasant enough, Vesuvius to-day sent forth vapours of a delicate rose-tint, floating far and breaking seaward into soft little fleeces of cirrus. The cone, covered with sulphur, gleamed bright yellow against cloudless blue.

The voyage was resumed at dinner-time; when I came upon deck again, night had fallen. We were somewhere near Sorrento; behind us lay the long curve of faint-glimmering lights on the Naples shore; ahead was Capri. In profound gloom, though under a sky all set with stars, we passed between the island and Cape Minerva; the haven of Capri showed but a faint glimmer; over it towered mighty crags, an awful blackness, a void amid constellations. From my seat near the stern of the vessel I could discern no human form; it was as though I voyaged quite alone in the silence of this magic sea.

Silence so all-possessing that the sound of the ship's engine could not reach my ear, but was blended with the water-splash into a lulling murmur. The stillness of a dead world laid its spell on all that lived. To-day seemed an unreality, an idle impertinence; the real was that long-buried past which gave its meaning to all about me, touching the night with infinite pathos. Best of all, one's own being became lost to consciousness; the mind knew only the phantasmal forms it shaped, and was at peace in vision.

QUESTIONS

1. Gissing uses the first person singular much more often than is inevitable in a personal essay. Does he seem to use it egotistically, assertively, or modestly? (Consider the effect of changing the opening of the second paragraph to read: Tomorrow the Messina boat, which calls at Paola, leaves. It is now more than a twelve-month since a trip to Paola began to seem an inviting prospect.)

2. Characterize the contrasting outlooks of Gissing and the Neapolitan family in the third paragraph. What are the assumptions behind the objections raised by the family? Do Gissing's replies respond directly to these assumptions?

3. What seems to be Gissing's attitude towards the Neapolitan family? Is it disdainful? aloof? reserved? warm? friendly? Show that his attitude towards groups of people (on the street, in the restaurant) is similar. Show that his liking for solitude is consistent with his liking for crowds.

4. Identify the several changes that Gissing says "it is dispiriting to note" (paragraph four). From what standpoints might they not be dispiriting?

5. On what basis can Gissing at once like vulgar music (paragraph five) and dislike vulgar cosmopolitanism (paragraph four)? Frame your answer as an assumption about the way men ought to live.

6. What sort of outlook is displayed in such lines as "I pass the Santa Lucia with downcast eyes" (paragraph four), "I cannot read without a dimming of the eyes" (paragraph seven), and "Best of all, one's own being became lost to consciousness" (final paragraph)?

7. What light does the opening paragraph of the second section throw on Gissing's attitudes in the first section? Which sentences here are particularly revealing?

8. The first and last paragraphs of the second section make certain assumptions about the good life. What are they? To what extent are they qualified by other assumptions in the second paragraph in the second section?

9. What mood predominates in the essay? Go over two or three passages in which Gissing expresses radically different moods and see whether that predominant mood accompanies or underlies them.

10. On the basis of your answers to the previous questions, describe the broad preferences that Gissing displays in the essay. Are they consistent with one another? Do you know a term that is commonly used to embrace all or most of them? Frame Gissing's preferences as assumptions about the way people ought to live.

London

HENRY JAMES

James' decision to leave America for Europe was a momentous
one, and in his essays, travel books, and fiction he returned
again and again to the theme of the American in Europe, pon-
dering it from every possible point of view. *Daisy Miller* contrasts the openness of manner of an American girl with the
decorous ways of Europeanized Americans; *The American* sets
an unsophisticated American against sophisticated and sometimes corrupt Europeans; *The Ambassadors* shows the growth
in awareness, during a stay in Europe, of a middle-aged New
Englander. James himself settled in London, having found
Paris too distracting for his work, but ventured occasionally
to the Continent. He retained his American citizenship until
1915, when, in protest against America's delayed entry into the
War, he became a British subject. (Further headnote information on James appears on pp. 28, 446.)

There is a certain evening that I count as virtually a first impression
—the end of a wet, black Sunday, twenty years ago, about the first
of March. There had been an earlier vision, but it had turned gray,
like faded ink, and the occasion I speak of was a fresh beginning.
No doubt I had a mystic prescience of how fond of the murky modern Babylon I was one day to become; certain it is that as I look
back I find every small circumstance of those hours of approach and

From *Italian Hours* by Henry James. Reprinted by permission of the Houghton
Mifflin Company.

arrival still as vivid as if the solemnity of an opening era had
breathed upon it. The sense of approach was already almost intolerably strong at Liverpool, where, as I remember, the perception of
the English character of everything was as acute as a surprise,
though it could only be a surprise without a shock. It was expectation exquisitely gratified, superabundantly confirmed. There was a
kind of wonder, indeed, that England should be as English as, for
my entertainment, she took the trouble to be; but the wonder would
have been greater, and all the pleasure absent, if the sensation had
not been violent. It seems to sit there again like a visiting presence,
as it sat opposite to me at breakfast at a small table in a window of
the old coffee-room of the Adelphi Hotel—the unextended (as it
then was), the unimproved, the unblushingly local Adelphi. Liverpool is not a romantic city, but that smoky Saturday returns to me
as a supreme success, measured by its association with the kind of
emotion in the hope of which, for the most part, we betake ourselves to far countries.

It assumed this character at an early hour—or rather, indeed,
twenty-four hours before—with the sight, as one looked across the
wintry ocean, of the strange, dark, lonely freshness of the coast of
Ireland. Better still, before we could come up to the city, were the
black steamers knocking about in the yellow Mersey, under a sky so
low that they seemed to touch it with their funnels, and in the
thickest, windiest light. Spring was already in the air, in the town;
there was no rain, but there was still less sun—one wondered what
had become, on this side of the world, of the big white splotch in
the heavens; and the gray mildness, shading away into black at
every pretext, appeared in itself a promise. This was how it hung
about me, between the window and the fire, in the coffee-room of
the hotel—late in the morning for breakfast, as we had been long
disembarking. The other passengers had dispersed, knowingly
catching trains for London (we had only been a handful); I had
the place to myself, and I felt as if I had an exclusive property in
the impression. I prolonged it, I sacrificed to it, and it is perfectly recoverable now, with the very taste of the national muffin,

the creak of the waiter's shoes as he came and went (could anything be so English as his intensely professional back? it revealed a country of tradition), and the rustle of the newspaper I was too excited to read.

I continued to sacrifice for the rest of the day; it didn't seem to me a sentient thing, as yet, to inquire into the means of getting away. My curiosity must indeed have languished, for I found myself on the morrow in the slowest of Sunday trains, pottering up to London with an interruptedness which might have been tedious without the conversation of an old gentleman who shared the carriage with me and to whom my alien as well as comparatively youthful character had betrayed itself. He instructed me as to the sights of London, and impressed upon me that nothing was more worthy of my attention than the great cathedral of St. Paul. "Have you seen St. Peter's in Rome? St. Peter's is more highly embellished, you know; but you may depend upon it that St. Paul's is the better building of the two." The impression I began with speaking of was, strictly, that of the drive from Euston, after dark, to Morley's Hotel in Trafalgar Square. It was not lovely—it was in fact rather horrible; but as I move again through dusky, tortuous miles, in the greasy four-wheeler to which my luggage had compelled me to commit myself, I recognize the first step in an initiation of which the subsequent stages were to abound in pleasant things. It is a kind of humiliation in a great city not to know where you are going, and Morley's Hotel was then, to my imagination, only a vague ruddy spot in the general immensity. The immensity was the great fact, and that was a charm; the miles of housetops and viaducts, the complication of junctions and signals through which the train made its way to the station had already given me the scale. The weather had turned to wet, and we went deeper and deeper into the Sunday night. The sheep in the fields, on the way from Liverpool, had shown in their demeanor a certain consciousness of the day; but this momentous cab drive was an introduction to rigidities of custom. The low black houses were as inanimate as so many rows of coal-scuttles, save where at frequent corners, from a gin shop, there

was a flare of light more brutal still than the darkness. The custom of gin—that was equally rigid, and in this first impression the
public-houses counted for much.

Morley's Hotel proved indeed to be a ruddy spot; brilliant, in my
recollection, is the coffee-room fire, the hospitable mahogany, the
sense that in the stupendous city this, at any rate for the hour, was
a shelter and a point of view. My remembrance of the rest of the
evening—I was probably very tired—is mainly a remembrance of a
vast four-poster. My little bedroom candle, set in its deep basin,
caused this monument to project a huge shadow and to make me
think, I scarce knew why, of *The Ingoldsby Legends*. If at a tolerably early hour the next day I found myself approaching St.
Paul's, it was not wholly in obedience to the old gentleman in the
railway carriage: I had an errand in the City, and the City was
doubtless prodigious. But what I mainly recall is the romantic consciousness of passing under Temple Bar and the way two lines of
Henry Esmond repeated themselves in my mind as I drew near
the masterpiece of Sir Christopher Wren. "The stout, red-faced
woman" whom Esmond had seen tearing after the stag-hounds
over the slopes at Windsor was not a bit like the effigy "which turns
its stony back upon St. Paul's and faces the coaches struggling up
Ludgate Hill." As I looked at Queen Anne over the apron of my
hansom—she struck me as very small and dirty, and the vehicle
ascended the mild incline without an effort—it was a thrilling
thought that the statue had been familiar to the hero of the incomparable novel. All history appeared to live again, and the continuity
of things to vibrate through my mind.

To this hour, as I pass along the Strand, I take again the walk I
took there that afternoon. I love the place today, and that was the
commencement of my passion. It appeared to me to present phenomena and to contain objects of every kind, of an inexhaustible interest; in particular it struck me as desirable and even indispensable
that I should purchase most of the articles in most of the shops. My
eyes rest with a certain tenderness on the places where I resisted
and on those where I succumbed. The fragrance of Mr. Rimmel's

establishment is again in my nostrils; I see the slim young lady (I hear her pronunciation) who waited upon me there. Sacred to me today is the particular aroma of the hair wash that I bought of her. I pause before the granite portico of Exeter Hall (it was unexpectedly narrow and wedge-like), and it evokes a cloud of associations which are none the less impressive because they are vague; coming from I don't know where—from *Punch*, from Thackeray, from old volumes of the *Illustrated London News* turned over in childhood; seeming connected with Mrs. Beecher Stowe and *Uncle Tom's Cabin*. Memorable is a rush I made into a glover's at Charing Cross —the one you pass going eastward, just before you turn into the station; that, however, now that I think of it, must have been in the morning, as soon as I issued from the hotel. Keen within me was a sense of the importance of deflowering, of despoiling the shop.

A day or two later, in the afternoon, I found myself staring at my fire, in a lodging of which I had taken possession on foreseeing that I should spend some weeks in London. I had just come in, and, having attended to the distribution of my luggage, sat down to consider my habitation. It was on the ground floor, and the fading daylight reached it in a sadly damaged condition. It struck me as stuffy and unsocial, with its moldy smell and its decoration of lithographs and wax flowers—an impersonal black hole in the huge general blackness. The uproar of Piccadilly hummed away at the end of the street, and the rattle of a heartless hansom passed close to my ears. A sudden horror of the whole place came over me, like a tiger-pounce of homesickness which had been watching its moment. London was hideous, vicious, cruel, and above all overwhelming; whether or no she was "careful of the type," she was as indifferent as Nature herself to the single life. In the course of an hour I should have to go out to my dinner, which was not supplied on the premises, and that effort assumed the form of a desperate and dangerous quest. It appeared to me that I would rather remain dinnerless, would rather even starve, than sally forth into the infernal town, where the natural fate of an obscure stranger would be to be trampled to death in Piccadilly and his carcass thrown into the Thames.

I did not starve, however, and I eventually attached myself by a hundred human links to the dreadful, delightful city. That momentary vision of its smeared face and stony heart has remained memorable to me, but I am happy to say that I can easily summon up others.

QUESTIONS

1. James writes at once from the point of view of the man looking back on an experience and from the point of view of the man engaged in that experience. Which point of view predominates in the first two paragraphs? (Isolate passages that belong distinctly to one or the other.) Is there any paragraph in the essay in which the other predominates? To what extent do the two points of view blend in the essay?

2. Consider in their contexts the following phrases from the opening paragraph: "mystic prescience," "sense of approach . . . almost intolerably strong," "exquisitely gratified," "supreme success." What sort of person do they suggest? Is this person the younger James, the older James, or both?

3. What aspects of Liverpool might a newcomer notice that James ignores (for instance, the dockworkers)? What degree of interest does James show in physical conveniences, food, the customs of the country? What seems to be his predominant interest? (A consideration of the final sentences of the first two paragraphs will be helpful.)

4. How would you characterize the point of view of the old gentleman whom James meets? How does his outlook compare with that which James as a young man has displayed thus far? What in the point of view of the essay suggests why James does not describe St. Paul's later on?

5. What sort (or sorts) of judgment does the younger James pass upon the visible scene? (Consider his descriptions of the steamers on the Mersey, the houses and gin-shop on the way to the hotel, the statue of Queen Anne.) How might other people judge the same sights?

6. To what extent are past and present distinguished in the fifth paragraph? How would you characterize the treatment of point of view

here? Compare the subtlety of its use here with the subtlety of its use in the first paragraph.

7. James sees Liverpool and London with something of a painter's eye. Compare his relative interest in line, color, mass, perspective, and composition. How detailed, sensuous, picturesque, or delicate are the images he creates?

8. How surprising is the turnabout in the final paragraph? Would you say that it alters the point of view of the younger James that has prevailed thus far? In what respect might you say that it does not? What is the point of view of the last three sentences?

9. How largely does the "certain evening" (the first line in the essay) figure in the whole essay? Examine the organization of the essay in the light of James' remark about the continuity of things vibrating in his mind (paragraph four).

10. In view of your answers to the previous questions, particularly Questions 6 and 7, would you say that the point of view of the younger James is predominantly esthetic or sentimental? Or is it something else? How seriously does James take his younger self?

Porro Unum . . .

MAX BEERBOHM

Though Max Beerbohm (1872-1956) was knighted in 1939, his greatest impact as wit and satirist occurred in the two decades or so preceding the First World War. Fastidious and irreverent, his essays and drawings early established him as something of an institution—the "incomparable Max." In 1898, he succeeded George Bernard Shaw as drama critic for a notable London weekly. He resigned in 1910, when he moved to Rapallo, Italy, where he lived principally until his death. Among his better-known works are *A Christmas Garland*, a series of parodies of contemporary authors; *Zuleika Dobson*, a brilliantly ironical novel of undergraduate life at Oxford (his own university); and *The Poet's Corner*, a collection of remarkable caricatures of nineteenth-century authors.

By graceful custom, every newcomer to a throne in Europe pays a round of visits to his neighbours. When King Edward came back from seeing the Tsar at Reval, his subjects seemed to think that he had fulfilled the last demand on his civility. That was in the days of Abdul Hamid. None of us wished the King to visit Turkey. Turkey is not internationally powerful, nor had Abdul any Guelph blood in him; and so we were able to assert, by ignoring her and him, our

Reprinted from *Yet Again* by Max Beerbohm by permission of Alfred A. Knopf, Inc. Published 1951 by Alfred A. Knopf, Inc., and by permission of William Heinemann, Ltd., London.

humanitarianism and passion for liberty, quite safely, quite politely. Now that Abdul is deposed from "his infernal throne," it is taken as a matter of course that the King will visit his successor. Well, let His Majesty betake himself and his tact and a full cargo of Victorian Orders to Constantinople, by all means. But, on the way, nestling in the very heart of Europe, perfectly civilised and strifeless, jewelled all over with freedom, is another country which he has not visited since his accession—a country which, oddly enough, none but I seems to expect him to visit. Why, I ask, should Switzerland be cold-shouldered?

I admit she does not appeal to the romantic imagination. She never has, as a nation, counted for anything. Physically soaring out of sight, morally and intellectually she has lain low and said nothing. Not one idea, not one deed, has she to her credit. All that is worth knowing of her history can be set forth without compression in a few lines of a guide-book. Her one and only hero—William Tell—never, as we now know, existed. He has been proved to be a myth. Also, he is the one and only myth that Switzerland has managed to create. He exhausted her poor little stock of imagination. Living as pigmies among the blind excesses of Nature, living on sufferance there, animalculae, her sons have been overwhelmed from the outset, have had no chance whatsoever of development. Even if they had a language of their own, they would have no literature. Not one painter, not one musician, have they produced; only couriers, guides, waiters, and other parasites. A smug, tame, sly, dull, mercenary little race of men, they exist by and for the alien tripper. They are the fine flower of commercial civilisation, the shining symbol of international comity, and have never done anybody any harm. I cannot imagine why the King should not give them the incomparable advertisement of a visit.

Not that they are badly in need of advertisement over here. Every year the British trippers to Switzerland vastly outnumber the British trippers to any other land—a fact which shows how little the romantic imagination tells as against cheapness and comfort of hotels and the notion that a heart strained by climbing is good for the health. And this fact does but make our Sovereign's abstention the more remarkable. Switzerland is not "smart," but a King is not the figure-head merely of his *entourage:* he is the whole nation's figure-head. Switzerland, alone among nations, is a British institution, and King Edward ought not to snub her. That we expect him to do so without protest from us, seems to me a rather grave symptom of flunkeyism.

Fiercely resenting that imputation, you proceed to raise difficulties. "Who," you ask, "would there be to receive the King in the name of the Swiss nation?" I promptly answer, "The President of the Swiss Republic." You did not expect that. You had quite forgotten, if indeed you had ever heard, that there was any such person. For the life of you, you could not tell me his name. Well, his name is not very widely known even in Switzerland. A friend of mine, who was there lately, tells me that he asked one Swiss after another what was the name of the President, and that they all sought refuge in polite astonishment at such ignorance, and, when pressed for the name, could only screw up their eyes, snap their fingers, and feverishly declare that they had it on the tips of their tongues. This is just as it should be. In an ideal republic there should be no one whose name might not at any moment slip the memory of his fellows. Some sort of foreman there must be, for the State's convenience; but the more obscure he be, and the more automatic, the better for the ideal of equality. In the Republics of France and of America the President is of an extrusive kind. His office has been fashioned on the monarchic model, and his whole position is anomalous. He has to try to be ornamental as well as useful, a symbol as well as a pivot. Obviously, it is absurd to single out one man as a symbol of the equality of all men. And not less unreasonable is it to expect him to be inspiring as a patriotic symbol, an incarnation of his country. Only an anointed king, whose forefathers were kings too, can be that. In France, where kings have been, no one can get up the slightest pretence of emotion for the

President. If the President is modest and unassuming, and doesn't, as did the late M. Faure, make an ass of himself by behaving in a kingly manner, he is safe from ridicule: the amused smiles that follow him are not unkind. But in no case is any one proud of him. Never does any one see France in him. In America, where no kings have been, they are able to make a pretence of enthusiasm for a President. But no real chord of national sentiment is touched by this eminent gentleman who has no past or future eminence, who has been shoved forward for a space and will anon be sent packing in favour of some other upstart. Let some princeling of a foreign State set foot in America, and lo! all the inhabitants are tumbling over one another in their desire for a glimpse of him—a desire which is the natural and pathetic outcome of their unsatisfied inner craving for a dynasty of their own. Human nature being what it is, a monarchy is the best expedient, all the world over. But, given a republic, let the thing be done thoroughly, let the appearance be well kept up, as in Switzerland. Let the President be, as there, a furtive creature and insignificant, not merely coming no man knows whence, nor merely passing no man knows whither, but existing no man knows where; and existing not even as a name—except on the tip of the tongue. National dignity, as well as the republican ideal, is served better thus. Besides, it is less trying for the President.

And yet, stronger than all my sense of what is right and proper is the desire in me that the President of the Swiss Republic should, just for once, be dragged forth, blinking, from his burrow in Berne (Berne is the capital of Switzerland), into the glare of European publicity, and be driven in a landau to the railway station, there to await the King of England and kiss him on either cheek when he dismounts from the train, while the massed orchestras of all the principal hotels play our national anthem—and also a Swiss national anthem, hastily composed for the occasion. I want him to entertain the King, that evening, at a great banquet, whereat His Majesty will have the President's wife on his right hand, and will make a brief but graceful speech in the Swiss language (English,

French, German, and Italian, consecutively) referring to the glorious and never-to-be-forgotten name of William Tell (embarrassed silence), and to the vast number of his subjects who annually visit Switzerland (loud and prolonged cheers). Next morning, let there be a review of twenty thousand waiters from all parts of the country, all the head-waiters receiving a modest grade of the Victorian Order. Later in the day, let the King visit the National Gallery—a hall filled with picture post-cards of the most picturesque spots in Switzerland; and thence let him be conducted to the principal factory of cuckoo-clocks, and, after some of the clocks have been made to strike, be heard remarking to the President, with a hearty laugh, that the sound is like that of the cuckoo. How the second day of the visit would be filled up, I do not know; I leave that to the President's discretion. Before his departure to the frontier, the King will of course be made honorary manager of one of the principal hotels.

I hope to be present in Berne during these great days in the President's life. But, if anything happen to keep me here, I shall content myself with the prospect of his visit to London. I long to see him and his wife driving past, with the proper escort of Life Guards, under a vista of quadrilingual mottoes, bowing acknowledgments to us. I wonder what he is like. I picture him as a small spare man, with a slightly grizzled beard, and pleasant though shifty eyes behind a pince-nez. I picture him frock-coated, bowler-hatted, and evidently nervous. His wife I cannot at all imagine.

QUESTIONS

1. What point of view is implicit in the use of such phrases as "by graceful custom," "round of visits," "quite politely," and "cold-shouldered" (paragraph one)?

2. What attitude towards the king is expressed in the sentence "Well, let His Majesty . . ."? Distinguish it from the attitude towards Switzerland displayed in the succeeding sentence. Are the two attitudes ir-

reconcilable? Are they, individually or together, consistent with the point of view implicit in the phrases mentioned in Question 1? What shift in point of view—if any—is implied by Beerbohm's abandonment of first person plural for first person singular at the end of the paragraph?

3. Compare the values implicit in such terms as "civility," "passion for liberty," and "strifeless" (paragraph one) with the values implicit in "not one idea" and "no literature" (paragraph two). What does your answer suggest generally about point of view in the two paragraphs? On the basis of your answer define the point of view from which the writer says that the Swiss are "the fine flower of commercial civilization." What accompanying phrases in the second paragraph support your interpretation?

4. What is the central argument in the third paragraph for the propriety of a state visit? To what extent is the argument vitiated by other points made in the paragraph? What point of view emerges?

5. Discuss the effect on point of view of the presence of "you" at the beginning of the fourth paragraph and the absence of "I" in the latter part of it.

6. What assumption about human nature does the writer entertain in his phrase in the fourth paragraph, "human nature being what it is"? What are the assumed political values upon which he builds his argument in the paragraph?

7. The fifth paragraph differs from those before in lacking both argument and explicit evaluation. How, then, does it proceed? Examine some of the varying means within the paragraph by which Beerbohm establishes a point of view. (Consider "dragged forth, blinking, from his burrow," "Berne is the capital of Switzerland," "massed orchestras of all the principal hotels," "glorious . . . embarrassed.")

8. The final paragraph reverses the setting. To what effect? Why is the reversal left until the end? How well does the president embody the characteristics suggested in the fourth and fifth paragraphs? Why can't the writer imagine the wife?

9. The humor in the essay rests mainly upon the interplay between Beerbohm's assumed points of view and his presumed actual point of view that underlies them. At what point in the essay are you first aware of the discrepancy? On what basis are you able to distinguish the as-

sumed from the actual? At what points in the essay—if any—does irony disappear?

10. Relying upon your analysis in Question 9, describe what you think to be Beerbohm's own assumptions about the proper commercial, social, moral, cultural, and political conduct of man.

Audubon's Happy Land

KATHERINE ANNE PORTER

Katherine Anne Porter (1894—) was born in Indian Creek, a small town in Texas, was reared there and in Louisiana, and received her education in small convent schools. She admits to being the great-great-great-granddaughter of Daniel Boone, and to having begun writing stories as soon as she could put words to paper. Since then she has established herself as one of the most meticulous and distinguished short-story writers of her time. Her fiction, often set in the Southwest, has been collected in *Flowering Judas, Pale Horse, Pale Rider,* and *The Leaning Tower.* She has also written essays and movie scripts, and has done several translations.

The center of St. Francisville is ugly as only small towns trying frantically to provide gasoline and sandwiches to passing motorists can be, but its lane-like streets unfold almost at once into grace and goodness. On the day of our visit, the only sign of special festivity was a splendid old Negro, in top hat, frock coat with nosegay in buttonhole, a black cotton umbrella shading his venerable head, seated before the casually contrived small office where we bought our tickets for the Audubon pilgrimage and were joined by our guide. The old Negro rose, bowed, raised his hat at arm's length to an angle of forty-five degrees more or less, playing his role in the ceremonies not only as a detail of the scene, but as part also of its history. Our guide appeared in a few minutes, tying a flowered kerchief under her chin, *babushka* fashion, as she came. She was dark and thin and soft-voiced, so typically Louisiana French that we thought she must be from New Orleans, or the Bayou Teche country. It turned out that she was from Idaho, lately married to a cousin of the Percys at "Greenwood." No matter; she belonged also, by virtue of love and attachment, as well as appearance, to the scene and its history.

Saint Francis, who preached to the birds, and Audubon, who painted them as no one before or since, are both commemorated in this place. In 1779, the monks of Saint Francis founded the town and christened it. Spain ruled the territory then, though the brothers Le Moyne—Iberville and Bienville—had claimed it three-quarters of a century before for France. The Spanish government made a classical error with the classical result. It invited wealthy foreign investors to help settle the country, and the foreign investors ended by taking final possession. These particular foreigners bore such names as Ratliff, Barrow, Wade, Hamilton, Percy; they were all men of substance and of worldly mind, mostly from Virginia and the Carolinas, who obtained by Spanish grant splendid parcels of land of about twelve thousand acres each. These acres formed a subtropical jungle to the very banks of the Mississippi. A man could not, said an old woodsman, sink his hunting knife to the hilt in it anywhere.

The newcomers had on their side the strong arm of slave labor, and definite views on caste, property, morals, and manners. They pushed back the Louisiana jungle mile by mile, uncovered rich lands, and raised splendid crops. They built charming houses and filled them with furniture from France and England. Their silver and porcelain and linen were such as befitted their pride, which was high, and their tastes, which were delicate and expensive. Their daughters sang, danced, and played the harpsichord; their

sons played the flute and fought duels; they collected libraries,
they hunted and played chess, and spent the winter season in New
Orleans. They traveled much in Europe, and brought back always
more and more Old World plunder. Everywhere, with ceaseless,
intensely personal concern, they thought, talked, and played politics.

In a few short years, these wealthy, nostalgic Americans were, in
the phrase of the day, "groaning under the galling yoke of Spain."
They forgathered evening after evening in one or another of their
mansions and groaned; that is to say, discussed the matter with
shrewdness, realism, and a keen eye to the possibilities. They called
upon President Madison to lend a hand in taking this territory
from Spain, which continued to hold it for some reason long after
the Louisiana Purchase. "President Madison," says a local historian
of that day, "remained deaf to their cries." The Feliciana planters
then stopped crying, organized a small army, and marched on the
Spanish capital, Baton Rouge. Harsh as it sounds in such a gentle-
manly sort of argument, they caused the Spanish Commandant to
be killed as proof of the seriousness of their intentions. They then
declared for themselves the Independent Republic of West Florida,
with St. Francisville as its capital. A certain Mr. Fulwar Skipwith
was elected President. All was done in form, with a Constitution, a
Body of Laws, and a flag designed for the occasion. The strategy
was a brilliant success. President Madison sent friendly troops to
annex the infant republic to the United States of America. This
Graustarkian event took place in 1810.

The next year, a Roosevelt (Nicholas), partner in an Eastern
steamship company, sent the first steamboat into the Mississippi,
straight past St. Francisville and her sister town, Bayou Sara. The
days of opulence and glory began in earnest, based solidly on land,
money crops, and transportation, to flourish for just half a century.

It is quite finished as to opulence, and the glory is now a gentle
aura, radiating not so much from the past as from the present, for
St. Francisville lives with graceful competence on stored wealth
that is not merely tangible. The legend has, in fact, magnified the

opulence into something more than it really was, to the infinite damage of a particular truth: that wealth in the pre-War South was very modest by present standards, and it was not ostentatious, even then. The important thing to know about St. Francisville, as perhaps a typical survivor of that culture, is this: no one there tells you about steamboat wealth, or wears the air of poverty living on its memories, or (and this is the constant, rather tiresome accusation of busy, hasty observers) "yearns for the good old days."

The town's most treasured inhabitant was Aubudon, and its happiest memory. This is no afterthought, based on his later reputation. And it is the more interesting when we consider what kind of reputation Audubon's was, almost to the end; nothing at all that a really materialistic society would take seriously. He was an artist, but not a fashionable one, never successful by any worldly standards; but the people of St. Francisville loved him, recognized him, took him to themselves when he was unknown and almost in despair. And now in every house, they will show you some small souvenir of him, some record that he was once a guest there. The Pirries, of New Orleans and Oakley, near St. Francisville, captured him in New Orleans at the moment when he was heading East, disheartened, and brought him to Oakley for the pleasant employment of teaching their young daughter, Miss Eliza, to dance and draw, of mornings. His afternoons, and some of his evenings, he spent in the Feliciana woods, and we know what he found there.

The Feliciana country is not a jungle now, nor has it been for a great while. The modest, occasional rises of earth, called hills, are covered with civilized little woods, fenced grazing-fields for fine cattle, thatches of sugar cane, of corn, and orchards. Both Felicianas, east and west, are so handsome and amiable you might mistake them for one, instead of twins. For fear they will be confounded in the stranger's eye, the boundaries are marked plainly along the highway. The difference was to me that West Feliciana was holding a spring festival in honor of Audubon, and I, a returned Southerner, in effect a tourist, went straight through East Feliciana, which had not invited visitors, to West Feliciana, which had.

You are to think of this landscape as an April garden, flowering with trees and shrubs of the elegant, difficult kind that live so securely in this climate: camellias, gardenias, crêpe myrtle, fine old-fashioned roses; with simpler things, honeysuckle, dogwood, wisteria, magnolia, bridal-wreath, oleander, redbud, leaving no fence or corner bare. The birds of Saint Francis and of Audubon fill the air with their light singing and their undisturbed flight. The great, dark oaks spread their immense branches fronded with moss; the camphor and cedar trees add their graceful shapes and their dry, spicy odors; and yes, just as you have been told, perhaps too often, there are the white, pillared houses seated in dignity, glimpsed first at a distance through their park-like gardens.

The celebrated oak *allées* are there at "Live Oak," at "Waverly," at "Rosedown," perhaps the finest grove of all at "Highland"—the wide, shaded driveways from the gate to the great door, all so appropriately designed for the ritual events of life, a wedding or a funeral procession, the christening party, the evening walks of betrothed lovers. W. B. Yeats causes one of his characters to reflect, in face of a grove of ancient trees, "that a man who planted trees, knowing that no descendant nearer than his great-grandson could stand under their shade, had a noble and generous confidence." That kind of confidence created this landscape, now as famous, as banal, if you like, as the horse-chestnuts along the Champs Elysées, as the perfume gardens of Grasse, as the canals of Venice, as the lilies-of-the-valley in the forest of Saint-Cloud. It possesses, too, the appeal of those much-visited scenes, and shares their nature, which is to demand nothing by way of arranged tribute; each new-comer may discover it for himself; but this landscape shares its peculiar treasure only with such as know there is something more here than mere hungry human pride in mahogany staircases and silver doorknobs. The real spirit of the place planted those oaks, and keeps them standing.

The first thing that might strike you is the simplicity, the comparative smallness of even the largest houses (in plain figures, "Greenwood" is one hundred feet square; there is a veranda one hundred and ten feet long at "The Myrtles," a long, narrow house), compared not only to the grandeur of their legend, but to anything of corresponding fame you may have seen, such as the princely houses of Florence or the Spanish palaces in Mexico, or, as a last resort, the Fifth Avenue museums of the fantastically rich of two or three generations ago. Their importance is of another kind—that of the oldest New York houses, or the Patrizieren houses in Basel; with a quality nearly akin to the Amalienburg in the forest near Munich, quite the loveliest house I ever saw, or expect to see. These St. Francisville houses are examples of pure domestic architecture, somehow urban in style, graceful, and differing from city houses in this particular, that they sit in landscapes designed to show them off; they are meant to be observed from every point of view. No two of them are alike, but they were all built to be lived in, by people who had a completely aristocratic sense of the house as a dwelling-place.

They are ample and their subtle proportions give them stateliness not accounted for in terms of actual size. They are placed in relation to the south wind and the morning sun. Their ceilings are high, because high ceilings are right for this kind of architecture, and this kind of architecture is right for a hot climate. Their fireplaces are beautiful, well placed, in harmony with the rooms, and meant for fine log fires in the brief winters. Their windows are many, tall and rightly spaced for light and air, as well as for the view outward. All of them, from "Live Oak," built in 1779, to "The Myrtles," built in the 1840's, have in common the beauty and stability of cypress, blue poplar, apparently indestructible brick made especially for the chimneys and foundations, old methods of mortising and pinning, hand-forged nails.

"Live Oak" stands on a green knoll, and, from the front door, one looks straight through the central room to the rolling meadow bordered with iris in profuse bloom. This house is really tired, worn down to the bare grain, the furniture just what might have been left from some remote disaster, but it is beautiful, a place to live in, with its wide, double porches and outside staircase in the early style of the Spanish in Louisiana, its dark paneling, and its air of gentle remoteness.

"Waverly" is another sort of thing altogether, a bright place full of color, where the old furniture is set off with gaily flowered rugs, and the heavy old Louisiana four-poster beds—of a kind to be found nowhere else—are dressed sprucely in fresh curtains. The white pillars of "Waverly" are flat and slender, and the graceful fan-lights of the front door are repeated on the second floor, with an especially airy effect. The vestiges of the old boxwood maze are being coaxed back to life there, and gardenias grow in hedges, as they should.

At "The Myrtles," the flowery iron grille of the long veranda sets the Victorian tone; the long dining-room still wears, between the thin moldings, its French wallpaper from 1840—sepia-colored panels from floor to ceiling of game birds and flowers. The cypress floor is honey-colored, the Italian marble mantelpiece was that day banked with branches of white dogwood. All the rooms are long, full of the softest light lying upon the smooth surfaces of old fruit-wood and mahogany. From the back veranda, an old-fashioned back yard, full of country living, lay in the solid shade of grape arbors and trees rounded like baskets of flowers. Chickens roamed and picked there; there was a wood-pile with a great iron wash-pot up-ended against it, near the charred spot where the fire is still built to heat the water.

At "Virginia," we saw George Washington's account-book, made, I believe, at Valley Forge, with all the detailed outlay of that troublesome episode. "Virginia" is by way of being an inn now—

that is to say, if travelers happen along they will be put up in tall, canopied beds under fine old quilted coverlets. The large silver spoons in the dining-room came from an ancestor of the Fisher family—Baron de Würmser, who had them as a gift from Frederick the Great. Generous-sized ladles they are, too, paper-thin and flexible. Like so many old coin silver spoons, they appear to have been chewed, and they have been. A thin silver spoon was once considered the ideal object for an infant to cut his teeth upon. But there were dents in a de Würmser soup ladle which testified that some Fisher infant must have been a saber-toothed tiger. "Surely no teething child did that," I remarked. "No," said the hostess, a fleeting shade of severity on her brow. "It was thrown out with the dish-water once, and the pigs got it." Here is the French passport for a Fisher grandfather, dated 1836. It was then he brought back the splendid flowered wallpaper, even now fresh in its discreet colors, the hand-painted mauve linen window-shades on rollers, then so fashionable, replacing the outmoded Venetian blinds; the ornate, almost morbidly feminine drawing-room chairs and sofas.

At "Greenwood," the host was engaged with a group of oil prospectors, for, beneath their charming, fruitful surfaces, the Felicianas are suspected of containing the dark, the sinister new treasure more powerful than gold. If so, what will become of the oaks and the flourishing fields and the gentle cattle? What will become of these lovely houses? "They make syrup and breed cattle here," said our guide; "that keeps 'Greenwood' going very well. Some people (she named them) wanted Mr. Percy to make a dude ranch of this place, but he wouldn't hear of it."

We mentioned our premonitions about St. Francisville if oil should be discovered. Our guide spoke up with the quiet recklessness of faith. "It wouldn't do any harm," she said. "The Feliciana people have had what money can buy, and they have something money can't buy, and they know it. They have nothing to sell. Tourists come here from all over and offer them thousands of dollars for their little things, just little things they don't need and hardly ever look at, but they won't sell them."

"Greenwood" is the typical Southern mansion of too many songs, too many stories—with the extravagant height of massive, round pillar, the too-high ceiling, the gleaming sweep of central hall, all in the 1830 Greek, gilded somewhat, but lightly. There is bareness; space dwarfing the human stature and breathing a faint bleakness. Yet the gentle groves and small hills are framed with overwhelming effect between those columns; effect grandiose beyond what the measuring eye knows is actually there.

It seems now that the builders should have known that this house was the end, never the beginning. It is quite improbable that anyone should again build a house like "Greenwood" to live in. But there it is, with the huge beams of the gallery being replaced, oil prospectors roaming about, and the hostess sitting in her drawing-room with the green-and-gold chairs, the lace curtains fine as bride veils drifting a little; the young girls in jodhpurs are going out to ride. Here, as everywhere else, there were no radios or gramophones going, no telephones visible or ringing; and it seemd to me suddenly that this silence, the silence of a house in order, of people at home, the silence of leisure, is the most desirable of all things we have lost.

At "Highland," descendants in the fourth generation stand in the shade of the oaks planted, as the old House Book records, in January 1832. The house is older. It has its share of drum tables, fiddle-backed chairs, carved door-frames and wainscoting, but its real beauty lies in the fall of light into the ample, square rooms, the rise of the stair tread, the energy and firmness of its structure. The paneled doors swing on their hand-forged hinges as they did the day they were hung there; the edge of the first doorstep—an immense log of cypress square-hewn—is as sharp as though feet had not stepped back and forth over it for one hundred and forty years.

"Rosedown" is more formal, with its fish pool and eighteenth-century statuary set along the *allée,* and in a semicircle before the conventionally planted garden. The office still stands there, and the "slave bell" in its low wooden frame. The "slave bell" was the dinner-bell for the whole plantation. Above all, at "Rosedown," the Ancestors still rule, still lend their unquenchable life to a little world of fabulous old ladies and a strange overgrowth of knick-knacks sprouting like small, harmless fungi on a tree-trunk. Their portraits—Sully seems to have been the preferred painter—smile at you, or turn their attentive heads toward one another; as hand-some and as gallant and elegantly dressed a set of young men and women as you would be apt to find blood-kin under one roof. "My great-great-grandfather," said the old, old lady, smiling back again at the high-headed, smooth-cheeked young beau in the frilled shirt-bosom and deep blue, sloping-shouldered coat. His eyes are the same bright hazel as her own. This was the only house in which the past lay like a fine dust in the air.

Steamboats brought wealth and change to St. Francisville once, and oil may do it again. In that case, we are to suppose that new grand pianos would replace the old, square, black Steinways of 1840, as they had in turn replaced the harpsichords. There would be a great deal of shoring up, replacement, planting, pruning, and adding. There would be travel again, and humanistic education. The young people who went away cannot, alas, come back young, but the young there now would not have to go away.

And what else would happen to this place, so occupied, so self-sufficient, so reassuringly solid and breathing? St. Francisville is not a monument, nor a *décor*, nor a wailing-wall for mourners for the past. It is a living town, moving at its own pace in a familiar world. But it was comforting to take a last glance backward as we turned into the main highway, at Audubon's Happy Land, reflecting that, for the present, in the whole place, if you except the fruits of the earth and the picture postcards at "Rosedown," there was nothing, really nothing, for sale.

QUESTIONS

1. At what point in the first paragraph does Miss Porter first make her presence felt? What details in the first paragraph suggest a woman's point of view rather than a man's?

2. What contributions do the following phrases make towards establishing Miss Porter's point of view: "the constant, rather tiresome accusation of busy, hasty observers" (paragraph six), "I, a returned Southerner" (paragraph eight), and "this landscape shares its peculiar treasure only with such as know . . ." (paragraph ten)?

3. Miss Porter does not often refer to herself in the first person. Occasionally she identifies herself as one of a group ("On the day of our visit"). More often she refers to herself as "you." Insofar as "you" might also be taken to refer to any visitor to the mansions and to the reader of the essay, her use of it has particular consequences in establishing a point of view. Consider what these consequences are in the paragraph beginning "You are to think of this landscape."

4. Miss Porter expresses no direct opinion about the "newcomers" in the third paragraph, but the stylistic self-consciousness of that paragraph (the repetitions and the juxtapositions) suggests an opinion. What is it?

5. What is Miss Porter's point of view towards the events that she describes in the fourth paragraph? Consider the following elements: irony, direct judgment, and rapidity of narration.

6. What sort of judgment is Miss Porter making in paragraph seven when she says Audubon would not have been taken seriously in a materialistic society? What is she assuming about the tastes of such a society? What does her statement of Audubon's acceptance in St. Francisville imply about its tastes?

7. Miss Porter says in the eleventh paragraph that the mansions are "to be observed from every point of view," but she observes them from a particular one. What architectural standards are implicit in such phrases as "subtle proportions," "right for a hot climate," and "harmony" (paragraph twelve)? What values attach to such phrases as "fine log fires," "indestructible brick," and "old methods of mortising" (paragraph twelve)? Show that the same standards apply to Miss Porter's descriptions

of "Waverly" and "Greenwood." Do you know of any esthetic, social, or economic standards upon which one might condemn Southern mansions?

8. In the last paragraph, Miss Porter says that "St. Francisville is not a monument, nor a *décor*, nor a wailing-wall for mourners for the past." In what sense does this assertion imply a judgment? To what extent does that judgment govern her attitudes towards the different mansions? (Consider especially "Live Oak," "Greenwood," and "Rosedown.")

9. On what basis does Miss Porter speak of "the sinister new treasure" (in the paragraph beginning "At 'Greenwood' ")? Is her viewpoint consistent with that which she holds towards the "wealthy, nostalgic Americans" of the fourth paragraph? Is it consistent with her image of the future in the next to last paragraph?

10. Would you say that Miss Porter's attachment to St. Francisville is reserved or enthusiastic? Would you say that her sentimentalism is abundant or restrained? Would you say that her point of view in these respects is consistent with her values as they have been seen in the previous questions?

Impressions of Japan

WILLIAM FAULKNER

William Faulkner (1897—) is generally acknowledged the greatest living American novelist. Born near Oxford, Mississippi, he has passed most of his life there, and to good purpose, drawing on its history and traditions in creating his mythical Yoknapatawpha County, the setting of much of his fiction—*The Sound and the Fury, Light in August, The Hamlet*. Though he restricts his scene, and by his subject-matter encourages a sociological interest in his work, his concern is ultimately with—in his own words—the "human heart in conflict with itself," the "old universal truths lacking which any story is ephemeral and doomed—love and honor and pity and pride and compassion and sacrifice." In 1951 he received the Nobel Prize. In 1955 he visited Japan under the auspices of the State Department, and at that time wrote the prose reprinted below.

The engines are long since throttled back; the overcast sinks slowly upward with no semblance whatever of speed until suddenly you see the aircraft's shadow scudding the cottony hillocks; and now speed has returned again, aircraft and shadow now rushing toward one another as toward one mutual headlong destruction.

To break through the overcast and fling that shadow once more down, upon an island. It looks like land, like any other air-found landfall, yet you know it is an island, almost as if you saw both sea-bound flanks of it at the same instant, like a transparent slide; an island more miraculously found in the waste of water than Wake or Guam even, since here is a civilization, an ordered and ancient homogeny of the human race.

It is visible and audible, spoken and written too: a communication between man and man because human speaks it; you hear and see them. But to this one western ear and eye it means nothing because it resembles nothing which that western eye remembers; there is nothing to measure it against, nothing for memory and habit to say, "Why this looks like the word for house or home or happiness"; not even just cryptic but acrostic too, as though the splashed symbols of the characters held not mere communication but something urgent and important beyond just information, promising toward some ultimate wisdom or knowledge containing the secret of man's salvation. But then no more, because there is nothing for western memory to measure it against; so not the mind to listen but only the ear to hear that chirrup and skitter of syllables like the cries of birds in the mouths of children, like music in the mouths of women and young girls.

The faces: Van Gogh and Manet would have loved them: that of the pilgrim with staff and pack and dusty with walking, mounting the stairs toward the Temple in the early sunlight; the Temple lay-brother or perhaps servant, his gown tucked about his thighs, squatting in the gate of the compound before beginning, or perhaps having already set it into motion, the day; that of the old woman vending peanuts beneath the gate for tourists to feed the pigeons with: a face worn with living and remembering, as though not one life had been long enough but rather every separate breath had been needed to etch into it all those fine and myriad lines; a face durable and now even a comfort to her, as if it had by now blotted up whatever had ever ached or sorrowed behind it, leaving it free now of the anguishes and the griefs and the enduring: here is one anyway who never read Faulkner and neither knows nor cares why he came to Japan nor gives one single damn what he thinks of Ernest Hemingway.

He is much too busy to have time to bother about whether he is happy or not, quite dirty, perhaps five years old, pastless and apparently immune even from parents, playing in the gutter with the stub of a cigarette.

The bowl of mountains containing the lake is as full of hard rapid air as the mouth of a wind-tunnel; for some time now we have been thinking that maybe it is already too late to take a reef in the mainsail: yet there it is. It is only a skiff yet to the western eye it is as invincibly and irrevocably alien as a Chinese junk, driven by a battered U.S. made outboard engine and containing a woman in a kimono beneath an open paper parasol such as would have excited no comment in a sunny reach of the English Thames, as fragile and invulnerable in the center of that hard blue bowl of wind as a butterfly in the eye of a typhoon.

The geisha's mass of blueblack lacquered hair encloses the painted face like a helmet, surmounts, crowns the slender body's ordered and ritual posturing like a grenadier's bearskin busby, too heavy in appearance for that slender throat to bear, the painted fixed expressionless face immobile and immune also above the studied posturing: yet behind that painted and lifeless mask is something quick and alive and elfin: or more than elfin: puckish: or more than puckish even: sardonic and quizzical, a gift for comedy, and more: for burlesque and caricature: for a sly and vicious revenge on the race of men.

Kimono. It covers her from throat to ankles; with a gesture as feminine as the placing of a flower or as female as the cradling of a child, the hands themselves can be concealed into the sleeves until there remains one unbroken chalice-shape of modesty proclaiming her femininity where nudity would merely parade her mammalian femaleness. A modesty which flaunts its own immodestness like the crimson rose tossed by no more than one white flick of hand, from the balcony window—modesty, than which there is nothing

more immodest and which therefore is a woman's dearest possession; she should defend it with her life.

Loyalty. In her western clothes, blouse and skirt, she is merely
one dumpy and nondescript young woman though in kimono at the
deft balanced rapid tripping glide she too comes into her own share
of that national heritage of feminine magic. Though she has more
than that; she partakes of her share of that other quality which
women have in this land which was not given them by what they
have on: loyalty, constancy, fidelity, not for, but at least one hopes
not without, reward. She does not speak my language nor I hers, yet
in two days she knows my countryman's habit of waking soon after
first light so that each morning when I open my eyes a coffee tray
is already on the balcony table; she knows I like a fresh room to
breakfast in when I return from walking, and it is so: the room done
for the day and the table set and the morning paper ready; she
asks without words why I have no clothes to be laundered today,
and without words asks permission to sew the buttons and darn the
socks; she calls me wise man and teacher, who am neither, when
speaking of me to others; she is proud to have me for her client and,
I hope, pleased that I try to deserve that pride and match with
courtesy that loyalty. There is a lot of loose loyalty in this land.
Even a little of it is too valuable to be ignored. I would wish that
all of it were deserved or at least appreciated as I have tried to do.

This is the same rice paddy which I know back home in Arkansas
and Mississippi and Louisiana, where it replaces now and then the
cotton. This one is merely a little smaller and a little more fiercely
cultivated, right up to the single row of beans which line the very
edge of the irrigation canals, the work here done by hand where in
my country machines do it since we have more machines than we
have people; nature is the same: only the economy is different.

And the names are the same names too: Jonathan and Winesap
and Delicious; the heavy August foliage is blue gray with the same
spray which we use. But there the resemblance ceases: every single
apple enclosed in this twist of paper until that whole tree to this

western eye becomes significant and festive and ceremonial like the symbolical tree of the western rite of Christmas. Only it is more significant here: where in the West there is one small often artificial tree to a family, wrested from the living dirt to be decked in ritual tinsel and then to die as though the tree were not the protagonist of a rite but the victim of a sacrifice, here not one tree to a family but every tree of all is dressed and decked to proclaim and salute older gods than Christ: Demeter and Ceres.

Briefer and faster now, toward the journey's nearing end: goldenrod, as evocative of dust and autumn and hay fever as ever in Mississippi, against a tall bamboo fence.

The scenery is beautiful but the faces are better still.

The swift supple narrow grace with which the young girl bows and in that same one glowing motion recovers, tougher through very tenderness than the rigid culture which bent her as is the willow bough itself to the hard gust which can never do more than sway it.

The tools they use evoke the ones Noah must have built his ark with, yet the framework of the house seems to rise and stand without nails in the fitted joints nor even the need for nails, as if here were a magic, an art in the simple building of man's habitations which our western ancestors seemed to have lost somewhere when they moved.

And always the water, the sound, the plash and drip of it, as if here were a people making constant oblation to water as some peoples do to what they call their luck.

So kind the people that with three words the guest can go anywhere and live: Gohan; Sake: Arrigato. And one more word:

Tomorrow now the aircraft lightens, a moment more and the wheels will wrench free of the ground, already dragging its shadow back toward the overcast before the wheels are even tucked up, into the overcast and then through it, the land, the island gone now which memory will always know though eye no longer remembers. Sayonara.

QUESTIONS

1. Try to relate the physical perspective upon Japan in the first two paragraphs to the mental outlook of the third paragraph and to the general outlook that pervades the essay. At what points does Faulkner resume a comparable physical perspective?

2. In what different respects is Faulkner interested in the two men and the woman in the fourth paragraph? His reference to the painters Van Gogh and Manet might seem to suggest that his interests are esthetic. Are they? At what points in the first six paragraphs would you say Faulkner's interests are most explicitly esthetic? How close does he seem to be to the people he describes in these paragraphs?

3. Is Faulkner's judgment upon the geisha in the seventh paragraph moral? Is it esthetic? Does he disapprove more of the outward woman or the inward? What assumed values underlie his judgment?

4. What are the distinctions between feminine and female that Faulkner makes in the eighth paragraph? What assumptions about women underlie the distinctions? Would you say that Faulkner is judging appearance versus reality here on the same basis that he judges them in the preceding paragraph? What about his judgment in the succeeding paragraph?

5. What aspects of rice paddies does Faulkner ignore that someone else might be preoccupied with? What is his broad interest in them? In what way might it be said that his interest in the rice paddies is consistent with, perhaps the same as, his interest in the little boy in the fifth paragraph?

6. What are the three or four assumed standards by which Faulkner passes judgment against the West in the paragraph beginning "And the names"? To what extent generally in the essay does he seem to praise Japan at the expense of the West? In what respect is he most critical of Japan? Where is he impartial in discussing Japan and the West? (In answering the three preceding questions, state as explicitly as possible Faulkner's assumed standards or values.)

7. The interests of another visitor to Japan might well have been predominantly philosophical, sociological, or cultural. What is Faulkner's predominant interest? Explain how it applies to paragraphs four through seven.

8. Analyze the development of Faulkner's references to himself. Would you say that the changes make for inconsistency in point of view? What modification in point of view might have resulted had he used one or another of the forms of reference consistently?

9. Examine the essay for its reliance upon contrast and paradox (for example, "no semblance whatever of speed . . . and now speed has returned," "it looks like land . . . yet"). How sharp or subtle do the contrasts and paradoxes seem? What do they suggest about a point of view?

10. Examine the seventh paragraph for its syntax, rhythm, and movement of thought. What effect does Faulkner achieve by making the paragraph a single sentence? Express the effect as point of view.

The Dance

D. H. LAWRENCE

Born and brought up in an ugly little mining village, Lawrence early witnessed the dehumanizing effects of industrial-
ism, and much of his later effort was spent in battle against
the conditions he found characteristic of modern industrial
existence—mechanization, thwarting of the self, distortion of
the human affections. The battle he pursued in a variety of
literary forms: poetry, novels (*Women in Love, Lady Chatter-
ley's Lover*), short stories, and essays. The ethos underlying
his work is perhaps best suggested by his own words, "My
great religion is a belief in the blood, the flesh, as being wiser
than the intellect." Lawrence's literary friendships, at once
intimate and stormy, included those with Aldous Huxley, Bertrand Russell, and Katherine Mansfield. (Further headnote information on Lawrence appears on pp. 33, 413.)

Maria had no real licence for San Gaudenzio, yet the peasants always called for wine. It is easy to arrange in Italy. The penny is paid
another time.

The wild old road that skirts the lake-side, scrambling always
higher as the precipice becomes steeper, climbing and winding to
the villages perched high up, passes under the high boundary-wall
of San Gaudenzio, between that and the ruined church. But the

From *Twilight in Italy* by D. H. Lawrence. Reprinted by permission of The
Viking Press, Inc., Laurence Pollinger, Ltd., and the Estate of the late Mrs.
Frieda Lawrence.

road went just as much between the vines and past the house as outside, under the wall; for the high gates were always open, and men or women and mules come into the property to call at the door of the homestead. There was a loud shout, "Ah—a—a—ah—Mari—'a. O—O—Oh Pa'o'!" from outside, another wild, inarticulate cry from within, and one of the Fiori appeared in the doorway to hail the newcomer.

It was usually a man, sometimes a peasant from Mugiano, high up, sometimes a peasant from the wilds of the mountain, a wood-cutter, or a charcoal-burner. He came in and sat in the house-place, his glass of wine in his hand between his knees, or on the floor between his feet, and he talked in a few wild phrases, very shy, like a hawk indoors, and unintelligible in his dialect.

Sometimes we had a dance. Then, for the wine to drink, three men came with mandolins and guitars, and sat in a corner playing their rapid tunes, while all danced on the dusty brick floor of the little parlour. No strange women were invited, only men; the young bloods from the big village on the lake, the wild men from above. They danced the slow, trailing, lilting polka-waltz round and round the small room, the guitars and mandolins twanging rapidly, the dust rising from the soft bricks. There were only the two English-women: so men danced with men, as the Italians love to do. They love even better to dance with men, with a dear blood-friend, than with women.

"It's better like this, two men?" Giovanni says to me, his blue eyes hot, his face curiously tender.

The wood-cutters and peasants take off their coats, their throats are bare. They dance with strange intentness, particularly if they have for partner an English Signora. Their feet in thick boots are curiously swift and significant. And it is strange to see the English-women, as they dance with the peasants, transfigured with a kind of brilliant surprise. All the while the peasants are very courteous, but quiet. They see the women dilate and flash, they think they have found a footing, they are certain. So the male dancers are quiet, but even grandiloquent, their feet nimble, their bodies wild and confident.

They are at a loss when the two English Signoras move together and laugh excitedly at the end of the dance.

"Isn't it fine?"

"Fine! Their arms are like iron, carrying you round."

"Yes! Yes! And the muscles on their shoulders! I never knew there were such muscles! I'm almost frightened."

"But it's fine, isn't it? I'm getting into the dance."

"Yes—yes—you've only to let them take you."

Then the glasses are put down, the guitars give their strange, vibrant, almost painful summons, and the dance begins again.

It is a strange dance, strange and lilting, and changing as the music changed. But it had always a kind of leisurely dignity, a trail·ing kind of polka-waltz, intimate, passionate, yet never hurried, never violent in its passion, always becoming more intense. The women's faces changed to a kind of transported wonder, they were in the very rhythm of delight. From the soft bricks of the floor the red ochre rose in a thin cloud of dust, making hazy the shadowy dancers; the three musicians, in their black hats and their cloaks, sat obscurely in the corner, making a music that came quicker and quicker, making a dance that grew swifter and more intense, more subtle, the men seeming to fly and to implicate other strange inter-rhythmic dance into the women, the women drifting and palpitating as if their souls shook and resounded to a breeze that was subtly rushing upon them, through them; the men worked their feet, their thighs swifter, more vividly, the music came to an almost intolerable climax, there was a moment when the dance passed into a possession, the men caught up the women and swung them from the earth, leapt with them for a second, and then the next phase of the dance had begun, slower again, more subtly interwoven, taking perfect, oh, exquisite delight in every interrelated movement, a rhythm within a rhythm, a subtle approaching and drawing nearer to a climax, nearer, till, oh, there was the surpassing lift and swing of the women, when the woman's body seemed like a boat lifted over the powerful, exquisite wave of the man's body, perfect, for a moment, and then once more the slow, intense, nearer movement of the dance began, always nearer, nearer, always to a more perfect climax.

And the women waited as if in transport for the climax, when they would be flung into a movement surpassing all movement. They were flung, borne away, lifted like a boat on a supreme wave, into the zenith and nave of the heavens, consummate.

Then suddenly the dance crashed to an end, and the dancers stood stranded, lost, bewildered, on a strange shore. The air was full of red dust, half-lit by the lamp on the wall; the players in the corner were putting down their instruments to take up their glasses.

And the dancers sat round the wall, crowding in the little room, faint with the transport of repeated ecstasy. There was a subtle smile on the face of the men, subtle, knowing, so finely sensual that the conscious eyes could scarcely look at it. And the women were dazed, like creatures dazzled by too much light. The light was still on their faces, like a blindness, a reeling, like a transfiguration. The men were bringing wine, on a little tin tray, leaning with their proud, vivid loins, their faces flickering with the same subtle smile. Meanwhile, Maria Fiori was splashing water, much water, on the red floor. There was the smell of water among the glowing, transfigured men and women who sat gleaming in another world, round the walls.

The peasants have chosen their women. For the dark, handsome Englishwoman, who looks like a slightly malignant Madonna, comes Il Duro; for the "bella bionda," the wood-cutter. But the peasants have always to take their turn after the young well-to-do men from the village below.

Nevertheless, they are confident. They cannot understand the middle-class diffidence of the young men who wear collars and ties and finger-rings.

The wood-cutter from the mountain is of medium height, dark, thin, and hard as a hatchet, with eyes that are black like the very flaming thrust of night. He is quite a savage. There is something strange about his dancing, the violent way he works one shoulder. He has a wooden leg, from the knee-joint. Yet he dances well, and is inordinately proud. He is fierce as a bird, and hard with energy as a thunderbolt. He will dance with the blonde Signora. But he never speaks. He is like some violent natural phenomenon rather than a person. The woman begins to wilt a little in his possession.

"È bello—il ballo?" he asks at length, one direct, flashing question.

"Si—molto bello," cries the woman, glad to have speech again.

The eyes of the wood-cutter flash like actual possession. He seems now to have come into his own. With all his senses, he is dominant, sure.

He is inconceivably vigorous in body, and his dancing is almost perfect, with a little catch in it, owing to his lameness, which brings almost a pure intoxication. Every muscle in his body is supple as steel, supple, as strong as thunder, and yet so quick, so delicately swift, it is almost unbearable. As he draws near to the swing, the climax, the ecstasy, he seems to lie in wait, there is a sense of a great strength crouching ready. Then it rushes forth, liquid, perfect, transcendent, the woman swoons over in the dance, and it goes on, enjoyment, infinite, incalculable enjoyment. He is like a god, a strange natural phenomenon, most intimate and compelling, wonderful.

But he is not a human being. The woman, somewhere shocked in her independent soul, begins to fall away from him. She has another being, which he has not touched, and which she will fall back upon. The dance is over, she will fall back on herself. It is perfect, too perfect.

During the next dance, while she is in the power of the educated Ettore, a perfect and calculated voluptuary, who knows how much he can get out of this Northern woman, and only how much, the wood-cutter stands on the edge of the darkness, in the open doorway, and watches. He is fixed upon her, established, perfect. And all the while she is aware of the insistent hawk-like poising of the face of the wood-cutter, poised on the edge of the darkness, in the doorway, in possession, unrelinquishing.

And she is angry. There is something stupid, absurd, in the hard, talon-like eyes watching so fiercely and so confidently in the doorway, sure, unmitigated. Has the creature no sense?

The woman reacts from him. For some time she will take no notice of him. But he waits, fixed. Then she comes near to him, and his will seems to take hold of her. He looks at her with a strange, proud, inhuman confidence, as if his influence with her was already accomplished.

"Venga—venga un po'," he says, jerking his head strangely to the darkness.

"What?" she replies, and passes shaken and dilated and brilliant, consciously ignoring him, passes away among the others, among those who are safe.

There is food in the kitchen, great hunks of bread, sliced sausage that Maria has made, wine, and a little coffee. But only the quality come to eat. The peasants may not come in. There is eating and drinking in the little house, the guitars are silent. It is eleven o'clock.

Then there is singing, the strange bestial singing of these hills. Sometimes the guitars can play an accompaniment, but usually not. Then the men lift up their heads and send out the high, half-howling music, astounding. The words are in dialect. They argue among themselves for a moment: will the Signora understand? They sing. The Signora does not understand in the least. So with a strange, slightly malignant triumph, the men sing all the verses of their song, sitting round the walls of the little parlour. Their throats move, their faces have a slight mocking smile. The boy capers in the doorway like a faun, with glee, his straight black hair falling over his forehead. The elder brother sits straight and flushed, but even his eyes glitter with a kind of yellow light of laughter. Paolo also sits quiet, with the invisible smile on his face. Only Maria, large and active, prospering now, keeps collected, ready to order a shrill silence in the same way as she orders the peasants, violently, to keep their places.

The boy comes to me and says:

"Do you know, Signore, what they are singing?"

"No," I say.

So he capers with furious glee. The men with the watchful eyes, all roused, sit round the wall and sing more distinctly:

> "Si verrà la primavera
> Fiorann' le mandoline,
> Vienn' di basso le Trentine
> Coi 'taliani far' l'amor."

But the next verses are so improper that I pretend not to understand. The women, with wakened, dilated faces, are listening, listening hard, their two faces beautiful in their attention, as if listening to something magical, a long way off. And the men sitting round the wall sing more plainly, coming nearer to the correct Italian. The song comes loud and vibrating and maliciously from their reedy throats, it penetrates everybody. The foreign women can understand the sound, they can feel the malicious, suggestive mockery. But they cannot catch the words. The smile becomes more dangerous on the faces of the men.

Then Maria Fiori sees that I have understood, and she cries, in her loud, overriding voice:

"Basta—basta."

The men get up, straighten their bodies with a curious, offering movement. The guitars and mandolins strike the vibrating strings. But the vague Northern reserve has come over the Englishwomen. They dance again, but without the fusion in the dance. They have had enough.

The musicians are thanked, they rise and go into the night. The men pass off in pairs. But the wood-cutter, whose name and whose nickname I could never hear, still hovered on the edge of the darkness.

Then Maria sent him also away, complaining that he was too wild, *proprio selvatico,* and only the "quality" remained, the well-to-do youths from below. There was a little more coffee, and a talking, a story of a man who had fallen over a declivity in a lonely part going home drunk in the evening, and had lain unfound for eighteen hours. Then a story of a donkey who had kicked a youth in the chest and killed him.

But the women were tired, they would go to bed. Still the two young men would not go away. We all went out to look at the night.

The stars were very bright overhead, the mountain opposite and the mountains behind us faintly outlined themselves on the sky. Below, the lake was a black gulf. A little wind blew cold from the Adige.

In the morning the visitors had gone. They had insisted on staying the night. They had eaten eight eggs each and much bread at one o'clock in the morning. Then they had gone to sleep, lying on the floor in the sitting-room.

In the early sunshine they had drunk coffee and gone down to the village on the lake. Maria was very pleased. She would have made a good deal of money. The young men were rich. Her cupidity seemed like her very blossom.

QUESTIONS

1. In the first paragraph Lawrence is perhaps a cynical, knowing observer of Italian life. What is he in the second paragraph? How does the quick shift seem to affect the point of view of the first paragraph? Would you say that the last sentence in the essay expresses the point of view of the first paragraph, the second, or both?

2. What seems to be the focus of Lawrence's attention in the fourth paragraph: the visible scene? physical description? the kind of music? Italian custom and behavior? Which of these things—if any of them—

preoccupies him in the third paragraph and in the fifth and sixth? Taking the four paragraphs together, can you define Lawrence's dominant interest?

3. From what physical perspective is it likely that Lawrence is observing the dance in the fourteenth paragraph ("It is a strange dance . . .")? How much of the detail of the paragraph may be said to depend upon that perspective?

4. The fourteenth paragraph has interesting qualities: apparent contradictions (the dance is "leisurely" yet "intense," "had always a kind of . . . dignity" yet "passed into a possession," grows "swifter and more intense" at the same time that the women are "drifting"), extreme use of repetition and qualification ("a trailing kind of polka-waltz, intimate, passionate, yet never hurried, never violent in its passion, always becoming more intense"), odd metaphors ("women . . . palpitating," "worked . . . their thighs . . . more vividly"), the employment of one long sentence, covering most of the paragraph, to describe the dance. What point of view do these qualities establish? What relationship of Lawrence to the dancers is suggested in the following lines: "taking perfect, oh, exquisite delight . . . and drawing nearer to a climax, nearer, till, oh, there was the surpassing lift"?

5. What sort of judgment or feeling about the wood-cutter is implicit in the descriptive phrase "eyes that are black like the very flaming thrust of night" (paragraph twenty)? What three or four other descriptive phrases in paragraphs twenty through twenty-eight suggest a similar judgment or feeling?

6. At one point in paragraphs twenty through twenty-eight Lawrence speaks in a tone of voice—hence from a point of view—that is not his own. Where is it? How do you know? Where else in these same paragraphs might it be said that Lawrence comes close to assuming someone else's tone of voice? If it were asserted that in these paragraphs Lawrence's identity dissolves into that of one of the persons he describes, who do you suppose would be meant: the wood-cutter, the woman, or Ettore? Justify your answer; show that it is consistent with your other answers here.

7. What values are at issue in the relationship between the woman and the wood-cutter in paragraphs twenty through twenty-eight? Whose side is Lawrence on? How do you know?

8. What pejorative weight does Lawrence give to "bestial," "half-howling," and "malignant" in the long paragraph preceding the verse?

9. What appears to be Lawrence's attitude toward the immediate situation in the one extended passage toward the end in which he is directly involved in the scene? Is this attitude consistent with what you have judged to be his attitude during the dancing of the wood-cutter and the Englishwoman? With your answers to previous questions in mind, what would you say is the effect upon point of view of Lawrence's avoidance of reference to himself in most of the essay?

10. With your answers to previous questions in mind, what would you say are Lawrence's assumptions about the values that should govern human existence?

Notes on the English Character

E. M. FORSTER

Forster's interest in the English character, reflected in the essay that follows, has been a lasting one, and has influenced the concerns of his fiction, where his habit is frequently to explore his countrymen as they respond under the pressures of a foreign setting—Italy in both *Where Angels Fear to Tread* and *A Room with a View,* India in *A Passage to India.* In *Howards End,* he shifts his focus to England, providing a penetrating glimpse into English social history of the late nineteenth, early twentieth centuries. Forster himself has spent much of his later life in leisurely retirement, at Abinger, a small village in Surrey, and at Cambridge. (Further headnote information on Forster appears on pp. 137, 151.)

First Note. I had better let the cat out of the bag at once and record my opinion that the character of the English is essentially middle-class. There is a sound historical reason for this, for, since the end of the eighteenth century, the middle classes have been the dominant force in our community. They gained wealth by the Industrial Revolution, political power by the Reform Bill of 1832; they are connected with the rise and organization of the British Empire; they are responsible for the literature of the nineteenth century. Solidity, caution, integrity, efficiency. Lack of imagination, hypocrisy. These qualities characterize the middle classes in every country, but in

England they are national characteristics also, because only in England have the middle classes been in power for one hundred and fifty years. Napoleon, in his rude way, called us "a nation of shopkeepers." We prefer to call ourselves "a great commercial nation"—it sounds more dignified—but the two phrases amount to the same. Of course there are other classes: there is an aristocracy, there are the poor. But it is on the middle classes that the eye of the critic rests—just as it rests on the poor in Russia and on the aristocracy in Japan. Russia is symbolized by the peasant or by the factory worker; Japan by the samurai; the national figure of England is Mr. Bull with his top hat, his comfortable clothes, his substantial stomach, and his substantial balance at the bank. Saint George may caper on banners and in the speeches of politicians, but it is John Bull who delivers the goods. And even Saint George— if Gibbon is correct—wore a top hat once; he was an army contractor and supplied indifferent bacon. It all amounts to the same in the end.

Second Note. Just as the heart of England is the middle classes, so the heart of the middle classes is the public-school system. This extraordinary institution is local. It does not even exist all over the British Isles. It is unknown in Ireland, almost unknown in Scotland (countries excluded from my survey), and though it may inspire other great institutions—Aligarh, for example, and some of the schools in the United States—it remains unique, because it was created by the Anglo-Saxon middle classes, and can flourish only where they flourish. How perfectly it expresses their character—far better, for instance, than does the university, into which social and spiritual complexities have already entered. With its boarding-houses, its compulsory games, its system of prefects and fagging, its insistence on good form and on *esprit de corps,* it produces a type whose weight is out of all proportion to its numbers.

On leaving his school, the boy either sets to work at once—goes into the army or into business, or emigrates—or else proceeds to the university, and after three or four years there enters some other profession—becomes a barrister, doctor, civil servant, schoolmaster, or journalist. (If through some mishap he does not become a manual worker or an artist.) In all these careers his education, or the absence of it, influences him. Its memories influence him also. Many men look back on their school days as the happiest of their lives. They remember with regret that golden time when life, though hard, was not yet complex; when they all worked together and played together and thought together, so far as they thought at all; when they were taught that school is the world in miniature, and believed that no one can love his country who does not love his school. And they prolong that time as best they can by joining their Old Boys' society; indeed, some of them remain Old Boys and nothing else for the rest of their lives. They attribute all good to the school. They worship it. They quote the remark that "the battle of Waterloo was won on the playing-fields of Eton." It is nothing to them that the remark is inapplicable historically and was never made by the Duke of Wellington, and that the Duke of Wellington was an Irishman. They go on quoting it because it expresses their sentiments; they feel that if the Duke of Wellington didn't make it he ought to have, and if he wasn't an Englishman he ought to have been. And they go forth into a world that is not entirely composed of public-school men or even of Anglo-Saxons, but of men who are as various as the sands of the sea; into a world of whose richness and subtlety they have no conception. They go forth into it with well-developed bodies, fairly developed minds, and undeveloped hearts. And it is this undeveloped heart that is largely responsible for the difficulties of Englishmen abroad. An undeveloped heart—not a cold one. The difference is important, and on it my next note will be based.

For it is not that the Englishman can't feel—it is that he is afraid to feel. He has been taught at his public school that feeling is bad form. He must not express great joy or sorrow, or even open his mouth too wide when he talks—his pipe might fall out if he did. He must bottle up his emotions, or let them out only on a very special occasion.

Once upon a time (this is an anecdote) I went for a week's

holiday on the Continent with an Indian friend. We both enjoyed ourselves and were sorry when the week was over, but on
parting our behavior was absolutely different. He was plunged in
despair. He felt that because the holiday was over all happiness
was over until the world ended. He could not express his sorrow
too much. But in me the Englishman came out strong. I reflected
that we should meet again in a month or two, and could write in
the interval if we had anything to say; and under these circumstances I could not see what there was to make a fuss about. It
wasn't as if we were parting forever or dying. "Buck up," I said,
"do buck up." He refused to buck up, and I left him plunged in
gloom.

The conclusion of the anecdote is even more instructive. For
when we met the next month our conversation threw a good deal
of light on the English character. I began by scolding my friend. I
told him that he had been wrong to feel and display so much emotion upon so slight an occasion; that it was inappropriate. The word
"inappropriate" roused him to fury. "What?" he cried. "Do you
measure out your emotions as if they were potatoes?" I did not like
the simile of the potatoes, but after a moment's reflection I said,
"Yes, I do; and what's more, I think I ought to. A small occasion
demands a little emotion, just as a large occasion demands a great
one. I would like my emotions to be appropriate. This may be
measuring them like potatoes, but it is better than slopping them
about like water from a pail, which is what you did." He did not
like the simile of the pail. "If those are your opinions, they part us
forever," he cried, and left the room. Returning immediately, he
added: "No—but your whole attitude toward emotion is wrong.
Emotion has nothing to do with appropriateness. It matters only
that it shall be sincere. I happened to feel deeply. I showed it. It
doesn't matter whether I ought to have felt deeply or not."

This remark impressed me very much. Yet I could not agree
with it, and said that I valued emotion as much as he did, but used
it differently; if I poured it out on small occasions I was afraid of
having none left for the great ones, and of being bankrupt at the

crises of life. Note the word "bankrupt." I spoke as a member of a prudent middle-class nation, always anxious to meet my liabilities. But my friend spoke as an Oriental, and the Oriental has behind him a tradition, not of middle-class prudence, but of kingly munificence and splendour. He feels his resources are endless, just as John Bull feels his are finite. As regards material resources, the Oriental is clearly unwise. Money isn't endless. If we spend or give away all the money we have, we haven't any more, and must take the consequences, which are frequently unpleasant. But, as regards the resources of the spirit, he may be right. The emotions may be endless. The more we express them, the more we have to express.

> *True love in this differs from gold and clay,*
> *That to divide is not to take away,*

says Shelley. Shelley, at all events, believes that the wealth of the spirit is endless; that we may express it copiously, passionately, and always; and that we can never feel sorrow or joy too acutely.

In the above anecdote, I have figured as a typical Englishman. I will now descend from that dizzy and somewhat unfamiliar height, and return to my business of note-taking. A note on the *slowness* of the English character. The Englishman appears to be cold and unemotional because he is really slow. When an event happens, he may understand it quickly enough with his mind, but he takes quite a while to feel it. Once upon a time a coach, containing some Englishmen and some Frenchmen, was driving over the Alps. The horses ran away, and as they were dashing across a bridge the coach caught on the stonework, tottered, and nearly fell into the ravine below. The Frenchmen were frantic with terror: they screamed and gesticulated and flung themselves about, as Frenchmen would. The Englishmen sat quite calm. An hour later the coach drew up at an inn to change horses, and by that time the situations were exactly reversed. The Frenchmen had forgotten all about the danger, and were chattering gaily; the Englishmen had just begun to feel it, and one had a nervous breakdown and was obliged to go to bed. We have here a clear physical difference between the two races—a difference that goes deep into character. The Frenchmen responded at once; the Englishmen responded in time. They were slow and they were also practical. Their instinct forbade them to throw themselves about in the coach, because it was more likely to tip over if they did. They had this extraordinary appreciation of *fact* that we shall notice again and again. When a disaster comes, the English instinct is to do what can be done first, and to postpone the feeling as long as possible. Hence they are splendid at emergencies. No doubt they are brave—no one will deny that—but bravery is partly an affair of the nerves, and the English nervous system is well equipped for meeting a physical emergency. It acts promptly and feels slowly. Such a combination is fruitful, and anyone who possesses it has gone a long way toward being brave. And when the action is over, then the Englishman can feel.

There is one more consideration—a most important one. If the English nature is cold, how is it that it has produced a great literature that is particularly great in poetry? Judged by its prose, English literature would not stand in the first rank. It is its poetry that raises it to the level of Greek, Persian, or French. And yet the English are supposed to be so unpoetical. How is this? The nation that produced the Elizabethan drama and the Lake Poets cannot be a cold, unpoetical nation. We can't get fire out of ice. Since literature always rests upon national character, there must be in the English nature hidden springs of fire to produce the fire we see. The warm sympathy, the romance, the imagination, that we look for in Englishmen whom we meet, and too often vainly look for, must exist in the nation as a whole, or we could not have this outburst of national song. An undeveloped heart—not a cold one.

The trouble is that the English nature is not at all easy to understand. It has a great air of simplicity, it advertises itself as simple, but the more we consider it, the greater the problems we shall encounter. People talk of the mysterious East, but the West also is mysterious. It has depths that do not reveal themselves at the first gaze. We know what the sea looks like from a distance: it is of one colour, and level, and obviously cannot contain such creatures as fish. But if we look into the sea over the edge of a boat, we see a dozen colours, and depth below depth, and fish swimming in them. That sea is the English character—apparently imperturbable and even. The depths and the colours are the English romanticism and the English sensitiveness—we do not expect to find such things, but they exist. And—to continue my metaphor—the fish are the English emotions, which are always trying to get up to the surface, but don't quite know how. For the most part we see them moving far below, distorted and obscure. Now and then they succeed and we exclaim, "Why, the Englishman has emotions! He actually can feel!" And occasionally we see that beautiful creature the flying fish, which rises out of the water altogether into the air and the sunlight. English literature is a flying fish. It is a sample of the life that goes on day after day beneath the surface; it is a proof that beauty and emotion exist in the salt, inhospitable sea.

And now let's get back to terra firma. The Englishman's attitude toward criticism will give us another starting-point. He is not annoyed by criticism. He listens or not as the case may be, smiles and passes on, saying, "Oh, the fellow's jealous"; "Oh, I'm used to Bernard Shaw; monkey tricks don't hurt me." It never occurs to him that the fellow may be accurate as well as jealous, and that he might do well to take the criticism to heart and profit by it. It never strikes him—except as a form of words—that he is capable of improvement; his self-complacency is abysmal. Other nations, both Oriental and European, have an uneasy feeling that they are not quite perfect. In consequence they resent criticism. It hurts them; and their snappy answers often mask a determination to improve themselves. Not so the Englishman. He has no uneasy feeling. Let the critics bark. And the "tolerant humorous attitude" with which he confronts them is not really tolerant, because it is insensitive, and not really humorous, because it is bounded by the titter and the guffaw.

Turn over the pages of *Punch*. There is neither wit, laughter, nor satire in our national jester—only the snigger of a suburban householder who can understand nothing that does not resemble himself. Week after week, under Mr. Punch's supervision, a man falls off his horse, or a colonel misses a golf ball, or a little girl makes a mistake in her prayers. Week after week ladies show not too much of their legs, foreigners are deprecated, originality condemned. Week after week a bricklayer does not do as much work as he ought and a futurist does more than he need. It is all supposed to be so good-tempered and clean; it is also supposed to be funny. It is actually an outstanding example of our attitude toward criticism: the middle-class Englishman, with a smile on his clean-shaven lips, is engaged in admiring himself and ignoring the rest of mankind. If, in those colourless pages, he came across anything that really was funny—a drawing by Max Beerbohm, for instance —his smile would disappear, and he would say to himself, "The fellow's a bit of a crank," and pass on.

This particular attitude reveals such insensitiveness as to suggest a more serious charge: is the Englishman altogether indifferent to the things of the spirit? Let us glance for a moment at his religion —not, indeed, at his theology, which would not merit inspection, but at the action on his daily life of his belief in the unseen. Here again his attitude is practical. But an innate decency comes out: he is thinking of others rather than of himself. Right conduct is his aim. He asks of his religion that it shall make him a better man in daily life; that he shall be more kind, more just, more merciful, more desirous to fight what is evil and to protect what is good. No one could call this a low conception. It is, as far as it goes, a spiritual one. Yet—and this seems to me typical of the race—it is only half the religious idea. Religion is more than an ethical code with a divine sanction. It is also a means through which man may get into direct connection with the divine, and, judging by history, few Englishmen have succeeded in doing this. We have produced no series of prophets, as has Judaism or Islam. We have not even produced a Joan of Arc, or a Savonarola. We have produced few saints. In Germany the Reformation was due to the passionate conviction of Luther. In England it was due to a palace intrigue. We can show a steady level of piety, a fixed determination to live decently according to our lights—little more.

Well, it is something. It clears us of the charge of being an unspiritual nation. That facile contrast between the spiritual East and the materialistic West can be pushed too far. The West also is spiritual. Only it expresses its belief, not in fasting and visions, not in prophetic rapture, but in the daily round, the common task. An incomplete expression, if you like. I agree. But the argument underlying these scattered notes is that the Englishman is an incomplete person. Not a cold or an unspiritual one. But undeveloped, incomplete.

The attitude of the average orthodox Englishman is often misunderstood. It is thought that he must know that a doctrine—say, like that of the Trinity—is untrue. Moslems in particular feel that his faith is a dishonest compromise between polytheism and monotheism. The answer to this criticism is that the average orthodox Englishman is no theologian. He regards the Trinity as a mystery that it is not his place to solve. "I find difficulties enough in daily life," he will say. "I concern myself with those. As for the Trinity, it is a doctrine handed down to me from my fathers, whom I respect, and I hope to hand it down to my sons, and that they will respect me. No doubt it is true, or it would not have been handed down. And no doubt the clergy could explain it to me if I asked them; but, like myself, they are busy men, and I will not take up their time."

In such an answer there is confusion of thought, if you like, but no conscious deceit, which is alien to the English nature. The Englishman's deceit is generally unconscious.

For I have suggested earlier that the English are sometimes hypocrites, and it is now my duty to develop this rather painful subject. Hypocrisy is the prime charge that is always brought against us. The Germans are called brutal, the Spanish cruel, the Americans superficial, and so on; but we are perfide Albion, the island of hypocrites, the people who have built up an Empire with

a Bible in one hand, a pistol in the other, and financial conces-
sions in both pockets. Is the charge true? I think it is; but while
making it we must be quite clear as to what we mean by hypocrisy.
Do we mean *conscious* deceit? Well, the English are comparatively
guiltless of this; they have little of the Renaissance villain about
them. Do we mean *unconscious* deceit? Muddle-headedness? Of
this I believe them to be guilty. When an Englishman has been
led into a course of wrong action, he has nearly always begun by
muddling himself. A public-school education does not make for
mental clearness, and he possesses to a very high degree the power of
confusing his own mind. We have seen this tendency at work in the
domain of theology; how does it work in the domain of conduct?

Jane Austen may seem an odd authority to cite, but Jane Austen
has, within her limits, a marvellous insight into the English mind.
Her range is limited, her characters never attempt any of the more
scarlet sins. But she has a merciless eye for questions of conduct,
and the classical example of two English people muddling themselves before they embark upon a wrong course of action is to be
found in the opening chapters of *Sense and Sensibility*. Old Mr.
Dashwood has just died. He has been twice married. By his first
marriage he has a son, John; by his second marriage three daughters. The son is well off; the young ladies and their mother—for
Mr. Dashwood's second wife survives him—are badly off. He has
called his son to his death-bed and has solemnly adjured him to
provide for the second family. Much moved, the young man promises, and mentally decides to give each of his sisters a thousand
pounds; and then the comedy begins. For he announces his generous intention to his wife, and Mrs. John Dashwood by no means
approves of depriving their own little boy of so large a sum. The
thousand pounds are accordingly reduced to five hundred. But even
this seems rather much. Might not an annuity to the stepmother
be less of a wrench? Yes—but though less of a wrench it might be
more of a drain, for "she is very stout and healthy, and scarcely
forty." An occasional present of fifty pounds will be better, "and
will, I think, be amply discharging my promise to my father." Or,

better still, an occasional present of fish. And in the end nothing is done, nothing; the four impecunious ladies are not even helped in the moving of their furniture.

Well, are the John Dashwoods hypocrites? It depends upon our definition of hypocrisy. The young man could not see his evil impulses as they gathered force and gained on him. And even his wife, though a worse character, is also self-deceived. She reflects that old Mr. Dashwood may have been out of his mind at his death. She thinks of her own little boy—and surely a mother ought to think of her own child. She has muddled herself so completely that in one sentence she can refuse the ladies the income that would enable them to keep a carriage and in the next can say that they will not be keeping a carriage and so will have no expenses. No doubt men and women in other lands can muddle themselves, too, yet the state of mind of Mr. and Mrs. John Dashwood seems to me typical of England. They are slow—they take time even to do wrong; whereas people in other lands do wrong quickly.

There are national faults as there are national diseases, and perhaps one can draw a parallel between them. It has always impressed me that the national diseases of England should be cancer and consumption—slow, insidious, pretending to be something else; while the diseases proper to the South should be cholera and plague, which strike at a man when he is perfectly well and may leave him a corpse by evening. Mr. and Mrs. John Dashwood are moral consumptives. They collapse gradually without realizing what the disease is. There is nothing dramatic or violent about their sin. You cannot call them villains.

Here is the place to glance at some of the other charges that have been brought against the English as a nation. They have, for instance, been accused of treachery, cruelty, and fanaticism. In these charges I have never been able to see the least point, because treachery and cruelty are conscious sins. The man knows he is doing wrong, and does it deliberately, like Tartuffe or Iago. He betrays his friend because he wishes to. He tortures his prisoners because he enjoys seeing the blood flow. He worships the Devil because he prefers evil to good. From villainies such as these the average Englishman is free. His character, which prevents his rising to certain heights, also prevents him from sinking to these depths. Because he doesn't produce mystics he doesn't produce villains either; he gives the world no prophets, but no anarchists, no fanatics—religious or political.

Of course there are cruel and treacherous people in England— one has only to look at the police courts—and examples of public infamy can be found, such as the Amritsar massacre. But one does not look at the police courts or the military mind to find the soul of any nation; and the more English people one meets the more convinced one becomes that the charges as a whole are untrue. Yet foreign critics often make them. Why? Partly because they fix their eyes on the criminal classes, partly because they are annoyed with certain genuine defects in the English character, and in their irritation throw in cruelty in order to make the problem simpler. Moral indignation is always agreeable, but nearly always misplaced. It is indulged in both by the English and by the critics of the English. They all find it great fun. The drawback is that while they are amusing themselves the world becomes neither wiser nor better.

The main point of these notes is that the English character is incomplete. No national character is complete. We have to look for some qualities in one part of the world and others in another. But the English character is incomplete in a way that is particularly annoying to the foreign observer. It has a bad surface—self-complacent, unsympathetic, and reserved. There is plenty of emotion further down, but it never gets used. There is plenty of brain power, but it is more often used to confirm prejudices than to dispel them. With such an equipment the Englishman cannot be popular. Only I would repeat: there is little vice in him and no real coldness. It is the machinery that is wrong.

I hope and believe myself that in the next twenty years we shall see a great change, and that the national character will alter into something that is less unique but more lovable. The supremacy of the middle classes is probably ending. What new element the working classes will introduce one cannot say, but at all events they will not have been educated at public schools. And whether these notes praise or blame the English character—that is only incidental. They are the notes of a student who is trying to get at the truth and would value the assistance of others. I believe myself that the truth is great and that it shall prevail. I have no faith in official caution and reticence. The cats are all out of their bags, and diplomacy cannot recall them. The nations *must* understand one another, and quickly; and without the interposition of their governments, for the shrinkage of the globe is throwing them into one another's arms. To that understanding these notes are a feeble contribution—notes on the English character as it has struck a novelist.

QUESTIONS

1. Forster lets two cats out of the bag: at the beginning and at the end. With what seriousness does he use the expression on each occasion? What point of view is suggested? If you see a difference in point of view, which one would you say is more characteristic of the essay?

2. At the end of the essay Forster identifies his point of view as that of a novelist. What aspects of the form of the essay and the means of argument and illustration suggest a novelist's point of view rather than, say, a sociologist's? Do you find Forster's point of view as a younger man, in his experience with his Indian friend, significantly different from his general point of view in the essay?

3. The basic assumption of the essay is implicit in the title phrase "English character." State the assumption in terms broad enough to include French and American character as well. At what point in the essay does Forster himself most seriously challenge the assumption?

4. If before the end of the eighteenth century the dominant force in England was the aristocracy, what—according to Forster's reasoning in the second sentence of the first paragraph—would have been the essential character of the English people then? State the assumption that underlies his reasoning. Can you think of a country where such an assumption would not apply?

5. The Introduction to the present section of the text discusses the assumption that underlies Forster's assertion that the public school "produces a type" (paragraph two). What is that assumption? What assumption underlies Forster's assertion in the same paragraph that the public school expresses the character of the middle class? Are his two assumptions consistent with each other?

6. Is the anecdote about the French and English people in the carriage funny because it is convincing or convincing because it is funny? Would its illustrative value be seriously damaged if one of the Frenchmen had drunk to excess at the inn? To what extent would you say Forster's point depends upon the validity of the anecdote as he has told it?

7. Consider the following syllogisms: (1) The qualities of the English middle class are the qualities of the English nation; one of the qualities of the English middle class is unimaginativeness; hence one of the qualities of the English nation is unimaginativeness. (2) An unimaginative nation cannot produce great poetry; the English nation produces great poetry; hence the English nation cannot be unimaginative. To what extent do the views in each syllogism reflect Forster's assumptions and reasoning in paragraphs one and nine? Has he contradicted himself? With what degree of success does the eleventh paragraph overcome the real or apparent contradiction?

8. In paragraph ten Forster might have written: We know what a volcano looks like from a distance: it is of one color. . . . What qualities of English poetry are suggested by the flying fish that might not be suggested by the overflow of lava? What special qualities of poetry might be better suggested by the overflow of lava?

9. How detailed is Forster's analogy between English poetry and a flying fish? How much further might it be extended before it became untenable? Why is it so convincing as it stands?

10. What assumptions about the relationship of character to behavior, action, and thought underlie Forster's discussion of the Englishman's response to criticism, his spirituality, and his theology? Can you think of any contrasting assumptions that would seem reasonable? Are Forster's assumptions here consistent with his assumptions about public schools (Question 5)?

11. What does Forster assume about the relationship of literature to life when he uses *Punch* to support his argument? What contrasting as-

sumption might preclude his using the magazine so? What slightly different assumption about the relationship of literature to life does Forster make in discussing *Sense and Sensibility*? Do you find one assumption more convincing than the other? Do you find one illustration (*Punch* or *Sense and Sensibility*) more convincing than the other? Why?

12. What elements in the earlier "notes" prepare the reader for the sense of urgency to which the essay rises at the end? How would you describe Forster's overall point of view in the essay?

Civilisation in the United States

MATTHEW ARNOLD

The son of Thomas Arnold, the famous headmaster of Rugby,
Matthew Arnold (1822-1888) was probably the most active
man of letters in nineteenth-century England. Though he began as a poet, he turned in mid-life to the writing of literary
and then social criticism (*Essays in Criticism, Culture and
Anarchy*), and later to writing on religious matters. As he conceived it, his great battle was against the practicality and
literal-mindedness of the middle classes, a battle he fought in
print with remarkable gusto and ingenuity. He twice visited
the United States, in 1883 and 1886, on lecture tours, and
wrote a number of essays on American subjects. The following
is the larger part of one such essay.

Two or three years ago I spoke in this Review on the subject of
America; and after considering the institutions and the social condition of the people of the United States, I said that what, in the
jargon of the present day, is called the political and social problem,
does seem to be solved there with remarkable success. I pointed
out the contrast which in this respect the United States offer to our
own country, a contrast, in several ways, much to their advantage.
But I added that the solution of the political and social problem, as
it is called, ought not so to absorb us as to make us forget the human problem; and that it remained to ask how the human problem
is solved in the United States. It happened that Sir Lepel Griffin, a
very acute and distinguished Indian official, had just then been

travelling in the United States, and had published his opinion, from what he saw of the life there, that there is no country calling itself civilised where one would not rather live than in America, except Russia. Certainly then, I said, one cannot rest satisfied, when one finds such a judgment passed on the United States as this, with admiring their institutions and their solid social condition, their freedom and equality, their power, energy, and wealth. One must, further, go on to examine what is done there towards solving the human problem, and must see what Sir Lepel Griffin's objection comes to.

And this examination I promised that I would one day make. However, it is so delicate a matter to discuss how a sensitive nation solves the human problem, that I found myself inclined to follow the example of the Greek moralist Theophrastus, who waited, before composing his famous *Characters,* until he was ninety-nine years old. I thought I had perhaps better wait until I was about that age, before I discussed the success of the Americans in solving the human problem. But ninety-nine is a great age; it is probable that I may never reach it, or even come near it. So I have determined, finally, to face the question without any such long delay, and thus I come to offer to the readers of this Review the remarks following. With the same frankness with which I discussed here the solution of the political and social problem by the people of the United States, I shall discuss their success in solving the human problem.

Perhaps it is not likely that any one will now remember what I said three years ago here about the success of the Americans in solving the political and social problem. I will sum it up in the briefest possible manner. I said that the United States had constituted themselves in a modern age; that their institutions complied well with the form and pressure of those circumstances and conditions which a modern age presents. Quite apart from all question how much of the merit for this may be due to the wisdom and virtue of the American people, and how much to their good fortune, it is undeniable that their institutions do work well and happily. The play of their institutions suggests, I said, the image of a man in a suit of

clothes which fits him to perfection, leaving all his movements un-
impeded and easy; a suit of clothes loose where it ought to be
loose, and sitting close where its sitting close is an advantage; a
suit of clothes able, moreover, to adapt itself naturally to the
wearer's growth, and to admit of all enlargements as they succes-
sively arise.

So much as to the solution, by the United States, of the political
problem. As to the social problem, I observed that the people of
the United States were a community singularly free from the distinction of classes, singularly homogeneous; that the division between rich and poor was consequently less profound there than in
countries where the distinction of classes accentuates that division.
I added that I believed there was exaggeration in the reports of
their administrative and judicial corruption; and altogether, I concluded, the United States, politically and socially, are a country
living prosperously in a natural modern condition, and conscious of
living prosperously in such a condition. And being in this healthy
case, and having this healthy consciousness, the community there
uses its understanding with the soundness of health; it in general,
as to its own political and social concerns, sees clear and thinks
straight. Comparing the United States with ourselves, I said that
while they are in this natural and healthy condition, we on the contrary are so little homogeneous, we are living with a system of
classes so intense, with institutions and a society so little modern,
so unnaturally complicated, that the whole action of our minds is
hampered and falsened by it; we are in consequence wanting in
lucidity, we do not see clear or think straight, and the Americans
have here much the advantage of us.

Yet we find an acute and experienced Englishman saying that
there is no country, calling itself civilised, where one would not
rather live than in the United States, except Russia! The civilisation of the United States must somehow, if an able man can think
thus, have shortcomings, in spite of the country's success and
prosperity. What is civilisation? It is the humanisation of man in society, the satisfaction for him, in society, of the true law of human

nature. Man's study, says Plato, is to discover the right answer to the question *how to live?* our aim, he says, is very and true life. We are more or less civilised as we come more or less near to this aim, in that social state which the pursuit of our aim essentially demands. But several elements or powers, as I have often insisted, go to build up a complete human life. There is the power of conduct, the power of intellect and knowledge, the power of beauty, the power of social life and manners; we have instincts responding to them all, requiring them all. And we are perfectly civilised only when all these instincts in our nature, all these elements in our civilisation, have been adequately recognised and satisfied. But of course this adequate recognition and satisfaction of all the elements in question is impossible; some of them are recognised more than others, some of them more in one community, some in another; and the satisfactions found are more or less worthy.

And meanwhile, people use the term *civilisation* in the loosest possible way, for the most part attaching to it, however, in their own mind some meaning connected with their own preferences and experiences. The most common meaning thus attached to it is perhaps that of a satisfaction, not of all the main demands of human nature, but of the demand for the comforts and conveniences of life, and of this demand as made by the sort of person who uses the term.

Now we should always attend to the common and prevalent use of an important term. Probably Sir Lepel Griffin had this notion of the comforts and conveniences of life much in his thoughts when he reproached American civilisation with its shortcomings. For men of his kind, and for all that large number of men, so prominent in this country and who make their voice so much heard, men who have been at the public schools and universities, men of the professional and official class, men who do the most part of our literature and our journalism, America is not a comfortable place of abode. A man of this sort has in England everything in his favour; society appears organised expressly for his advantage. A Rothschild or a Vanderbilt can buy his way anywhere, and can have what comforts and luxuries he likes whether in America or in England.

But it is in England that an income of from three or four to fourteen or fifteen hundred a year does so much for its possessor, enables him to live with so many of the conveniences of far richer people. For his benefit, his benefit above all, clubs are organised and hansom cabs ply; service is abundant, porters stand waiting at the railway stations. In America all luxuries are dear except oysters and ice; service is in general scarce and bad; a club is a most expensive luxury; the cab-rates are prohibitive—more than half of the people who in England would use cabs must in America use the horse-cars, the tram. The charges of tailors and mercers are about a third higher than they are with us. I mention only a few striking points as to which there can be no dispute, and in which a man of Sir Lepel Griffin's class would feel the great difference between America and England in the conveniences at his command. There are a hundred other points one might mention, where he would feel the same thing. When a man is passing judgment on a country's civilisation, points of this kind crowd to his memory, and determine his sentence.

On the other hand, for that immense class of people, the great bulk of the community, the class of people whose income is less than three or four hundred a year, things in America are favourable. It is easier for them there than in the Old World to rise and to make their fortune; but I am not now speaking of that. Even without making their fortune, even with their income below three or four hundred a year, things are favourable to them in America, society seems organised there for their benefit. To begin with, the humbler kind of work is better paid in America than with us, the higher kind worse. The official, for instance, gets less, his office-keeper gets more. The public ways are abominably cut up by rails and blocked with horse-cars; but the inconvenience is for those who use private carriages and cabs, the convenience is for the bulk of the community who but for the horse-cars would have to walk. The ordinary railway cars are not delightful, but they are cheap, and they are better furnished and in winter are warmer than third-class carriages in England. Luxuries are, as I have said, very dear—above all, European luxuries; but a working man's clothing is nearly as cheap as in England, and plain food is on the whole cheaper. Even luxuries of a certain kind are within a labouring man's easy reach. I have mentioned ice, I will mention fruit also. The abundance and cheapness of fruit is a great boon to people of small incomes in America. Do not believe the Americans when they extol their peaches as equal to any in the world, or better than any in the world; they are not to be compared to peaches grown under glass. Do not believe that the American Newtown pippins appear in the New York and Boston fruit-shops as they appear in those of London and Liverpool; or that the Americans have any pear to give you like the Marie Louise. But what labourer, or artisan, or small clerk, ever gets hot-house peaches, or Newtown pippins, or Marie Louise pears? Not such good pears, apples, and peaches as those, but pears, apples, and peaches by no means to be despised, such people and their families do in America get in plenty.

Well, now, what would a philosopher or a philanthropist say in this case? which would he say was the more civilised condition— that of the country where the balance of advantage, as to the comforts and conveniences of life, is greatly in favour of the people with incomes below three hundred a year, or that of the country where it is greatly in favour of those with incomes above that sum?

Many people will be ready to give an answer to that question without the smallest hesitation. They will say that they are, and that all of us ought to be, for the greatest happiness of the greatest number. However, the question is not one which I feel bound now to discuss and answer. Of course, if happiness and civilisation consist in being plentifully supplied with the comforts and conveniences of life, the question presents little difficulty. But I believe neither that happiness consists, merely or mainly, in being plentifully supplied with the comforts and conveniences of life, nor that civilisation consists in being so supplied; therefore I leave the question unanswered.

I prefer to seek for some other and better tests by which to try the civilisation of the United States. I have often insisted on the need of more equality in our own country, and on the mischiefs caused by inequality over here. In the United States there is not our intense division of classes, our inequality; there is great equality. Let me mention two points in the system of social life and manners over there in which this equality seems to me to have done good. The first is a mere point of form, but it has its significance. Every one knows it is the established habit with us in England, if we write to people supposed to belong to the class of gentlemen, of addressing them by the title of *Esquire,* while we keep *Mr.* for people not supposed to belong to that class. If we think of it, could one easily find a habit more ridiculous, more offensive? The title of *Esquire,* like most of our titles, comes out of the great frippery shop of the Middle Ages; it is alien to the sound taste and manner of antiquity, when men said *Pericles* and *Camillus.* But unlike other titles, it is applied or withheld quite arbitrarily. Surely, where a man has no specific title proper to him, the one plain title of *Master* or *Mr.* is enough, and we need not be encumbered with a second title of *Esquire,* now quite unmeaning, to draw an invidious and impossible line of distinction between those who are gentlemen and those who are not; as if we actually wished to provide a source of embarrassment for the sender of a letter, and of mortification for the receiver of it.

The French, those great authorities in social life and manners, find *Mr.* enough, and the Americans are more and more, I am glad to say, following the French example. I only hope they will persevere, and not be seduced by *Esquire* being "so English, you know." And I do hope, moreover, that we shall one day take the same course and drop our absurd *Esquire.*

The other point goes deeper. Much may be said against the voices and intonations of American women. But almost every one acknowledges that there is a charm in American women—a charm which you find in almost all of them, wherever you go. It is the charm of a natural manner, a manner not self-conscious, artificial, and constrained. It may not be a beautiful manner always, but it is almost always a natural manner, a free and happy manner; and this gives pleasure. Here we have, undoubtedly, a note of civilisation, and an evidence, at the same time, of the good effect of equality upon social life and manners. I have often heard it observed that a perfectly natural manner is as rare among Englishwomen of the middle classes as it is general among American women of like condition with them. And so far as the observation is true, the reason of its truth no doubt is, that the Englishwoman is living in presence of an upper class, as it is called—in presence, that is, of a class of women recognised as being the right thing in style and manner, and whom she imagines criticising *her* style and manner, finding this or that to be amiss with it, this or that to be vulgar. Hence self-consciousness and constraint in her. The American woman lives in presence of no such class; there may be circles trying to pass themselves off as such a class, giving themselves airs as such, but they command no recognition, no authority. The American woman in general is perfectly unconcerned about their opinion, is herself, enjoys her existence, and has consequently a manner happy and natural. It is her great charm; and it is moreover, as I have said, a real note of civilisation, and one which has to be reckoned to the credit of American life, and of its equality.

But we must get nearer still to the heart of the question raised as to the character and worth of American civilisation. I have said how much the word civilisation really means—the humanisation of man in society; his making progress there towards his true and full humanity. Partial and material achievement is always being put forward as civilisation. We hear a nation called highly civilised by reason of its industry, commerce, and wealth, or by reason of its liberty or equality, or by reason of its numerous churches, schools, libraries, and newspapers. But there is something in human nature, some instinct of growth, some law of perfection, which rebels against this narrow account of the matter. And perhaps what human nature demands in civilisation, over and above all those obvious things which first occur to our thoughts—what human nature, I say, demands in civilisation, if it is to stand as a high and satisfying civilisation, is best described by the word *interesting*. Here is the extraordinary charm of the old Greek civilisation—that it is so *interesting*. Do not tell me only, says human nature, of the magnitude of your industry and commerce; of the beneficence of your institutions, your freedom, your equality; of the great and growing number of your churches and schools, libraries and newspapers; tell me also if your civilisation—which is the grand name you give to all this development—tell me if your civilisation is *interesting*.

An American friend of mine, Professor Norton, has lately published the early letters of Carlyle. If anyone wants a good antidote to the unpleasant effect left by Mr. Froude's *Life of Carlyle*, let him read those letters. Not only of Carlyle will those letters make him think kindly, but they will also fill him with admiring esteem for the qualities, character, and family life, as there delineated, of the Scottish peasant. Well, the Carlyle family were numerous, poor, and struggling. Thomas Carlyle, the eldest son, a young man in wretched health and worse spirits, was fighting his way in Edinburgh. One of his younger brothers talked of emigrating. "The very best thing he could do!" we should all say. Carlyle dissuades him. "You shall never," he writes, "you shall never seriously meditate crossing the great Salt Pool to plant yourself in the Yankee-land. That is a miserable fate for any one, at best; never dream of it. Could you banish yourself from all that is interesting to your mind, forget the history, the glorious institutions, the noble principles of old Scotland—that you might eat a better dinner, perhaps?"

There is our word launched—the word *interesting*. I am not saying that Carlyle's advice was good, or that young men should not emigrate. I do but take note, in the word *interesting*, of a requirement, a cry of aspiration, a cry not sounding in the imaginative Carlyle's own breast only, but sure of a response in his brother's breast also, and in human nature.

Amiel, that contemplative Swiss whose journals the world has been reading lately, tells us that "the human heart is, as it were, haunted by confused reminiscences of an age of gold; or rather, by aspirations towards a harmony of things which everyday reality denies to us." He says that the splendour and refinement of high life is an attempt by the rich and cultivated classes to realise this ideal, and is "a form of poetry." And the interest which this attempt awakens in the classes which are not rich or cultivated, their indestructible interest in the pageant and fairy tale, as to them it appears, of the life in castles and palaces, the life of the great, bears witness to a like imaginative strain in them also, a strain tending after the elevated and the beautiful. In short, what Goethe describes as "was uns alle bändigt, *das Gemeine*—that which holds us all in bondage, the common and ignoble," is, notwithstanding its admitted prevalence, contrary to a deep-seated instinct of human nature and repelled by it. Of civilisation, which is to humanise us in society, we demand, before we will consent to be satisfied with it —we demand, however much else it may give us, that it shall give us, too, the *interesting*.

Now, the great sources of the *interesting* are distinction and beauty: that which is elevated, and that which is beautiful. Let us take the beautiful first, and consider how far it is present in American civilisation. Evidently this is that civilisation's weak side. There is little to nourish and delight the sense of beauty there. In the long-settled States east of the Alleghenies the landscape in general is not interesting, the climate harsh and in extremes. The Americans are restless, eager to better themselves and to make fortunes; the inhabitant does not strike his roots lovingly down into the soil, as in rural England. In the valley of the Connecticut you will find farm after farm which the Yankee settler has abandoned in order to go West, leaving the farm to some new Irish immigrant. The charm of beauty which comes from ancientness and permanence of rural life the country could not yet have in a high degree, but it has it in an even less degree than might be expected. Then the Americans come originally, for the most part, from that great class in English society amongst whom the sense for conduct and business is much more strongly developed than the sense for beauty. If we in England were without the cathedrals, parish churches, and castles of the catholic and feudal age, and without the houses of the Elizabethan age, but had only the towns and buildings which the rise of our middle class has created in the modern age, we should be in much the same case as the Americans. We should be living with much the same absence of training for the sense of beauty through the eye, from the aspect of outward things. The American cities have hardly anything to please a trained or a natural sense for beauty. They have buildings which cost a great deal of money and produce a certain effect—buildings, shall I say, such as our Midland Station at St. Pancras; but nothing such as Somerset House or Whitehall. One architect of genius they had—Richardson. I had the pleasure to know him; he is dead, alas! Much of his work was injured by the conditions under which he was obliged to execute it; I can recall but one building, and that of no great importance, where he seems to have had his own way, to be fully himself; but that is indeed excellent. In general, where the Americans succeed best in their architecture—in that art so indicative and educative of a people's sense for beauty—is in the fashion of their villa-cottages in wood. These are often original and at the same time very pleasing, but they are pretty and coquettish, not beautiful. Of the really beautiful in the other arts, and in literature, very little has been produced there as yet. I asked a German portrait-painter, whom I found painting and prospering in America, how he liked the country? "How *can* an artist like it?" was his answer. The American artists live chiefly in Europe; all Americans of cultivation and wealth visit Europe more and more constantly. The mere nomenclature of the country acts upon a cultivated person like the incessant pricking of pins. What people in whom the sense for beauty and fitness was quick could have invented, or could tolerate, the hideous names ending in *ville*, the Briggsvilles, Higginsvilles, Jacksonvilles, rife from Maine to Florida; the jumble of unnatural and inappropriate names everywhere? On the line from Albany to Buffalo you have, in one part, half the names in the classical dictionary to designate the stations; it is said that the folly is due to a surveyor who, when the country was laid out, happened to possess a classical dictionary, but a people with any artist-sense would have put down that surveyor. The Americans meekly retain his names; and indeed his strange Marcellus or Syracuse is perhaps not much worse than their congenital Briggsville.

So much as to beauty, and as to the provision, in the United States, for the sense of beauty. As to distinction, and the interest which human nature seeks from enjoying the effect made upon it by what is elevated, the case is much the same. There is very little to create such an effect, very much to thwart it. Goethe says somewhere that "the thrill of awe is the best thing humanity has":—

Das Schaudern ist der Menschheit bestes Theil.

But, if there be a discipline in which the Americans are wanting, it is the discipline of awe and respect. An austere and intense religion imposed on their Puritan founders the discipline of respect, and so provided for them the thrill of awe; but this religion is dying out. The Americans have produced plenty of men strong, shrewd, upright, able, effective; very few who are highly distinguished. Alexander Hamilton is indeed a man of rare distinction; Washington, though he has not the high mental distinction of Pericles or Caesar, has true distinction of style and character. But these men belong to the pre-American age. Lincoln's recent American biographers declare that Washington is but an Englishman, an English officer; the typical American, they say, is Abraham Lincoln. Now Lincoln is shrewd, sagacious, humorous, honest, courageous, firm; he is a man with qualities deserving the most sincere esteem and praise, but he has not distinction.

In truth everything is against distinction in America, and against the sense of elevation to be gained through admiring and respecting it. The glorification of "the average man," who is quite a religion with statesmen and publicists there, is against it. The addiction to "the funny man," who is a national misfortune there, is against it. Above all, the newspapers are against it.

It is often said that every nation has the government it deserves. What is much more certain is that every nation has the newspapers it deserves. The newspaper is the direct product of the want felt; the supply answers closely and inevitably to the demand. I suppose no one knows what the American newspapers are, who has not been obliged, for some length of time, to read either those newspapers or none at all. Powerful and valuable contributions occur scattered about in them. But on the whole, and taking the total impression and effect made by them, I should say that if one were searching for the best means to efface and kill in a whole nation the discipline of respect, the feeling for what is elevated, one could not do better than take the American newspapers. The absence of truth and soberness in them, the poverty in serious interest, the personality and sensation-mongering, are beyond belief. There are a few newspapers which are in whole, or in part, exceptions. The *New York Nation,* a weekly paper, may be paralleled with the *Saturday Review* as it was in its old and good days; but the *New York Nation* is conducted by a foreigner, and has an extremely small sale. In general, the daily papers are such that when one returns home one is moved to admiration and thankfulness not only at the great London papers, like the *Times* or the *Standard,* but quite as much at the great provincial newspapers too—papers like the *Leeds Mercury* and the *Yorkshire Post* in the north of England, like the *Scotsman* and the *Glasgow Herald* in Scotland.

The Americans used to say to me that what they valued was news, and that this their newspapers gave them. I at last made the reply: "Yes, news for the servants' hall!" I remember that a New York newspaper, one of the first I saw after landing in the country, had a long account, with the prominence we should give to the illness of the German Emperor or the arrest of the Lord Mayor of Dublin, of a young woman who had married a man who was a bag of bones, as we say, and who used to exhibit himself as a skeleton; of her growing horror in living with this man, and finally of her death. All this in the most minute detail, and described with all the writer's powers of rhetoric. This has always remained by me as a specimen of what the Americans call news.

You must have lived amongst their newspapers to know what

they are. If I relate some of my own experiences, it is because these will give a clear enough notion of what the newspapers over there are, and one remembers more definitely what has happened to one-self. Soon after arriving in Boston, I opened a Boston newspaper and came upon a column headed: "Tickings." By *tickings* we are to understand news conveyed through the tickings of the telegraph. The first "ticking" was: "Matthew Arnold is sixty-two years old"—an age, I must say in passing, which I had not then reached. The second "ticking" was: "Wales says, Mary is a darling;" the meaning being, that the Prince of Wales expressed great admiration for Miss Mary Anderson. This was at Boston, the American Athens. I proceeded to Chicago. An evening paper was given me soon after I arrived; I opened it, and found under a large-type heading, "*We have seen him arrive,*" the following picture of myself: "He has harsh features, supercilious manners, parts his hair down the middle, wears a single eyeglass and ill-fitting clothes." Notwithstanding this rather un-favourable introduction I was most kindly and hospitably received at Chicago. It happened that I had a letter for Mr. Medill, an elderly gentleman of Scotch descent, the editor of the chief news-paper in those parts, the *Chicago Tribune.* I called on him, and we conversed amicably together. Some time afterwards, when I had gone back to England, a New York paper published a criticism of Chicago and its people, purporting to have been contributed by me to the *Pall Mall Gazette* over here. It was a poor hoax, but many people were taken in and were excusably angry, Mr. Medill of the *Chicago Tribune* amongst the number. A friend telegraphed to me to know if I had written the criticism. I, of course, instantly tele-graphed back that I had not written a syllable of it. Then a Chicago paper is sent to me; and what I have the pleasure of reading, as the result of my contradiction, is this: "Arnold denies; Mr. Medill [my old friend] refuses to accept Arnold's disclaimer; says Arnold is a cur."

I once declared that in England the born lover of ideas and of light could not but feel that the sky over his head is of brass and iron. And so I say that, in America, he who craves for the *interesting* in civilisation, he who requires from what surrounds him satisfaction for his sense of beauty, his sense for elevation, will feel the sky over his head to be of brass and iron. The human problem, then, is as yet solved in the United States most imperfectly; a great void exists in the civilisation over there: a want of what is elevated and beautiful, of what is interesting.

QUESTIONS

1. Arnold says that his main intent is "to ask how the human problem is solved in the United States." How explicit is he in defining the nature of that problem? What would you say he means by it?

2. Arnold sets himself up to be a frank critic of the United States. What are the chief means by which he maintains a tactfully frank point of view rather than a brutally frank one? (Consider the presence of various kinds of material, the ordering of the general discussion, the degree of formality of his argument, the vocabulary of his criticism.)

3. In his phrase "true law of human nature" (paragraph five) Arnold assumes that there is such a thing as human nature. Does the assumption carry with it the suggestion of law? What is Arnold's true law? What would be the false law? What true law might the psychologist assume? Contrast Arnold's ideal man ("perfectly civilized"—paragraph five) with the Christian or the romantic ideal. Does he seem to disapprove of the genius who devotes his life to art?

4. To what words and phrases in the sixth paragraph does "true law" in the fifth stand in opposition? Would you say that Arnold's discussion in the fifth and sixth paragraphs lays a basis for dogmatism or modesty in judgment? What are the chief terms in his hierarchy of values, beginning with "comforts and conveniences" (paragraph six), that he discusses in the rest of the essay?

5. Why do you suppose Arnold refuses to make a decision for either the happy few or the happy multitude in paragraph ten? What evidence is there in the essay that he values one more than the other?

6. In paragraph thirteen Arnold speaks of "a natural manner" in American women as a consequence of equality. He calls it "a real note of civilization." In paragraph twenty he says that "everything is against

distinction in America," in particular "the glorification of 'the average man.'" Would you say his values are inconsistent? In other words, would you say that his true law of human nature (paragraph five) can lead at once to "a natural manner" and to "distinction" or that it can lead to only one of them?

7. Identify the standards (such as euphony) that underlie Arnold's particular judgments about beauty in paragraph eighteen.

8. Upon the basis of what definition of distinction does Arnold assert —in the nineteenth paragraph—that Lincoln lacks distinction? (It may be useful to recall his discussion of the complete human life in paragraph five.) Upon the basis of what definition of distinction might one judge Lincoln to possess more distinction than Washington? Considering the essay as a whole, would you say Arnold's inclinations are more aristocratic than democratic? Does his true law of human nature (paragraph five) seem to favor the development of an aristocracy or a democracy?

9. What standard of values would justify a newspaper's giving more space to the story of the woman who married the bag of bones than to the illness of the German Emperor? What is Arnold's criterion?

10. Arnold's key term, "interesting," is neither very interesting nor very precise. Can you justify his using it? Can you think of a better term that might have served his purpose?

11. Arnold gives more space to discussing comforts and conveniences than he gives to discussing beauty. On what basis would you criticize his doing so? On what basis could you justify it?

12. How would you describe Arnold's overall point of view in the essay? Justify your description by reference to his allusions, language, sentence structure, and particular likes and dislikes.

Materialism and Idealism
in American Life

GEORGE SANTAYANA

Though Santayana spent the last forty years of his life in Europe, having rebelled against much in the New England tradition, he was always conscious of his ties to America, on one occasion insisting that "It is as an American writer that I must be counted, if I am counted at all." His study of the American character and experience he pursued in many essays written after his departure; some are collected in *Character and Opinion in the United States*. His one novel, *The Last Puritan* (published when he was seventy-two), is set in New England and is a late attempt to clarify his own responses to the governing traditions of that region. The selection that follows, written during a stay in England in the early 1920's, is part of a larger study on the same subject. (Further headnote information on Santayana appears on p. 169.)

The language and traditions common to England and America are like other family bonds: they draw kindred together at the greater crises in life, but they also occasion at times a little friction and fault-finding. The groundwork of the two societies is so similar, that each nation, feeling almost at home with the other, and almost able to understand its speech, may instinctively resent what hin-

From *Character and Opinion* by George Santayana. Reprinted by permission of Constable & Co.. Ltd.

ders it from feeling at home altogether. Differences will tend to seem anomalies that have slipped in by mistake and through somebody's fault. Each will judge the other by his own standards, not feeling, as in the presence of complete foreigners, that he must make an effort of imagination and put himself in another man's shoes.

In matters of morals, manners, and art, the danger of comparisons is not merely that they may prove invidious, by ranging qualities in an order of merit which might wound somebody's vanity; the danger is rather that comparisons may distort comprehension, because in truth good qualities are all different in kind, and free lives are different in spirit. Comparison is the expedient of those who cannot reach the heart of the things compared; and no philosophy is more external and egotistical than that which places the essence of a thing in its relation to something else. In reality, at the center of every natural being there is something individual and incommensurable, a seed with its native impulses and aspirations, shaping themselves as best they can in their given environment. Variation is a consequence of freedom, and the slight but radical diversity of souls in turn makes freedom requisite. Instead of instituting in his mind any comparisons between the United States and other nations, I would accordingly urge the reader to forget himself and, in so far as such a thing may be possible for him or for me, to transport himself ideally with me into the outer circumstances of American life, the better to feel its inner temper, and to see how inevitably the American shapes his feelings and judgments, honestly reporting all things as they appear from his new and unobstructed station.

I speak of the American in the singular, as if there were not millions of them, north and south, east and west, of both sexes, of all ages, and of various races, professions, and religions. Of course the one American I speak of is mythical; but to speak in parables is inevitable in such a subject, and it is perhaps as well to do so frankly. There is a sort of poetic ineptitude in all human discourse when it tries to deal with natural and existing things. Practical men may not notice it, but in fact human discourse is intrinsically addressed not to natural existing things but to ideal essences, poetic or logical terms which thought may define and play with. When fortune or necessity diverts our attention from this congenial ideal sport to crude facts and pressing issues, we turn our frail poetic ideas into symbols for those terrible irruptive things. In that paper money of our own stamping, the legal tender of the mind, we are obliged to reckon all the movements and values of the world. The universal American I speak of is one of these symbols; and I should be still speaking in symbols and creating moral units and a false simplicity, if I spoke of classes pedantically subdivided, or individuals ideally integrated and defined. As it happens, the symbolic American can be made largely adequate to the facts; because, if there are immense differences between individual Americans—for some Americans are black—yet there is a great uniformity in their environment, customs, temper, and thoughts. They have all been uprooted from their several soils and ancestries and plunged together into one vortex, whirling irresistibly in a space otherwise quite empty. To be an American is of itself almost a moral condition, an education, and a career. Hence a single ideal figment can cover a large part of what each American is in his character, and almost the whole of what most Americans are in their social outlook and political judgments.

The discovery of the new world exercised a sort of selection among the inhabitants of Europe. All the colonists, except the Negroes, were voluntary exiles. The fortunate, the deeply rooted, and the lazy remained at home; the wilder instincts or dissatisfaction of others tempted them beyond the horizon. The American is accordingly the most adventurous, or the descendant of the most adventurous, of Europeans. It is in his blood to be socially a radical, though perhaps not intellectually. What has existed in the past, especially in the remote past, seems to him not only not authoritative, but irrelevant, inferior, and outworn. He finds it rather a sorry waste of time to think about the past at all. But his enthusiasm for the future is profound; he can conceive of no more decisive way of recommending an opinion or a practice than to say that it is what everybody is coming to adopt. This expectation of what he approves, or approval of what he expects, makes up his optimism. It is the necessary faith of the pioneer.

Such a temperament is, of course, not maintained in the nation merely by inheritance. Inheritance notoriously tends to restore the average of a race, and plays incidentally many a trick of atavism. What maintains this temperament and makes it national is social contagion or pressure—something immensely strong in democracies. The luckless American who is born a conservative, or who is drawn to poetic subtlety, pious retreats, or gay passions, nevertheless has the categorical excellence of work, growth, enterprise, reform, and prosperity dinned into his ears: every door is open in this direction and shut in the other; so that he either folds up his heart and withers in a corner—in remote places you sometimes find such a solitary gaunt idealist—or else he flies to Oxford or Florence or Montmartre to save his soul—or perhaps not to save it.

The optimism of the pioneer is not limited to his view of himself and his own future: it starts from that; but feeling assured, safe, and cheery within, he looks with smiling and most kindly eyes on everything and everybody about him. Individualism, roughness, and self-trust are supposed to go with selfishness and a cold heart; but I suspect that is a prejudice. It is rather dependence, insecurity, and mutual jostling that poison our placid gregarious brotherhood; and fanciful passionate demands upon people's affections, when they are disappointed, as they soon must be, breed ill will and a final meanness. The milk of human kindness is less apt to turn sour if the vessel that holds it stands steady, cool, and separate, and is not too often uncorked. In his affections the American is seldom passionate, often deep, and always kindly. If it were given me to look into the depths of a man's heart, and I did not find goodwill at the bottom, I should say without any hesitation, You are not an American. But as the American is an individualist his goodwill is not officious. His instinct is to think well of everybody, and to wish everybody well, but in a spirit of rough comradeship, expecting every man to stand on his own legs and to be helpful in his turn. When he has given his neighbor a·chance he thinks he has done enough for him; but he feels it is an absolute duty to do that. It will take some hammering to drive a coddling socialism into America.

As self-trust may pass into self-sufficiency, so optimism, kindness, and goodwill may grow into a habit of doting on everything. To the good American many subjects are sacred: sex is sacred, women are sacred, children are sacred, business is sacred, America is sacred, Masonic lodges and college clubs are sacred. This feeling grows out of the good opinion he wishes to have of these things, and serves to maintain it. If he did not regard all these things as sacred he might come to doubt sometimes if they were wholly good. Of this kind, too, is the idealism of single ladies in reduced circumstances who can see the soul of beauty in ugly things, and are perfectly happy because their old dog has such pathetic eyes, their minister is so eloquent, their garden with its three sunflowers is so pleasant, their dead friends were so devoted, and their distant relations are so rich.

Consider now the great emptiness of America: not merely the primitive physical emptiness, surviving in some regions, and the continental spacing of the chief natural features, but also the moral emptiness of a settlement where men and even houses are easily moved about, and no one, almost, lives where he was born or believes what he has been taught. Not that the American has jettisoned these impedimenta in anger; they have simply slipped from him as he moves. Great empty spaces bring a sort of freedom to both soul and body. You may pitch your tent where you will; or if ever you decide to build anything, it can be in a style of your own devising. You have room, fresh materials, few models, and no critics. You trust your own experience, not only because you must, but because you find you may do so safely and prosperously; the forces that determine fortune are not yet too complicated for one man to explore. Your detachable condition makes you lavish with money and cheerfully experimental; you lose little if you lose all, since you remain completely yourself. At the same time your absolute initiative gives you practice in coping with novel situations, and in being original; it teaches you shrewd management. Your life and mind will become dry and direct, with few decorative flourishes. In your works everything will be stark and pragmatic; you will not understand why anybody should make those little sacrifices to instinct or custom which we call grace. The fine arts will seem to you academic luxuries, fit to amuse the ladies, like Greek and Sanskrit; for while you will perfectly appreciate generosity in men's purposes, you will not admit that the execution of these purposes can be anything but business. Unfortunately the essence of the fine arts is that the execution should be generous too, and delightful in itself; therefore the fine arts will suffer, not so much in their express professional pursuit—for then they become practical tasks and a kind of business—as in that diffused charm which qualifies all human action when men are artists by nature. Elaboration, which is something to accomplish, will be preferred to simplicity, which is something to rest in; manners will suffer somewhat; speech will suffer horribly. For the American the urgency of his novel attack upon matter, his zeal in gathering its fruits, precludes meanderings in primrose paths; devices must be short cuts, and symbols must be mere symbols. If his wife wants luxuries, of course she may have them; and if he has vices, that can be provided for too; but they must all be set down under those headings in his ledgers.

At the same time, the American is imaginative; for where life is intense, imagination is intense also. Were he not imaginative he would not live so much in the future. But his imagination is practical, and the future it forecasts is immediate; it works with the clearest and least ambiguous terms known to his experience, in terms of number, measure, contrivance, economy, and speed. He is an idealist working on matter. Understanding as he does the material potentialities of things, he is successful in invention, conservative in reform, and quick in emergencies. All his life he jumps into the train after it has started and jumps out before it has stopped; and he never once gets left behind, or breaks a leg.

There is an enthusiasm in his sympathetic handling of material forces which goes far to cancel the illiberal character which it might otherwise assume. The good workman hardly distinguishes his artistic intention from the potency in himself and in things which is about to realise that intention. Accordingly his ideals fall into the form of premonitions and prophecies; and his studious prophecies often come true. So do the happy workmanlike ideals of the American. When a poor boy, perhaps, he dreams of an education, and presently he gets an education, or at least a degree; he dreams of growing rich, and he grows rich—only more slowly and modestly, perhaps, than he expected; he dreams of marrying his Rebecca and, even if he marries a Leah instead, he ultimately finds in Leah his Rebecca after all. He dreams of helping to carry on and to accelerate the movement of a vast, seething, progressive society, and he actually does so. Ideals clinging so close to nature are almost sure of fulfilment; the American beams with a certain self-confidence and sense of mastery; he feels that God and nature are working with him.

Idealism in the American accordingly goes hand in hand with present contentment and with foresight of what the future very likely will actually bring. He is not a revolutionist; he believes he is already on the right track and moving towards an excellent destiny. In revolutionists, on the contrary, idealism is founded on dissatisfaction and expresses it. What exists seems to them an absurd jumble of irrational accidents and bad habits, and they want the future to be based on reason and to be the pellucid embodiment of all their maxims. All their zeal is for something radically different from the actual and (if they only knew it) from the possible; it is ideally simple, and they love it and believe in it because their nature craves it. They think life would be set free by the destruction of all its organs. They are therefore extreme idealists in the region of hope, but not at all, as poets and artists are, in the region of perception and memory. In the atmosphere of civilized life they miss all the refraction and all the fragrance; so that in their conception of actual things they are apt to be crude realists; and their ignorance and inexperience of the moral world, unless it comes of ill-luck, indicates their incapacity for education. Now incapacity for education, when united with great inner vitality, is one root of idealism. It is what condemns us all, in the region of sense, to substitute perpetually what we are capable of imagining for what things may be in themselves; it is what condemns us, wherever it extends, to think *a priori;* it is what keeps us bravely and incorrigibly pursuing what we call the good—that is, what would fulfil the demands of our nature—however little provision the fates may have made for it. But the want of insight on the part of revolutionists touching the past and the present infects in an important particular their idealism about the future; it renders their dreams of the future unrealizable. For in human beings—this may not be true of other animals, more perfectly preformed—experience is necessary to pertinent and concrete thinking; even our primitive instincts are blind until they stumble upon some occasion that solicits them; and they can be much transformed or deranged by their first partial satisfactions. Therefore a man who does not idealize his experience, but idealizes *a priori,* is incapable of true prophecy; when he dreams he raves, and the more he criticizes the less he helps. American idealism, on the contrary, is nothing if not helpful, nothing if not pertinent to practicable transformations; and when the American frets, it is because whatever is useless and impertinent, be it idealism or inertia, irritates him; for it frustrates the good results which he sees might so easily have been obtained.

The American is wonderfully alive; and his vitality, not having often found a suitable outlet, makes him appear agitated on the surface; he is always letting off an unnecessarily loud blast of incidental steam. Yet his vitality is not superficial; it is inwardly prompted, and as sensitive and quick as a magnetic needle. He is inquisitive, and ready with an answer to any question that he may put to himself of his own accord; but if you try to pour instruction into him, on matters that do not touch his own spontaneous life, he shows the most extraordinary powers of resistance and oblivescence; so that he often is remarkably expert in some direc-

tions and surprisingly obtuse in others. He seems to bear lightly
the sorrowful burden of human knowledge. In a word, he is young.

What sense is there in this feeling, which we all have, that the
American is young? His country is blessed with as many elderly
people as any other, and his descent from Adam, or from the Darwinian rival of Adam, cannot be shorter than that of his European
cousins. Nor are his ideas always very fresh. Trite and rigid bits of
morality and religion, with much seemly and antique political lore,
remain axiomatic in him, as in the mind of a child; he may carry all
this about with an unquestioning familiarity which does not com-
port understanding. To keep traditional sentiments in this way in-
sulated and uncriticized is itself a sign of youth. A good young man
is naturally conservative and loyal on all those subjects which his
experience has not brought to a test; advanced opinions on politics,
marriage, or literature are comparatively rare in America; they are
left for the ladies to discuss, and usually to condemn, while the
men get on with their work. In spite of what is old-fashioned in his
more general ideas, the American is unmistakably young; and this,
I should say, for two reasons: one, that he is chiefly occupied with
his immediate environment, and the other, that his reactions upon it
are inwardly prompted, spontaneous, and full of vivacity and self-
trust. His views are not yet lengthened; his will is not yet broken or
transformed. The present moment, however, in this, as in other
things, may mark a great change in him; he is perhaps now reaching his majority, and all I say may hardly apply today, and may
not apply at all tomorrow. I speak of him as I have known him; and
whatever moral strength may accrue to him later, I am not sorry to
have known him in his youth. The charm of youth, even when it is a
little boisterous, lies in nearness to the impulses of nature, in a
quicker and more obvious obedience to that pure, seminal principle
which, having formed the body and its organs, always directs their
movements, unless it is forced by vice or necessity to make them
crooked, or to suspend them. Even under the inevitable crust of
age the soul remains young, and, wherever it is able to break
through, sprouts into something green and tender. We are all as

young at heart as the most youthful American, but the seed in his case has fallen upon virgin soil, where it may spring up more bravely and with less respect for the giants of the wood. Peoples seem older when their perennial natural youth is encumbered with more possessions and prepossessions, and they are mindful of the many things they have lost or missed. The American is not mindful of them.

QUESTIONS

1. In his opening sentences Santayana relies upon two metaphors, "family bonds" and "groundwork," to describe a relationship between England and America that he assumes to exist. What evidence that he presents in paragraphs two and three might be used to argue against the assumption? Can you think of any other counter-evidence? How important is the assumption to the main body of the essay?

2. Consider the following substitution for the third and fourth sentences in the second paragraph: In reality, at the center of all natural beings there are the same impulses, which are shaped variously according to environment; variation among nations is a long-term consequence of local climate, geography, material wealth, etc. (which lead to differing social and cultural conditions); variation can be mitigated by the establishment of a world state. What differences and similarities do the two statements show in their assumptions about human nature, the influence of environment, and the proper conduct of life?

3. Where does Santayana state most explicitly the assumptions upon which he justifies discussing America alone and discussing a mythical American? What assumption does he make about the perception of reality by the mind in the third paragraph, especially where he talks about "ideal essences"? Does that assumption govern his reference to "the heart of the things . . . , the essence of a thing," in the second paragraph?

4. To what extent, if any, does Santayana's image of the American in the latter part of paragraph three contradict his notions about human nature and the influence of environment in paragraph two? If you find a discrepancy, can you justify it in any way?

5. What single assumption about human conduct underlies Santayana's assertion at the beginning of paragraph four that "the fortunate, the deeply rooted, and the lazy remained at home"? Can you imagine a circumstance under which a lazy person might have emigrated? By strict logic, if it was the fortunate, the deeply rooted, and the lazy who stayed home, it was the unfortunate, the shallowly rooted, and the energetic who emigrated. That Santayana uses instead the term "the most adventurous" suggests that he makes another assumption about the consequence of a man's being fortunate, deeply rooted, or lazy. What is that assumption? Does it seem valid?

6. What assumption does Santayana make in paragraph five about the conditions under which an artist thrives? Can you think of any notable cases that would support, or refute, his assumption? Is his assumption here consistent with his remarks on poets and artists in the tenth paragraph?

7. Examine Santayana's metaphor of the milk of human kindness in the sixth paragraph. Does he employ it as argument, a means of repetition, illumination, or humor?

8. What assumption in paragraph two covers the assertion in paragraph eight that "Great empty spaces bring a sort of freedom to both soul and body"? Can you match some of the assertions about American life in paragraph eight with contrasting assertions that might seem equally valid (for instance: great empty spaces enervate the soul, bring chaos to it)?

9. In paragraph nine Santayana links thinking about the future to imagination; in paragraph four he links thinking about the future to indifference to the past. Express these connections as assumptions. How convincing do you find his illustrations of practical imagination in America? What other *kind* of illustration might he have adduced? Does his particular kind of illustration, as it is employed here and elsewhere in the essay, seem more appropriate? Why?

10. In paragraph ten Santayana says that the American "is not a revolutionist." In paragraph four he says that "it is in his blood to be socially a radical, though perhaps not intellectually." Is the contradiction real or apparent? What assumed values underlie Santayana's preference of American idealism over revolutionary idealism in the tenth paragraph?

11. In composing his mythical American Santayana declines to draw more than one portrait (see paragraph three). Does his American, nevertheless, seem to be rather more like one particular group of Americans than another? Do you know of any significant group whose qualities might seem contradictory to those he establishes? Taking into account that he is describing America of about 1920, would you say that his broad description seems accurate?

12. How similar are Santayana's own qualities, as you infer them from the essay, to those of the mythical American he describes?

The American Political Tradition

CARL BECKER

Probably the most shaping influence on Becker's thought occurred during his student days at the University of Wisconsin,
where he studied with the great historian Frederick Jackson
Turner, daily sharing, as he later wrote, in "the inestimable
privilege of watching an original and penetrating intelligence
at work." From Turner's theories about the frontier, Becker
gained a lasting interest in American history and particularly
in American democracy, subjects he returned to in many essays (some collected in *Every Man His Own Historian* and
New Liberties for Old) and in a number of books—*The Eve
of the Revolution, The Declaration of Independence, Modern
Democracy*. His last work, *Freedom and Responsibility in the
American Way of Life*, from which the following is a selection,
was originally a series of lectures he delivered at the University of Michigan. (Further headnote information on Becker
appears on p. 125.)

On certain conventional occasions we rise and sing to the land of
the free and the home of the brave, land of the Pilgrim's pride, land
where our fathers died. No doubt there is as much symbolic truth
in these phrases as one can reasonably expect to find in a patriotic
hymn. But it is worth noting that in all the stages of our history our

fathers, if we go back a few generations, mostly died somewhere else. We are a collection of people from all the nations of Europe, and even of the world—people who have in successive generations come here in order to escape oppression or to improve the material conditions of life. Goethe expressed this general feeling when he exclaimed: "America, you have it better!" I once asked a Greek who had recently come to this country how he liked it here. He agreed with Goethe. "I like it fine," he said. "I am a Greek Jew. So what? No one asks am I a Greek Jew. In America is everything better for poor people like me." This is the essential fact: in America everything has always been better for poor people. It is this conviction, no doubt, that makes us a united nation, although by all the rules known to an Adolf Hitler we should be neither united nor a nation. Native- and foreign-born alike are united by the profound conviction that America has the best of it. We are attached to the U.S.A. less for what it is than for what it has to offer, less because of its sacred rills and templed hills than because it is the place in the world where all comers can find the best opportunity to do what they like and get what they want. In this sense it has always been, and has always been thought by the peoples of Europe to be, the land of the free because it is the land of opportunity.

It was in this light—a somewhat too glamorous light, no doubt—that the first settlers looked to the new world of America. John Winthrop tells us that he and his associates decided to remove from England for two reasons mainly. One was that they wished to escape from the hopeless struggle with bishops and king in order to establish a "due form of government both civil and ecclesiastical." The other was that he (and no doubt other men in his position) found "his means heer soe shortened as he shall not be able to continue in that place and employment where he now is." Winthrop was a man of substantial estate, and if his means were shortened, how much more so were those of ordinary men! "This lande," he says, "grows weary of her inhabitants, soe as man is heer of less price amongst us than a horse or sheep. . . . We stand here striving for places of habitation . . . and in ye mean tyme suffer a

whole continent as fruitful and convenient for the use of man to lie
waste without any improvement." To be free of oppression or to
better their fortunes—for these reasons chiefly the first settlers came
to America, and from that time to this the poor and oppressed
classes of Europe have continued to come for the same reasons.

The first settlers found plenty of freedom in the new world—so
much indeed that in the first years it nearly wiped them out. But
they were for the most part a hardy lot. As William Bradford said:
"They are too delicate and unfitte to beginne new Plantations and
Collonies that cannot endure the biting of a muskeeto." They stuck
it out, the hardy ones, enduring all things—the mosquitoes and the
Indians, the climate, even in some winters near starvation. They
stuck it out and established the form of government that seemed to
them due and proper. No doubt they were still subjects of the king
and limited by the terms of royal charters, but king and Parliament and bishops were three thousand miles away, and efforts on
their part to interfere with the due form of government could be
ignored or, with sufficient ingenuity, made of slight effect. And if
there were in any colony men too cantankerous to submit to the
due form of government, they could always get out. In the New
World men did not need to stand striving for places of habitation.
And so Anne Hutchinson, who, "speaking from a mere motion of
the spirit," criticized the ministers for preaching a covenant of
works, and Roger Williams, who believed in soul liberty and even
went so far as to say that the land belonged to the Indians, got out
of Massachusetts Bay, or were forced out, and went to Rhode Island,
where another due form of government was easily improvised and
set up. And then there was Thomas Hooker, who had no great objection to the due form of government in Massachusetts Bay, but
who found his town second to Boston and himself overtopped in influence by Winthrop and Cotton. He and the people of Newtown,
therefore, as we are told, began to "have a hankering" after the
Connecticut Valley; and in 1634 they requested from the General
Court permission to leave Massachusetts Bay, advancing three
reasons—"their want of accommodation for their cattle, the fruit-

fulness and commodiousness of Connecticut, and the *strong bent of
their spirits to remove thither.*"

The migration of the people of Newtown to the Connecticut
Valley was in miniature a repetition of the migration of the first
settlers from England to the New World and the prototype of all
the later migrations from the older settlements to the uninhabited
hinterland. Whenever people in the older settlements found the conditions of life unsatisfactory, whether for lack of accommodation for
their cattle or some other reason, they were apt to have a "hankering" for some more fruitful and commodious region farther west.
Nothing then restrained them from following the "strong bent of
their spirits"; and so for three centuries the frontier of settlement
was always moving on—into the upcountry of Virginia, into western
New York and Pennsylvania, over the Alleghenies into the vast and
fertile woodland and prairie country of the Middle West, across the
Rockies to the Pacific coast. The difficulties and hardships encoun-
tered in this quest for new fortunes were many, and the conditions
of life on the edge of the frontier were often hazardous and always
bleak and primitive. But every successive frontier was a new "new
world" which offered to its first settlers essentially the same advantages that New England and Virginia offered to the first settlers
from England. It offered them freedom—free land, so that they
need not stand striving for places of habitation; freedom from the
social and religious conventions and restraints of a more settled
society; and freedom within broad limits to establish a due form of
government, a government that seemed to them suitable and adequate for people living on terms of equality and in something close
to a primitive state of nature.

The decisive factors in securing so much freedom and equality
for the people of the United States were the country's geographic
isolation from Europe, its vast extent, and its rich and seemingly
unlimited natural resources. It is related that an Englishman riding
from New York to San Francisco, having after a two days' journey
finally arrived at Santa Fe, remarked that the discovery of America
by Columbus seemed in no way remarkable, since it was difficult to

see how anyone could have missed it. The people of the United States have never been troubled by the problem of *Lebensraum*. There has always been room enough; until recently there has always been (and this is the essential point) plenty of free or relatively free land to be had for the taking. Speculators have done their best at various times to buy it up and hold it for monopoly prices, but with slight success. There was always too much of it, and the consequence is that for the greater part of its history the United States has been predominantly a nation of small farmers owning their land in fee simple—farmers to whom the term "tenant" or "peasant" was unknown and to whom it was in no sense applicable.

Benjamin Franklin, with his sure grasp of economic influences, foresaw this development. He noted the fact that industrialized cities of the European type, with their hopelessly impoverished working classes crowded together in slums, could never develop in America so long as any man with a little gumption could go elsewhere and become the independent owner of a farm. It was this situation that defeated every attempt to transplant and perpetuate in the New World the aristocratic social structure and upper-class political domination that prevailed in the old. In Franklin's time there were, it is true, pale replicas of the English class system in most of the colonies. Political control and social prestige were the prerogatives of a few interrelated landowning and merchant families—people of comparative wealth, living in fine houses, who preserved the social amenities and were conversant with the ideas then current among the educated upper classes in England. They thought of themselves as "the better sort" and looked with benevolent condescension on the "populace" of small farmers in the country and artisans and mechanics in the towns. "A poor man," according to a Philadelphia humorist writing in 1775, "has rarely the honor of speaking to a gentleman on any terms and never with familiarity but for a few weeks before election. How many . . . mechanics have been made happy within this fortnight by a shake of the hand, a pleasing smile, and a little familiar chat with gentlemen who have not for these seven years past condescended to look at them." [1] But, for all that, poverty and servility in the European sense were virtually unknown, and any young man of character and ability could, as the saying was, "get ahead" and "make something of himself"—could acquire an education (perhaps, signing himself Cassius, write a piece for the newspaper describing a certain condescension in gentlemen), could acquire a little property, and so edge himself, or at all events his children, into the reserved precincts of the "better sort." Even this mild species of unstable distinctions was seriously impaired by the American Revolution, which was as much an uprising of the populace against the better sort as it was an uprising of the better sort against British control, and it virtually disappeared as a political force in 1828 with the election of Andrew Jackson.

The election of Jackson represented the triumph of the masses over the classes, of the agricultural democracy of the newer West and South over the industrial and moneyed aristocracy of the older East, of the untutored backwoodsman over the cultivated and fastidious gentleman and scholar. At the inaugural reception given by the new president, so we are told, "the White House was invaded by a mob of men, women, and boys who stood on chairs in their muddy boots, fought for the refreshments, and trod glass and porcelain underfoot. 'It would have done Mr. Wilberforce's heart good,' wrote an onlooker, 'to have seen a stout black wench eating in this free country a jelly with a gold spoon in the President's house.' Jackson was glad to escape by a window; and the mob was drawn off like flies to honey, by tubs of punch being placed on the lawn. Washington society thought of the Tuileries on the 10th of August, and shuddered." [2] This episode may be taken to symbolize the fact that the Middle West was emerging as the central and dominant political force in the United States, and that the rough-and-ready and unabashed freedom and equality of the frontier would make short shrift of ceremony, of distinctions of rank

[1] Charles and Mary Beard, *The Rise of American Civilization*, I, 131.
[2] Samuel Eliot Morison and Henry Steele Commager, *The Growth of the American Republic*, 355 [Edition of 1930].

and office, and of the inherited European code of gentility and good manners so highly prized and carefully observed by the better sort.

Such were the essential aspects of the historical experience of the American people that have had a fundamental influence in shaping their ideas about freedom and equality, the function of the government, and the liberty and responsibility of the individual. Since there was for so long a time more fertile land than there were people to cultivate it, it was always relatively easy for the common man to make his own way and pay his own score, unassisted by *noblesse oblige* or communal charity and without benefit of a watchful, paternalistic government: always relatively easy, therefore, for the common man to be and to feel independent, a free man and be damned to you, stranger! Since the people were always on the move from the more settled to the undeveloped regions of the country, successive generations of common men were forced to discard settled customs and fixed habits, to break with family ties and old associations, and, relying on their own initiative and common sense, to reshape social institutions and forms of governments to suit the practical needs of life in new and relatively primitive conditions. In few countries have the common people been so little hampered by tradition in their thought and action, or had so often to adapt their lives to new and often hazardous conditions, or had so often the opportunity to follow the bent of their spirits in framing fundamental constitutional laws and new forms of governments. It is this peculiar historical experience that has disposed the American people to emphasize the freedom and responsibility of the individual and to minimize the function and authority of the government: that is to say, to take it for granted that freedom of thought and conduct is the natural right of the individual, and that government, so far from being something transcendent or divine, is essentially a homespun affair, a convenient committee appointed by the people to perform certain specified communal services, and in the nature of the case bound not to go beyond its instructions.

This conception of the function of government and the freedom and responsibility of the individual, although firmly enough grounded in the historical experience of the American people, is also supported by a political philosophy—a philosophy clearly formulated at the very time when the United States became an independent nation, and purporting to set forth the imprescriptible rights of all men and the essential purpose of all just governments. The confidence of the people of the United States in the rightness of their institutions and freedoms, sufficiently great in any case, is therefore all the greater because they can be reminded every Fourth of July that their institutions and freedoms are the kind of institutions and freedoms best suited to all mankind because prescribed by the law of nature and the will of God.

The natural rights political philosophy was of European origin. The Protestant Reformation was based on the doctrine of justification by faith—the doctrine that the individual becomes a good man by adhering to the law of God rather than by submitting to the laws and conventions of society. In the seventeenth century this doctrine was employed to justify the English revolution against the established authority of church and king, and at that time the law of God was often identified with the law of nature. But it was in the eighteenth century, in connection with the revolt against the despotic power of kings claiming to rule by divine right and supported by a privileged aristocracy of priests and nobles, that the natural rights philosophy was the most clearly formulated, and was given official sanction, as one may say, by the French Declaration of the Rights of Man and the Citizen and the American Declaration of Independence.

In the Declaration of Independence Jefferson expressed what he called "the common sense of the subject" in the following brief passage:

We hold these truths to be self-evident; that all men are created equal; that they are endowed by their Creator with inherent and unalienable rights; that among these are life, liberty, and the pursuit of happiness; that to secure these rights governments are in-

stituted among men. deriving their just powers from the consent of the governed; that whenever any form of government becomes destructive of these ends, it is the right of the people to alter or to abolish it, and to institute a new government, laying its foundation on such principles and organizing its powers in such form as to them shall seem most likely to effect their safety and happiness.

This statement may be reduced to four fundamental principles: (1) that the universe, including man, is subject to the law of nature, which is a revelation of the will of God; (2) that all men have certain natural or God-given rights; (3) that governments exist to secure these rights; and (4) that all just governments derive their authority from the consent of the governed.

This is the essence of the political philosophy formulated in the eighteenth century to justify the liberal-democratic revolution of modern times. It was revolutionary only in the sense that it was a reinterpretation in secular and liberal terms of the Christian doctrine of the origin, nature, and destiny of man. It denied that man is naturally prone to evil and error, and for that reason incapable, apart from the compulsion of state and church, of arriving at the truth or living the good life. It affirmed, on the contrary, that men are endowed by their Creator with reason in order that they may progressively discover that which is true, and with conscience in order that they may be disposed, in the measure of their enlightenment, to follow that which is good. If Jefferson and his contemporaries entertained a somewhat too optimistic faith in the natural intelligence and goodness of men, the reason is that they were living at a time when in most countries men were too much governed—a time when the oppressions suffered by the majority of men were those imposed by the organized authority of church and state. For the majority of men, liberty could therefore be most easily conceived in terms of the emancipation of the individual from governmental constraint, and in order to justify such emancipation it was necessary to assume that men were by nature sufficiently rational and sufficiently good for the restraints of law and custom safely to be reduced to a minimum.

For Jefferson and his contemporaries the essential freedoms were, naturally enough, those which had been the most commonly denied. Of these, there were three principal ones—freedom of opinion in order that the truth might prevail; freedom of occupation and economic enterprise in order that careers might be open to talent; and freedom from arbitrary government in order that no man might be compelled against his will. These freedoms were precisely what Jefferson meant by "liberty" as one of the inherent and inalienable rights of man, and it was through the fullest enjoyment of these freedoms that the "pursuit of happiness" would be the most likely to result in the greatest happiness for the greatest number of men. And so we arrive at the central idea of the natural rights philosophy in respect to the function of government and the freedom and responsibility of the individual: the happy idea that the best way to secure the inalienable rights of man is just to leave the individual as free as possible to do what he likes, and that accordingly no form of government can secure them so well as the one that governs least.

The natural rights philosophy made its way in America with far less opposition than it did in Europe. It was accepted as a convenient theory for justifying the political separation of the American colonies from Great Britain; but with that object attained no further revolution of serious import, such as occurred in France, was required to bring the social and political institutions of the United States into harmony with the philosophy that presided at its birth as an independent nation. The state and Federal constitutions were scarcely more than a codification of colonial institutions with the Parliament and king left out, and the natural rights philosophy of the Declaration of Independence was accepted without much opposition as the obvious and necessary foundation of the new political structure. If the colonies had ever been governed by a king, it was only by a king *in absentia* exercising a merely nominal control. Monarchical absolutism and the theory of divine right, the vested interest of a ruling landed aristocracy based on birth, the moral and political influence of an organized state religion—none of these obstacles to political and social democracy, which had to be overcome in all European countries, was ever in any real sense a part of the American political practice or tradition. The people of the United States never had to live with the resistant survivals of an *ancien régime:* never had, like the British, to place a king in cold storage in order to keep a Pretender off their backs, or, like the French, to make terms with powerful royalist and clerical parties openly or secretly bent on destroying the republic. The natural rights philosophy was therefore accepted by the people of the United States, as one may say, without debate and by a rising vote. It seemed to them, as Jefferson said, merely the "common sense of the subject"; and it seemed to them the common sense of the subject because it was scarcely more than an ideological description of institutions and a way of life to which they had long been accustomed and to which they were entirely devoted.

QUESTIONS

1. Does "symbolic truth," rather than merely "truth," contribute to or minimize the skeptical point of view that Becker takes in the second sentence of the selection? Where in the first sentence do you find hints of his skepticism? Do you find any further skepticism in the first paragraph? What other passages in the selection—if any—are notable for their skepticism?

2. To what extent does Becker assume, and to what extent does he attempt to prove, that Americans believe they have the best of it (paragraph one)? To what extent does he assume or attempt to prove that America is a united nation? What logical assumption does he seem to make about the relationship between belief and unity? To what extent, if any, would the validity of his assumptions be affected by the assertion that many people came to America to escape justice, to avoid responsibilities, or to be with their husbands?

3. It is generally agreed that the Puritans who came to this country to escape religious persecution set up a theocratic government that was itself intolerant. Would you say that Becker's description of the colonists' setting up "the form of government that seemed to them due and proper" (paragraph three) is meant—implicitly—to apply to the Puritans? What does Becker seem to be assuming about the character, or motives, of the colonists who set up the due and proper form of government? What differing assumed qualities of character underlie his reference to the "young man of character" in paragraph six? Distinguish the roles in American history that Becker ascribes to the two character types.

4. In his discussion in paragraphs five and six does Becker assume that men control external events or that external events control men? Show that the assumption applies to life in Europe as well as to life in America. What corollary assumption does Becker seem to make in the same paragraphs about the way human beings generally behave towards each other? Does his view here seem consistent with his view of the colonies explored in Question 3?

5. Given the assumptions established in the preceding question, what prediction might be made about the future of democracy in America? To what extent does Becker's description of the course of American history in paragraphs three to eight support your answer?

6. Beginning with paragraphs nine and ten, Becker is primarily concerned with freedom as a force motivating men rather than as a consequence. On the basis of these and the preceding paragraphs, what would you say are the three or four broad forces—applicable to the development of all kinds of government—that Becker assumes to dominate the course of history? (Your answer to Question 4 will help you here.) Can you think of other forces to which other historians have attached greater significance (for instance, the great man, such as Napoleon)? To which of the three or four forces does Becker attribute the greatest significance in the past history of America? To which does he seem to ascribe the more enduring power? Upon which must he rely if he believes that American democracy will survive?

7. Becker's description of the history of the doctrine of the rights of man relies upon an assumption about historical continuity. From an analysis of paragraph ten, define that assumption as precisely as you can. Show that it applies to the discussion in the final paragraph of the acceptance of the doctrine of the rights of man both in America and in

Europe. Show that Becker discounts historical continuity in his major argument in the first eight paragraphs. Is there any evidence in the first eight paragraphs—explicit or inadvertent—of such continuity? What, presumably, would have been the history of America had continuity been the over-riding historical force? To which of the forces identified in Question 6 is the force of continuity intimately related?

8. What assumption about the development of ideas underlies Becker's reasoning in the sentence "If Jefferson and his contemporaries . . ." (paragraph twelve) and his similar reasoning in the opening sentence of paragraph thirteen? Does this assumption complement or contradict the assumption about historical continuity explored in the previous question?

9. Defend the view that Becker's basic assumptions (explored mainly in Questions 4, 6, and 7) make him a skeptic. Is this skepticism the same as the skepticism identified in Question 1? Can you explain why the selection as a whole does not convey the impression of skepticism?

SECTION V

Tone and Style

Tone and Style

Every so often a teacher says to a well-intentioned student:
"Your papers are unified, coherent, well-organized, well-developed,
thoughtful, brave, clean, and reverent. They are flat and uninterest-
ing. Try to get involved in what you are saying, try to assume an
attitude towards your subject and your reader, try to indulge a
mood as you write, try to see your theme as an experience instead
of as an assignment." The next theme he gets from the student is
all style and tone: loud and clear.

The advice and the response address themselves to the most
elusive and the most engaging aspect of composition. In one respect,
tone and style are the heart of every course in reading and writing:
they underlie discussions of informality, simplicity, precision, and
economy. But as qualities that the individual theme might possess—
distinguishing its informality and simplicity from those qualities in
another theme—they seldom receive attention. They are matters to
attend to when the student learns to write grammatically and
coherently. Or the teacher knows that they cannot—and should not
—be taught: he has had too much experience with the well-intentioned student. Yet how gratifying it is to read the occasional theme
that does distinguish itself from the mass; how gratifying to hear
the political speech—by a former student—that was written by a
person rather than by a committee, a ghost, or an IBM machine;
how important to know the difference between false notes and true,
between Timestyle and—what? Since tone and style are sometimes

the essence of an essay and never a negligible part of it, they deserve the student's attention.

Tone in writing may most easily be thought of as the writer's tone of voice; it is the attitude that he assumes towards his subject and his reader. When one well-intentioned student wrote, "Say now, did it ever strike you that George Orwell and Carl Becker operate on the same wave length," he was assuming a breezy tone. He could have said—and meant the same thing, "Offhand it might not seem so, but George Orwell and Carl Becker have a lot in common"; or, "A careful comparison between George Orwell and Carl Becker displays many points of agreement between the two men." "Say now" is colloquial; in contrast to "offhand" it does not contribute directly to the meaning of its sentence; it serves only to establish an air of familiar address, as though writer and reader were in conversation. "Strike you" is on the borderline between colloquial and informal written language; "operate on the same wave length" is a vivid and perhaps tasteless metaphor, casually tossed off, irreverent. (For reverence, see "A careful comparison between George Orwell. . . .") Sometimes in analyzing tone we merely want to be able to say: the tone is thus and such because of thus and such elements. Sometimes we want to know why a particular tone was adopted: to meet—or to counteract—a frivolous subject, occasion, audience. At other times we want to pass judgment upon the tone: it is vulgarly irreverent; it is stuffily reverent; it is uncertain, confused.

A writer establishes the tone of a piece of writing by a variety of means, some of them deliberate and artful, some of them unconscious and automatic. He knows, for instance, that "ain't" is regarded by parents, teachers, and some philologists as a vulgar colloquialism. If he uses it in a piece of writing, other than reportage of conversation, he can achieve certain effects: a tone of casual humor, or of disrespect, or of utter familiarity. Of course if he doesn't know about "ain't," he cannot deliberately achieve these effects; he is likely instead to produce a jumble of uncontrolled tones. Few students in college will have trouble controlling "ain't," but they may have trouble with other words. What contrasts in tone are suggested by the following pairs: offhand, at first blush; tasteless, vulgar; jumble, hodge-podge?

Diction affects tone. Tone affects diction. The tone that a writer embraces may induce him—sometimes without his thinking about it—to choose one sort of word rather than another. It must have been easy for Lincoln, with his legal background and with a solemn occasion to contemplate, to find his formal, magisterial, abstractly metaphorical language: "Fourscore and seven years ago our fathers brought forth on this continent. . . ." How easy it is for all of us, when we are angry, to use language unbecoming to our normal civilized selves. More than diction is involved, too. The long balanced sentences of Lincoln contribute to his solemn tone, and the short, irregular phrases of an angry man suggest his passion. Diction may be the most obvious and most important element in tone, but sentence structure, rhythm, and sound are also significant. With all of these elements, the degree of conscious control is variable. It is not in the nature of man to be entirely deliberate in his writing; and among those who try to be most deliberate, few achieve anything like mastery of the complexities confronting them.

Tone, it may appear, is closely allied with point of view. When we say that the tone of the Gettysburg Address is formal, magisterial, we suggest a point of view. The distinction, nevertheless, is real. Tone is to be thought of as the mood, or perhaps the manner, of the writer; point of view is his stated (or implicit) outlook. Tone may vary considerably within an essay. Point of view is more likely to remain constant; variation in it will more quickly raise the question of consistency.

Some years after George Santayana's death, Bertrand Russell said of him, "There was always something rather prim about Santayana. His clothes were always neat, and even in country lanes he wore patent-leather button boots. I think a person of sufficient intelligence might perhaps have guessed these characteristics from his literary style." Any student who wants to may test his intelligence by re-reading the two Santayana essays in this text; and he may be forced to decide that Russell is wrong. But whether Russell is wrong or right about Santayana, he is re-phrasing a common opinion, one that received its classic expression in Buffon's words: the style is the man himself. The opinion is not easy to explain or defend.

Santayana may be a poor example. Consider the three selections by D. H. Lawrence in the text. They were chosen for their excellence, but they may have been chosen badly. Consider "Etna." Isn't the word "whither" in the first paragraph too poetical? Isn't the phrase "because why?" in the second too colloquial? Aren't there too many adjectives, too many exclamation points? Isn't there too much enthusiasm and exaggeration? Doesn't the passage seem labored, precious? The answer to this argument is to say that it too is enthusiastic and exaggerated. Doesn't "Etna" succeed because of the playful balance that Lawrence achieves between the poetical and the colloquial? Doesn't he intend that his adjectives and exclamation points should undercut themselves? Doesn't he mock his enthusiasm (without minimizing it)? No doubt both arguments are right. We have terms—such as poetical and colloquial—that critics on both sides of the fence can agree upon; and we can find illustrations other than from Lawrence that most critics would describe and evaluate similarly. Even unskilled readers would agree about Sir Arthur Quiller-Couch's famous example: "Regret to inform you, the hand that rocked the cradle has kicked the bucket." But D. H. Lawrence, along with many other writers, is another, subtle problem. In the end, each critic goes his own way, with his argument intact.

The reason for the impasse is that with sophisticated, complex prose, the critic proceeds beyond description and conventional evaluation. His judgment becomes subjective, the response of a man to the presence of another man. Many of the marks of style are nameable; they can be pointed to and practised upon: write a paragraph employing metaphor in the manner of D. H. Lawrence. But the marks are ultimately the marks of an individual man. The recurring presence of conspicuous metaphor in an essay, the easy profusion of sensuous metaphor, suggest a particular mentality. (Within five lines of "Etna" we have "why can't one sit still," "sunny . . . sea," "jewel of Calabria," "like a fire-opal," "dog-star laying a . . . gleam," "as if baying at us," "Orion marching.") In judging a sophisticated style the critic responds as a person to another person; and in such an act he shows preferences that are personal rather than conventional or universal. It is thus that we explain that the style is the man.

Style refers to the way a man writes rather than to what he writes about or what he affirms; it refers to manner rather than to matter, to form rather than to content. (But without content, there can be no form; to discuss style is inevitably to discuss substance.) Style is likewise to be distinguished from structure. Although the line of demarcation is never sharp, structure refers mainly to the organizational form of an essay, style to paragraph and sentence patterns, diction, rhythm, and sound. It is clear, then, that the elements of style are the same as the elements of tone; and artfulness and unconsciousness describe the creation of style just as they do that of tone. But in spite of the intimate bond between style and tone, they are not the same thing. Style underlies tone; tone does not underlie style. Although we sometimes speak of the style of this or that essay, we usually believe that a writer's style remains consistent from essay to essay or that over a period of time it changes gradually; whereas we assume that the tone of the essay he writes today may be solemn, that of tomorrow frivolous, that of the next day variable. Underlying the differences of tone will be a basic unity of style. The man's mood may change, and hence his tone may change; but the man remains the same, and hence his style remains the same. As the man changes, his style changes.

Finally, it must be said of style, as it was said of tone, that it is allied with point of view. Objectively, of course, style refers to things quite different from point of view: metaphor, sentence rhythm, etc. We say that a writer's style is highly metaphorical; we do not say his point of view is. By the same token, we say that a writer writes from the point of view of an old man looking back cynically over his past history; we do not describe his style in such terms. And if we use point of view to include assumptions, we speak of a socialistic point of view; we do not speak of a socialistic style. But when we make inferences about style, about, say, the presence of irony in an essay, do we have a man or a point of view? And if point of view can be assumed, how do we know whether we have hold of a man or a mask? The answer to the first question is that on occasion the two terms may, to all intents and purposes, mean the same thing. The answer to the second is that we cannot know. In general, point of view can be considered to be susceptible to easy variation; so that a writer's point of view may indeed be a mask: one for today, one for tomorrow. But the objective marks of a writer's style are to be thought of as less susceptible to variation; so that it may be appropriate to infer from his style something more permanent, more fundamental, than the term point of view suggests. To infer the man from his style is to run the same risk as inferring him from his habits, manners, and behavior. One inevitably accepts the risk.

Because style and tone concern the way a writer writes, they may seem to be unrelated to meaning—if inevitable accompaniments of it. But just as they require substance in which to manifest themselves, so meaning resides in them. An obvious illustration is the stylistic and tonal device of irony, through which stated meanings are modified. In the absence of irony, style and tone support or reinforce stated meanings. When intended irony fails in student themes ("You've written 'Absurd' there, sir, but I was being ironical"), the explanation is usually that the style and tone of the rest of the theme have given no clue that the lone statement is ironical. Sometimes Jonathan Swift's irony fails; but then the fault lies with the reader.

The bearing that style and tone have upon meaning may be apparent if one thinks of the connection between tone and point of view; it may seem subtle if one thinks of style and the man. Consider "Etna" again. Almost nothing of what Lawrence asserts is to be taken literally. The reader realizes that "comes over one an absolute necessity to move," "that wicked witch," "not many men can really stand her," mainly serve to express feelings. Substitute abstract language, "a fascinating physical phenomenon," for Lawrence's playful metaphor, "that wicked witch," and the feeling is lost. If the reader examines the style and tone of the passage he can distinguish a variety of qualities of the man who is expressing his feelings: impatience, implied by the ellipsis in the opening phrase and by the recurring questions; volatility, implied by the rapid shifts in tone; intensity, similarly implied and further suggested by the piled-up adjectives and the sentences that tumble over each other; playful self-consciousness, implied by certain artificialities ("looks at one, looks at one") and incongruities ("glamorous and fierce"). These qualities contribute to the total meaning of the passage, which can be phrased thus: Lawrence is attracted to nature because of that which is elemental within himself, and simultaneously he is aware of his distinct ego; he recognizes that the attraction to nature is a threat to his ego; by his stylistic exhibition of his ego he says that he will not abandon himself to nature: he will leave Etna.

If it is true that style is the man and that style contributes to meaning, the absence of the man implies an absence of style and a loss of meaning. Nevertheless, hopeful people are building machines that will be able to write. Short years ago it was believed to be a mathematical certainty that if a monkey sat in front of a typewriter and punched the keys at random long enough, he would produce *King Lear*. The certainty has been refuted: mathematics now shows that a forest of monkeys could not in finite time produce so much as "Never, never, never, never, never." But IBM machines are more impressive than monkeys, and already they know how to translate *King Lear* into Russian. The absence of man may mean the absence of style, but does it matter? Anyone who cares will distinguish himself from the machine—from nature too—stylistically.

Given below are some terms commonly used in discussing tone and style. No student should expect that familiarity with them and occasional practice upon them will assure him of the same sort of mastery that he might expect from comparable attention to the problem of organization. To know what irony is, to be able to exhibit its various forms and moods (sarcasm, understatement; lightness, gravity), will guarantee very little in the way of stylistic excellence. Nowhere is the fact that good writing is an art rather than a craft more inescapable than in matters of style. The student may hope from his study of the essays in this section of the text to move in the direction of art.

Tone. The following terms represent extremes between which a writer varies (some of them are often applied to style): impersonal, formal, serious, reserved, vs. personal, informal, light, intimate.
Style: Learned, involved, didactic, elevated, allusive, poetical, elegant, ironical, witty, vs. simple, clear, plain, economical.

Diction
  Anglo-Saxon vs. Latinate
  Colloquial vs. Formal
  Common vs. Special (Archaism, Dialect, Jargon, Localism, Slang)
  Concrete vs. Abstract
  Denotative vs. Connotative
  Literal vs. Figurative (Irony, Metaphor)

Phrase and Sentence Patterns
  Balanced/Antithetical vs. Loose
  Periodic vs. Non-periodic
  Rhythmical vs. Non-rhythmical
  Simple vs. Complex

First Start in Life

H. G. WELLS

Born in Bromley, a London suburb, H. G. Wells (1866-1946) was the son of a small shopkeeper; his mother had been a ladies' maid. He began working at the age of thirteen, and with the aid of a scholarship attended the Royal College of Science, graduating with first-class honors. He taught science for a time, turned to journalism, joined the Fabian Society (a socialist group that also included George Bernard Shaw), and began writing novels: science fiction (*The War of the Worlds, The Invisible Man*), still read today, and more realistic novels of everyday life (*Mr. Polly*—which draws on his experiences touched upon below). Wells' best novel is probably *Tono Bungay*, in which he satirizes modern business ethics; he is also the author of *The Outline of History*, a popular account of world history from a distinctly rationalist point of view.

My first start in life was rather hastily improvised. My mother had a second cousin, Thomas Pennicott, "Uncle Tom" we called him, who had always been very much in the margin of her world. I think he had admired her and been perhaps helped by her when they were young folk at Midhurst. He was one of the witnesses to her marriage. He was a fat, round-faced, clean-shaven, black-haired man, illiterate, good humoured and shrewd. He had followed the ruling tendency in my mother's family to keep inns, and he had

From *Experiment in Autobiography* by H. G. Wells, The Macmillan Company, 1934. Reprinted by permission of the Executors of the Estate of H. G. Wells.

kept the Royal Oak opposite the South Western Railway Station at Windsor to such good effect, that he was able to buy and rebuild a riverside inn, called Surly Hall, much affected by the Eton wet-bobs, during the summer term. He built it as a gabled house and the gables were decorated with blue designs and mottoes glorifying Eton in the Latin tongue, very elegant and correct. The wet-bobs rowed up in the afternoons and choked the bar and swarmed over the lawn, vociferously consuming squashed flies and other strangely named refreshments. There was a ferry, a number of tethered punts and boats, green tables under the trees, a decaying collection of stuffed birds, ostrich eggs, wampum and sundries, in an outhouse of white plaster and tarred weather boarding, called the Museum, an eyot and a willow-bordered paddock for campers. Surly Hall has long since disappeared from the banks of the Thames, though I believe that Monkey Island, half a mile further up, still carries on.

It was Uncle Tom's excellent custom to invite Sarah's boys for the holidays; it was not an invariable custom but it happened most years, and we had a thoroughly healthy and expansive three weeks or a month, hanging about his licensed premises in an atmosphere faintly flavoured by sawdust and beer. My brothers' times fell into the Royal Oak days, but my lot was to visit Surly Hall for the last three of my school years. There I learnt to punt, paddle and row, but the current was considered too swift for me to attempt swimming without anyone to teach me. I did not learn to swim until I was past thirty.

My uncle was a widower, but he had two grown-up daughters in their early twenties, Kate and Clara; they shared the duties of the one or two barmaids he also employed. They all found me a very amusing temporary younger brother. Kate was the serious sister, a blonde with intellectual aspirations, and she did very much to stimulate me to draw and read. There was a complete illustrated set of Dickens which I read in abundantly, and a lot of bound up *Family Heralds,* in which I best remember a translation of Eugene Sue's *Mysteries of Paris,* which seemed to me at the time, the greatest romance in the world. All these young women encouraged me to talk, because I said such unexpected things. They pretended to flirt with me, they used me as a convenient chaperon when enterprising men customers wanted to gossip on the lawn in the twilight, and Miss King, the chief barmaid, and Clara became competitive for my sentimental devotion. It all helped to educate me.

One day there appeared on the lawn a delightful vision in fluttering muslin, like one of the ladies in Botticelli's *Primavera*. It was that great actress, Ellen Terry, then in her full loveliness, who had come to Surly Hall to study a part and presently be visited there by Mr. Henry Irving. I ceased to consider myself engaged to Miss King forthwith; I had pledged myself heedlessly; and later on I was permitted to punt the goddess about, show her where white lilies were to be found and get her a great bunch of wet forget-me-nots. There was an abundance of forget-me-nots among the sedges, and in a bend above us were smooth brown water surfaces under great trees and a spread of yellow (and some white) water-lilies in which dragon-flies hovered. It was far finer, I thought, than the Keston Fish Ponds, which had hitherto been the most beautiful place in my world, and at Keston there was no boat with oars, paddle and boat-hook complete, in which I could muck about for hours together.

Often when I was going for walks along the rather trite and very pebbly footpaths about Bromley, thirty miles away, I would let my imagination play with the idea that round the next corner and a little further on and then a bit more, I should find myself with a cry of delighted recognition on the road that led immediately to Surly Hall in summer and all its pleasantness. And how was I to suspect that Uncle Tom was losing money and his temper over the place, having borrowed to rebuild it rather too pretentiously, and that he was quarrelling with both his daughters about their lovers and that dark-eyed Clara, dreadfully bored and distressed temperamentally, was taking to drink? I knew nothing of all that, nor how greyly and dismally the Thames sluices by these riverside inns in the winter months.

But this is a mere glimpse of summer paradise on the way to my first start in life. My mother, I think I have made it clear, was within her limits a very determined little woman. Almost as unquestioning as her belief in Our Father and Our Saviour, was her belief in drapers. I know not whether that heartless trifler of her early years was a draper, but she certainly thought that to wear a black coat and tie behind a counter was the best of all possible lots attainable by man—at any rate by man at our social level. She had bound my brother Frank, resisting weakly, to Mr. Crowhurst in the Market Square, Bromley, for five years and she had bound my brother Freddy to Mr. Sparrowhawk of the Pavement for four, to obey those gentlemen as if they were parents and learn the whole art and mystery of drapery from them, and she was now making a very resolute attempt to incarcerate me and determine my future in the same fashion. It did not dawn upon her that my queer gifts of drawing and expression were of any value at all. But as poor father was to be all alone in Atlas House now—the use he made of his eight years of solitude does not concern this story—a Bromley shop was no longer a suitable soil in which to pop me in order to grow up the perfect draper. She did not like to send me away where there was no one to look after me, for she knew there are dangers that waylay the young who are not supervised. So she found a hasty solution to her problem by sending me on trial, with a view to apprenticeship, to Messrs. Rodgers and Denyer of Windsor, opposite the Castle. There my morals would be under the observation of Surly Hall. And from Messrs. Rodgers and Denyer I got my first impressions of the intensely undesirable life for which she designed me. I had no idea of what I was in for. I went to my fate as I was told, unquestioningly, as my brothers had done before me.

I am told that for lots of poor boys, leaving school and going into employment about thirteen or fourteen is a very exhilarating experience. But that is because they get pay, freedom in the evening and on Sundays, and an enhanced dietary. And they are released from the irksomeness of lessons and school tasks. But I had rather liked lessons and school tasks and drapers' apprentices did not get pay. An immense fuss, entirely unjustifiable, was made about the valuable trade apprentices were going to learn, and in the past the parents of the victim, if he "lived in," usually paid a premium of forty or fifty pounds or so for his immolation. I knew that the new start meant a farewell to many childish things. I had seen both my brothers pass into servitude, and I can still remember my brother Freddy having a last game of "marble runs" with toy bricks on the tilted kitchen table, a game of which he was particularly fond, before he submitted to the yoke of Mr. Sparrowhawk and began that ritual of stock-keeping, putting things away, tidying things up, bending over the counter, being attentive and measuring off, that lasted thereafter for forty-odd years of his life. He knew what he was going to, did my brother Fred; and that game was played with sacrificial solemnity. "I enjoyed that game," said Freddy, who has always displayed a certain gentle stoicism. "It's supper time Bert. . . . Let's put the things away."

Now it was my turn to put the things away, put the books away, give up drawing and painting and every sort of free delight, stop writing stories and imitations of *Punch*, give up all vain hopes and dreams, and serve an employer.

I hated this place into which I had been put from the outset, but I was far too childish, as yet, to make any real resistance to the closing in of the prison about me. But I would not, I could not, give myself satisfactorily to this strange restricted life. It was just by the luck of that incapacity that the prison rejected me.

I was set down from Uncle Pennicott's dog-cart, with a small portmanteau containing all my earthly goods, at the side door of the establishment of Messrs. Rodgers and Denyer, I was taken up a narrow staircase to the men's dormitory, in which were eight or ten beds and four miserable wash-hand stands, and I was shown a dismal little sitting room with a ground glass window opening on a blank wall, in which the apprentices and assistants might "sit" of an evening, and then I was conducted downstairs to an underground dining-room, lit by naked gas-jets and furnished with two long tables covered with American cloth, where the eating was to be done. Then I was introduced to the shop and particularly to the cash desk, where it had been arranged for the first year of my apprenticeship that I was to sit on a tall stool and receive money, give change, enter the amount on a sheet and stamp receipts. I was further instructed in a ritual of dusting and window cleaning. I was to come down at half past seven in the morning, I learnt, without fail, dust, clean windows, eat a bread-and-butter breakfast at half past eight, prepare my cash sheet and so to the routine of the day. I had to add up my cash at the end of the day, count the money in the till, make sheet and cash agree, help to wrapper-up and sweep out the shop, and so escape at half-past seven or eight to drink the delights of freedom until ten, when I had to be in. Lights out at half past ten. And this was to go on day after day—for ever it seemed to me— with an early closing day once a week at five, and Sunday free.

I did not rise to these demands upon me. My mind withdrew itself from my duties. I did my utmost to go on living within myself and leave my duties to do themselves. My disposition to reverie increased. I dusted abominably; whenever I could manage it I did not dust at all. I smuggled books into my desk or did algebraic problems from my battered Todhunter's Larger Algebra; I gave change absent-mindedly and usually I gave inaccurate change, and I entered wrong figures on the cash sheet out of sheer slovenliness.

The one bright moment during the day was when the Guards fifes and drums went past the shop and up to the Castle. These fifes and drums swirled me away campaigning again. Dispatch riders came headlong from dreamland, brooking no denial from the shopwalker. "Is General Bert Wells here? The Prussians have landed!"

I obeyed, I realize, all the impulses of a developing claustrophobia during that first phase of servitude. I would abandon my desk to sneak down into the warehouse, where I spent an unconscionable time seated in a convenient place of reflection, reading. Or I just stood about down there behind stacks of unpacked bales.

As the afternoon dragged on, the hour of reckoning when the cash sheet was added up drew near. It never by any chance corresponded with the money in the till. There had to be a checking of bills, a scrutiny of figures. Wrong sums had been set down. The adding had been wild work. At first the total error would be anything —more or less. After some weeks it became constantly a shortage. The booking clerk, and one of the partners who did the business correspondence and supervised things, would stay late to wrestle with the problem. They were impatient and reproachful. I had to stay too, profoundly apathetic. Either I was giving change in excess, or in some way the money was seeping away. I did not care a rap. I had always hated money sums and long additions and now I detested them. I just wanted to get out of that shop before it was ten o'clock and time to return to the house. I did not realize the dreadful suspicions that were gathering above my head, nor the temptation my inaccuracies were offering to anyone who had access to my desk while I was at meals or otherwise absent. Nobody thought of that, unless perhaps it was the booking clerk.

Every early closing night, every Sunday, at every opportunity I had, I cut off to Surly Hall and took refuge with my cousins. I went with joy and returned with heavy feet. I did not want to talk about business there and when they asked me how I was getting on I said "Oh all right," and turned the talk to more agreeable topics. I did the long two miles from Windsor to and fro after dark for the one or two bright hours I spent there. My cousin Kate or Miss King would play the piano and sing. They would talk to me as though I was not the lowest thing on earth. There, I was still esteemed clever, and the queer things I said were applauded. My cousins, delighted at my appreciation, sang "Sweet Dreamland Faces," and "Juanita," to me and I sat on a little stool close to the piano in a state of rapt appreciation—of the music, the shaded lamp, the comfort and the ease of it.

In this world of gramophones, pianolas and the radio, it is worth noting that at the age of thirteen I had heard no music at all except an occasional brass band, the not very good music of hymn singing and organ voluntaries in Bromley Church and these piano songs at Surly Hall.

Then came a terrible inquisition at the shop. I was almost

charged with pilfering. But my uncle Tom defended me stoutly. "You better not go saying *that*," said my uncle Tom, and indeed, except that there was now a continual shortage in the cash desk, there was no evidence against me. I had no expensive vices; I had no criminal associates, I was extremely shabby and untidy; no marked money—if they used marked money—or indeed any money except the weekly sixpence allowed me for pocket money, had ever been found upon me and my bearing was one of unconscious but convincing rectitude. Indeed I never realized fully what all the fuss was about until afterwards. Yet the fact remains that as a cash desk clerk I had leaked abominably and somebody—I suppose— had got away with the leakage.

It was plain also that I shirked all my other tasks. And while my start in life was thus already faltering, I had some sort of difference with the junior porter, which resulted in a conspicuous black eye for me. It was a gross breach of social conventions for an apprentice to fight a porter. I had great difficulty in explaining that black eye to my own satisfaction at Surly Hall. Moreover the clothes I had come to Windsor in were anything but stylish, and Mr. Denyer, the most animated of the partners, liked the look of me less and less. I wore a black velvet cap with a peak and that was all wrong. It became plain that my mother's first attempt to give me a start in life had failed. I was not starting. I was not fitted, said Messrs. Rodgers and Denyer, with perfect truth, to be a draper. I was not refined enough.

I do not recall that at Windsor from first to last I made more than the slightest effort to do what was expected of me. It was not so much a resistance as an aversion. And it is a queer thing about that place that though I stayed there a couple of months, I do not remember the name of a single individual except one assistant named Nash, who happened to be the son of a Bromley draper and wore a long moustache. But all the other figures who sat with him at the downstairs dinner table are now blank nameless figures. Did I look at them? Did I listen to them? Nor can I remember the positions of the counters or the arrangement of the goods in the shop. I made no friends. Mr. Denyer, young Mr. Rodgers and old Mr. Rodgers left impressions, because they were like great pantomime heads always looking for me and saying disagreeable things to me, and I was always engaged in getting away from them. They disliked me; I think everybody in that place came to dislike me as a tiresome boring little misfit who made trouble and didn't do his share and was either missing when he was wanted or in the way when he wasn't. My self-conceit, I suppose, has blotted out all the other humiliating details from my memory. I do not even remember whether I felt any chagrin at my failure. All that seems effaced beyond recall. And yet that nocturnal tramp along the Maidenhead Road, which I took whenever I could, is real and living to me still. I could draw a map of the whole way down the hill and through Clewer. I could show where the road was wider and where it narrowed down.

Like most undernourished growing boys I was cowardly and I found the last stretch from Clewer to the inn terrifyingly dark and lonely. It was black on the moonless nights and eerie by moonlight and often it was misty from the river. My imagination peopled the dark fields on either hand with crouching and pursuing foes. Chunks of badly trimmed hedge took on formidable shapes. Sometimes I took to my heels and ran. For a week or so that road was haunted by a rumour of an escaped panther—from Lady Florence Dixie's riverside home, the Fisheries. That phantom panther waited for me patiently; it followed me like a noiseless dog, biding its time. And one night on the other side of the hedge a sleeping horse sighed deeply, a gigantic sigh, and almost frightened me out of my wits.

But nothing of that sort kept me from going at every opportunity to Surly Hall, where there was something to touch my imagination and sustain my self-respect. I was hanging on subconsciously long before I held on consciously, to that life of books and expression and creative living from which the close exactions and economies of employment for private profit were sucking me down. And nothing that my mother and cousins could say to move and encourage me, could induce me to fix my attention on the little flimsy bits of paper with carbon duplicates, that were being slapped down at the guichet of the cash desk.

"One eleven half—two and six. Quick please."

QUESTIONS

1. Define the tone of the first paragraph on the basis of answers to the following questions. What is the general level of diction, and how much variation is there from that level? How complex are the sentence structures? On what basis is the paragraph developed? How striking are the metaphors?

2. Describe the differences in tone and style that result from the following revision of the sixth sentence in the first paragraph: He built it as a gabled house and decorated the gables with blue designs and mottoes glorifying Eton in the Latin tongue; he considered the effect to be very elegant and correct. Describe the differences in tone and style that result from the following revision of the first sentence in the second paragraph: It was Uncle Tom's custom to invite Sarah's boys for the holidays; and we had expansive times there, hanging about his premises in an atmosphere flavored by sawdust and beer.

3. From what points of view does Wells speak of "a delightful vision in fluttering muslin," "that great actress," "I had pledged myself heedlessly," and "later on I was permitted to punt the goddess about" (paragraph four)? How do you know? What contribution do the shifts make to the tone of the paragraph?

4. What differences in quality of irony do you observe in such phrases as "summer paradise," "belief in Our Father and Our Savior," "belief in drapers," and "heartless trifler" (paragraph six)? Where else in the paragraph do you find irony?

5. How complexly does Wells develop his prison metaphor in paragraphs six through ten. (Note the other metaphors that he connects it to.) What contribution do the metaphors make to the tone of, say, paragraph seven? Does that tone dominate the paragraph? Why?

6. How would you account for the differences in structure and rhythm of the sentences in the tenth ("I was set down . . .") and eleventh

paragraphs? How different in structure and rhythm is either paragraph from the first paragraph? Which of the three would you say is characteristic of the essay?

7. What is the general level of diction in the essay? In what sense does that general level assist Wells in achieving the particular effects that he aims at in the paragraph beginning "It was plain" and in the next to last paragraph?

8. Consider how seriously Wells seems to be taking himself in the following passages: "I did not learn to swim until I was past thirty" (paragraph two), "It all helped to educate me" (paragraph three), "my queer gifts of drawing and expression" (paragraph six), and "I hated this place into which I had been put" (paragraph nine). What limitations does the general tone that Wells employs impose upon his varying estimates of himself in the essay?

9. To what extent does either Surly Hall or the Rodgers and Denyer establishment take on the quality of a symbol? What are the particular qualities of its concreteness? What does your answer suggest about Wells' style?

10. On the basis of your answers to previous questions, characterize Wells' style. How highly ironical or metaphorical is it? How varied, complex? How graceful or how intense? What might you infer about the man from it?

German Relations

ROBERT GRAVES

Born at Wimbledon, England, and educated at Oxford, Robert Graves (1895—) has made his home for the last thirty years on the island of Majorca. During a long literary career, he has written poetry, essays, and historical novels (*I, Claudius*), has translated the classics (*Iliad, The Golden Ass*), and has made original contributions in the areas of anthropology and poetics (*The Greek Myths, The White Goddess*). His autobiography, *Goodbye to All That*, from which the following is a chapter, shocked the literary world on its appearance (1929), and has since become a minor classic of candid irreverence. Graves was recently elected Professor of Poetry at Oxford, a mark of his growing influence and reputation.

My mother took us abroad to stay at my grandfather's house in Germany five times between my second and twelfth year. Then he died, and we never went again. He owned a big old manor-house at Deisenhofen, ten miles from Munich; by name "Laufzorn," which means "Begone, anger!" Our summers there were easily the best things of my early childhood. Pine forests and hot sun, red deer, black and red squirrels, acres of blueberries and wild strawberries; nine or ten different kinds of edible mushrooms which we went into the forest to pick, and unfamiliar flowers in the fields—Munich lies high—and outcrops of Alpine flowers occur here and there; a farm with all the usual animals except sheep; drives through the countryside in a brake behind my grandfather's greys; and bathing in the Isar under a waterfall. The Isar was bright green, and said to be the fastest river of Europe. We used to visit the uncles who kept a peacock farm a few miles away; and a grand-uncle, Johannes von Ranke, the ethnologist, who lived on the lake shores of Tegernsee, where everyone had buttercup-blond hair; and occasionally my Aunt Agnes, Freifrau Baronin von Aufsess, of Aufsess Castle, some hours away by train, high up in the Bavarian Alps.

Aufsess, built in the ninth century, stood so remote that it had never been sacked, but remained Aufsess property ever since. To the original building, a keep with only a ladder-entrance half-way up, a mediaeval castle had been added. Its treasures of plate and armour were amazing. My Uncle Siegfried showed us children the chapel: its walls hung with enamelled shields of each Aufsess baron, impaled with the arms of the noble family into which he had married. He pointed to a stone in the floor which pulled up by a ring, and said: "That is the family vault where all Aufsesses go when they die. I'll be down there one day." He scowled comically. (But he got killed in the War as an officer of the Imperial German Staff and, I believe, they never found his body.) Uncle Siegfried had a peculiar sense of humour. One day we children saw him on the garden path, eating pebbles. He told us to go away, but of course we stayed, sat down, and tried to eat pebbles too; only to be told very seriously that children should not eat pebbles: we would break our teeth. We agreed, after trying one or two; so he found us each a pebble which looked just like all the rest, but which crushed easily and had a chocolate centre. This was on condition that we went away and left him to his picking and crunching. When we returned, later in the day, we searched and searched, but found only the ordinary hard pebbles. He never once let us down in a joke.

Among the castle treasures were a baby's lace cap that had taken two years to make; and a wine glass which my uncle's old father had found in the Franco-Prussian War standing upright in the middle of the square in an entirely ruined French village. For dinner, when we went there, we ate some enormous trout. My father, a practised fisherman, asked my uncle in astonishment where they came from. He explained that an underground river welled up close to the castle, and the fish which emerged with it were quite white from the darkness, of extraordinary size, and stone-blind.

They also gave us jam made of wild rose-berries, which they called "Hetchi-Petch," and showed us an iron chest in a small, thick-walled, whitewashed room at the top of the keep—a tremendous chest, twice the size of the door, and obviously made inside the room, which had no windows except arrow-slits. It had two keys, and must have been twelfth- or thirteenth-century work. Tradition ruled that it should never be opened, unless the castle stood in the most extreme danger. The baron held one key; his steward, the other. The chest could be opened only by using both keys, and nobody knew what lay inside; it was even considered unlucky to speculate. Of course, we speculated. It might be gold; more likely a store of corn in sealed jars; or even some sort of weapon—Greek fire, perhaps. From what I know of the Aufsesses and their stewards, it is inconceivable that the chest ever got the better of their curiosity. A ghost walked the castle, the ghost of a former baron known as the "Red Knight"; his terrifying portrait hung half-way up the turret staircase which led to our bedrooms. We slept on feather-beds for the first time in our lives.

Laufzorn, which my grandfather had bought and restored from a ruinous condition, could not compare in tradition with Aufsess, though it had for a time been a shooting lodge of the Bavarian kings. Still, two ghosts went with the place; the farm labourers used to see them frequently. One of them was a carriage which drove furiously along without horses and, before the days of motor cars, spread real horror. Not having visited the banqueting hall since childhood, I find it difficult to recall its true dimensions. It seemed as big as a cathedral, with stained-glass armorial windows,

and bare floor-boards were furnished only at the four corners with
small islands of tables and chairs; swallows had built rows of nests
all along the sides of the ceiling. There were roundels of coloured
light from the windows, the many-tined stags' heads (shot by my
grandfather) mounted on the walls, swallow-droppings under the
nests, and a little harmonium in one corner where we sang German songs. These concentrate my memories of Laufzorn. The bottom storey formed part of the farm. A carriage-drive ran right
through it, with a wide, covered courtyard in the centre, where
cattle were once driven to safety in times of baronial feud. On one
side of the drive lay the estate steward's quarters, on the other the
farm servants' inn and kitchen. In the middle storey lived my
grandfather and his family. The top storey was a store for corn,
apples, and other farm produce; and up here my cousin Wilhelm
—later shot down in an air battle by a school-fellow of mine—
used to lie for hours picking off mice with an air-gun.

Bavarian food had a richness and spiciness that we always missed
on our return to England. We loved the rye bread, the dark pine
honey, the huge ice-cream puddings made with fresh raspberry
juice and the help of snow stored during the winter in an ice-house,
my grandfather's venison, the honey cakes, the pastries, and particularly the sauces rich with different kinds of mushrooms. Also the
pretzels, the carrots cooked in sugar, and summer pudding of cran-
berries and blueberries. In the orchard, close to the house, we
could eat as many apples, pears, and greengages as we liked.
There were also rows of black-currant and gooseberry bushes in the
garden. The estate, despite the recency of my grandfather's tenure,
his liberalism, and his experiments in modern agricultural methods,
remained feudalistic. The poor, sweaty, savage-looking farm servants, who talked a dialect we could not understand, frightened
us. They ranked lower even than the servants at home; and as for
the colony of Italians, settled about half a mile from the house,
whom my grandfather had imported as cheap labour for his brick
factory—we associated them in our minds with "the gipsies in the
wood" of the song. My grandfather took us over the factory one day

and made me taste a lump of Italian *polenta*. My mother told us afterwards—when milk pudding at Wimbledon came to table burned, and we complained—"Those poor Italians in your grandfather's brick yard used to burn their *polenta* on purpose, sometimes, just for a change of flavour."

Beyond the farm buildings at Laufzorn lay a large pond, fringed with irises and full of carp; my uncles netted it every three or four years. Once we watched the fun, and shouted when we saw the net pulled closer and closer to the shallow landing corner. It bulged with wriggling carp, and a big pike threshed about among them. I waded in to help, and came out with six leeches, like black rubber tubes, fastened to my legs; salt had to be put on their tails before they would leave go. The farm labourers grew wildly excited; one of them gutted a fish with his thumb, and ate it raw. I also remember the truck line between the railway station, two miles away, and the brick yard. Since the land had a fall of perhaps one in a hundred between the factory and the station, the Italians used to load the trucks with bricks; then a squad of them would give the trucks a hard shove and run along the track pushing for twenty or thirty yards; after which the trucks sailed off all by themselves down to the station.

We were allowed to climb up into the rafters of the big hay barn, and jump down into the springy hay; we gradually increased the height of the jumps. It was exciting to feel our insides left behind us in the air. Once we visited the Laufzorn cellar, not the ordinary beer cellar, but another into which one descended from the courtyard—quite dark except for a little slit window. A huge heap of potatoes lay on the floor; to get to the light, they had put out a twisted mass of long white feelers. In one corner was a dark hole closed by a gate: a secret passage from the house to a ruined monastery, a mile away—so we were told. My uncles had once been down some distance, but the air got bad and they came back; the gate had been put up to prevent others from trying it and losing their senses. Come to think of it, they were probably teasing us, and the hole led to the bottom of the *garde-robe*—which is a polite name for a mediaeval earth-closet.

When we drove out with my grandfather, he was acclaimed with *"Grüss Gott, Herr Professor!"* by the principal personages of each village we went through. It always had a big inn with a rumbling skittle-alley, and a tall Maypole, banded like a barber's pole with blue and white, the Bavarian national colours. Apple and pear trees lined every road. The idea of these unguarded public fruit trees astonished us. We could not understand why any fruit remained on them. On Wimbledon Common even the horse-chestnut trees were pelted with sticks and stones, long before the chestnuts ripened, and in defiance of an energetic common keeper. What we least liked in Bavaria were the wayside crucifixes with their realistic blood and wounds, and the *ex-voto* pictures, like sign-boards, of naked souls in purgatory, grinning with anguish among high red and yellow flames. Though taught to believe in hell, we did not like to be reminded of it.

Munich we found sinister—disgusting fumes of beer and cigar smoke, and intense sounds of eating in the restaurants; the hotly dressed, enormously stout population in trams and trains; the ferocious officials. Then the terrifying Morgue, which children were not allowed to visit. Any notable who died was taken to the Morgue, they told us, and put in a chair, to sit in state for a day or two. If a general, he had his uniform on; or if a burgomaster's wife, she had on her silks and jewels. Strings were tied to their fingers, and the slightest movement of a single string would ring a great bell, in case any life remained in the corpse after all. I have never verified the truth of this, but it was true enough to me. When my grandfather died, about a year after our last visit, I pictured him in the Morgue with his bushy white hair, his morning coat, his striped trousers, his decorations, and his stethoscope. And perhaps, I thought, a silk hat, gloves, and cane on a table beside him. Trying, in a nightmare, to be alive; but knowing himself dead.

The Headmaster of Rokeby School, who caned me for forgetting my gymnastic shoes, loved German culture, and impressed this feeling on the school, so that it stood to my credit that I could speak German and had visited Germany. At my other preparatory schools this German connexion seemed something at least excusable, and perhaps even interesting. Only at Charterhouse did it rank as a social offence. My history from the age of fourteen, when I went to Charterhouse, until just before the end of the War, when I began to think for myself, is a forced rejection of the German in me. I used to insist indignantly on being Irish, and took my self-protective stand on the technical point that solely the father's nationality counted. Of course, I also accepted the whole patriarchal system of things, convinced of the natural supremacy of male over female. My mother took the "love, honour, and obey" contract literally; my sisters were brought up to wish themselves boys, to be shocked at the idea of woman's suffrage, and not to expect so expensive an education as their brothers. The final decision in any domestic matter always rested with my father. My mother would say: "If two ride together, one must ride behind."

We children did not talk German well; our genders and minor parts of speech were shaky, and we never learned to read Gothic characters or script. Yet we had the sense of German so strongly that I feel I know German far better than French, though able to read French almost as fast as I can read English, and German only very painfully and slowly, with the help of a dictionary. I use different parts of my mind for the two languages. French is a surface acquirement which I could forget quite easily if I had no reason to speak it every now and then.

QUESTIONS

1. Define the range and general level of diction in the first paragraph. Define the degree to which the language is connotative and figurative.

2. Arrange the following descriptive phrases from the first paragraph according to their degree of precision: "acres of blueberries," "outcrops

of Alpine flowers," "the Isar was bright green," "buttercup-blond hair." Arrange the phrases according to their vividness. Which phrase is most typical of the description in the paragraph? Which is least?

3. How would you describe the sentence rhythms in the first paragraph? (Consider repeated sentence structures, series consisting of paired or tripled phrases, and significant consistency or variation in sentence length.)

4. Assess the relative amounts of descriptive detail, generalization, reflection, opinion, and feeling in the first paragraph. On the basis of your assessment and your answers to the first three questions, define the tone of the paragraph.

5. Graves succeeds in characterizing his Uncle Siegfried without apparent effort. What are his means of characterization? In what significant respects are his approaches to his characterization indirect? What stylistic features that you have examined in previous questions might be said to contribute to the unobtrusiveness of the characterization?

6. On what is Graves commenting in his parenthetical remarks about his uncle in paragraph two and his cousin in paragraph five? What effect does he achieve by setting the remarks off the way he does? To what other material in the essay do the remarks relate thematically?

7. From whose point of view and in what tone does Graves say, "his terrifying portrait hung half-way up the turret staircase" (paragraph four), "Still, two ghosts went with the place" (paragraph five), "It seemed as big as a cathedral" (paragraph five), "The poor, sweaty, savage-looking farm servants . . . frightened us" (paragraph six)? What point of view predominates in the essay?

8. Define the quality of the metaphorical language in paragraphs seven and eight. Is its quality consistent with the other qualities of Graves' style that you have explored?

9. What unusual qualities of diction (of connotation and metaphor), sentence structure, and sentence rhythm do you find in the tenth paragraph ("Munich we found sinister . . .")? Do you find this paragraph more successful than the rest of the writing in the essay? Why?

10. On the basis of your answers to previous questions, characterize Graves' style. What is its most outstanding quality? Would you say his

style suits his task of autobiographical revelation? What other tasks might it suit, or not suit? If you have read the selection by H. G. Wells in this section of the text, compare specific elements of the styles of the two men: use of irony and metaphor, connotativeness of diction, flexibility of sentence structure.

In the Days of My Youth

GEORGE BERNARD SHAW

Shaw once characterized himself as the "upstart son of a downstart," and in so doing wittily linked both his later career and his heritage. Related to men of wealth and position in Ireland, he early saw the value of his connections disappear under the stress of his father's spendthrift ways and liking for alcohol. He left Dublin—"not enamored of poverty, of ostracism, of contempt"—to join his mother in London, where she was helping to support the family as a teacher of music. Ten years of undistinguished literary work were followed by success as critic and playwright, and as eccentric public figure. Shaw the upstart sported a red beard, advocated teetotalism and vegetarianism, spouted barbed witticisms, and in his many plays (and in the Prefaces he wrote for them) deliberately set about undercutting the conventional views and pretensions of the age. His best plays include *Man and Superman, Major Barbara,* and *Saint Joan.* He received the Nobel Prize in 1925. (Further headnote information on Shaw appears on p. 60.)

From the late T. P. O'Connor's magazine entitled M.A.P. (Mainly About People), the date of my contribution being 17 September 1898.

MY DEAR T. P.,

All autobiographies are lies. I do not mean unconscious, uninten-

From *Sixteen Self Sketches* by George Bernard Shaw. Reprinted by permission of The Public Trustee and The Society of Authors, London.

tional lies: I mean deliberate lies. No man is bad enough to tell the truth about himself during his lifetime, involving, as it must, the truth about his family and his friends and colleagues. And no man is good enough to tell the truth to posterity in a document which he suppresses until there is nobody left alive to contradict him.

I speak with the more confidence on the subject because I have myself tried the experiment, within certain timid limits, of being candidly autobiographical. But I have produced no permanent impression, because nobody has ever believed me. I once told a fellow-critic [A. B. Walkley] some facts about my family.

My paternal grandmother had fifteen children in the first twenty-two years of her marriage, and would perhaps have had fifteen more had her husband survived that experience. Of the fifteen she managed to bring up eleven, thus providing me with all but a dozen uncles and aunts and innumerable cousins on my father's side alone. My maternal grandfather married twice and had eight children, of whom only one died unmarried and childless.

Such families are rare nowadays; but in Ireland in the middle of the nineteenth century we thought nothing of them, ill as we could afford them. Like most fertile clans mine did not consist exclusively of teetotallers; nor did all its members remain until death up to the very moderate standard of legal sanity. One of them discovered a perfectly original method of suicide. It was simple to the verge of triteness; yet no human being had ever thought of it before. It was also amusing. But in the act of carrying it out my relative jammed the mechanism of his heart and died about a second before he succeeded in killing himself. The coroner's jury found that he died "from natural causes"; and the secret of the suicide was kept, not only from the public, but from most of the family.

I revealed that secret in private conversation to Walkley. He shrieked with laughter, and printed the whole story in his next *causerie*. It never for a moment occurred to him that it was true. Meanwhile, the extent to which I stood compromised with my relative's widow and brothers and sisters may be imagined.

Twice in my life I have given prosaically truthful instructions to solicitors, and been surprised to find that they were not carried out. They thought I must be romancing or joking.

If I were to attempt to write genuine autobiography here, the same difficulty would arise. I should give mortal offence to the few relatives who would know that I was writing the truth; and nobody else would believe me.

I am in the further difficulty that I have not yet ascertained the truth about myself. For instance, how far am I mad, and how far sane? I do not know. My specific talent has enabled me to cut a figure in my profession in London; but a man may, like Don Quixote, be clever enough to cut a figure, and yet be stark mad.

A critic recently described me as having "a kindly dislike of my fellow creatures." Dread would have been nearer the mark than dislike; for man is the only animal of which I am thoroughly and cravenly afraid. I have never thought much of the courage of a lion tamer. Inside the cage he is at least safe from other men. There is less harm in a well-fed lion. It has no ideals, no sect, no party, no nation, no class: in short, no reason for destroying anything it does not want to eat. In the Mexican war, the Americans burnt the Spanish fleet, and finally had to drag wounded men out of hulls which had become furnaces. The effect of this on one of the American commanders was to make him assemble his men and tell them that he wished to declare before them that he believed in God Almighty. No lion would have done that. On reading it, and observing that the newspapers, representing normal public opinion, seemed to consider it a very creditable, natural, and impressively pious incident, I came to the conclusion that I must be mad. At all events, if I am sane, the rest of the world ought not to be at large. We cannot both see things as they really are.

My father was an Irish Protestant gentleman of the downstart race of younger sons. He had no inheritance, no profession, no manual skill, no qualification of any sort for any definite social function. He must have had some elementary education; for he could read and write and keep accounts more or less inaccurately; and he spoke and dressed like an Irish educated gentleman and not like a railway porter. But he certainly had not a university degree; and I never heard him speak of any school or college of which he could claim to be an alumnus. He had, however, been brought up to believe that there was an inborn virtue of gentility in all Shaws as partisans of William the Conqueror (the Dutch William of glorious pious and immortal memory, not the Norman adventurer) and owners of landed estates in Ireland or their relatives. Such younger sons as had outstanding ability made for Dublin, where one of them founded the Royal Bank, which old people in my boyhood still called Shaw's Bank. He was made a baronet, and founded the Dublin Shaws in a family seat called Bushy Park out Rathfarnham way. My father was a second cousin of the baronet, and was privileged to hire a carriage and attend the Bushy Park funerals, besides having a right to an invitation to certain family parties there. Necessarily all the Shaws were Protestants and snobs.

On the strength of his snobbery my father, after condescending to a clerkship or two, managed to assert his family claim on the State with sufficient success to obtain a post in the Four Courts (the Irish *Palais de Justice*). The post was abolished; and he was pensioned off. He sold the pension, and embarked with the proceeds in the corn trade, of which he had not the slightest knowledge; nor did he acquire much, as far as I can judge, to the day of his death. There was a mill a little way out in the country, which perhaps paid its own rent, since the machinery was kept in motion. But its chief use, I believe, was to amuse me and my two boon companions, the sons of my father's partner.

I believe Ireland, as far as the Protestant gentry is concerned, to be the most irreligious country in the world. I was christened by my uncle; and as my godfather was intoxicated and did not turn up, the sexton was ordered to promise and vow in his place, precisely as my uncle might have ordered him to put more coals on the vestry fire. I was never confirmed; and I believe my parents never were either. Of the seriousness with which English families took this rite I had no conception; for Irish Protestantism was not then a religion: it was a side in political faction, a class prejudice, a conviction that Roman Catholics are socially inferior persons who will go to hell when they die and leave Heaven in the exclusive possession of Protestant ladies and gentlemen. In my childhood I was sent every Sunday to a Sunday-school where genteel little children repeated texts, and were rewarded with cards inscribed with them. After an hour of this we were marched into the adjoining church (the Molyneux in Upper Leeson Street), to sit round the altar rails and fidget there until our neighbors must have wished the service over as heartily as we did. I suffered this, not for my salvation, but because my father's respectability demanded it. When we went to live in Dalkey we broke with the observance and never resumed it.

What helped to make "church" a hotbed of all the social vices was that no working folk ever came there. In England the clergy go among the poor, and sometimes do try desperately to get them to come to church. In Ireland the poor are Roman Catholics (Papists my Orange grandfather called them). The Protestant Church has nothing to do with them. I cannot say that in Ireland in my time there all the Protestants were the worse for what they called their religion. I can only answer for those I knew.

Imagine being taught to despise a workman, and to respect a gentleman, in a country where every rag of excuse for gentility is stripped off by poverty! Imagine being taught that there is one God, a Protestant and a perfect gentleman, keeping Heaven select for the gentry against an idolatrous impostor called the Pope! Imagine the pretensions of the English peerage on the incomes of the English middle class! I remember Stopford Brooke one day telling me that he discerned in my books an intense and contemptuous hatred for society. No wonder!

If I had not suffered from these things in my childhood, perhaps I could keep my temper about them. To an outsider there is nothing but comedy in the spectacle of a forlorn set of Protestant merchants in a Catholic country, led by a petty plutocracy of stockbrokers, doctors, and landagents, and camouflaged by that section of the landed gentry who, too heavily mortgaged to escape to London, play at being a Court and an aristocracy reigned over by a Vice-Regal exile persuaded to accept the post of Lord-Lieutenant at a salary of £20,000 a year, leaving him heavily out of pocket but making his wife a deputy queen. To such pretences, involving continual lying as to incomes and social standing, were sacrificed all the realities of life.

And now, what power did I find in Ireland religious enough to redeem me from this abomination of desolation? Quite simply, the power of Art. My mother, as it happened, had a considerable musical talent. In order to exercise it seriously, she had to associate with other people who had musical talent. My first doubt as to whether God could really be a good Protestant was suggested by the fact that the best voices available for combination with my mother's in the works of the great composers had been unaccountably vouchsafed to Roman Catholics. Even the Divine gentility was presently called in question; for some of these vocalists were undeniably shopkeepers. If the best tenor, undeniably a Catholic, was at least an accountant, the buffo was a frank stationer.

There was no help for it: if my mother was to do anything but sing silly ballads in drawing rooms, she had to associate herself on an entirely unsectarian footing with people of like artistic gifts without the smallest reference to creed or class. She must actually permit herself to be approached by Roman Catholic priests, and at their invitation to enter that house of Belial, the Roman Catholic chapel, and sing the Masses of Mozart there. If religion is that which binds men to one another, and irreligion that which sunders, then must I testify that I found the religion of my country in its musical genius, and its irreligion in its churches and drawing rooms.

Let me add a word of gratitude to that cherished asylum of my boyhood, the National Gallery of Ireland. I believe I am the only Irishman who has ever been in it, except the officials. But I know that it did much more for me than the two confiscated medieval Cathedrals so magnificently "restored" out of the profits of the drink trade.

From Nature, too, one learns everywhere. She makes many an Irishman melancholy, and sets him snivelling about "the days that are over." Only the other day it was proposed to me that I should help to uplift my downtrodden country by assembling with other Irishmen to romance about 1798. I do not take the slightest interest in 1798. Until Irishmen apply themselves seriously to what the condition of Ireland is to be in 1998 they will get very little patriotism out of

yours sincerely,

G. BERNARD SHAW

QUESTIONS

1. The tone of the first paragraph is humorous. What else, or what more precisely, is it? (Include in your answer the relationship that it establishes between Shaw and the reader.) What are the three or four notable means by which the tone is achieved?

2. What is the tonal effect of Shaw's use of numbers in the third paragraph? Explain the basis of the chief point of humor in the paragraph. What similarities do you observe between Shaw's means of achieving tone in this paragraph and in the first?

3. What do the following phrases contribute to the tone of the fourth paragraph: "fertile clans," "moderate standard of legal sanity," "jammed the mechanism of his heart"? Distinguish between Shaw's attitude towards his reader and his attitude towards his subject here. What of interest do you discover when you compare his attitude towards his subject with the attitude that Walkley took (paragraph five)?

4. Do you find the tone of Shaw's reflections upon himself in paragraph eight different from the tone of his comment on mankind in paragraph nine? Would you say that his tone in the first nine paragraphs is generally more conducive to an examination of the self or to an expression of the self? Does the general substance of the essay support your opinion?

5. Identify the paradox, analogy, metaphor, exaggeration, and logic upon which Shaw builds the humor of his attack in the ninth paragraph. What effect does he achieve by re-introducing the lion after the two

sentences on the Mexican war? In what way does he connect the animal image to the subject of the eighth paragraph? Which of the above elements (paradox, etc.) would you say is rarely employed in the rest of the essay?

6. Consider the following presentments: the lion and the Mexican War (paragraph nine), the history of the Shaws (paragraph ten), the author's christening (paragraph twelve). What degrees of vagueness, clarity, and suggestiveness attach to them? What does the way they are presented and developed suggest about the quality of Shaw's powers of visualization? (If you have read the Dylan Thomas essay in this section, it will prove helpful to consider how he would have presented and developed the same material.)

7. What range in formality of diction do you observe in the tenth paragraph? To what extent does the characteristic level dominate the paragraph? What is the range in length and complexity of sentences? What kinds of transitions are most in evidence? On the basis of your answers, establish a generalization about Shaw's style. Examine the respect in which each characteristic supports—or fails to support—Shaw's tone as you have defined it in answer to Questions 1, 2, and 3.

8. On the basis of a comparison of paragraphs ten and fifteen, answer the following questions. Is irony or invective Shaw's more characteristic mode of attack? Is the irony subtle or obvious? Is the invective harsh or light? In what respect does the presence of one modify the quality of the other?

9. Would you say Shaw's sentence rhythms are graceful, energetic, or conversational? Compare paragraphs thirteen and fourteen for these qualities, analyzing such features as the employment of idiomatic or colloquial expression, ease or abruptness of transition, use of balanced and paired phrasing (on the one hand . . . and on the other; rich and comfortable, middle-class and smug).

10. What is the tone of the fourteenth paragraph? How does it differ from that of the first paragraph? In what broad way does the tone of the fourteenth and the last paragraph differ from that of the first eight paragraphs?

11. Characterize Shaw's style: is it plain? formal? complex? evocative? flexible? To what extent, or in what respect, would you say Shaw's style

is suited to autobiographical revelation? How strong a sense of the man does the style itself give? (Would you say that his style in any way suggests the madman he says he might be?)

12. Is there any evidence that Shaw's tone and style are affected by the fact that he has cast the sketch in the form of a letter?

At the Farm

MARK TWAIN

Though Mark Twain spent much of his mature life in the East, principally in Connecticut, his richest work springs from recollections of his youth and early manhood. Both *Tom Sawyer* and *Huckleberry Finn* take their setting from Hannibal, Missouri, a small river town on the Mississippi to which his family moved when he was a child; *Life on the Mississippi* draws largely on his experiences as a steamboat pilot in the 1850's. The following, a portion of his *Autobiography*, was written much later in life, during a time generally of unhappiness and despair, but it has obvious affinities with Twain's earlier works. (Further headnote information on Twain appears on pp. 8, 66.)

My uncle, John A. Quarles, was a farmer and his place was in the country four miles from Florida. He had eight children and fifteen or twenty Negroes and was also fortunate in other ways, particularly in his character. I have not come across a better man than he was. I was his guest for two or three months every year, from the fourth year after we removed to Hannibal till I was eleven or twelve years old. I have never consciously used him or his wife in a book, but his farm has come very handy to me in literature once or twice. In *Huck Finn* and in *Tom Sawyer, Detective* I moved it down to Arkansas. It was all of six hundred miles but it was no trouble; it was not a very large farm, five hundred acres perhaps, but I could have done it if it had been twice as large. And as for the morality of it, I cared nothing for that; I would move a state if the exigencies of literature required it.

It was a heavenly place for a boy, that farm of my uncle John's. The house was a double log one with a spacious floor (roofed in) connecting it with the kitchen. In the summer the table was set in the middle of that shady and breezy floor, and the sumptuous meals—well, it makes me cry to think of them. Fried chicken, roast pig, wild and tame turkeys, ducks and geese, venison just killed, squirrels, rabbits, pheasants, partridges, prairie-chickens, biscuits, hot batter-cakes, hot buckwheat cakes, hot "wheat bread," hot rolls, hot corn pone; fresh corn boiled on the ear, succotash, butter-beans, string-beans, tomatoes, peas, Irish potatoes, sweet potatoes; buttermilk, sweet milk; "clabber"; watermelons, muskmelons, cantaloupes—all fresh from the garden—apple pie, peach pie, pumpkin pie, apple dumplings, peach cobbler—I can't remember the rest. The way that the things were cooked was perhaps the main splendor, particularly a certain few of the dishes. For instance the corn bread, the hot biscuits and wheat bread, and the fried chicken. These things have never been properly cooked in the North—in fact no one there is able to learn the art, so far as my experience goes. The North thinks it knows how to make corn bread but this is mere superstition. Perhaps no bread in the world is quite so good as Southern corn bread, and perhaps no bread in the world is quite so bad as the Northern imitation of it. The North seldom tries to fry chicken and this is well; the art cannot be learned north of the line of Mason and Dixon, nor anywhere in Europe. This is not hearsay; it is experience that is speaking. In Europe it is imagined that the custom of serving various kinds of bread blazing hot is "American" but that is too broad a spread; it is custom in the South but is much less than that in the North. In the North and in Europe hot bread is considered unhealthy. This is probably another fussy superstition, like the European superstition that ice-water is unhealthy. Europe does not need ice-water and

does not drink it; and yet notwithstanding this its word for it is
better than ours, because it describes it, whereas ours doesn't.
Europe calls it "iced" water. Our word describes water made from
melted ice—a drink which has a characterless taste and which we
have but little acquaintance with.

It seems a pity that the world should throw away so many good
things merely because they are unwholesome. I doubt if God has
given us any refreshment which, taken in moderation, is unwholesome, except microbes. Yet there are people who strictly deprive
themselves of each and every eatable, drinkable, and smokable
which has in any way acquired a shady reputation. They pay this
price for health. And health is all they get for it. How strange it is.
It is like paying out your whole fortune for a cow that has gone
dry.

The farm-house stood in the middle of a very large yard and the
yard was fenced on three sides with rails and on the rear side with
high palings; against these stood the smoke-house; beyond the
palings was the orchard; beyond the orchard were the Negro
quarter and the tobacco fields. The front yard was entered over a
stile made of sawed-off logs of graduated heights; I do not remember any gate. In a corner of the front yard were a dozen lofty
hickory trees and a dozen black walnuts, and in the nutting
season riches were to be gathered there.

Down a piece, abreast the house, stood a little log cabin against
the rail fence; and there the woody hill fell sharply away, past the
barns, the corn-crib, the stables, and the tobacco-curing house, to a
limpid brook which sang along over its gravelly bed and curved
and frisked in and out and here and there and yonder in the deep
shade of overhanging foliage and vines—a divine place for wading, and it had swimming-pools too, which were forbidden to us
and therefore much frequented by us. For we were little Christian
children and had early been taught the value of forbidden fruit.

In the little log cabin lived a bedridden white-headed slave
woman whom we visited daily and looked upon with awe, for we
believed she was upward of a thousand years old and had talked

with Moses. The younger Negroes credited these statistics and had furnished them to us in good faith. We accommodated all the details which came to us about her, and so we believed that she had lost her health in the long desert trip coming out of Egypt and had never been able to get it back again. She had a round bald place on the crown of her head, and we used to creep around and gaze at it in reverent silence and reflect that it was caused by fright through seeing Pharaoh drowned. We called her "Aunt" Hannah, Southern fashion. She was superstitious, like the other Negroes; also, like them, she was deeply religious. Like them, she had great faith in prayer and employed it in all ordinary exigencies, but not in cases where a dead certainty of result was urgent. Whenever witches were around she tied up the remnant of her wool in little tufts with white thread, and this promptly made the witches impotent.

All the Negroes were friends of ours and with those of our own age we were in effect comrades. I say in effect, using the phrase as a modification. We were comrades and yet not comrades; color and condition interposed a subtle line which both parties were conscious of and which rendered complete fusion impossible. We had a faithful and affectionate good friend, ally, and adviser in "Uncle Dan'l," a middle-aged slave whose head was the best one in the Negro quarter, whose sympathies were wide and warm, and whose heart was honest and simple and knew no guile. He has served me well these many, many years. I have not seen him for more than half a century, and yet spiritually I have had his welcome company a good part of that time and have staged him in books under his own name and as Jim and carted him all around, to Hannibal, down the Mississippi on a raft, and even across the Desert of Sahara in a balloon—and he has endured it all with the patience and friendliness and loyalty which were his birthright. It was on the farm that I got my strong liking for his race and my appreciation of certain of its fine qualities. This feeling and this estimate have stood the test of sixty years and more, and have suffered no impairment. The black face is as welcome to me now as it was then.

In my school-boy days I had no aversion to slavery. I was not aware that there was anything wrong about it. No one arraigned it in my hearing; the local papers said nothing against it; the local pulpit taught us that God approved it, that it was a holy thing, and that the doubter need only look in the Bible if he wished to settle his mind—and then the texts were read aloud to us to make the matter sure; if the slaves themselves had an aversion to slavery, they were wise and said nothing. In Hannibal we seldom saw a slave misused; on the farm, never.

There was, however, one small incident of my boyhood days which touched this matter and it must have meant a good deal to me or it would not have stayed in my memory, clear and sharp, vivid and shadowless, all these slow-drifting years. We had a little slave boy whom we had hired from some one, there in Hannibal. He was from the Eastern Shore of Maryland and had been brought away from his family and his friends, halfway across the American continent, and sold. He was a cheery spirit, innocent and gentle, and the noisiest creature that ever was perhaps. All day long he was singing, whistling, yelling, whooping, laughing—it was maddening, devastating, unendurable. At last, one day, I lost all my temper and went raging to my mother and said Sandy had been singing for an hour without a single break, and I couldn't stand it, and *wouldn't* she please shut him up. The tears came into her eyes and her lip trembled, and she said something like this:

"Poor thing, when he sings it shows that he is not remembering, and that comforts me; but when he is still I am afraid he is thinking and I cannot bear it. He will never see his mother again; if he can sing, I must not hinder it but be thankful for it. If you were older, you would understand me; then that friendless child's noise would make you glad."

It was a simple speech and made up of small words but it went home, and Sandy's noise was not a trouble to me any more. She never used large words but she had a natural gift for making small ones do effective work. She lived to reach the neighborhood of ninety years and was capable with her tongue to the last, es-

pecially when a meanness or an injustice roused her spirit. She has
come handy to me several times in my books, where she figures as
Tom Sawyer's Aunt Polly. I fitted her out with a dialect and tried to
think up other improvements for her, but did not find any. I used
Sandy once, also; it was in *Tom Sawyer*. I tried to get him to whitewash the fence but it did not work. I do not remember what name
I called him by in the book.

I can see the farm yet with perfect clearness. I can see all its
belongings, all its details: the family room of the house with a
"trundle" bed in one corner and a spinning-wheel in another, a
wheel whose rising and falling wail, heard from a distance, was the
mournfulest of all sounds to me and made me homesick and low-
spirited and filled my atmosphere with the wandering spirits of the
dead; the vast fireplace, piled high on winter nights with flaming
hickory logs from whose ends a sugary sap bubbled out but did
not go to waste, for we scraped it off and ate it; the lazy cat spread
out on the rough hearth-stones; the drowsy dogs braced against the
jambs and blinking; my aunt in one chimney corner, knitting; my
uncle in the other, smoking his corn-cob pipe; the slick and carpet-
less oak floor faintly mirroring the dancing flame-tongues and
freckled with black indentations where fire-coals had popped out
and died a leisurely death; half a dozen children romping in the
background twilight; split-bottomed chairs here and there, some
with rockers; a cradle, out of service but waiting with confidence;
in the early cold mornings a snuggle of children in shirts and
chemises occupying the hearth-stone and procrastinating—they
could not bear to leave that comfortable place and go out on the
wind-swept floor-space between the house and kitchen where the
general tin basin stood, and wash.

Along outside of the front fence ran the country road, dusty in
the summertime and a good place for snakes—they liked to lie in
it and sun themselves; when they were rattlesnakes or puff adders,
we killed them; when they were black snakes or racers or belonged
to the fabled "hoop" breed, we fled, without shame; when they
were "house-snakes" or "garters" we carried them home and put

them in Aunt Patsy's work-basket for a surprise; for she was prejudiced against snakes and always when she took the basket in her lap and they began to climb out of it, it disordered her mind. She never could seem to get used to them, her opportunities went for nothing. And she was always cold toward bats, too, and could not bear them; and yet I think a bat is as friendly a bird as there is. My mother was Aunt Patsy's sister and had the same wild superstitions. A bat is beautifully soft and silky; I do not know any creature that is pleasanter to the touch or is more grateful for caressings, if offered in the right spirit. I know all about these coleoptera because our great cave, three miles below Hannibal, was multitudinously stocked with them and often I brought them home to amuse my mother with. It was easy to manage if it was a school-day, because then I had ostensibly been to school and hadn't any bats. She was not a suspicious person but full of trust and confidence, and when I said, "There's something in my coat-pocket for you," she would put her hand in. But she always took it out again, herself; I didn't have to tell her. It was remarkable, the way she couldn't learn to like private bats. The more experience she had, the more she could not change her views.

I think she was never in the cave in her life; but everybody else went there. Many excursion parties came from considerable distances up and down the river to visit the cave. It was miles in extent and was a tangled wilderness of narrow and lofty clefts and passages. It was an easy place to get lost in; anybody could do it, including the bats. I got lost in it myself, along with a lady, and our last candle burned down to almost nothing before we glimpsed the search-party's lights winding about in the distance.

"Injun Joe," the half-breed, got lost in there once and would have starved to death if the bats had run short. But there was no chance of that, there were myriads of them. He told me all his story. In the book called *Tom Sawyer* I starved him entirely to death in the cave but that was in the interest of art: it never happened. "General" Gaines, who was our first town drunkard before Jimmy Finn got the place, was lost in there for the space of a week and finally pushed his handkerchief out of a hole in a hilltop near Saverton, several miles down the river from the cave's mouth, and somebody saw it and dug him out. There is nothing the matter with his statistics except the handkerchief. I knew him for years and he hadn't any. But it could have been his nose. That would attract attention.

The cave was an uncanny place for it contained a corpse, the corpse of a young girl of fourteen. It was in a glass cylinder inclosed in a copper one which was suspended from a rail which bridged a narrow passage. The body was preserved in alcohol, and it was said that loafers and rowdies used to drag it up by the hair and look at the dead face. The girl was the daughter of a St. Louis surgeon of extraordinary ability and wide celebrity. He was an eccentric man and did many strange things. He put the poor thing in that forlorn place himself.

QUESTIONS

1. Define the tonal effect of revising the first sentence in the first two paragraphs in the following way: My uncle, John A. Quarles, was a farmer who lived in the country four miles from Florida. That farm of my uncle John's was a heavenly place for a boy.

2. Explain the stylistic impropriety—according to ordinary standards—of Twain's use of "and" in the first and second sentences in the first paragraph ("a farmer and his place"; "twenty Negroes and was also fortunate"). What effect is Twain aiming at in each instance? Examine the improprieties of his use of "it" in the last two sentences in the paragraph.

3. Twain's humor is a decisive element defining the tone of the first paragraph. Is the humor pointed or casual, extravagant or mild, economical or repetitious? Identify the irony and metaphor that are its basis.

4. What words and phrases in the second paragraph seem inappropriate to the tone suggested by the structure of the first sentence in the paragraph? What words and phrases seem most appropriate? Justify the inconsistency.

5. On the basis of your answers to the previous questions, describe the tone of the first two paragraphs.

6. Distinguish the points of view present in the sixth paragraph. What effects does Twain obtain by juxtaposing them?

7. Examine the metaphorical language in the seventh paragraph. Would you say that the paragraph is highly metaphorical? Are the metaphors common or striking, simple or complex? How differently does Twain use his chief metaphor from the way he uses the chief metaphor in the first paragraph?

8. What contrasts in tone and style are there between the three paragraphs given to Sandy and Twain's mother, and the paragraph about the snakes and bats? Which presentation seems more typical of the essay? Which seems the more successful and genuine?

9. To what extent would you say Twain's humor is verbal—depending on metaphor and verbal irony? To what extent does it depend upon point of view and situation? (Consider the two paragraphs "Along outside of the front fence . . ." and " 'Injun Joe,' the half-breed. . . .")

10. What is Twain's general outlook on life? What are his values? (Answer in terms of the views stated or implicit in paragraphs three, seven, and eleven.) To what extent might you infer his outlook from the characteristics of his style?

11. The last paragraph in the sketch could easily be omitted. Could any other material? What would you say is the principle on which Twain has organized the sketch? (Try re-arranging some of the material.) What would you say is the chief factor giving unity to the sketch? Do your answers to these questions call to mind any of Twain's stylistic characteristics?

À Very Young Person

RUDYARD KIPLING

Rudyard Kipling (1865-1936) is best remembered for his poetry (*Barrack-Room Ballads*), short stories (*Soldiers Three*), and novels (*Kim*) relating to India. Born in Bombay, of English parents, he was sent to England for his education, but returned to India in preference to attending an English university. He became, at seventeen, a reporter for a local newspaper, and also began writing poetry and short stories, issuing no less than fifteen volumes in the years 1888-1891. These captured the life of India as no Western writer had previously, and brought him early fame. Though he soon left India for world travel, a stay in the United States, and finally a home in England, he continued to draw on his early experiences, perhaps most memorably in the *Jungle Books* and *Kim*. He received the Nobel Prize in 1907.

Give me the first six years of a child's life and you can have the rest.

Looking back from this my seventieth year, it seems to me that every card in my working life has been dealt me in such a manner that I had but to play it as it came. Therefore, ascribing all good fortune to Allah the Dispenser of Events, I begin:—

My first impression is of daybreak, light and colour and golden and purple fruits at the level of my shoulder. This would be the memory of early morning walks to the Bombay fruit market with my *ayah* and later with my sister in her perambulator, and of our returns with our purchases piled high on the bows of it. Our *ayah* was a Portuguese Roman Catholic who would pray—I beside her —at a wayside Cross. Meeta, my Hindu bearer, would sometimes go into little Hindu temples where, being below the age of caste, I held his hand and looked at the dimly seen, friendly Gods.

Our evening walks were by the sea in the shadow of palm-groves which, I think, were called the Mahim Woods. When the wind blew the great nuts would tumble, and we fled—my *ayah* and my sister in her perambulator—to the safety of the open. I have always felt the menacing darkness of tropical eventides, as I have loved the voices of night-winds through palm or banana leaves, and the song of the tree-frogs.

There were far-going Arab dhows on the pearly waters, and gaily dressed Parsees wading out to worship the sunset. Of their creed I knew nothing, nor did I know that near our little house on the Bombay Esplanade were the Towers of Silence, where their Dead are exposed to the waiting vultures on the rim of the towers, who scuffle and spread wings when they see the bearers of the Dead below. I did not understand my mother's distress when she found "a child's hand" in our garden, and said I was not to ask questions about it. I wanted to see that child's hand. But my *ayah* told me.

In the afternoon heats before we took our sleep, she or Meeta would tell us stories and Indian nursery songs all unforgotten, and we were sent into the dining-room after we had been dressed, with the caution "Speak English now to Papa and Mamma." So one spoke "English," haltingly translated out of the vernacular idiom that one thought and dreamed in. The Mother sang wonderful songs at a black piano and would go out to Big Dinners. Once she came back, very quickly, and told me, still awake, that "the big Lord Sahib" had been killed and there was to be no Big Dinner.

This was Lord Mayo, assassinated by a native. Meeta explained afterwards that he had been "hit with a knife." Meeta unconsciously saved me from any night terrors or dread of the dark. Our *ayah*, with a servant's curious mixture of deep affection and shallow device, had told me that a stuffed leopard's head on the nursery wall was there to see that I went to sleep. But Meeta spoke of it scornfully as "the head of an animal," and I took it off my mind as a fetish, good or bad, for it was only some unspecified "animal."

Far across green spaces round the house was a marvellous place filled with smells of paints and oils, and lumps of clay with which I played. That was the atelier of my Father's School of Art, and a Mr. "Terry Sahib" his assistant, to whom my small sister was devoted, was our great friend. Once, on the way there alone, I passed the edge of a huge ravine a foot deep, where a winged monster as big as myself attacked me, and I fled and wept. My Father drew for me a picture of the tragedy with a rhyme beneath:—

> There was a small boy in Bombay
> Who once from a hen ran away.
>   When they said: "You're a baby,"
>   He replied: "Well, I may be:
> But I don't like these hens of Bombay."

This consoled me. I have thought well of hens ever since.

Then those days of strong light and darkness passed, and there was a time in a ship with an immense semi-circle blocking all vision on each side of her. (She must have been the old paddle-wheel P. & O. *Ripon*.) There was a train across a desert (the Suez Canal was not yet opened) and a halt in it, and a small girl wrapped in a shawl on the seat opposite me, whose face stands out still. There was next a dark land, and a darker room full of cold, in one wall of which a white woman made naked fire, and I cried aloud with dread, for I had never before seen a grate.

Then came a new small house smelling of aridity and emptiness, and a parting in the dawn with Father and Mother, who said that I must learn quickly to read and write so that they might send me letters and books.

I lived in that house for close on six years. It belonged to a woman who took in children whose parents were in India. She was married to an old Navy Captain, who had been a midshipman at Navarino, and had afterwards been entangled in a harpoon-line while whale-fishing, and dragged down till he miraculously freed himself. But the line had scarred his ankle for life—a dry, black scar, which I used to look at with horrified interest.

The house itself stood in the extreme suburbs of Southsea, next to a Portsmouth unchanged in most particulars since Trafalgar— the Portsmouth of Sir Walter Besant's *By Celia's Arbour*. The timber for a Navy that was only experimenting with iron-clads such as the *Inflexible* lay in great booms in the Harbour. The little training-brigs kept their walks opposite Southsea Castle, and Portsmouth Hard was as it had always been. Outside these things lay the desolation of Hayling Island, Lumps Fort, and the isolated hamlet of Milton. I would go for long walks with the Captain, and once he took me to see a ship called the *Alert* (or *Discovery*) returned from Arctic explorations, her decks filled with old sledges and lumber, and her spare rudder being cut up for souvenirs. A sailor gave me a piece, but I lost it. Then the old Captain died, and I was sorry, for he was the only person in that house as far as I can remember who ever threw me a kind word.

It was an establishment run with the full vigour of the Evangelical as revealed to the Woman. I had never heard of Hell, so I was introduced to it in all its terrors—I and whatever luckless little slavey might be in the house, whom severe rationing had led to steal food. Once I saw the Woman beat such a girl who picked up the kitchen poker and threatened retaliation. Myself I was regularly beaten. The Woman had an only son of twelve or thirteen as religious as she. I was a real joy to him, for when his mother had finished with me for the day he (we slept in the same room) took me on and roasted the other side.

If you cross-examine a child of seven or eight on his day's doings (specially when he wants to go to sleep) he will contradict himself very satisfactorily. If each contradiction be set down as a lie and retailed at breakfast, life is not easy. I have known a certain amount of bullying, but this was calculated torture—religious as well as scientific. Yet it made me give attention to the lies I soon found it necessary to tell: and this, I presume, is the foundation of literary effort.

But my ignorance was my salvation. I was made to read without explanation, under the usual fear of punishment. And on a day that I remember it came to me that "reading" was not "the Cat lay on the Mat," but a means to everything that would make me happy. So I read all that came within my reach. As soon as my pleasure in this was known, deprivation from reading was added to my punishments. I then read by stealth and the more earnestly.

There were not many books in that house, but Father and Mother as soon as they heard I could read sent me priceless volumes. One I have still, a bound copy of *Aunt Judy's Magazine* of the early 'seventies, in which appeared Mrs. Ewing's *Six to Sixteen*. I owe more in circuitous ways to that tale than I can tell. I knew it, as I know it still, almost by heart. Here was a history of real people and real things. It was better than Knatchbull-Hugesson's *Tales at Tea-time*, better even than *The Old Shikarri* with its steel engravings of charging pigs and angry tigers. On another plane was an old magazine with Wordsworth's "I climbed the dark brow of the mighty Helvellyn." I knew nothing of its meaning but the words moved and pleased. So did other extracts from the poems of "A. Tennyson."

A visitor, too, gave me a little purple book of severely moral tendency called *The Hope of the Katzikopfs*—about a bad boy made virtuous, but it contained verses that began, "Farewell Rewards and Fairies," and ended with an injunction "To pray for the 'noddle' of William Churne of Staffordshire." This bore fruit afterwards.

And somehow or other I came across a tale about a lion-hunter in

South Africa who fell among lions who were all Freemasons, and with them entered into a confederacy against some wicked baboons. I think that, too, lay dormant until the *Jungle Books* began to be born.

There comes to my mind here a memory of two books of verse about child-life which I have tried in vain to identify. One—blue and fat—described "nine white wolves" coming "over the wold" and stirred me to the deeps; and also certain savages who "thought the name of England was something that could not burn."

The other book—brown and fat—was full of lovely tales in strange metres. A girl was turned into a water-rat "as a matter of course"; an Urchin cured an old man of gout by means of a cool cabbage-leaf, and somehow "forty wicked Goblins" were mixed up in the plot; and a "Darling" got out on the house-leads with a broom and tried to sweep stars off the skies. It must have been an unusual book for that age, but I have never been able to recover it, any more than I have a song that a nursemaid sang at low-tide in the face of the sunset on Littlehampton Sands when I was less than six. But the impression of wonder, excitement and terror and the red bars of failing light is as clear as ever.

Among the servants in the House of Desolation was one from Cumnor, which name I associated with sorrow and darkness and a raven that "flapped its wings." Years later I identified the lines: "And thrice the Raven flapped her wing Around the towers of Cumnor Hall." But how and where I first heard the lines that cast the shadow is beyond me—unless it be that the brain holds everything that passes within reach of the senses, and it is only ourselves who do not know this.

When my Father sent me a *Robinson Crusoe* with steel engravings I set up in business alone as a trader with savages (the wreck parts of the tale never much interested me), in a mildewy basement room where I stood my solitary confinements. My apparatus was a cocoanut shell strung on a red cord, a tin trunk, and a piece of packing-case which kept off any other world. Thus fenced about, everything inside the fence was quite real, but mixed with the smell of damp cupboards. If the bit of board fell, I had to begin the magic all over again. I have learned since from children who play much alone that this rule of "beginning again in a pretend game" is not uncommon. The magic, you see, lies in the ring or fence that you take refuge in.

Once I remember being taken to a town called Oxford and a street called Holywell, where I was shown an Ancient of Days who, I was told, was the Provost of Oriel; wherefore I never understood, but conceived him to be some sort of idol. And twice or thrice we went, all of us, to pay a day-long visit to an old gentleman in a house in the country near Havant. Here everything was wonderful and unlike my world, and he had an old lady sister who was kind, and I played in hot, sweet-smelling meadows and ate all sorts of things.

After such a visit I was once put through the third degree by the Woman and her son, who asked me if I had told the old gentleman that I was much fonder of him than was the Woman's son. It must have been the tail-end of some sordid intrigue or other—the old gentleman being of kin to that unhappy pair—but it was beyond my comprehension. My sole concern had been a friendly pony in the paddock. My dazed attempts to clear myself were not accepted and, once again, the pleasure that I was seen to have taken was balanced by punishments and humiliation—above all humiliation. That alternation was quite regular. I can but admire the infernal laborious ingenuity of it all. *Exempli gratia.* Coming out of church once I smiled. The Devil-Boy demanded why. I said I didn't know, which was child's truth. He replied that I *must* know. People didn't laugh for nothing. Heaven knows what explanation I put forward; but it was duly reported to the Woman as a "lie." Result, afternoon upstairs with the Collect to learn. I learned most of the Collects that way and a great deal of the Bible. The son after three or four years went into a Bank and was generally too tired on his return to torture me, unless things had gone wrong with him. I learned to know what was coming from his step into the house.

But, for a month each year I possessed a paradise which I verily believe saved me. Each December I stayed with my Aunt Georgy, my mother's sister, wife of Sir Edward Burne-Jones, at The Grange, North End Road. At first I must have been escorted there, but later I went alone, and arriving at the house would reach up to the open-work iron bell-pull on the wonderful gate that let me into all felicity. When I had a house of my own, and The Grange was emptied of meaning, I begged for and was given that bell-pull for my entrance, in the hope that other children might also feel happy when they rang it.

At The Grange I had love and affection as much as the greediest, and I was not very greedy, could desire. There were most wonderful smells of paints and turpentine whiffing down from the big studio on the first floor where my Uncle worked; there was the society of my two cousins, and a sloping mulberry tree which we used to climb for our plots and conferences. There was a rocking-horse in the nursery and a table that, tilted up on two chairs, made a toboggan-slide of the best. There were pictures finished or half finished of lovely colours; and in the rooms chairs and cupboards such as the world had not yet seen, for William Morris (our Deputy "Uncle Topsy") was just beginning to fabricate these things. There was an incessant come and go of young people and grown-ups all willing to play with us—except an elderly person called "Browning" who took no proper interest in the skirmishes which happened to be raging on his entry. Best of all, immeasurably, was the beloved Aunt herself reading us *The Pirate* or *The Arabian Nights* of evenings, when one lay out on the big sofas sucking toffee, and calling our cousins "Ho, Son," or "Daughter of my Uncle" or "O True Believer."

Often the Uncle, who had a "golden voice," would assist in our evening play, though mostly he worked at black and white in the middle of our riots. He was never idle. We made a draped chair in the hall serve for the seat of "Norna of the Fitful Head" and addressed her questions till the Uncle got inside the rugs and gave us answers which thrilled us with delightful shivers, in a voice deeper than all the boots in the world. And once he descended in

broad daylight with a tube of "Mummy Brown" in his hand, saying
that he had discovered it was made of dead Pharaohs and we must
bury it accordingly. So we all went out and helped—according to
the rites of Mizraim and Memphis, I hope—and—to this day I
could drive a spade within a foot of where that tube lies.

At bedtime one hastened along the passages, where unfinished
cartoons lay against the walls. The Uncle often painted in their
eyes first, leaving the rest in charcoal—a most effective presentation.
Hence our speed to our own top-landing, where we could hang over
the stairs and listen to the loveliest sound in the world—deep-
voiced men laughing together over dinner.

It was a jumble of delights and emotions culminating in being
allowed to blow the big organ in the studio for the beloved Aunt,
while the Uncle worked, or "Uncle Topsy" came in full of some
business of picture-frames or stained glass or general denunciations.
Then it was hard to keep the little lead weight on its string below
the chalk mark, and if the organ ran out in squeals the beloved
Aunt would be sorry. Never, *never* angry!

As a rule Morris took no notice of anything outside what was in
his mind at the moment. But I remember one amazing exception.
My cousin Margaret and I, then about eight, were in the nursery
eating pork-dripping on brown bread, which is a dish for the Gods,
when we heard "Uncle Topsy" in the hall calling, as he usually did,
for "Ned" or "Georgie." The matter was outside our world. So we
were the more impressed when, not finding the grown-ups, he came
in and said he would tell us a story. We settled ourselves under the
table which we used for a toboggan-slide and he, bravely as ever,
climbed on to our big rocking-horse. There, slowly surging back
and forth while the poor beast creaked, he told us a tale full of fascinating horrors, about a man who was condemned to dream bad
dreams. One of them took the shape of a cow's tail waving from a
heap of dried fish. He went away as abruptly as he had come.
Long afterwards, when I was old enough to know a maker's pains,
it dawned on me that we must have heard the Saga of Burnt Njal,
which was then interesting him. In default of grown-ups, and

pressed by need to pass the story between his teeth and clarify it, he had used us.

But on a certain day—one tried to fend off the thought of it— the delicious dream would end, and one would return to the House of Desolation, and for the next two or three mornings there cry on waking up. Hence more punishments and cross-examinations.

Often and often afterwards, the beloved Aunt would ask me why I had never told anyone how I was being treated. Children tell little more than animals, for what comes to them they accept as eternally established. Also, badly-treated children have a clear notion of what they are likely to get if they betray the secrets of a prison-house before they are clear of it.

In justice to the Woman I can say that I was adequately fed. (I remember a gift to her of some red "fruit" called "tomatoes" which, after long consideration, she boiled with sugar; and they were very beastly. The tinned meat of those days was Australian beef with a crumbly fat, and string-boiled mutton, hard to get down.) Nor was my life an unsuitable preparation for my future, in that it demanded constant wariness, the habit of observation, and attendance on moods and tempers; the noting of discrepancies between speech and action; a certain reserve of demeanour; and automatic suspicion of sudden favours. Brother Lippo Lippi, in his own harder case, as a boy discovered:—

> *Why, soul and sense of him grow sharp alike,*
> *He learns the look of things and none the less*
> *For admonition.*

So it was with me.

My troubles settled themselves in a few years. My eyes went wrong, and I could not well see to read. For which reason I read the more and in bad lights. My work at the terrible little day-school where I had been sent suffered in consequence, and my monthly reports showed it. The loss of "reading-time" was the worst of my "home" punishments for bad school-work. One report was so bad that I threw it away and said that I had never received it. But this is a hard world for the amateur liar. My web of deceit was swiftly exposed—the Son spared time after banking-hours to help in the auto-da-fé—and I was well beaten and sent to school through the streets of Southsea with the placard "Liar" between my shoulders. In the long run these things, and many more of the like, drained me of any capacity for real, personal hate for the rest of my days. So close must any life-filling passion lie to its opposite. "Who having known the Diamond will concern himself with glass?"

Some sort of nervous breakdown followed for I imagined I saw shadows and things that were not there, and they worried me more than the Woman. The beloved Aunt must have heard of it, and a man came down to see me as to my eyes and reported that I was half-blind. This, too, was supposed to be "showing-off," and I was segregated from my sister—another punishment—as a sort of moral leper. Then—I do not remember that I had any warning— the Mother returned from India. She told me afterwards that when she first came up to my room to kiss me good-night, I flung up an arm to guard off the cuff that I had been trained to expect.

I was taken at once from the House of Desolation, and for months ran wild in a little farmhouse on the edge of Epping Forest, where I was not encouraged to refer to my guilty past. Except for my spectacles, which were uncommon in those days, I was completely happy with my Mother and the local society, which included for me a gipsy of the name of Saville, who told me tales of selling horses to the ignorant; the farmer's wife; her niece Patty who turned a kind blind eye on our raids into the dairy; the postman; and the farm-boys. The farmer did not approve of my teaching one of his cows to stand and be milked in the field. My Mother drew the line at my return to meals red-booted from assisting at the slaughter of swine, or reeking after the exploration of attractive muck-heaps. These were the only restrictions I recall.

A cousin, afterwards to be a Prime Minister, would come down on visits. The farmer said that we did each other "no good." Yet the worst I can remember was our self-sacrificing war against a wasp's nest on a muddy islet in a most muddy pond. Our only weapons were switches of broom, but we defeated the enemy unscathed. The trouble at home centred round an enormous current roly-poly —a "spotted dog" a foot long. We took it away to sustain us in action and we heard a great deal about it from Patty in the evening.

Then we went to London and stayed for some weeks in a tiny lodging-house in the semi-rural Brompton Road, kept by an ivory-faced, lordly-whiskered ex-butler and his patient wife. Here, for the first time, it happened that the night got into my head. I rose up and wandered about that still house till daybreak, when I slipped out into the little brick-walled garden and saw the dawn break. All would have been well but for Pluto, a pet toad brought back from Epping Forest, who lived mostly in one of my pockets. It struck me that he might be thirsty, and I stole into my Mother's room and would have given him drink from a water-jug. But it slipped and broke and very much was said. The ex-butler could not understand why I had stayed awake all night. I did not know then that such night-wakings would be laid upon me through my life; or that my fortunate hour would be on the turn of sunrise, with a sou'-west breeze afoot.

The sorely tried Mother got my sister and me season-tickets for the old South Kensington Museum which was only across the road. (No need in those days to caution us against the traffic.) Very shortly we two, on account of our regular attendance (for the weather had turned wet), owned that place and one policeman in special. When we came with any grown-ups he saluted us magnificently. From the big Buddha with the little door in his back, to the towering dull-gilt ancient coaches and carven chariots in long dark corridors—even the places marked "private" where fresh treasures were always being unpacked—we roved at will, and divided the treasures child-fashion. There were instruments of music inlaid with lapis, beryl and ivories; glorious gold-fretted spinets and clavichords; the bowels of the great Glastonbury clock; mechanical models; steel- and silver-butted pistols, daggers and arquebusses— the labels alone were an education; a collection of precious stones and rings—we quarrelled over those—and a big bluish book which was the manuscript of one of Dickens' novels. That man seemed to me to have written very carelessly; leaving out lots which he had to squeeze in between the lines afterwards.

These experiences were a soaking in colour and design with, above all, the proper Museum smell; and it stayed with me. By the end of that long holiday I understood that my Mother had written verses, that my Father "wrote things" also; that books and pictures were among the most important affairs in the world; that I could read as much as I chose and ask the meaning of things from anyone I met. I had found out, too, that one could take pen and set down what one thought, and that nobody accused one of "showing off" by so doing. I read a good deal; *Sidonia the Sorceress;* Emerson's poems; and Bret Harte's stories; and I learned all sorts of verses for the pleasure of repeating them to myself in bed.

QUESTIONS

1. Consider the following revision of the first paragraph of Kipling's sketch: Looking back over seventy years, I can see that my success hasn't required special effort on my part: a kind fate dealt me a good hand. What are the differences in diction, rhythm, handling of metaphor, and use of irony? On the basis of your answers, define the tone of Kipling's paragraph.

2. Would you say that scene or feeling dominates the second and third paragraphs? (Consider the focus of attention in the sentences, consistency and quality of sentence rhythm, precision of image.) On the basis of your answers define the point of view in the two paragraphs. Where does the diction most noticeably indicate that point of view? Where does another point of view most strongly emerge?

3. Would you say that the contrast between the "gaily dressed Parsees" and the "Dead . . . exposed to the waiting vultures" (paragraph four) is vivid or reflective, ironic or dramatic? Or is it something else? Is its quality muted or heightened by the sentence rhythms? What is the particular effect of the modified sentence rhythm of the last two sentences?

4. Analyze the metaphorical language in the first six paragraphs. How unusual, vivid, or complex is it? What immediate functions do the two or three major metaphors serve? Would you say that the general quality of the metaphorical language is consonant with the general quality that you have attributed to the images (scenes) in Questions 2 and 3?

5. Show how Kipling's use or avoidance of detail serves his fluctuating point of view in both paragraphs five and ten.

6. Examine the irony in paragraphs eleven ("It was an establishment . . .") and twelve. What is its range in seriousness and subtlety? Does it, or does diction or sentence rhythm, dominate the tone of the paragraphs?

7. Taking paragraphs five, twenty-two ("After such a visit . . ."), and twenty-four to be typical, distinguish Kipling's tone in treating of India, Portsmouth, and the Grange. What, broadly, are the reasons for the differences? What would you say are the chief stylistic devices that determine the tone of each of the three paragraphs?

8. Contrast the structure and rhythm of the sentences in the seventh paragraph and in the last. What particular appropriateness does each rhythm have? Which rhythm would you say is closer to the norm in the sketch?

9. Kipling organizes the essay both chronologically and in another way. How would you describe the latter method? What reasons would you give for saying the one or the other is the more meaningful and dramatic? Which of the two seems more consonant with the major qualities of his style? Explain your answer.

10. What particular aspects of Kipling's tone and style might suggest a seventy-year-old man? What particular sort of one?

11. What aspects of Kipling's growth have prepared him for his literary career? What traces of his experience do you find in his style?

Shooting an Elephant

GEORGE ORWELL

> Orwell's experiences in India, as a youth and later as a member of the Indian Imperial Police, gave him first-hand knowledge of both Indian and Anglo-Indian life; they also turned him into a sharply critical commentator on British Imperialism, which he came to characterize as "very largely a racket." His first novel, *Burmese Days,* presents a thoroughly devastating picture of the hypocrisy and futility of English colonial existence. "Shooting an Elephant," written several years after Orwell had left India for Europe, may be profitably compared with another of his essays, "Marrakech" (pp. 92-99), written slightly later. Both suggest why he has been called the "conscience of his generation." (Further headnote information on Orwell appears on pp. 92, 175.)

In Moulmein, in Lower Burma, I was hated by large numbers of people—the only time in my life that I have been important enough for this to happen to me. I was sub-divisional police officer of the town, and in an aimless, petty kind of way anti-European feeling was very bitter. No one had the guts to raise a riot, but if a European woman went through the bazaars alone somebody would probably spit betel juice over her dress. As a police officer I was an obvious target and was baited whenever it seemed safe to do so. When a nimble Burman tripped me up on the football field and the referee (another Burman) looked the other way, the crowd yelled with hideous laughter. This happened more than once. In the end the sneering yellow faces of young men that met me everywhere, the insults hooted after me when I was at a safe distance, got badly on my nerves. The young Buddhist priests were the worst of all. There were several thousands of them in the town and none of them seemed to have anything to do except stand on street corners and jeer at Europeans.

All this was perplexing and upsetting. For at that time I had already made up my mind that imperialism was an evil thing and the sooner I chucked up my job and got out of it the better. Theoretically—and secretly, of course—I was all for the Burmese and all against their oppressors, the British. As for the job I was doing, I hated it more bitterly than I can perhaps make clear. In a job like that you see the dirty work of Empire at close quarters. The wretched prisoners huddling in the stinking cages of the lock-ups, the grey, cowed faces of the long-term convicts, the scarred buttocks of the men who had been flogged with bamboos—all these oppressed me with an intolerable sense of guilt. But I could get nothing into perspective. I was young and ill-educated and I had had to think out my problems in the utter silence that is imposed on every Englishman in the East. I did not even know that the British Empire is dying, still less did I know that it is a great deal better than the younger empires that are going to supplant it. All I knew was that I was stuck between my hatred of the empire I served and my rage against the evil-spirited little beasts who tried to make my job impossible. With one part of my mind I thought of the British Raj as an unbreakable tyranny, as something clamped down, in *saecula saeculorum*, upon the will of prostrate peoples; with another part I thought that the greatest joy in the world would be to drive a bayonet into a Buddhist priest's guts. Feelings like these are the normal by-products of imperialism; ask any Anglo-Indian official, if you can catch him off duty.

One day something happened which in a roundabout way was

enlightening. It was a tiny incident in itself, but it gave me a better glimpse than I had had before of the real nature of imperialism— the real motives for which despotic governments act. Early one morning the sub-inspector at a police station the other end of the town rang me up on the 'phone and said that an elephant was rav- aging the bazaar. Would I please come and do something about it? I did not know what I could do, but I wanted to see what was hap- pening and I got on to a pony and started out. I took my rifle, an old .44 Winchester and much too small to kill an elephant, but I thought the noise might be useful *in terrorem*. Various Burmans stopped me on the way and told me about the elephant's doings. It was not, of course, a wild elephant, but a tame one which had gone "must." It had been chained up, as tame elephants always are when their attack of "must" is due, but on the previous night it had broken its chain and escaped. Its mahout, the only person who could manage it when it was in that state, had set out in pursuit, but had taken the wrong direction and was now twelve hours' jour- ney away, and in the morning the elephant had suddenly reap- peared in the town. The Burmese population had no weapons and were quite helpless against it. It had already destroyed somebody's bamboo hut, killed a cow and raided some fruit-stalls and devoured the stock; also it had met the municipal rubbish van and, when the driver jumped out and took to his heels, had turned the van over and inflicted violences upon it.

The Burmese sub-inspector and some Indian constables were waiting for me in the quarter where the elephant had been seen. It was a very poor quarter, a labyrinth of squalid bamboo huts, thatched with palm-leaf, winding all over a steep hillside. I re- member that it was a cloudy, stuffy morning at the beginning of the rains. We began questioning the people as to where the elephant had gone and, as usual, failed to get any definite information. That is invariably the case in the East, a story always sounds clear enough at a distance, but the nearer you get to the scene of events the vaguer it becomes. Some of the people said that the elephant had gone in one direction, some said that he had gone in another.

some professed not even to have heard of any elephant. I had almost made up my mind that the whole story was a pack of lies,
when we heard yells a little distance away. There was a loud, scan-
dalized cry of "Go away, child! Go away this instant!" and an old
woman with a switch in her hand came round the corner of a hut,
violently shooing away a crowd of naked children. Some more
women followed, clicking their tongues and exclaiming; evidently
there was something that the children ought not to have seen. I
rounded the hut and saw a man's dead body sprawling in the mud.
He was an Indian, a black Dravidian coolie, almost naked, and he
could not have been dead many minutes. The people said that the
elephant had come suddenly upon him round the corner of the hut,
caught him with its trunk, put its foot on his back and ground him
into the earth. This was the rainy season and the ground was soft,
and his face had scored a trench a foot deep and a couple of yards
long. He was lying on his belly with arms crucified and head
sharply twisted to one side. His face was coated with mud, the eyes
wide open, the teeth bared and grinning with an expression of unendurable agony. (Never tell me, by the way, that the dead look
peaceful. Most of the corpses I have seen looked devilish.) The
friction of the great beast's foot had stripped the skin from his back
as neatly as one skins a rabbit. As soon as I saw the dead man I
sent an orderly to a friend's house nearby to borrow an elephant
rifle. I had already sent back the pony, not wanting it to go mad
with fright and throw me if it smelt the elephant.

The orderly came back in a few minutes with a rifle and five cartridges, and meanwhile some Burmans had arrived and told us that
the elephant was in the paddy fields below, only a few hundred
yards away. As I started forward practically the whole population
of the quarter flocked out of the houses and followed me. They had
seen the rifle and were all shouting excitedly that I was going to
shoot the elephant. They had not shown much interest in the elephant when he was merely ravaging their homes, but it was different now that he was going to be shot. It was a bit of fun to them,
as it would be to an English crowd; besides they wanted the meat.

It made me vaguely uneasy. I had no intention of shooting the elephant—I had merely sent for the rifle to defend myself if necessary—and it is always unnerving to have a crowd following you. I marched down the hill, looking and feeling a fool, with the rifle over my shoulder and an ever-growing army of people jostling at my heels. At the bottom, when you got away from the huts, there was a metalled road and beyond that a miry waste of paddy fields a thousand yards across, not yet ploughed but soggy from the first rains and dotted with coarse grass. The elephant was standing eight yards from the road, his left side towards us. He took not the slightest notice of the crowd's approach. He was tearing up bunches of grass, beating them against his knees to clean them and stuffing them into his mouth.

I had halted on the road. As soon as I saw the elephant I knew with perfect certainty that I ought not to shoot him. It is a serious matter to shoot a working elephant—it is comparable to destroying a huge and costly piece of machinery—and obviously one ought not to do it if it can possibly be avoided. And at that distance, peacefully eating, the elephant looked no more dangerous than a cow. I thought then and I think now that his attack of "must" was already passing off; in which case he would merely wander harmlessly about until the mahout came back and caught him. Moreover, I did not in the least want to shoot him. I decided that I would watch him for a little while to make sure that he did not turn savage again, and then go home.

But at that moment I glanced round at the crowd that had followed me. It was an immense crowd, two thousand at the least and growing every minute. It blocked the road for a long distance on either side. I looked at the sea of yellow faces above the garish clothes—faces all happy and excited over this bit of fun, all certain that the elephant was going to be shot. They were watching me as they would watch a conjurer about to perform a trick. They did not like me, but with the magical rifle in my hands I was momentarily worth watching. And suddenly I realized that I should have to shoot the elephant after all. The people expected it of me and I had got to do it; I could feel their two thousand wills pressing me forward, irresistibly. And it was at this moment, as I stood there with the rifle in my hands, that I first grasped the hollowness, the futility of the white man's dominion in the East. Here was I, the white man with his gun, standing in front of the unarmed native crowd— seemingly the leading actor of the piece; but in reality I was only an absurd puppet pushed to and fro by the will of those yellow faces behind. I perceived in this moment that when the white man turns tyrant it is his own freedom that he destroys. He becomes a sort of hollow, posing dummy, the conventionalized figure of a sahib. For it is the condition of his rule that he shall spend his life in trying to impress the "natives," and so in every crisis he has got to do what the "natives" expect of him. He wears a mask; and his face grows to fit it. I had got to shoot the elephant. I had committed myself to doing it when I sent for the rifle. A sahib has got to act like a sahib; he has got to appear resolute, to know his own mind and do definite things. To come all that way, rifle in hand, with two thousand people marching at my heels, and then to trail feebly away, having done nothing—no, that was impossible. The crowd would laugh at me. And my whole life, every white man's life in the East, was one long struggle not to be laughed at.

But I did not want to shoot the elephant. I watched him beating his bunch of grass against his knees, with that preoccupied grandmotherly air that elephants have. It seemed to me that it would be murder to shoot him. At that age I was not squeamish about killing animals, but I had never shot an elephant and never wanted to. (Somehow it always seems worse to kill a *large* animal.) Besides, there was the beast's owner to be considered. Alive, the elephant was worth at least a hundred pounds; dead, he would only be worth the value of his tusks, five pounds, possibly. But I had got to act quickly. I turned to some experienced-looking Burmans who had been there when we arrived, and asked them how the elephant had been behaving. They all said the same thing: he took no notice of you if you left him alone, but he might charge if you went too close to him.

It was perfectly clear to me what I ought to do. I ought to walk up to within, say, twenty-five yards of the elephant and test his behavior. If he charged, I could shoot; if he took no notice of me, it would be safe to leave him until the mahout came back. But also I knew that I was going to do no such thing. I was a poor shot with a rifle and the ground was soft mud into which one would sink at every step. If the elephant charged and I missed him, I should have about as much chance as a toad under a steam-roller. But even then I was not thinking particularly of my own skin, only of the watchful yellow faces behind. For at that moment, with the crowd watching me, I was not afraid in the ordinary sense, as I would have been if I had been alone. A white man mustn't be frightened in front of "natives"; and so, in general, he isn't frightened. The sole thought in my mind was that if anything went wrong those two thousand Burmans would see me pursued, caught, trampled on and reduced to a grinning corpse like that Indian up the hill. And if that happened it was quite probable that some of them would laugh. That would never do. There was only one alternative. I shoved the cartridges into the magazine and lay down on the road to get a better aim.

The crowd grew very still, and a deep, low, happy sigh, as of people who see the theatre curtain go up at last, breathed from innumerable throats. They were going to have their bit of fun after all. The rifle was a beautiful German thing with cross-hair sights. I did not then know that in shooting an elephant one would shoot to cut an imaginary bar running from ear-hole to ear-hole. I ought, therefore, as the elephant was sideways on, to have aimed straight at his ear-hole; actually I aimed several inches in front of this, thinking the brain would be further forward.

When I pulled the trigger I did not hear the bang or feel the kick —one never does when a shot goes home—but I heard the devilish roar of glee that went up from the crowd. In that instant, in too short a time, one would have thought, even for the bullet to get there, a mysterious, terrible change had come over the elephant. He neither stirred nor fell, but every line of his body had altered.

He looked suddenly stricken, shrunken, immensely old, as though the frightful impact of the bullet had paralysed him without knocking him down. At last, after what seemed a long time—it might have been five seconds, I dare say—he sagged flabbily to his knees. His mouth slobbered. An enormous senility seemed to have settled upon him. One could have imagined him thousands of years old. I fired again into the same spot. At the second shot he did not collapse but climbed with desperate slowness to his feet and stood weakly upright, with legs sagging and head drooping. I fired a third time. That was the shot that did for him. You could see the agony of it jolt his whole body and knock the last remnant of strength from his legs. But in falling he seemed for a moment to rise, for as his hind legs collapsed beneath him he seemed to tower upward like a huge rock toppling, his trunk reaching skywards like a tree. He trumpeted, for the first and only time. And then down he came, his belly towards me, with a crash that seemed to shake the ground even where I lay.

I got up. The Burmans were already racing past me across the mud. It was obvious that the elephant would never rise again, but he was not dead. He was breathing very rhythmically with long rattling gasps, his great mound of a side painfully rising and falling. His mouth was wide open—I could see far down into caverns of pale pink throat. I waited a long time for him to die, but his breathing did not weaken. Finally I fired my two remaining shots into the spot where I thought his heart must be. The thick blood welled out of him like red velvet, but still he did not die. His body did not even jerk when the shots hit him, the tortured breathing continued without a pause. He was dying, very slowly and in great agony, but in some world remote from me where not even a bullet could damage him further. I felt that I had got to put an end to that dreadful noise. It seemed dreadful to see the great beast lying there, powerless to move and yet powerless to die, and not even to be able to finish him. I sent back for my small rifle and poured shot after shot into his heart and down his throat. They seemed to make no impression. The tortured gasps continued as steadily as the ticking of a clock.

In the end I could not stand it any longer and went away. I heard later that it took him half an hour to die. Burmans were bringing dahs and baskets even before I left, and I was told they had stripped his body almost to the bones by the afternoon.

Afterwards, of course, there were endless discussions about the shooting of the elephant. The owner was furious, but he was only an Indian and could do nothing. Besides, legally I had done the right thing, for a mad elephant has to be killed, like a mad dog, if its owner fails to control it. Among the Europeans opinion was divided. The older men said I was right, the younger men said it was a damn shame to shoot an elephant for killing a coolie, because an elephant was worth more than any damn Coringhee coolie. And afterwards I was very glad that the coolie had been killed; it put me legally in the right and it gave me a sufficient pretext for shooting the elephant. I often wondered whether any of the others grasped that I had done it solely to avoid looking a fool.

QUESTIONS

1. What sort of tone would such language as "guts," "hideous," "sneering," and "hooted" (paragraph one) ordinarily help establish? Why do these words fail to contribute to such a tone in the context of the paragraph? What sort of relationship to the reader does Orwell establish by using them in the special way that he does?

2. Compare the complexity, formality, rhythm, and dramatic focus of the first two sentences in the essay with the following revision; then state the attendant tonal differences: In Moulmein, in Lower Burma, anti-European feeling, although expressed in an aimless, petty kind of way, was very bitter. I myself, as subdivisional police officer of the town, held—for the only time in my life—an important enough position so that I was hated by large numbers of people.

3. What variety in diction do you observe in the second paragraph? Can you account for it? Identify the level of formality of those words

and phrases that seem to you to establish the dominant tone of the paragraph. What would you say is the tonal effect of the repeated structure and language in the five sentences beginning "But I could get nothing"? What shift in tone comes with the last sentence? How does Orwell achieve the shift?

4. Examine the transitions within the third paragraph. Are they clear or hidden, graceful or abrupt, plain or elaborate? Compare them with the transitions from paragraph to paragraph in the essay. Do you see any notable differences? Would you say their qualities are consonant with the stylistic qualities that the previous questions have explored?

5. To what extent does Orwell employ irony in the seventh paragraph ("But at that moment . . .")? Does he use his chief metaphor in the paragraph—puppet, dummy, mask—as a means of argument, illumination, or emphasis? How complex is the metaphor? How striking? How unusual and how effective are the other metaphors in the paragraph?

6. The two most vivid passages in the essay are the descriptions of the dead coolie and the dying elephant. Compare them in the following respects: level of diction, prevalence of modifying adjectives and adverbs, use of repeated description, complexity of sentence construction, prevalence and originality of metaphor. How markedly different from the other passages that you have analyzed is either of these passages stylistically? In which respects, if any?

7. Contrast the tones of the passages describing the dead coolie and the dying elephant. Is the tone within each passage consistent? In what individual respect does the tone of each passage contribute to the seriousness of the depicted scene? In which instance do you think Orwell employs his tone more originally? In which more effectively?

8. What stylistic features mark the shifts in tone in the final paragraph? What is the main basis upon which you recognize the shifts? What attitude towards the reader is implicit in the way in which Orwell handles the shifts? Is it the same attitude that Question 1 explores? Would you say it is characteristic of the essay?

9. On the basis of your answers to previous questions, what would you say Orwell's style is: simple? formal? flexible? complex? colorful? What might you infer about the man from his style?

10. Taking the subject of Orwell's essay to be "the real nature of imperialism—the real motives for which despotic governments act" (para-

graph three), explain the function of the first two paragraphs. Do you think that the subsequent experience that he describes is adequate to his argument? What material in the essay is extraneous to his subject? To what extent does this extraneous material contribute to the power of the essay? Is, then, the essay defective?

Reminiscences of Childhood

DYLAN THOMAS

Dylan Thomas (1914-1953) published his first book of poetry when he was twenty and his second two years later. He then did odd jobs, spent some time as a journalist, and worked for the British Broadcasting Company. In marked contrast to the intellectualized manner of many of his contemporaries, his writings are impassioned and highly subjective; often they show the influence of his native South Wales. By the time of his early death, he had established himself as a poet of importance and as an erratic and flamboyant public figure, with a particularly large following in the United States, where he is remembered for his exuberant public readings. His prose has been collected in *Portrait of the Artist as a Young Dog* and *Quite Early One Morning;* shortly before his death he wrote a verse play, *Under Milk Wood.*

I like very much people telling me about their childhood, but they'll have to be quick or else I'll be telling them about mine.

I was born in a large Welsh town at the beginning of the Great War—an ugly, lovely town (or so it was and is to me), crawling, sprawling by a long and splendid curving shore where truant boys and sandfield boys and old men from nowhere, beachcombed, idled and paddled, watched the dock-bound ships or the ships steaming away into wonder and India, magic and China, countries bright with oranges and loud with lions; threw stones into the sea for the barking outcast dogs; made castles and forts and harbours and race tracks in the sand; and on Saturday summer afternoons listened to the brass band, watched the Punch and Judy, or hung about on the fringes of the crowd to hear the fierce religious speakers who shouted at the sea, as though it were wicked and wrong to roll in and out like that, white-horsed and full of fishes.

One man, I remember, used to take off his hat and set fire to his hair every now and then, but I do not remember what it proved, if it proved anything at all, except that he was a very interesting man.

This sea-town was my world; outside a strange Wales, coal-pitted, mountained, river-run, full, so far as I knew, of choirs and football teams and sheep and storybook tall hats and red flannel petticoats, moved about its business which was none of mine.

Beyond that unknown Wales with its wild names like peals of bells in the darkness, and its mountain men clothed in the skins of animals perhaps and always singing, lay England which was London and the country called the Front, from which many of our neighbours never came back. It was a country to which only young men travelled.

At the beginning, the only "front" I knew was the little lobby before our front door. I could not understand how so many people never returned from there, but later I grew to know more, though still without understanding, and carried a wooden rifle in the park and shot down the invisible unknown enemy like a flock of wild birds. And the park itself was a world within the world of the sea-town. Quite near where I lived, so near that on summer evenings I could listen in my bed to the voices of older children playing ball on the sloping paper-littered bank, the park was full of terrors and treasures. Though it was only a little park, it held within its borders of old tall trees, notched with our names and shabby from our climbing, as many secret places, caverns and forests, prairies and deserts, as a country somewhere at the end of the sea.

And though we would explore it one day, armed and desperate, from end to end, from the robbers' den to the pirates' cabin, the highwayman's inn to the cattle ranch, or the hidden room in the undergrowth, where we held beetle races, and lit the wood fires and roasted potatoes and talked about Africa, and the makes of motor cars, yet still the next day, it remained as unexplored as the Poles—a country just born and always changing.

There were many secret societies but you could belong only to one; and in blood or red ink, and a rusty pocketknife, with, of course, an instrument to remove stones from horses' feet, you signed your name at the foot of a terrible document, swore death to all the other societies, crossed your heart that you would divulge no secret and that if you did, you would consent to torture by slow fire, and undertook to carry out by yourself a feat of either daring or endurance. You could take your choice: would you climb to the top of the tallest and most dangerous tree, and from there hurl stones and insults at grown-up passers-by, especially postmen, or any other men in uniform? Or would you ring every doorbell in the terrace, not forgetting the doorbell of the man with the red face who kept dogs and ran fast? Or would you swim in the reservoir, which was forbidden and had angry swans, or would you eat a whole old jam jar full of mud?

There were many more alternatives. I chose one of endurance and for half an hour, it may have been longer or shorter, held up off the ground a very heavy broken pram we had found in a bush. I thought my back would break and the half hour felt like a day, but I preferred it to braving the red face and the dogs, or to swallowing tadpoles.

We knew every inhabitant of the park, every regular visitor, every nursemaid, every gardener, every old man. We knew the hour when the alarming retired policeman came in to look at the dahlias and the hour when the old lady arrived in the Bath chair with six Pekinese, and a pale girl to read aloud to her. I think she read the newspaper, but we always said she read the *Wizard*. The face of the old man who sat summer and winter on the bench looking over

the reservoir, I can see clearly now and I wrote a poem long long
after I'd left the park and the sea-town called:

THE HUNCHBACK IN THE PARK

The hunchback in the park
A solitary mister
Propped between trees and water
From the opening of the garden lock
That lets the trees and water enter
Until the Sunday sombre ball at dark

Eating bread from a newspaper
Drinking water from the chained cup
That the children filled with gravel
In the fountain basin where I sailed my ship
Slept at night in a dog kennel
But nobody chained him up.

Like the park birds he came early
Like the water he sat down
And Mister they called Hey mister
The truant boys from the town
Running when he had heard them clearly
On out of sound

Past lake and rockery
Laughing when he shook his paper
Hunchbacked in mockery
Through the loud zoo of the willow groves
Dodging the park-keeper
With his stick that picked up leaves.

And the old dog sleeper
Alone between nurses and swans

While the boys among willows
Made the tigers jump out of their eyes
To roar on the rockery stones
And the groves were blue with sailors

Made all day until bell-time
A woman figure without fault
Straight as a young elm
Straight and tall from his crooked bones
That she might stand in the night
After the locks and the chains

All night in the unmade park
After the railings and shrubberies
The birds the grass the trees and the lake
And the wild boys innocent as strawberries
Had followed the hunchback
To his kennel in the dark.

And that park grew up with me; that small world widened as I learned its secrets and boundaries, as I discovered new refuges and ambushes in its woods and jungles; hidden homes and lairs for the multitudes of imagination, for cowboys and Indians, and the tall terrible half-people who rode on nightmares through my bedroom. But it was not the only world—that world of rockery, gravel path, play-bank, bowling green, bandstands, reservoir, dahlia garden, where an ancient keeper, known as Smoky, was the whiskered snake in the grass one must keep off. There was another world where with my friends I used to dawdle on half holidays along the bent and Devon-facing seashore, hoping for gold watches or the skull of a sheep or a message in a bottle to be washed up with the tide; and another where we used to wander whistling through the packed streets, stale as station sandwiches, round the impressive gasworks and the slaughter house, past by the blackened monuments and the museum that should have been in a museum. Or we scratched at a kind of cricket on the bald and cindery surface of the recreation ground, or we took a tram that shook like an iron jelly down to the gaunt pier, there to clamber under the pier, hanging perilously onto its skeleton legs or to run along to the end where patient men with the seaward eyes of the dockside unemployed capped and muffled, dangling from their mouths pipes that had long gone out, angled over the edge for unpleasant tasting fish.

Never was there such a town as ours, I thought, as we fought on the sandhills with rough boys or dared each other to climb up the scaffolding of half-built houses soon to be called Laburnum Beaches. Never was there such a town, I thought, for the smell of fish and chips on Saturday evenings; for the Saturday afternoon cinema matinees where we shouted and hissed our threepences away; for the crowds in the streets with leeks in their hats on international nights; for the park, the inexhaustible and mysterious, bushy red-Indian hiding park where the hunchback sat alone and the groves were blue with sailors. The memories of childhood have no order, and so I remember that never was there such a dame school as ours, so firm and kind and smelling of galoshes, with the sweet and fumbled music of the piano lessons drifting down from upstairs to the lonely schoolroom, where only the sometimes tearful wicked sat over undone sums, or to repeat a little crime—the pulling of a girl's hair during geography, the sly shin kick under the table during English literature. Behind the school was a narrow lane where only the oldest and boldest threw pebbles at windows, scuffled and boasted, fibbed about their relations—

"My father's got a chauffeur."

"What's he want a chauffeur for? He hasn't got a car."

"My father's the richest man in the town."

"My father's the richest man in Wales."

"My father owns the world."

And swapped gob-stoppers for slings, old knives for marbles, kite strings for foreign stamps.

The lane was always the place to tell your secrets; if you did not have any, you invented them. Occasionally now I dream that I am turning out of school into the lane of confidences when I say to the boys of my class, "At last, I have a real secret."

"What is it—what is it?"

"I can fly."

And when they do not believe me, I flap my arms and slowly leave the ground only a few inches at first, then gaining air until I fly waving my cap level with the upper windows of the school, peering in until the mistress at the piano screams and the metronome falls to the ground and stops, and there is no more time.

And I fly over the trees and chimneys of my town, over the dockyards skimming the masts and funnels, over Inkerman Street, Sebastopol Street, and the street where all the women wear men's caps, over the trees of the everlasting park, where a brass band shakes the leaves and sends them showering down on to the nurses and the children, the cripples and the idlers, and the gardeners, and the shouting boys: over the yellow seashore, and the stone-chasing dogs, and the old men, and the singing sea.

The memories of childhood have no order, and no end.

QUESTIONS

1. Where else in the essay do you find the playful egotism of the opening paragraph? What function, then, does it serve in the essay?

2. In which of the following pairs from the second paragraph could one term be eliminated with negligible loss to literal meaning: "ugly, lovely," "crawling, sprawling," "wonder and India," "wicked and wrong"? What effect—other than rhythmic—do you suppose Thomas is trying to achieve with each pair?

3. Examine the whole of the second paragraph for the presence of paired or tripled words and phrases. What sort of rhythm do they create: involved or regular, slow or energetic? What is the contributory effect of the length of the sentence? What sort of tone does the rhythm serve? On what basis would you say the tone is appropriate to the subject of the essay?

4. Try re-arranging the items in the two series in the fourth paragraph ("coal-pitted . . . ," "choirs . . ."). What is the effect? What would

be the effect of adding "tree-blossoming" to the first series and "trains" to the second? What would be the effect of removing an item from each series? On the basis of your answers, what generalizations might you hazard about the tightness, orderliness, and economy of Thomas' sentences?

5. What is the difference in relationship of the items among themselves in the two series in paragraph four? What is the difference in rhythm in the two series? Which rhythm, would you say, dominates the essay so far? In what way might you relate the quality of the third paragraph in the essay to the quality of the relationship among the items in the second series?

6. Is it Thomas the man or the child who speaks of "Wales, with its wild names like peals of bells in the darkness" (paragraph five) and who says that "the park was full of terrors and treasures" (paragraph six)? Where in the first nine paragraphs does Thomas most thoroughly assume the point of view of the child? Would you say that Thomas' characteristic rhythm and tone abet or inhibit his assuming the point of view of the child? (In answering this question see whether that rhythm and tone dominate the passages in which he assumes the child's point of view.)

7. What aspects of the poem relate to qualities dealt with in Questions 3 and 5? Is the diction of the poem more or less formal than that of the two preceding paragraphs? What is the general level of diction of both the prose and the poem?

8. Examine the metaphorical language in the paragraph following the poem. Would you say that "tram that shook like an iron jelly" is a trite metaphor? In general, do the metaphors seem common, simple, unobtrusive? To which senses do they appeal? Is there a respect in which some do not appeal to the senses?

9. What material scattered throughout the essay anticipates the fantasy of the next to last paragraph? In what respect does the tone, or the point of view, of the essay prepare for it? Does seriousness or absurdity predominate in the paragraph? Do you seem to hear the mistress at the piano scream? (Your answers to these last two questions should depend in part on your analyzing the diction and rhythm of the paragraph.)

10. Characterize Thomas' style on the basis of your answers to previous questions. How formal is it? How poetical? How flexible? How

colorful? How difficult? What element gives it its most distinct flavor: irony? metaphor? diction?

11. Of what structural significance is it that Thomas begins with his birth and ends with his flight over the sea? What internal elements support this structure? To what extent does the general flavor of Thomas' style suggest the presence of such a structure?

The Return Journey

D. H. LAWRENCE

Lawrence's incessant wanderings, which took up the last ten years of his life, had a number of causes: search for a climate suitable to his delicate health, disgust with things English, anger at the police suppression of his novel, *The Rainbow*. Though he found few places satisfactory for very long, his travels did give him rich materials for his writings—the novels, *Kangaroo*, set in Australia, and *The Plumed Serpent*, set in Mexico; the essays that make up *Sea and Sardinia*, *Mornings in Mexico*, and *Etruscan Places*. The following excerpt from *Twilight in Italy*, written at a somewhat earlier period, makes clear the degree and quality of Lawrence's investment in foreign settings. (Further headnote information on Lawrence appears on pp. 33, 265.)

When one walks, one must travel west or south. If one turn northward or eastward it is like walking down a cul-de-sac, to the blind end.

So it has been since the Crusaders came home satiated, and the Renaissance saw the western sky as an archway into the future. So it is still. We must go westwards and southwards.

It is a sad and gloomy thing to travel even from Italy into France. But it is a joyful thing to walk south to Italy, south and west. It is

From *Twilight in Italy* by D. H. Lawrence. Reprinted by permission of The Viking Press, Inc., Laurence Pollinger, Ltd., and the estate of the late Mrs. Frieda Lawrence.

so. And there is a certain exaltation in the thought of going west, even to Cornwall, to Ireland. It is as if the magnetic poles were south-west and north-east, for our spirits, with the south-west, under the sunset, as the positive pole. So whilst I walk through Switzerland, though it is a valley of gloom and depression, a light seems to flash out under every footstep, with the joy of progression.

It was Sunday morning when I left the valley where the Italians lived. I went quickly over the stream, heading for Lucerne. It was a good thing to be out of doors, with one's pack on one's back, climbing uphill. But the trees were thick by the roadside; I was not yet free. It was Sunday morning, very still.

In two hours I was at the top of the hill, looking out over the intervening valley at the long lake of Zurich, spread there beyond with its girdle of low hills, like a relief-map. I could not bear to look at it, it was so small and unreal. I had a feeling as if it were false, a large relief-map that I was looking down upon, and which I wanted to smash. It seemed to intervene between me and some reality. I could not believe that that was the real world. It was a figment, a fabrication, like a dull landscape painted on a wall, to hide the real landscape.

So I went on, over to the other side of the hill, and I looked out again. Again there were the smoky-looking hills and the lake like a piece of looking-glass. But the hills were higher: that big one was the Rigi. I set off down the hill.

There was fat agricultural land and several villages. And church was over. The church-goers were all coming home: men in black broadcloth and old chimney-pot silk hats, carrying their umbrellas; women in ugly dresses, carrying books and umbrellas. The streets were dotted with these black-clothed men and stiff women, all reduced to a Sunday nullity. I hated it. It reminded me of that which I knew in my boyhood, that stiff, null "propriety" which used to come over us, like a sort of deliberate and self-inflicted cramp, on Sundays. I hated these elders in black broadcloth, with their neutral faces, going home piously to their Sunday dinners. I hated the feeling of these villages, comfortable, well-to-do, clean, and proper.

And my boot was chafing two of my toes. That always happens. I had come down to a wide, shallow valley-bed, marshy. So about a mile out of the village I sat down by a stone bridge, by a stream, and tore up my handkerchief, and bound up the toes. And as I sat binding my toes, two of the elders in black, with umbrellas under their arms, approached from the direction of the village.

They made me so furious, I had to hasten to fasten my boot, to hurry on again, before they should come near me. I could not bear the way they walked and talked, so crambling and material and mealy-mouthed.

Then it did actually begin to rain. I was just going down a short hill. So I sat under a bush and watched the trees drip. I was so glad to be there, homeless, without place or belonging, crouching under the leaves in the copse by the road, that I felt I had, like the meek, inherited the earth. Some men went by, with their coat-collars turned up, and the rain making still blacker their black broadcloth shoulders. They did not see me. I was as safe and separate as a ghost. So I ate the remains of my food that I had bought in Zurich, and waited for the rain.

Later, in the wet Sunday afternoon, I went on to the little lake, past many inert, neutral, material people, down an ugly road where trams ran. The blight of Sunday was almost intolerable near the town.

So on I went, by the side of the steamy, reedy lake, walking the length of it. Then suddenly I went in to a little villa by the water for tea. In Switzerland every house is a villa.

But this villa was kept by two old ladies and a delicate dog, who must not get his feet wet. I was very happy there. I had good jam and strange honey-cakes for tea, that I liked, and the little old ladies pattered round in a great stir, always whirling like two dry leaves after the restless dog.

"Why must he not go out?" I said.

"Because it is wet," they answered, "and he coughs and sneezes."

"Without a handkerchief, that is not *angenehm*," I said.

So we became bosom friends.

"You are Austrian?" they said to me.

I said I was from Graz; that my father was a doctor in Graz, and that I was walking for my pleasure through the countries of Europe.

I said this because I knew a doctor from Graz who was always wandering about, and because I did not want to be myself, an Englishman, to these two old ladies. I wanted to be something else. So we exchanged confidences.

They told me, in their queer, old, toothless fashion, about their visitors, a man who used to fish all day, every day for three weeks, fish every hour of the day, though many a day he caught nothing —nothing at all—still he fished from the boat; and so on, such trivialities. Then they told me of a third sister who had died, a third little old lady. One could feel the gap in the house. They cried; and I, being an Austrian from Graz, to my astonishment felt my tears slip over on to the table. I also *was* sorry, and I would have kissed the little old ladies to comfort them.

"Only in heaven it is warm, and it doesn't rain, and no one dies," I said, looking at the wet leaves.

Then I went away. I would have stayed the night at this house: I wanted to. But I had developed my Austrian character too far.

So I went on to a detestable brutal inn in the town. And the next day I climbed over the back of the detestable Rigi, with its vile hotel, to come to Lucerne. There, on the Rigi, I met a lost young Frenchman who could speak no German, and who said he could not find people to speak French. So we sat on a stone and became close friends, and I promised faithfully to go and visit him in his barracks in Algiers: I was to sail from Naples to Algiers. He wrote me the address on his card, and told me he had friends in the regiment, to whom I should be introduced, and we could have a good time, if I would stay a week or two, down there in Algiers.

How much more real Algiers was than the rock on the Rigi where we sat, or the lake beneath, or the mountains beyond. Algiers is very real, though I have never seen it, and my friend is my friend for ever, though I have lost his card and forgotten his name. He was a Government clerk from Lyons, making this his first foreign tour before he began his military service. He showed me his "circular excursion ticket." Then at last we parted, for he must get to the top of the Rigi, and I must get to the bottom.

Lucerne and its lake were as irritating as ever—like the wrapper round milk chocolate. I could not sleep even one night there: I took the steamer down the lake, to the very last station. There I found a good German inn, and was happy.

There was a tall thin young man, whose face was red and inflamed from the sun. I thought he was a German tourist. He had just come in; and he was eating bread and milk. He and I were alone in the eating-room. He was looking at an illustrated paper.

"Does the steamer stop here all night?" I asked him in German, hearing the boat bustling and blowing her steam on the water outside, and glancing round at her lights, red and white, in the pitch darkness.

He only shook his head over his bread and milk, and did not lift his face.

"Are you English, then?" I said.

No one but an Englishman would have hidden his face in a bowl of milk, and have shaken his red ears in such painful confusion.

"Yes," he said, "I am."

And I started almost out of my skin at the unexpected London accent. It was as if one suddenly found oneself in the Tube.

"So am I," I said. "Where have you come from?"

Then he began, like a general explaining his plans, to tell me. He had walked round over the Furka Pass, had been on foot four or five days. He had walked tremendously. Knowing no German, and nothing of the mountains, he had set off alone on this tour: he had a fortnight's holiday. So he had come over the Rhone Glacier across the Furka and down from Andermatt to the Lake. On this last day he had walked about thirty mountain miles.

"But weren't you tired?" I said, aghast.

He was. Under the inflamed redness of his sun- and wind- and snow-burned face he was sick with fatigue. He had done over a hundred miles in the last four days.

"Did you enjoy it?" I asked.

"Oh yes. I wanted to do it all." He wanted to do it, and he *had* done it. But God knows what he wanted to do it for. He had now one day at Lucerne, one day at Interlaken and Berne, then London.

I was sorry for him in my soul, he was so cruelly tired, so perishingly victorious.

"Why did you do so much?" I said. "Why did you come on foot all down the valley when you could have taken the train? Was it worth it?"

"I think so," he said.

Yet he was sick with fatigue and over-exhaustion. His eyes were quite dark, sightless: he seemed to have lost the power of seeing, to be virtually blind. He hung his head forward when he had to write a postcard, as if he felt his way. But he turned his postcard so that I should not see to whom it was addressed; not that I was interested; only I noticed his little, cautious, English movement of privacy.

"What time will you be going on?" I asked.

"When is the first steamer?" he said, and he turned out a guidebook with a time-table. He would leave at about seven.

"But why so early?" I said to him.

He must be in Lucerne at a certain hour, and at Interlaken in the evening.

"I suppose you will rest when you get to London?" I said.

He looked at me quickly, reservedly.

I was drinking beer: I asked him wouldn't he have something. He thought a moment, then said he would have another glass of hot milk. The landlord came—"And bread?" he asked.

The Englishman refused. He could not eat, really. Also he was poor; he had to husband his money. The landlord brought the milk and asked me, when would the gentleman want to go away. So I made arrangements between the landlord and the stranger. But the Englishman was slightly uncomfortable at my intervention. He did not like me to know what he would have for breakfast.

I could feel so well the machine that had him in its grip. He slaved for a year, mechanically, in London, riding in the Tube, working in the office. Then for a fortnight he was let free. So he rushed to Switzerland, with a tour planned out, and with just enough money to see him through, and to buy presents at Interlaken: bits of the edelweiss pottery: I could see him going home with them.

So he arrived, and with amazing, pathetic courage set forth on foot in a strange land, to face strange landlords, with no language but English at his command, and his purse definitely limited. Yet he wanted to go among the mountains, to cross a glacier. So he had walked on and on, like one possessed, ever forward. His name might have been Excelsior, indeed.

But then, when he reached his Furka, only to walk along the ridge and to descend on the same side! My God, it was killing to the soul. And here he was, down again from the mountains, beginning his journey home again: steamer and train and steamer and train and Tube, till he was back in the machine.

It hadn't let him go, and he knew it. Hence his cruel self-torture of fatigue, his cruel exercise of courage. He who hung his head in his milk in torment when I asked him a question in German, what courage had he not needed to take this his very first trip out of England, alone, on foot!

His eyes were dark and deep with unfathomable courage. Yet he was going back in the morning. He was going back. All he had courage for was to go back. He would go back, though he died by inches. Why not? It was killing him, it was like living loaded with irons. But he had the courage to submit, to die that way, since it was the way allotted to him.

The way he sank on the table in exhaustion, drinking his milk, his will nevertheless, so perfect and unblemished, triumphant, though his body was broken and in anguish, was almost too much to bear. My heart was wrung for my countryman, wrung till it bled.

I could not bear to understand my countryman, a man who worked for his living, as I had worked, as nearly all my country-men work. He would not give in. On his holiday he would walk, to fulfil his purpose, walk on; no matter how cruel the effort were, he would not rest, he would not relinquish his purpose nor abate his will, not by one jot or tittle. His body must pay whatever his will demanded, though it were torture.

It all seemed to me so foolish. I was almost in tears. He went to bed. I walked by the dark lake, and talked to the girl in the inn. She was a pleasant girl: it was a pleasant inn, a homely place. One could be happy there.

In the morning it was sunny, the lake was blue. By night I should be nearly at the crest of my journey. I was glad.

The Englishman had gone. I looked for his name in the book. It was written in a fair, clerkly hand. He lived at Streatham. Sud-denly I hated him. The dogged fool, to keep his nose on the grind-stone like that. What was all his courage but the very tip-top of cowardice? What a vile nature—almost Sadish, proud, like the in-famous Red Indians, of being able to stand torture.

The landlord came to talk to me. He was fat and comfortable and too respectful. But I had to tell him all the Englishman had done, in the way of a holiday, just to shame his own fat, ponderous, inn-keeper's luxuriousness that was too gross. Then all I got out of his enormous comfortableness was:

"Yes, that's a *very* long step to take."

So I set off myself, up the valley between the close, snow-topped mountains, whose white gleamed above me as I crawled, small as an insect, along the dark, cold valley below.

There had been a cattle fair earlier in the morning, so troops of cattle were roving down the road, some with bells tang-tanging, and with soft faces and startled eyes and a sudden swerving of horns. The grass was very green by the roads and by the streams; the shadows of the mountain slopes were very dark on either hand overhead, and the sky with snowy flanks and tips was high up.

Here, away from the world, the villages were quiet and obscure —left behind. They had the same fascinating atmosphere of being forgotten, left out of the world, that old English villages have. And buying apples and cheese and bread in a little shop that sold everything and smelled of everything, I felt at home again.

QUESTIONS

1. What effects would you say Lawrence achieves by the formality of his diction, his repetitiveness, and his variety in sentence length in the first three paragraphs? Do these effects in any way contribute to or qualify the believability of what he is affirming? What is the general tone of the three paragraphs?

2. Consider the following revisions: But because the trees were thick by the roadside, I did not yet feel free (paragraph four); I could not bear to look at it, because it was so small and unreal (paragraph five). Do the revised sentences express Lawrence's thought more accurately than the original sentences? Do they make more sense? What changes have resulted in point of view and tone?

3. By what three or four stylistic means does Lawrence emphasize his feeling of hatred in the seventh paragraph? Why isn't the tone of the paragraph one of hatred? What is its tone?

4. Estimate the preciseness, density, and economy of Lawrence's description of scene in the tenth paragraph. Identify the contradictions and incongruities upon which he builds his humor. Describe the quality of his diction and sentence rhythm (compare with the third paragraph). Show how the stylistic features of the paragraph serve a more important purpose than creation of either scene or humor.

5. Identify the point of view and tone of each of the following fragments from paragraphs twelve through twenty-four: "In Switzerland

every house is a villa"; "a delicate dog, who must not get his feet wet"; "Without a handkerchief, that is not *angenehm*"; "So we became bosom friends"; "in their queer, old, toothless fashion"; "and so on, such trivialities"; "Only in heaven it is warm"; "So I went on to a detestable brutal inn."

6. What is the difference in function of the following two similes: "the little old ladies pattered round in a great stir, always whirling like two dry leaves after the restless dog" (paragraph thirteen) and "Lucerne and its lake were as irritating as ever—like the wrapper round milk chocolate" (paragraph twenty-six)?

7. Examine Lawrence's use of the machine metaphor throughout the passage on the Englishman. What is the double reference that the metaphor contains? What are the particular complications of its use in the three paragraphs beginning "It hadn't let him go" and in the paragraph beginning "The Englishman had gone"? How original would you say the metaphor is? How seriously does Lawrence treat it? Does it serve mainly to say something about England or something about the Englishman? Is the metaphor strong visually? Is it strong in another way?

8. Throughout the selection Lawrence proceeds by a series of cause-effect relationships. Thus in paragraphs six through twenty-four we have: "So I went on," "So about a mile out of the village," "So I sat under a bush," "So I ate the remains," "So on I went," "So we became bosom friends," "So we exchanged confidences," "So I went on." State the precise relationship involved on each of these occasions. How clearly does Lawrence indicate each relationship? To what stylistic characteristics discussed in earlier questions does Lawrence's use and handling of such phrases relate?

9. Lawrence's rapidly shifting tone inevitably involves itself with his diction (its formality, figurativeness, connotativeness), sentence rhythm, and paragraphing. Show this assertion to be true of the last eight paragraphs in the selection. Show that rapid shifting typifies Lawrence's handling of individual incidents (consider that of the Englishman) and his handling of all of his material.

10. On the basis of your answers to previous questions, argue the view that Lawrence's style is extremely economical. Argue the view that it is extremely wordy and repetitious. Which view makes more sense? Why?

11. On the basis of your answers to previous questions, characterize Lawrence's style. Does your description differ in any significant respect from the description of the style of "Etna" in the Introduction to this section of the text?

Quincy

HENRY ADAMS

Descended from two presidents, the son of a famous diplomat,
Henry Adams (1838-1918) studied at Harvard and the University of Berlin, and spent the Civil War years in London as
secretary to his father, then Minister to England. Always diffi-
dent about his own accomplishments, he nevertheless taught
history at Harvard, edited the influential *North American Review,* wrote novels, biographies, historical essays, and a massive nine-volume *History of the United States During the Ad-
ministrations of Jefferson and Madison.* His most famous
works, written in old age, were intended as contrasts: *Mont-
Saint-Michel and Chartres,* in which he explores the unified,
coherent civilization of the Middle Ages, and *The Education
of Henry Adams,* in which he ponders the complexities of
modern existence by a study of his own past. What follows is
the opening chapter of the *Education.*

Under the shadow of Boston State House, turning its back on the
house of John Hancock, the little passage called Hancock Avenue
runs, or ran, from Beacon Street, skirting the State House grounds,
to Mount Vernon Street, on the summit of Beacon Hill; and there,
in the third house below Mount Vernon Place, February 16, 1838, a
child was born, and christened later by his uncle, the minister of

From *The Education of Henry Adams* by Henry Adams. Reprinted by permission of the Houghton Mifflin Company and Constable & Co., Ltd.

the First Church after the tenets of Boston Unitarianism, as Henry
Brooks Adams.

Had he been born in Jerusalem under the shadow of the Temple
and circumcised in the Synagogue by his uncle the high priest,
under the name of Israel Cohen, he would scarcely have been more
distinctly branded, and not much more heavily handicapped in the
races of the coming century, in running for such stakes as the century was to offer; but, on the other hand, the ordinary traveller,
who does not enter the field of racing, finds advantage in being, so
to speak, ticketed through life, with the safeguards of an old, established traffic. Safeguards are often irksome, but sometimes convenient, and if one needs them at all, one is apt to need them badly.
A hundred years earlier, such safeguards as his would have secured
any young man's success; and although in 1838 their value was
not very great compared with what they would have had in 1738,
yet the mere accident of starting a twentieth-century career from a
nest of associations so colonial—so troglodytic—as the First Church,
the Boston State House, Beacon Hill, John Hancock and John
Adams, Mount Vernon Street and Quincy, all crowding on ten
pounds of unconscious babyhood, was so queer as to offer a subject
of curious speculation to the baby long after he had witnessed the
solution. What could become of such a child of the seventeenth
and eighteenth centuries, when he should wake up to find himself
required to play the game of the twentieth? Had he been consulted,
would he have cared to play the game at all, holding such cards as
he held, and suspecting that the game was to be one of which
neither he nor any one else back to the beginning of time knew the
rules or the risks or the stakes? He was not consulted and was not
responsible, but had he been taken into the confidence of his parents, he would certainly have told them to change nothing as far as
concerned him. He would have been astounded by his own luck.
Probably no child, born in the year, held better cards than he.
Whether life was an honest game of chance, or whether the cards
were marked and forced, he could not refuse to play his excellent

hand. He could never make the usual plea of irresponsibility. He accepted the situation as though he had been a party to it, and under the same circumstances would do it again, the more readily for knowing the exact values. To his life as a whole he was a consenting, contracting party and partner from the moment he was born to the moment he died. Only with that understanding—as a consciously assenting member in full partnership with the society of his age—had his education an interest to himself or to others.

As it happened, he never got to the point of playing the game at all; he lost himself in the study of it, watching the errors of the players; but this is the only interest in the story, which otherwise has no moral and little incident. A story of education—seventy years of it—the practical value remains to the end in doubt, like other values about which men have disputed since the birth of Cain and Abel; but the practical value of the universe has never been stated in dollars. Although every one cannot be a Gargantua-Napoleon-Bismarck and walk off with the great bells of Notre Dame, every one must bear his own universe, and most persons are moderately interested in learning how their neighbors have managed to carry theirs.

This problem of education, started in 1838, went on for three years, while the baby grew, like other babies, unconsciously, as a vegetable, the outside world working as it never had worked before, to get his new universe ready for him. Often in old age he puzzled over the question whether, on the doctrine of chances, he was at liberty to accept himself or his world as an accident. No such accident had ever happened before in human experience. For him, alone, the old universe was thrown into the ash-heap and a new one created. He and his eighteenth-century, troglodytic Boston were suddenly cut apart—separated forever—in act if not in sentiment, by the opening of the Boston and Albany Railroad; the appearance of the first Cunard steamers in the bay; and the telegraphic messages which carried from Baltimore to Washington the news that Henry Clay and James K. Polk were nominated for the Presidency. This was in May, 1844; he was six years old; his new world was ready for use, and only fragments of the old met his eyes.

Of all this that was being done to complicate his education, he knew only the color of yellow. He first found himself sitting on a yellow kitchen floor in strong sunlight. He was three years old when he took this earliest step in education; a lesson of color. The second followed soon; a lesson of taste. On December 3, 1841, he developed scarlet fever. For several days he was as good as dead, reviving only under the careful nursing of his family. When he began to recover strength, about January 1, 1842, his hunger must have been stronger than any other pleasure or pain, for while in after life he retained not the faintest recollection of his illness, he remembered quite clearly his aunt entering the sick-room bearing in her hand a saucer with a baked apple.

The order of impressions retained by memory might naturally be that of color and taste, although one would rather suppose that the sense of pain would be first to educate. In fact, the third recollection of the child was that of discomfort. The moment he could be removed, he was bundled up in blankets and carried from the little house in Hancock Avenue to a larger one which his parents were to occupy for the rest of their lives in the neighboring Mount Vernon Street. The season was mid-winter, January 10, 1842, and he never forgot his acute distress for want of air under his blankets, or the noises of moving furniture.

As a means of variation from a normal type, sickness in childhood ought to have a certain value not to be classed under any fitness or unfitness of natural selection; and especially scarlet fever affected boys seriously, both physically and in character, though they might through life puzzle themselves to decide whether it had fitted or unfitted them for success; but this fever of Henry Adams took greater and greater importance in his eyes, from the point of view of education, the longer he lived. At first, the effect was physical. He fell behind his brothers two or three inches in height, and proportionally in bone and weight. His character and processes of mind seemed to share in this fining-down process of scale. He was not good in a fight, and his nerves were more delicate than boys' nerves ought to be. He exaggerated these weaknesses as he grew older. The habit of doubt; of distrusting his own judgment and of totally rejecting the judgment of the world; the tendency to regard every question as open; the hesitation to act except as a choice of evils; the shirking of responsibility; the love of line, form, quality; the horror of ennui; the passion for companionship and the antipathy to society—all these are well-known qualities of New England character in no way peculiar to individuals but in this instance they seemed to be stimulated by the fever, and Henry Adams could never make up his mind whether, on the whole, the change of character was morbid or healthy, good or bad for his purpose. His brothers were the type; he was the variation.

As far as the boy knew, the sickness did not affect him at all, and he grew up in excellent health, bodily and mental, taking life as it was given; accepting its local standards without a difficulty, and enjoying much of it as keenly as any other boy of his age. He seemed to himself quite normal, and his companions seemed always to think him so. Whatever was peculiar about him was education, not character, and came to him, directly and indirectly, as the result of that eighteenth-century inheritance which he took with his name.

The atmosphere of education in which he lived was colonial, revolutionary, almost Cromwellian, as though he were steeped, from his greatest grandmother's birth, in the odor of political crime. Resistance to something was the law of New England nature; the boy looked out on the world with the instinct of resistance; for numberless generations his predecessors had viewed the world chiefly as a thing to be reformed, filled with evil forces to be abolished, and they saw no reason to suppose that they had wholly succeeded in the abolition; the duty was unchanged. That duty implied not only resistance to evil, but hatred of it. Boys naturally look on all force as an enemy, and generally find it so, but the New Englander, whether boy or man, in his long struggle with a stingy or hostile universe, had learned also to love the pleasure of hating; his joys were few.

Politics, as a practice, whatever its professions, had always been the systematic organization of hatreds, and Massachusetts politics had been as harsh as the climate. The chief charm of New England was harshness of contrasts and extremes of sensibility—a cold that froze the blood, and a heat that boiled it—so that the pleasure of hating—one's self if no better victim offered—was not its rarest amusement; but the charm was a true and natural child of the soil, not a cultivated weed of the ancients. The violence of the contrast was real and made the strongest motive of education. The double exterior nature gave life its relative values. Winter and summer, cold and heat, town and country, force and freedom, marked two modes of life and thought, balanced like lobes of the brain. Town was winter confinement, school, rule, discipline; straight, gloomy streets, piled with six feet of snow in the middle; frosts that made the snow sing under wheels or runners; thaws when the streets became dangerous to cross; society of uncles, aunts, and cousins who expected children to behave themselves, and who were not always gratified; above all else, winter represented the desire to escape and go free. Town was restraint, law, unity. Country, only seven miles away, was liberty, diversity, outlawry, the endless delight of mere sense impressions given by nature for nothing, and breathed by boys without knowing it.

Boys are wild animals, rich in the treasures of sense, but the New England boy had a wider range of emotions than boys of more equable climates. He felt his nature crudely, as it was meant. To the boy Henry Adams, summer was drunken. Among senses, smell was the strongest—smell of hot pine-woods and sweet-fern in the scorching summer noon; of new-mown hay; of ploughed earth; of box hedges; of peaches, lilacs, syringas; of stables, barns, cowyards; of salt water and low tide on the marshes; nothing came amiss Next to smell came taste, and the children knew the taste of every thing they saw or touched; from pennyroyal and flagroot to the

shell of a pignut and the letters of a spelling-book—the taste of
A-B, AB, suddenly revived on the boy's tongue sixty years afterwards. Light, line, and color as sensual pleasures, came later and
were as crude as the rest. The New England light is glare, and the
atmosphere harshens color. The boy was a full man before he ever
knew what was meant by atmosphere; his idea of pleasure in light
was the blaze of a New England sun. His idea of color was a
peony, with the dew of early morning on its petals. The intense
blue of the sea, as he saw it a mile or two away, from the Quincy
hills; the cumuli in a June afternoon sky; the strong reds and greens
and purples of colored prints and children's picture-books, as the
American colors then ran; these were ideals. The opposites or antip-
athies, were the cold grays of November evenings, and the thick,
muddy thaws of Boston winter. With such standards, the Bostonian
could not but develop a double nature. Life was a double thing.
After a January blizzard, the boy who could look with pleasure
into the violent snow-glare of the cold white sunshine, with its intense light and shade, scarcely knew what was meant by tone. He
could reach it only by education.

Winter and summer, then, were two hostile lives, and bred two
separate natures. Winter was always the effort to live; summer was
tropical license. Whether the children rolled in the grass, or waded
in the brook, or swam in the salt ocean, or sailed in the bay, or
fished for smelts in the creeks, or netted minnows in the salt-
marshes, or took to the pine-woods and the granite quarries, or
chased muskrats and hunted snapping-turtles in the swamps, or
mushrooms or nuts on the autumn hills, summer and country were
always sensual living, while winter was always compulsory learning.
Summer was the multiplicity of nature; winter was school.

The bearing of the two seasons on the education of Henry Adams
was no fancy; it was the most decisive force he ever knew; it ran
through life, and made the division between its perplexing, warring,
irreconcilable problems, irreducible opposites, with growing emphasis to the last year of study. From earliest childhood the boy was
accustomed to feel that, for him, life was double. Winter and sum-

mer, town and country, law and liberty, were hostile, and the man who pretended they were not, was in his eyes a schoolmaster—that is, a man employed to tell lies to little boys. Though Quincy was but two hours' walk from Beacon Hill, it belonged in a different world. For two hundred years, every Adams, from father to son, had lived within sight of State Street, and sometimes had lived in it, yet none had ever taken kindly to the town, or been taken kindly by it. The boy inherited his double nature. He knew as yet nothing about his great-grandfather, who had died a dozen years before his own birth: he took for granted that any great-grandfather of his must have always been good, and his enemies wicked; but he divined his great-grandfather's character from his own. Never for a moment did he connect the two ideas of Boston and John Adams; they were separate and antagonistic; the idea of John Adams went with Quincy. He knew his grandfather John Quincy Adams only as an old man of seventy-five or eighty who was friendly and gentle with him, but except that he heard his grandfather always called "the President," and his grandmother "the Madam," he had no reason to suppose that his Adams grandfather differed in character from his Brooks grandfather who was equally kind and benevolent. He liked the Adams side best, but for no other reason than that it reminded him of the country, the summer, and the absence of re-straint. Yet he felt also that Quincy was in a way inferior to Bos-ton, and that socially Boston looked down on Quincy. The reason was clear enough even to a five-year old child. Quincy had no Boston style. Little enough style had either; a simpler manner of life and thought could hardly exist, short of cave-dwelling. The flint-and-steel with which his grandfather Adams used to light his own fires in the early morning was still on the mantelpiece of his study. The idea of a livery or even a dress for servants, or of an evening toilette, was next to blasphemy. Bathrooms, water-supplies, lighting, heating, and the whole array of domestic comforts, were unknown to Quincy. Boston had already a bathroom, a water-supply, a furnace, and gas. The superiority of Boston was evident, but a child liked it no better for that.

The magnificence of his grandfather Brooks's house in Pearl Street or South Street has long ago disappeared, but perhaps his country house at Medford may still remain to show what impressed the mind of a boy in 1845 with the idea of city splendor. The President's place at Quincy was the larger and older and far the more interesting of the two; but a boy felt at once its inferiority in fashion. It showed plainly enough its want of wealth. It smacked of colonial age, but not of Boston style or plush curtains. To the end of his life he never quite overcame the prejudice thus drawn in with his childish breath. He never could compel himself to care for nineteenth-century style. He was never able to adopt it, any more than his father or grandfather or great-grandfather had done. Not that he felt it as particularly hostile, for he reconciled himself to much that was worse; but because, for some remote reason, he was born an eighteenth-century child. The old house at Quincy was eighteenth century. What style it had was in its Queen Anne mahogany panels and its Louis Seize chairs and sofas. The panels belonged to an old colonial Vassall who built the house; the furniture had been brought back from Paris in 1789 or 1801 or 1817, along with porcelain and books and much else of old diplomatic remnants; and neither of the two eighteenth-century styles—neither English Queen Anne nor French Louis Seize—was comfortable for a boy, or for any one else. The dark mahogany had been painted white to suit daily life in winter gloom. Nothing seemed to favor, for a child's objects, the older forms. On the contrary, most boys, as well as grown-up people, preferred the new, with good reason, and the child felt himself distinctly at a disadvantage for the taste.

Nor had personal preference any share in his bias. The Brooks grandfather was as amiable and as sympathetic as the Adams grandfather. Both were born in 1767, and both died in 1848. Both were kind to children, and both belonged rather to the eighteenth than to the nineteenth centuries. The child knew no difference between them except that one was associated with winter and the other with summer; one with Boston, the other with Quincy. Even with Medford, the association was hardly easier. Once as a very

young boy he was taken to pass a few days with his grandfather
Brooks under charge of his aunt, but became so violently homesick
that within twenty-four hours he was brought back in disgrace.
Yet he could not remember ever being seriously homesick again.

The attachment to Quincy was not altogether sentimental or
wholly sympathetic. Quincy was not a bed of thornless roses. Even
there the curse of Cain set its mark. There as elsewhere a cruel
universe combined to crush a child. As though three or four vigorous brothers and sisters, with the best will, were not enough to
crush any child, every one else conspired towards an education
which he hated. From cradle to grave this problem of running order
through chaos, direction through space, discipline through freedom,
unity through multiplicity, has always been, and must always be,
the task of education, as it is the moral of religion, philosophy,
science, art, politics, and economy; but a boy's will is his life, and
he dies when it is broken, as the colt dies in harness, taking a new
nature in becoming tame. Rarely has the boy felt kindly towards
his tamers. Between him and his master has always been war.
Henry Adams never knew a boy of his generation to like a master,
and the task of remaining on friendly terms with one's own family,
in such a relation, was never easy.

All the more singular it seemed afterwards to him that his first
serious contact with the President should have been a struggle of
will, in which the old man almost necessarily defeated the boy, but
instead of leaving, as usual in such defeats, a lifelong sting, left
rather an impression of as fair treatment as could be expected from
a natural enemy. The boy met seldom with such restraint. He could
not have been much more than six years old at the time—seven at
the utmost—and his mother had taken him to Quincy for a long
stay with the President during the summer. What became of the
rest of the family he quite forgot; but he distinctly remembered
standing at the house door one summer morning in a passionate
outburst of rebellion against going to school. Naturally his mother
was the immediate victim of his rage; that is what mothers are for,
and boys also; but in this case the boy had his mother at unfair

disadvantage, for she was a guest, and had no means of enforcing obedience. Henry showed a certain tactical ability by refusing to start, and he met all efforts at compulsion by successful, though too vehement protest. He was in fair way to win, and was holding his own, with sufficient energy, at the bottom of the long staircase which led up to the door of the President's library, when the door opened, and the old man slowly came down. Putting on his hat, he took the boy's hand without a word, and walked with him, paralyzed with awe, up the road to the town. After the first moments of consternation at this interference in a domestic dispute, the boy reflected that an old gentleman close on eighty would never trouble himself to walk near a mile on a hot summer morning over a shadeless road to take a boy to school, and that it would be strange if a lad imbued with the passion of freedom could not find a corner to dodge around, somewhere before reaching the school door. Then and always, the boy insisted that this reasoning justified his apparent submission; but the old man did not stop, and the boy saw all his strategical points turned, one after another, until he found himself seated inside the school, and obviously the centre of curious if not malevolent criticism. Not till then did the President release his hand and depart.

The point was that this act, contrary to the inalienable rights of boys, and nullifying the social compact, ought to have made him dislike his grandfather for life. He could not recall that it had this effect even for a moment. With a certain maturity of mind, the child must have recognized that the President, though a tool of tyranny, had done his disreputable work with a certain intelligence. He had shown no temper, no irritation, no personal feeling, and had made no display of force. Above all, he had held his tongue. During their long walk he had said nothing; he had uttered no syllable of revolting cant about the duty of obedience and the wickedness of resistance to law, he had shown no concern in the matter; hardly even a consciousness of the boy's existence. Probably his mind at that moment was actually troubling itself little about his grandson's iniquities, and much about the iniquities of

President Polk, but the boy could scarcely at that age feel the whole satisfaction of thinking that President Polk was to be the vicarious victim of his own sins, and he gave his grandfather credit for intelligent silence. For this forbearance he felt instinctive respect. He admitted force as a form of right; he admitted even temper, under protest; but the seeds of a moral education would at that moment have fallen on the stoniest soil in Quincy, which is, as every one knows, the stoniest glacial and tidal drift known in any Puritan land.

Neither party to this momentary disagreement can have felt rancor, for during these three or four summers the old President's relations with the boy were friendly and almost intimate. Whether his older brothers and sisters were still more favored he failed to remember, but he was himself admitted to a sort of familiarity which, when in his turn he had reached old age, rather shocked him, for it must have sometimes tried the President's patience. He hung about the library; handled the books; deranged the papers; ransacked the drawers; searched the old purses and pocketbooks for foreign coins; drew the swordcane; snapped the travelling-pistols; upset everything in the corners, and penetrated the President's dressing-closet where a row of tumblers, inverted on the shelf, covered caterpillars which were supposed to become moths or butterflies, but never did. The Madam bore with fortitude the loss of the tumblers which her husband purloined for these hatcheries; but she made protest when he carried off her best cut-glass bowls to plant with acorns or peachstones that he might see the roots grow, but which, she said, he commonly forgot like the caterpillars.

At that time the President rode the hobby of tree-culture, and some fine old trees should still remain to witness it, unless they have been improved off the ground; but his was a restless mind, and although he took his hobbies seriously and would have been annoyed had his grandchild asked whether he was bored like an English duke, he probably cared more for the processes than for the results, so that his grandson was saddened by the sight and smell

of peaches and pears, the best of their kind, which he brought up
from the garden to rot on his shelves for seed. With the inherited
virtues of his Puritan ancestors, the little boy Henry conscientiously
brought up to him in his study the finest peaches he found in the
garden, and ate only the less perfect. Naturally he ate more by
way of compensation, but the act showed that he bore no grudge.
As for his grandfather, it is even possible that he may have felt a
certain self-reproach for his temporary rôle of schoolmaster—seeing
that his own career did not offer proof of the worldly advantages of
docile obedience—for there still exists somewhere a little volume of
critically edited Nursery Rhymes with the boy's name in full written in the President's trembling hand on the fly-leaf. Of course
there was also the Bible, given to each child at birth, with the
proper inscription in the President's hand on the fly-leaf; while their
grandfather Brooks supplied the silver mugs.

So many Bibles and silver mugs had to be supplied, that a new
house, or cottage, was built to hold them. It was "on the hill," five
minutes' walk above "the old house," with a far view eastward over
Quincy Bay, and northward over Boston. Till his twelfth year, the
child passed his summers there, and his pleasures of childhood
mostly centered in it. Of education he had as yet little to complain.
Country schools were not very serious. Nothing stuck to the mind
except home impressions, and the sharpest were those of kindred
children; but as influences that warped a mind, none compared
with the mere effect of the back of the President's bald head, as he
sat in his pew on Sundays, in line with that of President Quincy,
who, though some ten years younger, seemed to children about the
same age. Before railways entered the New England town, every
parish church showed half-a-dozen of these leading citizens, with
gray hair, who sat on the main aisle in the best pews, and had sat
there, or in some equivalent dignity, since the time of St. Augustine,
if not since the glacial epoch. It was unusual for boys to sit behind
a President grandfather, and to read over his head the tablet in
memory of a President great-grandfather, who had "pledged his
life, his fortune, and his sacred honor" to secure the independence

of his country and so forth; but boys naturally supposed, without much reasoning, that other boys had the equivalent of President grandfathers, and that churches would always go on, with the bald-headed leading citizens on the main aisle, and Presidents or their equivalents on the walls. The Irish gardener once said to the child: "You'll be thinkin' you'll be President too!" The casuality of the remark made so strong an impression on his mind that he never forgot it. He could not remember ever to have thought on the subject; to him, that there should be a doubt of his being President was a new idea. What had been would continue to be. He doubted neither about Presidents nor about Churches, and no one suggested at that time a doubt whether a system of society which had lasted since Adam would outlast one Adams more.

The Madam was a little more remote than the President, but more decorative. She stayed much in her own room with the Dutch tiles, looking out on her garden with the box walks, and seemed a fragile creature to a boy who sometimes brought her a note or a message, and took distinct pleasure in looking at her delicate face under what seemed to him very becoming caps. He liked her refined figure; her gentle voice and manner; her vague effect of not belonging there, but to Washington or to Europe, like her furniture, and writing-desk with little glass doors above and little eighteenth-century volumes in old binding, labelled "Peregrine Pickle" or "Tom Jones" or "Hannah More." Try as she might, the Madam could never be Bostonian, and it was her cross in life, but to the boy it was her charm. Even at that age, he felt drawn to it. The Madam's life had been in truth far from Boston. She was born in London in 1775, daughter of Joshua Johnson, an American merchant, brother of Governor Thomas Johnson of Maryland; and Catherine Nuth, of an English family in London. Driven from England by the Revolutionary War, Joshua Johnson took his family to Nantes, where they remained till the peace. The girl Louisa Catherine was nearly ten years old when brought back to London, and her sense of nationality must have been confused; but the influence of the Johnsons and the services of Joshua obtained for him from President Washington

the appointment of Consul in London on the organization of the
Government in 1790. In 1794 President Washington appointed John
Quincy Adams Minister to The Hague. He was twenty-seven years
old when he returned to London, and found the Consul's house a
very agreeable haunt. Louisa was then twenty.

At that time, and long afterwards, the Consul's house, far more
than the Minister's, was the centre of contact for travelling Americans, either official or other. The Legation was a shifting point, between 1785 and 1815; but the Consulate, far down in the City,
near the Tower, was convenient and inviting; so inviting that it
proved fatal to young Adams. Louisa was charming, like a Romney
portrait, but among her many charms that of being a New England woman was not one. The defect was serious. Her future
mother-in-law, Abigail, a famous New England woman whose authority over her turbulent husband, the second President, was
hardly so great as that which she exercised over her son, the sixth
to be, was troubled by the fear that Louisa might not be made of
stuff stern enough, or brought up in conditions severe enough, to
suit a New England climate, or to make an efficient wife for her
paragon son, and Abigail was right on that point, as on most others
where sound judgment was involved; but sound judgment is sometimes a source of weakness rather than of force, and John Quincy
already had reason to think that his mother held sound judgments
on the subject of daughters-in-law which human nature, since the
fall of Eve, made Adams helpless to realize. Being three thousand
miles away from his mother, and equally far in love, he married
Louisa in London, July 26, 1797, and took her to Berlin to be the
head of the United States Legation. During three or four exciting
years, the young bride lived in Berlin; whether she was happy or
not, whether she was content or not, whether she was socially successful or not, her descendants did not surely know; but in any case
she could by no chance have become educated there for a life in
Quincy or Boston. In 1801 the overthrow of the Federalist Party
drove her and her husband to America, and she became at last a
member of the Quincy household, but by that time her children

needed all her attention, and she remained there with occasional
winters in Boston and Washington, till 1809. Her husband was
made Senator in 1803, and in 1809 was appointed Minister to Russia. She went with him to St. Petersburg, taking her baby, Charles
Francis, born in 1807; but broken-hearted at having to leave her
two older boys behind. The life at St. Petersburg was hardly gay for
her; they were far too poor to shine in that extravagant society; but
she survived it, though her little girl baby did not, and in the
winter of 1814-15, alone with the boy of seven years old, crossed
Europe from St. Petersburg to Paris, in her travelling-carriage, passing through the armies, and reaching Paris in the *Cent Jours* after
Napoleon's return from Elba. Her husband next went to England
as Minister, and she was for two years at the Court of the Regent.
In 1817 her husband came home to be Secretary of State, and she
lived for eight years in F Street, doing her work of entertainer for
President Monroe's administration. Next she lived four miserable
years in the White House. When that chapter was closed in 1829,
she had earned the right to be tired and delicate, but she still had
fifteen years to serve as wife of a Member of the House, after her
husband went back to Congress in 1833. Then it was that the little
Henry, her grandson, first remembered her, from 1843 to 1848, sitting in her panelled room, at breakfast, with her heavy silver tea-
pot and sugar-bowl and cream-jug, which still exist somewhere as
an heirloom of the modern safety-vault. By that time she was
seventy years old or more, and thoroughly weary of being beaten
about a stormy world. To the boy she seemed singularly peaceful,
a vision of silver gray, presiding over her old President and her
Queen Anne mahogany; an exotic, like her Sèvres china; an object of deference to every one, and of great affection to her son
Charles; but hardly more Bostonian than she had been fifty years
before, on her wedding-day, in the shadow of the Tower of London.

Such a figure was even less fitted than that of her old husband,
the President, to impress on a boy's mind, the standards of the
coming century. She was Louis Seize, like the furniture. The boy
knew nothing of her interior life, which had been, as the venerable

Abigail, long since at peace, foresaw, one of severe stress and little pure satisfaction. He never dreamed that from her might come some of those doubts and self-questionings, those hesitations, those rebellions against law and discipline, which marked more than one of her descendants; but he might even then have felt some vague instinctive suspicion that he was to inherit from her the seeds of the primal sin, the fall from grace, the curse of Abel, that he was not of pure New England stock, but half exotic. As a child of Quincy he was not a true Bostonian, but even as a child of Quincy he inherited a quarter taint of Maryland blood. Charles Francis, half Marylander by birth, had hardly seen Boston till he was ten years old, when his parents left him there at school in 1817, and he never forgot the experience. He was to be nearly as old as his mother had been in 1845, before he quite accepted Boston, or Boston quite accepted him.

A boy who began his education in these surroundings, with physical strength inferior to that of his brothers, and with a certain delicacy of mind and bone, ought rightly to have felt at home in the eighteenth century and should, in proper self-respect, have rebelled against the standards of the nineteenth. The atmosphere of his first ten years must have been very like that of his grandfather at the same age, from 1767 till 1776, barring the battle of Bunker Hill, and even as late as 1846, the battle of Bunker Hill remained actual. The tone of Boston society was colonial. The true Bostonian always knelt in self-abasement before the majesty of English standards; far from concealing it as a weakness, he was proud of it as his strength. The eighteenth century ruled society long after 1850. Perhaps the boy began to shake it off rather earlier than most of his mates.

Indeed this prehistoric stage of education ended rather abruptly with his tenth year. One winter morning he was conscious of a certain confusion in the house on Mount Vernon Street, and gathered from such words as he could catch, that the President, who happened to be then staying there, on his way to Washington, had fallen and hurt himself. Then he heard the word paralysis. After that day he came to associate the word with the figure of his grandfather, in a tall-backed, invalid armchair, on one side of the spare bedroom fireplace, and one of his old friends, Dr. Parkman or P. P. F. Degrand, on the other side, both dozing.

The end of this first, or ancestral and Revolutionary, chapter came on February 21, 1848—and the month of February brought life and death as a family habit—when the eighteenth century, as an actual and living companion, vanished. If the scene on the floor of the House, when the old President fell, struck the still simple-minded American public with a sensation unusually dramatic, its effect on a ten-year-old boy, whose boy-life was fading away with the life of his grandfather, could not be slight. One had to pay for Revolutionary patriots; grandfathers and grandmothers; Presidents; diplomats; Queen Anne mahogany and Louis Seize chairs, as well as for Stuart portraits. Such things warp young life. Americans commonly believed that they ruined it, and perhaps the practical common-sense of the American mind judged right. Many a boy might be ruined by much less than the emotions of the funeral service in the Quincy church, with its surroundings of national respect and family pride. By another dramatic chance it happened that the clergyman of the parish, Dr. Lunt, was an unusual pulpit orator, the ideal of a somewhat austere intellectual type, such as the school of Buckminster and Channing inherited from the old Congregational clergy. His extraordinarily refined appearance, his dignity of manner, his deeply cadenced voice, his remarkable English and his fine appreciation, gave to the funeral service a character that left an overwhelming impression on the boy's mind. He was to see many great functions—funerals and festivals—in after-life, till his only thought was to see no more, but he never again witnessed anything nearly so impressive to him as the last services at Quincy over the body of one President and the ashes of another.

The effect of the Quincy service was deepened by the official ceremony which afterwards took place in Faneuil Hall, when the boy was taken to hear his uncle, Edward Everett, deliver a Eulogy. Like all Mr. Everett's orations, it was an admirable piece of oratory,

such as only an admirable orator and scholar could create; too
good for a ten-year-old boy to appreciate at its value; but already
the boy knew that the dead President could not be in it, and had
even learned why he would have been out of place there; for
knowledge was beginning to come fast. The shadow of the War of
1812 still hung over State Street; the shadow of the Civil War to
come had already begun to darken Faneuil Hall. No rhetoric could
have reconciled Mr. Everett's audience to his subject. How could
he say there, to an assemblage of Bostonians in the heart of mer-
cantile Boston, that the only distinctive mark of all the Adamses,
since old Sam Adams's father a hundred and fifty years before, had
been their inherited quarrel with State Street, which had again and
again broken out into riot, bloodshed, personal feuds, foreign and
civil war, wholesale banishments and confiscations, until the history of Florence was hardly more turbulent than that of Boston?
How could he whisper the word Hartford Convention before the
men who had made it? What would have been said had he suggested the chance of Secession and Civil War?

Thus already, at ten years old, the boy found himself standing
face to face with a dilemma that might have puzzled an early
Christian. What was he?—where was he going? Even then he felt
that something was wrong, but he concluded that it must be Boston. Quincy had always been right, for Quincy represented a moral
principle—the principle of resistance to Boston. His Adams ancestors must have been right, since they were always hostile to
State Street. If State Street was wrong, Quincy must be right! Turn
the dilemma as he pleased, he still came back on the eighteenth
century and the law of Resistance; of Truth; of Duty, and of Freedom. He was a ten-year-old priest and politician. He could under
no circumstances have guessed what the next fifty years had in
store, and no one could teach him; but sometimes, in his old age, he
wondered—and could never decide—whether the most clear and
certain knowledge would have helped him. Supposing he had seen a
New York stock-list of 1900, and had studied the statistics of railways, telegraphs, coal, and steel—would he have quitted his eight·

eenth-century, his ancestral prejudices, his abstract ideals, his semi-clerical training, and the rest, in order to perform an expiatory pilgrimage to State Street, and ask for the fatted calf of his grandfather Brooks and a clerkship in the Suffolk Bank?

Sixty years afterwards he was still unable to make up his mind. Each course had its advantages, but the material advantages, looking back, seemed to lie wholly in State Street.

QUESTIONS

1. Adams identifies several opposing forces at work in his education: eighteenth century and twentieth century, Quincy and Boston, winter and summer, force and freedom, Boston and Maryland, Adams and State Street. Explain what each term stands for.

2. Define as precisely as possible Adams' broad assumptions regarding free will versus determinism: the autonomy of the individual person versus the controlling influences of nature, social environment, and physical health; the influence of individual men upon history versus the inevitability of historical currents. In your answer consider the essay as a whole and then consider the discussion in paragraphs two and three.

3. Show that the point of view that Adams adopts towards himself in the essay is consonant with his views and assumptions that Questions 1 and 2 have explored. In what sense does the point of view that he maintains towards himself commit him to a certain general tone in the essay? What other tones is he consequently committed not to use?

4. Consider the following revision of the opening clause in the first paragraph: The little passage called Hancock Avenue, which lies under the shadow of Boston State House, turns its back on the house of John Hancock, and skirts the State House grounds, runs—or ran—from Beacon Street to Mount Vernon Street on the summit of Beacon Hill. Explain the differences in construction, and show that the focus and rhythm of the original better suit Adams' subject and tone (as you have defined his tone in the third question). To what extent does Adams repeat his construction in the rest of the sentence and in the first sentence of the next paragraph? Would you say the rhythm of the first paragraph or of the second is more distinctive? How would you account for the difference?

5. Examine Adams' use of the metaphor of the game in paragraphs two and three. Would you say that it makes mainly for brevity, clarity, humor, or irony? (Try eliminating it: What could become of such a child of the seventeenth and eighteenth centuries, when he should have to accommodate himself to the twentieth?) Where in the second paragraph might it be said that Adams carries the metaphor too far? Where in the two paragraphs does he use it contradictorily? What aspects of a card game could he probably not employ, given his particular application of it? What aspects might he have employed that he doesn't (for instance, that he occasionally was dealt a new card)? Defend the metaphor as it now stands.

6. Examine the metaphorical language, irony, paradox, and humor in the tenth paragraph ("Politics . . ."). How forceful and original are they? Contrast the sentence structure and rhythm in the paragraph with the sentence structure and rhythm in the opening sentences of the essay. How does the tone of the tenth paragraph differ from that of the opening sentences? What is the particular appropriateness of each tone?

7. Characterize the diction in paragraph thirteen ("The bearing of the two seasons . . .") according to four or five of the categories set forth in the Introduction to this section of the text (Anglo-Saxon versus Latinate, and so forth). Rewrite the first two or three sentences in the paragraph to illustrate opposing qualities.

8. Identify the several ironical touches by which Adams introduces humor into the account of his clash with his grandfather. Assuming that he might have treated the situation comically, explain why he does not. Show how point of view, tone, and style determine its actual quality. (Define that quality.)

9. In the latter portion of the essay Adams treats briefly several scenes that he might well have elaborated upon: his sitting behind his grandfather in church, his talking to the Irish gardener, his memory of his grandmother in her rooms, the Quincy funeral ceremony. Which of these scenes would you say Adams' style—as exhibited in the essay— is best suited to develop? Which least? Justify your answers. Considering Adams' aims and interests in the essay, which scene would you say most deserves to be developed? Explain his not developing it—on the grounds of either choice or inadequacy.

10. What tone governs the following passages: "He was a ten-year-old priest and politician" (next to last paragraph) and "he was to inherit

from her the seeds of primal sin, the fall from grace, the curse of Abel" (seven paragraphs from the end)? Analyze the method by which Adams achieves that tone. What parallel do you find between his method here and in the seventh paragraph? How would you explain the difference in tone?

11. Can you relate Adams' style in any way to the sort of person he describes himself as being in the seventh paragraph (in the sentence beginning "The habit of doubt")?

12. What evidence in the essay—either of manner or of opinion—suggests that Adams' generally aloof, contemplative point of view may be to some extent an assumed one?

Memories of the Past

HENRY JAMES

Much of James' later life was spent in carefully revising his earlier works, in composing a series of brilliant Prefaces to them (later collected as *The Art of the Novel*), and in writing the several volumes of his autobiography—*A Small Boy and Others, Notes of a Son and Brother,* and *The Middle Years* (left incomplete at the time of his death). Though these recollections do not advance very far chronologically, they do wonderfully recreate James' early years—the quality of life among the Jameses, the family's extensive travels, the relations of Henry and his brother William, who was to become a distinguished philosopher. And most of all, they provide the richest type of subject for James' highly individual "later style," as the following selection—the opening of *A Small Boy*—admirably demonstrates. (Further headnote information on James appears on pp. 28, 232.)

In the attempt to place together some particulars of the early life of William James and present him in his setting, his immediate native and domestic air, so that any future gathered memorials of him might become the more intelligible and interesting, I found one of the consequences of my interrogation of the past assert itself a good deal at the expense of some of the others. For it was to memory in the first place that my main appeal for particulars had to be made; I had been too near a witness of my brother's beginnings of life, and too close a participant, by affection, admiration and sympathy, in whatever touched and moved him, not to feel myself in possession even of a greater quantity of significant truth, a larger handful of the fine substance of history, than I could hope to express or apply. To recover anything like the full treasure of scattered, wasted circumstance was at the same time to live over the spent experience itself, so deep and rich and rare, with whatever sadder and sorer intensities, even with whatever poorer and thinner passages, after the manner of every one's experience; and the effect of this in turn was to find discrimination among the parts of my subject again and again difficult—so inseparably and beautifully they seemed to hang together and the comprehensive case to decline mutilation or refuse to be treated otherwise than handsomely. This meant that aspects began to multiply and images to swarm, so far at least as they showed, to appreciation, as true terms and happy values; and that I might positively and exceedingly rejoice in my relation to most of them, using it for all that, as the phrase is, it should be worth. To knock at the door of the past was in a word to see it open to me quite wide—to see the world within begin to "compose" with a grace of its own round the primary figure, see it people itself vividly and insistently. Such then is the circle of my commemoration and so much these free and copious notes a labor of love and loyalty. We were, to my sense, the blest group of us, such a company of characters and such a picture of differences, and withal so fused and united and interlocked, that each of us, to that fond fancy, pleads for preservation, and that in respect to what I speak of myself as possessing I think I shall be ashamed, as of a cold impiety, to find any element altogether negligible. To which I may add perhaps that I struggle under the drawback, innate and inbred, of seeing the whole content of memory and affection in each enacted and recovered moment, as who should say, in the vivid image and the very scene; the light of the only terms in which life has treated me to experience. And I cherish the moment and evoke the image and repaint the scene; though meanwhile indeed scarce able to convey how prevailingly and almost exclusively, during years and years, the field was animated and the adventure conditioned for me by my brother's nearness and that play of genius in him of which I had never had a doubt from the first.

The "first" then—since I retrace our steps to the start, for the pleasure, strangely mixed though it be, of feeling our small feet plant themselves afresh and artlessly stumble forward again— the first began long ago, far off, and yet glimmers at me there as out of a thin golden haze, with all the charm, for imagination and memory, of pressing pursuit rewarded, of distinctness in the dimness, of the flush of life in the grey, of the wonder of consciousness in everything; everything having naturally been all the while but the abject little matter of course. Partly doubtless as the effect of a life, now getting to be a tolerably long one, spent in the older world, I see the world of our childhood as very young indeed, young with its own juvenility as well as with ours; as if it wore the few and light garments and had gathered in but the scant properties and breakable toys of the tenderest age, or were at the most a very unformed young person, even a boisterous hobbledehoy. It exhaled at any rate a simple freshness, and I catch its pure breath, at our infantile Albany, as the very air of long summer afternoons— occasions tasting of ample leisure, still bookless, yet beginning to be bedless, or cribless; tasting of accessible garden peaches in a liberal backward territory that was still almost part of a country town; tasting of many-sized uncles, aunts, cousins, of strange legendary domestics, inveterately but archaically Irish, and whose familiar remarks and "criticism of life" were handed down, as well as of dim family ramifications and local allusions—mystifications always —that flowered into anecdote as into small hard plums; tasting above all of a big much-shaded savory house in which a softly-sighing widowed grandmother, Catherine Barber by birth, whose attitude was a resigned consciousness of complications and accretions, dispensed an hospitality seemingly as joyless as it was certainly boundless. What she *liked*, dear gentle lady of many cares and anxieties, was the "fiction of the day," the novels, at that time promptly pirated, of Mrs. Trollope and Mrs. Gore, of Mrs. Marsh, Mrs. Hubback and the Misses Kavanagh and Aguilar, whose very names are forgotten now, but which used to drive her away to quiet corners whence her figure comes back to me bent forward on a table with the book held out at a distance and a tall single candle placed, apparently not at all to her discomfort, in that age of sparer and braver habits, straight between the page and her eyes. There is a very animated allusion to one or two of her aspects in the fragment of a "spiritual autobiography," the reminiscences of a so-called Stephen Dewhurst printed by W. J. (1885) in The Literary Remains of Henry James; a reference which has the interest of being very nearly as characteristic of my father himself (which his references in almost any connection were wont to be) as of the person or the occasion evoked. I had reached my sixteenth year when she died, and as my only remembered grandparent she touches the chord of attachment to a particular vibration. She represented for us in our generation the only English blood—that of both her own parents—flowing in our veins; I confess that out of that association, for reasons and reasons, I feel her image most beneficently bend. We were, as to three parts, of two other stocks; and I recall how from far back I reflected—for I see I must have been always reflecting—that, mixed as such a mixture, our Scotch with our Irish, might be, it had had still a grace to borrow from the third infusion or dimension. If I could freely have chosen moreover it was precisely from my father's mother that, fond votary of the finest faith in the vivifying and characterizing force of mothers, I should have wished to borrow it; even while conscious that Catherine Barber's own people had drawn breath in American air for at least two generations before her. Our father's father, William James, an Irishman and a Protestant born (of county Cavan) had come to America, a very young man and then sole of his family, shortly after the Revolutionary War; my father, the second son of the third of the marriages to which the country of his adoption was liberally to help

him, had been born in Albany in 1811. Our maternal greatgrandfather on the father's side, Hugh Walsh, had reached our shores
from a like Irish home, Killyleagh, county Down, somewhat earlier,
in 1764, he being then nineteen; he had settled at Newburgh-on-
the-Hudson, half way to Albany, where some of his descendants till
lately lingered. Our maternal greatgrandfather on the mother's side
—that is our mother's mother's father, Alexander Robertson of Pol-
mont near Edinburgh—had likewise crossed the sea in the mid-
century and prospered in New York very much as Hugh Walsh
was prospering and William James was still more markedly to
prosper, further up the Hudson; as unanimous and fortunate be-
holders of the course of which admirable stream I like to think of
them. I find Alexander Robertson inscribed in a wee New York directory of the close of the century as Merchant; and our childhood in
that city was passed, as to some of its aspects, in a sense of the af-
terglow, reduced and circumscribed, it is true, but by no means
wholly inanimate, of his shining solidity.

The sweet taste of Albany probably lurked most in its being our
admired antithesis to New York; it was holiday, whereas New York
was home; at least that presently came to be the relation, for to my
very very first fleeting vision, I apprehend, Albany itself must have
been the scene exhibited. Our parents had gone there for a year or
two to be near our grandmother on their return from their first
(that is our mother's first) visit to Europe, which had quite immediately followed my birth, which appears to have lasted some
year and a half, and of which I shall have another word to say. The
Albany experiment would have been then their first founded house-
keeping, since I make them out to have betaken themselves for the
winter following their marriage to the ancient Astor House—not indeed at that time ancient, but the great and appointed modern
hotel of New York, the only one of such pretensions, and which
somehow continued to project its massive image, that of a great
square block of granite with vast dark warm interiors, across some
of the later and more sensitive stages of my infancy. Clearly—or
I should perhaps rather say dimly—recourse to that hospitality was

again occasionally had by our parents; who had originally had it to such a happy end that on January 9th, 1842, my elder brother had come into the world there. It remained a tradition with him that our father's friend from an early time, R. W. Emerson, then happening to be in New York and under that convenient roof, was proudly and pressingly "taken upstairs" to admire and give his blessing to the lately-born babe who was to become the second American William James. The blessing was to be renewed, I may mention, in the sense that among the impressions of the next early years I easily distinguish that of the great and urbane Emerson's occasional presence in Fourteenth Street, a center of many images, where the parental tent was before long to pitch itself and rest awhile. I am interested for the moment, however, in identifying the scene of our very first perceptions—of my very own at least, which I can here best speak for.

One of these, and probably the promptest in order, was that of my brother's occupying a place in the world to which I couldn't at all aspire—to any approach to which in truth I seem to myself ever conscious of having signally forfeited a title. It glimmers back to me that I quite definitely and resignedly thought of him as in the most exemplary manner already beforehand with me, already seated at his task when the attempt to drag me crying and kicking to the first hour of my education failed on the threshold of the Dutch House in Albany after the fashion I have glanced at in a collection of other pages than these (just as I remember to have once borrowed a hint from our grandmother's "interior" in a work of imagination). That failure of my powers or that indifference to them, my retreat shrieking from the Dutch House, was to leave him once for all already there an embodied demonstration of the possible—already wherever it might be that there was a question of my arriving, when arriving at all, belatedly and ruefully; as if he had gained such an advance of me in his sixteen months' experience of the world before mine began that I never for all the time of childhood and youth in the least caught up with him or overtook him. He was always round the corner and out of sight, coming back into view but at his hours of extremest ease. We were never in the same schoolroom, in the same game, scarce even in step together or in the same phase at the same time; when our phases overlapped, that is, it was only for a moment—he was clean out before I had got well in. How far he had really at any moment dashed forward it is not for me now to attempt to say; what comes to me is that I at least hung inveterately and woefully back, and that this relation alike to our interests and to each other seemed proper and preappointed. I lose myself in wonder at the loose ways, the strange process of waste, through which nature and fortune may deal on occasion with those whose faculty for application is all and only in their imagination and their sensibility. There may be during those bewildered and brooding years so little for them to "show" that I liken the individual dunce—as he so often must appear—to some commercial traveler who has lost the key to his packed case of samples and can but pass for a fool while other exhibitions go forward.

I achieve withal a dim remembrance of my final submission, though it is the faintest ghost of an impression and consists but of the bright blur of a dame's schoolroom, a mere medium for small piping shuffling sound and suffered heat, as well as for the wistfulness produced by "glimmering squares" that were fitfully screened, though not to any revival of cheer, by a huge swaying, yet dominant object. This dominant object, the shepherdess of the flock, was Miss Bayou or Bayhoo—I recover but the alien sound of her name, which memory caresses only because she may have been of like race with her temple of learning, which faced my grandmother's house in North Pearl Street and really justified its exotic claim by its yellow archaic gable-end: I think of the same as of brick baked in the land of dikes and making a series of small steps from the base of the gable to the point. These images are subject, I confess, to a soft confusion—which is somehow consecrated, none the less, and out of which, with its shade of contributory truth, some sort of scene insists on glancing. The very flush of the uneven bricks of the pavement lives in it, the very smell of the street cobbles, the imputed grace of the arching umbrage—I see it all as from under trees; the form of Steuben Street, which crossed our view, as steep even to the very essence of adventure, with a summit, and still more with a nethermost and riskiest incline, very far away. There lives in it the aspect of the other house—the other and much smaller than my grandmother's, conveniently near it and within sight; which was pinkish-red picked out with white, whereas my grandmother's was greyish-brown and very grave, and which must have stood back a little from the street, as I seem even now to swing, or at least to perch, on a relaxed gate of approach that was conceived to work by an iron chain weighted with a big ball; all under a spreading tree again and with the high, oh so high white stone steps (mustn't they have been marble?) and fan-lighted door of the pinkish-red front behind me. I lose myself in ravishment before the marble and the pink. There were other houses too—one of them the occasion of the first "paid" visit that struggles with my twilight of social consciousness; a call with my father, conveying me presumably for fond exhibition (since if my powers were not exhibitional my appearance and my long fair curls, of which I distinctly remember the lachrymose sacrifice, suppositiously were), on one of our aunts, the youngest of his three sisters, lately married and who, predestined to an early death, hovers there for me, softly spectral, in long light "front" ringlets, the fashion of the time and the capital sign of all our paternal aunts seemingly; with the remembered enhancement of her living in Elk Street, the name itself vaguely portentous, as through beasts of the forest not yet wholly exorcised, and more or less under the high brow of that Capitol which, as aloft somewhere and beneath the thickest shades of all, loomed, familiar yet impressive, at the end of almost any Albany vista of reference. I have seen other capitols since, but the whole majesty of the matter must have been then distilled into my mind—even though the connection was indirect and the concrete image, that of the primitive structure, long since pretentiously and insecurely superseded—so that, later on, the impression was to find itself, as the phrase is, discounted. Had it not moreover been reinforced at the time, for that particular Capitoline hour, by the fact that our uncle, our aunt's husband, was a son of Mr. Martin Van Buren, and that *he* was the President? This at least led the imagination on—or leads in any case my present imagination of that one; ministering to what I have called the soft confusion.

The confusion clears, however, though the softness remains, when, ceasing to press too far backward, I meet the ampler light of conscious and educated little returns to the place; for the education of New York, enjoyed up to my twelfth year, failed to blight its romantic appeal. The images I really distinguish flush through the maturer medium, but with the sense of them only the more wondrous. The other house, the house of my parents' limited early sojourn, becomes that of those of our cousins, numerous at that time, who pre-eminently figured for us; the various brood presided over by my father's second sister, Catherine James, who had married at a very early age Captain Robert Temple, U.S.A. Both these parents were to die young, and their children, six in number, the two eldest boys, were very markedly to people our preliminary scene, this being true in particular of three of them, the sharply differing brothers and the second sister, Mary Temple, radiant and rare, extinguished in her first youth, but after having made an impression on many persons, and on ourselves not least, which was to become in the harmonious circle, for all time, matter of sacred legend and reference, of associated piety. Those and others with them were the numerous dawnings on which in many cases the deepening and final darknesses were so soon to follow: our father's family was to offer such a chronicle of early deaths, arrested careers, broken promises, orphaned children. It sounds cold-blooded, but part of the charm of our grandmother's house for us—or I should perhaps but speak for myself—was in its being so much and so sociably a nurseried and playroomed orphanage. The children of her lost daughters and daughters-in-law overflowed there, mainly as girls; on whom the surviving sons-in-law and sons occasionally and most trustingly looked in. Parentally bereft cousins were somehow more thrilling than parentally provided ones; and most thrilling when, in the odd fashion of that time, they were sent to school in New York as a preliminary to their being sent to school in Europe. They spent scraps of holidays with us in Fourteenth Street, and I think my first childish conception of the enviable lot, formed amid these associations, was to be so little fathered or mothered, so little sunk in the short range, that the romance of life seemed to lie in some constant improvisation, by vague over-hovering authorities, of new situations and horizons. We were intensely domesticated, yet for the very reason perhaps that we felt our young bonds easy; and they were *so* easy compared to other small plights of which we had stray glimpses that my first assured conception of true richness was that we should be sent separately off among cold or even cruel aliens in order to be there thrillingly homesick. Homesickness was a luxury I remember craving from the tenderest age—a luxury of which I was unnaturally, or at least prosaically, deprived. Our motherless cousin Augustus Barker came up from Albany to the Institution Charlier—unless it was, as I suspect, a still earlier specimen, with a name that fades from me, of that type of French establishment for boys which then and for years after so incongruously flourished in New York; and though he professed a complete satisfaction with pleasures tasted in our innocent society I felt that he was engaged in a brave and strenuous adventure while we but hugged the comparatively safe shore.

QUESTIONS

1. Consider the following revision of the first two sentences in James' sketch: In preparing an account of the early years of William James that might be helpful to later biographers, I found that my closeness to him in those years resulted in my having more material about him than I could well use. What differences do you observe in diction, sentence rhythm, and meaning? What is the broad difference in tone?

2. Do you see any material in James' first four sentences that could be abbreviated or eliminated without significant loss to meaning or tone?

To what extent, or in what respect, would you say that either economy or wordiness is an apt term to describe his style?

3. Examine James' use of paired and tripled words and phrases in the first paragraph. To what extent would you say they dominate the rhythm of his sentences? To what extent would you say that modification and qualification dominate the rhythm? (If you have read the Dylan Thomas essay in this section of the text, compare the second paragraph of it with this first paragraph from James.) How would you describe the general flow and tempo of James' sentence rhythms?

4. Justify the variety in length of sentences in the first two paragraphs according to the material that James is treating. Explain how the general length and complexity of his sentences serve his broad intentions in the sketch.

5. What apparent cliché do you find in the opening sentence of the second paragraph? By what means does James try to give it life? How successful is he? Where else in the first two paragraphs do you find a similar handling of cliché?

6. By what reorganization of material about Catherine Barber might James have strengthened his pictorial image of her? What would you say his intention is in the way in which he does handle his material? Distinguish two or three means by which he restricts the vividness of description. (If you have read the Dylan Thomas and George Orwell essays in this section of the text, compare with James' their degrees of interest and precision in visual description.)

7. Show that the diction of the third paragraph may be described as characteristically formal, abstract, connotative, and figurative. In each case provide an instance of contrasting diction.

8. Judge the effectiveness of the following metaphors on the basis of originality, aptness, and consistency with the general tone of the surrounding writing: "larger handful of the fine substance of history" (paragraph one), "the first . . . glimmers at me there as out of a thin golden haze" (paragraph two), "she touches the chord of attachment to a particular vibration" (paragraph two), and "liken the . . . dunce . . . to some commercial traveler who has lost the key to his packed case of samples" (paragraph four). On the basis of your answers here and your answers to Question 5, what generalization might you hazard about the way James works with words?

9. Examine the image of light in the final paragraph. What is its basic meaning? How does it become associated with the image of sailing? To what other images is it related in the paragraph? What is its appropriateness to the sketch as a whole?

10. James' tone is serious but not altogether serious. Where does he lighten it? Where is he matter-of-fact? Likewise his tone is not entirely formal. Where does it become conversational? Where almost completely unreserved? In fact, "serious" and "formal" do not adequately describe James' general tone. What words do?

11. Examine the relationship of "the sweet taste of Albany" (the opening of the third paragraph) to material in the preceding paragraph. Examine the relationship of "final submission" (the opening of the fifth paragraph) to material in the preceding paragraph. Examine the basis on which James proceeds from subject to subject in the fifth paragraph. Apply your answers to a general description of the narrative flow of the sketch.

12. On the basis of your answers to previous questions, characterize James' style. Show how it contributes to the meaning of the sketch. What inferences about the man would you make from his style?